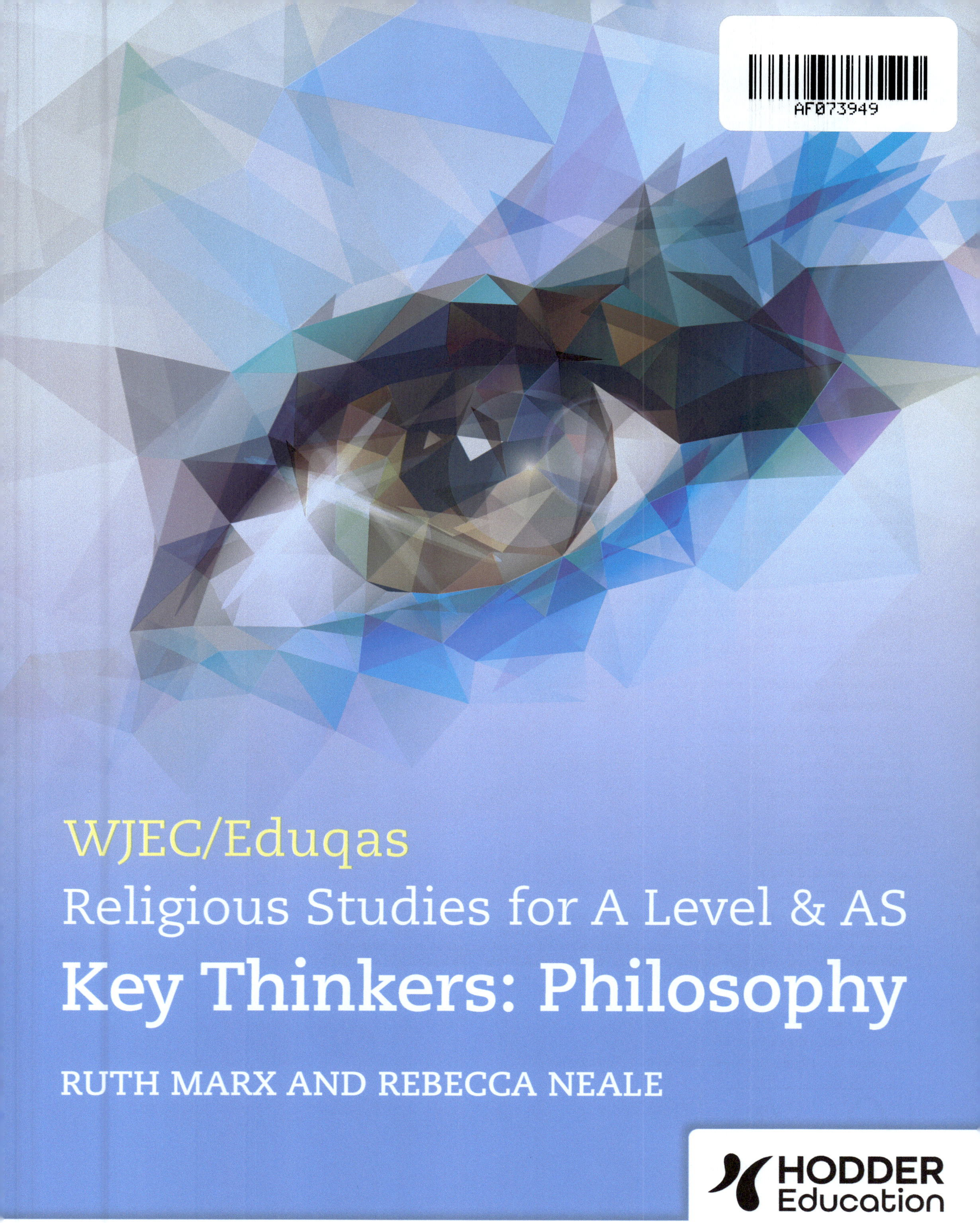

WJEC/Eduqas
Religious Studies for A Level & AS
Key Thinkers: Philosophy

RUTH MARX AND REBECCA NEALE

Every effort has been made to trace all copyright holders, but if any have been inadvertently overlooked, the Publishers will be pleased to make the necessary arrangements at the first opportunity.

Although every effort has been made to ensure that website addresses are correct at time of going to press, Hodder Education cannot be held responsible for the content of any website mentioned in this book. It is sometimes possible to find a relocated web page by typing in the address of the home page for a website in the URL window of your browser.

Hachette UK's policy is to use papers that are natural, renewable and recyclable products and made from wood grown in well-managed forests and other controlled sources. The logging and manufacturing processes are expected to conform to the environmental regulations of the country of origin.

Orders: please contact Hachette UK Distribution, Hely Hutchinson Centre, Milton Road, Didcot, Oxfordshire, OX11 7HH. Telephone: +44 (0)1235 827827. Email education@hachette.co.uk. Lines are open from 9 a.m. to 5 p.m., Monday to Friday.

You can also order through our website: www.hoddereducation.co.uk

ISBN: 9781913963019

© Ruth Marx and Rebecca Neale 2024

First published in 2024 by
Illuminate Publishing,
an imprint of Hodder Education,
An Hachette UK Company
Carmelite House
50 Victoria Embankment
London EC4Y 0DZ
www.hoddereducation.co.uk

Impression number 5 4 3 2 1

Year 2028 2027 2026 2025 2024

All rights reserved. Apart from any use permitted under UK copyright law, no part of this publication may be reproduced or transmitted in any form or by any means, electronic or mechanical, including photocopying and recording, or held within any information storage and retrieval system, without permission in writing from the publisher or under licence from the Copyright Licensing Agency Limited. Further details of such licences (for reprographic reproduction) may be obtained from the Copyright Licensing Agency Limited, www.cla.co.uk

Cover photo: © Antart/Shutterstock.com

Typeset by DC Graphic Design Limited, Hextable, Kent

Printed by Ashford Colour Press Ltd

A catalogue record for this title is available from the British Library.

Contents

How to use this book	4
1. St Thomas Aquinas	9
2. William Lane Craig	29
3. William Paley	35
4. F.R. Tennant	38
5. David Hume	43
6. Charles Darwin	60
7. St Anselm	64
8. René Descartes	72
9. Norman Malcolm	79
10. Gaunilo of Marmoutiers	86
11. Immanuel Kant	91
12. Epicurus	98
13. J.L. Mackie	101
14. William Rowe	105
15. Gregory S. Paul	109
16. John Hick on St Augustine and St Irenaeus	114
17. Sigmund Freud	132
18. Carl Jung	140
19. Richard Dawkins	148
20. Teresa of Avila	155
21. William James	161
22. Rudolf Otto	168
23. Caroline Franks Davis	174
24. R.F. Holland	183
25. Richard Swinburne	188
26. A.J. Ayer	205
27. Antony Flew	211
28. Richard Hare	217
29. Basil Mitchell	220
30. Ian Ramsey	224
31. John Randall Jr	230
32. Paul Tillich	237
33. Ludwig Wittgenstein	245
Acknowledgements	253
Index	254

How to use this book

This book helps you master one of the most important areas of your Religious Studies course in Philosophy: knowing the Key Thinkers. You'll find tips and insights to strengthen both your knowledge and your ability to evaluate each thinker – there's also a section on exam guidance so that you're ready to shine in your assessment at the end of the year.

You'll be able to push deeply into every area of scholarly knowledge required by the course – from grasping 'Key Ideas' to knowing how to best criticise a thinker's approach. You'll also find it easy to quickly 'brush up' on each thinker by reading the key points and summaries in the margins.

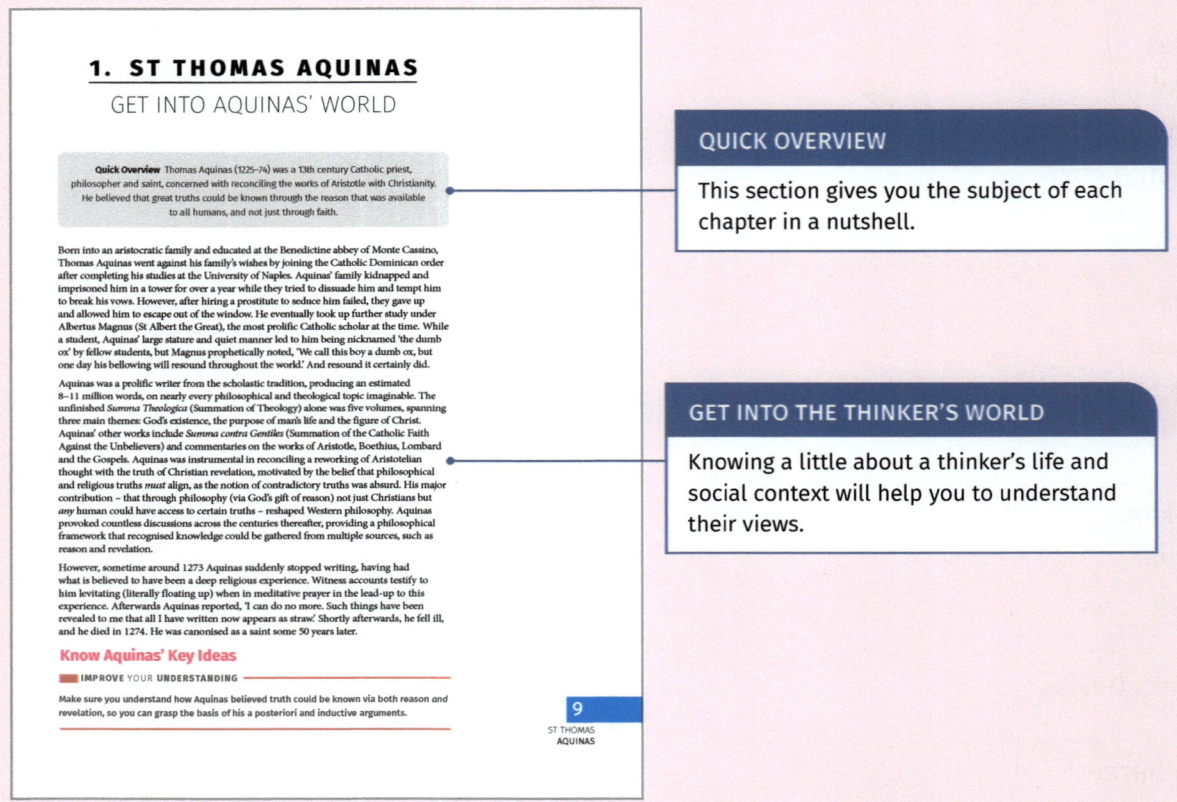

QUICK OVERVIEW

This section gives you the subject of each chapter in a nutshell.

GET INTO THE THINKER'S WORLD

Knowing a little about a thinker's life and social context will help you to understand their views.

■ INSIGHT

Richard Dawkins is a contemporary of Swinburne, and they have debated each other through publications and in person. Dawkins recognises that, even though they reach vastly different conclusions, Swinburne is committed to proper discussions of the existence of God rather than using 'flabby evasions' and 'obscurantism'.

Know Swinburne's Key Ideas
The God that Swinburne Believes In

In *The Coherence of Theism*, Swinburne set out his reasoning for why a belief in a theistic God is logically coherent and can be discussed through meaningful language. This significant contribution to philosophical discussions made Swinburne a voice of reasoned theism, providing solutions and responses to the problems posed to theistic belief from within philosophy. The book title does not imply that it is necessarily true that there is a theistic God, but that it can be a rational belief to hold and discuss.

■ INSIGHT

The Coherence of Theism was Swinburne's 1977 defence of how a belief in God can be rational and coherent. This includes his defence both of miracles and of religious language as meaningful.

A key element of Swinburne's defence of the existence of a theistic God is 'scientific principle'. When we are looking for a cause or reason behind a certain event, the simplest one will often suffice. Swinburne uses examples such as a detective sifting through evidence to find the likely criminal. The detective doesn't look for an over-complicated and convoluted solution, but simply follows the evidence. This mirrors the principle of Occam's razor – that simpler explanations require less verification and are therefore more likely to be true. For Swinburne, when faced with the philosophical problem of why there is a universe in the first place, and what caused life to develop and exist, an omnipotent and omnibenevolent God is the simplest and most complete answer. This has been challenged by scholars such as evolutionary biologist Richard Dawkins (see Chapter 19).

Despite the flaws in the arguments for God's existence, including the cosmological and teleological approaches, religious experience and miracles (Swinburne does not view the ontological argument as convincing for the existence of God), taken together they make a viable case for God's existence. This is referred to as a **cumulative argument** for the existence of God, and has influenced many other scholars such as Caroline Franks Davis (see Chapter 23). Swinburne points to an orderliness that runs throughout the universe, which he says can only exist due to an omnipotent and omnibenevolent being. Interestingly, Antony Flew (see Chapter 27) converted later in life from atheism to deism, and credited Swinburne's arguments around the orderliness of the universe as a contributing factor.

The belief that there is an omnipotent, omnibenevolent and omniscient God means that philosophical problems arise as to how God can have all of these attributes at once. Scholars such as J.L. Mackie (see Chapter 13) suggest there can be no solution to this conflict. If God is all powerful, for example, does that mean that God can sin? Can God do the logically impossible, too? If God is all knowing, and knows the future, where does that leave human free will? What is the point of prayer? Finally, if God is all loving, why is there such suffering in the world?

Swinburne states that looking at a range of evidence can show that it is more likely than less that there is a God – and that this is the simplest and most complete answer.

ESSENTIAL!

The **cumulative argument** for the existence of God states that 'God exists' is the best explanation for the universe, moral values and religious experiences, using a combination of varying arguments rather than an individual argument to prove God's existence.

189
RICHARD SWINBURNE

KNOW THE THINKER'S KEY IDEAS

Everything you need to know about the scholar in a few paragraphs – this is great for your AO1 skills (knowledge and understanding).

UNDERSTAND THE THINKER'S ARGUMENTS

Dig deeper into HOW the scholar justified their approach to ethics – when you really understand their arguments, you can evaluate and judge them for yourself. That's AO2 (evaluation) right there!

Gaunilo's Lost Island argument can be summarised as follows:

P1: There exists a lost island than which no greater can be conceived. It is the greatest possible island.

P2: The greatest possible island exists in the mind, but not in reality (*reductio ad absurdum*).

P3: Existence in reality is greater than existence in the mind alone.

C: Therefore this lost, greatest possible island must exist in reality.

Gaunilo used this parody to demonstrate how absurd Anselm's logic was. By replacing the term 'God' with the 'greatest possible island', the use of *reductio ad absurdum* shows that to deny the existence of the island is a logical absurdity. If the argument can be used to define anything into existence, which is clearly absurd, the argument must be faulty.

Understand Gaunilo's Arguments

Gaunilo was not objecting to Anselm's conclusion that God must exist in reality, as Gaunilo was a Christian and believed in God. However, as an empiricist, Gaunilo objected to the use of a priori knowledge and deductive logic to try to prove God's existence. By highlighting that Anselm's argument just appeared to define something into existence, which all evidence can disprove, Gaunilo was able to show that there was a fault with the logic. Therefore, the whole argument is invalid as a proof of God's existence. Gaunilo's response intended to show the following:

P1: If Anselm's argument were sound, it could prove the existence of other things that are the greatest that could be conceived.

P2: However, Anselm's argument was unable to prove the existence of the greatest possible conceivable island.

C: Therefore, Anselm's argument is not sound.

Gaunilo wrote that we would require evidence of such an island – 'real and indubitable fact' that this greatest possible island exists. Merely describing something as superlative (of the highest possible degree or quality) does not prove it exists.

■ WHAT DO YOU THINK?

Write down your thoughts on Gaunilo's arguments and revisit them shortly before the exam to see if your views have changed.

87
GAUNILO OF MARMOUTIERS

From his findings regarding the differences of individuals within a single species, Darwin went on to develop the concept of the tree of life, which explains how all species on earth are related and have evolved over time from a common ancestor. This idea also illustrates how species were closely or more distantly related. For example, humans and monkeys are all primates and therefore stem from the same 'branch' of the tree of life.

Understand Darwin's Arguments

■ IMPROVE YOUR UNDERSTANDING

Make sure that you know why Darwin's theory of evolution presents a challenge to teleological arguments.

With the publication of Darwin's theory of evolution, he was not attempting to challenge natural theology and religion outright, but was contributing to an already established perspective which, using evidence of extinct fossils, challenged a literal interpretation of Genesis. Many scientists were already considering creation as a slow, unfolding progress rather than a single event. Although Darwin did see natural selection as a replacement for Paley's argument, he did not rule out the role of a guiding creator and **beneficent** God. However, in the years that followed, Darwin's theory fuelled debate and controversy between religious and scientific thinkers, such as Thomas Huxley and Samuel Wilberforce, bishop of Oxford, in 1860. Huxley used Darwin's theory as a means to challenge the authority of the clergy in England at the time.

Read Darwin for Yourself

This passage is taken from Darwin's autobiography (often published as an appendix to *On the Origin of Species*). The notes in the margin will help you to grasp his ideas.

> Although I did not think much about the existence of a personal deity until a considerably later period of my life, I will here give the vague conclusions to which I have been driven. The old argument of design in nature, as given by Paley … fails, now that the law of natural selection has been discovered. We can no longer argue that, for instance, the beautiful hinge of a bivalve shell must have been made by an intelligent being, like the hinge of a door by man. There seems to be no more design in the variability of organic beings and in the action of natural selection, than in the course which the wind blows. Everything in nature is the result of fixed laws … But passing over the endless beautiful adaptations which we everywhere meet with, it may be asked how can the generally beneficent arrangement of the world be accounted for?

By 'personal deity' Darwin is referring to an interventionist God who responds to prayer, such as the Christian God.

Darwin is specifically referring to Paley's teleological argument from complex design.

As Paley made use of analogy, so too does Darwin. However, he argues, the reasoning is no longer comparable.

In Darwin's time there was no discernible pattern or wired behaviour to give the impression of 'design'.

By 'fixed laws' Darwin is referring to natural selection.

Darwin wondered what accounted for the overall beneficial arrangement of things on the world, which left room for the belief in a guiding and beneficent God.

Know Criticisms of Darwin

Some religious groups continue to this day to oppose the theory of evolution. Creationists, neo-creationists and intelligent design advocates argue that the theory of evolution can be challenged for several reasons, including the following.

Lack of evidence. Creationists argue that evolution itself has not been empirically observed, and that there are large gaps in the fossil records, meaning significant changes in species are unaccounted for. This undermines the theory, as there could be other explanations.

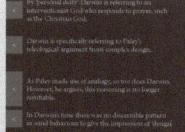

Beneficent means kind, generous and resulting in good. It describes a lesser form of good than 'omnibenevolent'.

■ TIP

Note that although Darwin, for the majority of his adult life, did not believe in the Christian God, he was not an outright atheist. His letters indicate that he believed it likely there was a divine first cause involved in creation.

61
CHARLES DARWIN

READ THE THINKER FOR YOURSELF

You'll deepen both your AO1 and AO2 skills by reading the scholar for yourself – there are also some notes in the margin to help you.

5

KNOW CRITICISMS OF THE THINKER

You'll be able to evaluate scholars by knowing how they've come under fire from those who developed alternative approaches to ethics.

WATCH OUT FOR TRAPS

This feature is based on previous years' examiners' reports. There are also powerful tips of how to stay on track.

EXAM GUIDANCE

This section shows you areas upon which exam questions are based so that you can revise efficiently. You'll also find loads of hints on how you should tackle different types of questions.

EVALUATING THE THINKER TODAY

This feature gives you arguments you can use for evaluation. It has been included for the thinkers most featured in the specification.

TIPS AND INSIGHTS

These features will help you stay on track and give added depth to your understanding.

ESSENTIAL!

Remember the essentials – key concepts are summarised for you.

STRENGTHEN YOUR GRASP

You'll upgrade your AO1 or AO2 skills with these practical tasks – they'll also get you in great shape for answering exam questions.

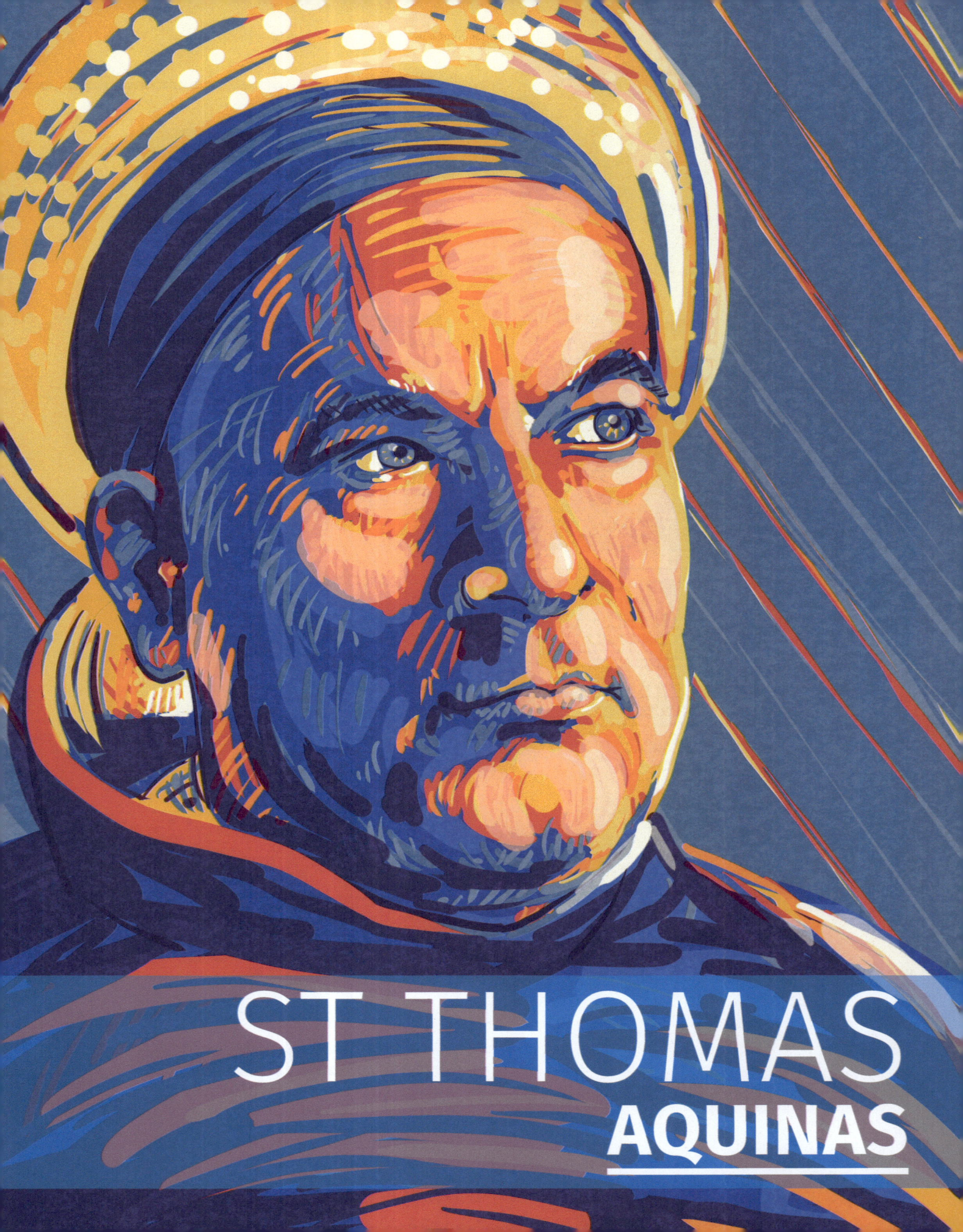

1. ST THOMAS AQUINAS
GET INTO AQUINAS' WORLD

> **Quick Overview** Thomas Aquinas (1225–74) was a 13th century Catholic priest, philosopher and saint, concerned with reconciling the works of Aristotle with Christianity. He believed that great truths could be known through the reason that was available to all humans, and not just through faith.

Born into an aristocratic family and educated at the Benedictine abbey of Monte Cassino, Thomas Aquinas went against his family's wishes by joining the Catholic Dominican order after completing his studies at the University of Naples. Aquinas' family kidnapped and imprisoned him in a tower for over a year while they tried to dissuade him and tempt him to break his vows. However, after hiring a prostitute to seduce him failed, they gave up and allowed him to escape out of the window. He eventually took up further study under Albertus Magnus (St Albert the Great), the most prolific Catholic scholar at the time. While a student, Aquinas' large stature and quiet manner led to him being nicknamed 'the dumb ox' by fellow students, but Magnus prophetically noted, 'We call this boy a dumb ox, but one day his bellowing will resound throughout the world.' And resound it certainly did.

Aquinas was a prolific writer from the scholastic tradition, producing an estimated 8–11 million words, on nearly every philosophical and theological topic imaginable. The unfinished *Summa Theologica* (Summation of Theology) alone was five volumes, spanning three main themes: God's existence, the purpose of man's life and the figure of Christ. Aquinas' other works include *Summa contra Gentiles* (Summation of the Catholic Faith Against the Unbelievers) and commentaries on the works of Aristotle, Boethius, Lombard and the Gospels. Aquinas was instrumental in reconciling a reworking of Aristotelian thought with the truth of Christian revelation, motivated by the belief that philosophical and religious truths *must* align, as the notion of contradictory truths was absurd. His major contribution – that through philosophy (via God's gift of reason) not just Christians but *any* human could have access to certain truths – reshaped Western philosophy. Aquinas provoked countless discussions across the centuries thereafter, providing a philosophical framework that recognised knowledge could be gathered from multiple sources, such as reason and revelation.

However, sometime around 1273 Aquinas suddenly stopped writing, having had what is believed to have been a deep religious experience. Witness accounts testify to him levitating (literally floating up) when in meditative prayer in the lead-up to this experience. Afterwards Aquinas reported, 'I can do no more. Such things have been revealed to me that all I have written now appears as straw.' Shortly afterwards, he fell ill, and he died in 1274. He was canonised as a saint some 50 years later.

Know Aquinas' Key Ideas

IMPROVE YOUR UNDERSTANDING

Make sure you understand how Aquinas believed truth could be known via both reason *and* revelation, so you can grasp the basis of his a posteriori and inductive arguments.

> **ESSENTIAL!**
>
> **A posteriori** refers to knowledge gained by reasoning backwards, from an effect back to the cause.
>
> **A priori** refers to knowledge which can be known via logical reasoning about what is already known prior to observation or experience.
>
> **Inductive** arguments point to a possible conclusion that is at best probable, so aim to persuade on rational grounds rather than as logical proof.

> **INSIGHT**
>
> Motion in this context doesn't just mean movement, rather things that undergo a state of change.

> **ESSENTIAL!**
>
> The **state of potentiality** is a state where something has the ability to become something else: for example, a block of marble.
>
> The **state of actuality** is a state where something is fully realised: for example, a marble statue.
>
> **Reductio ad absurdum** is a form of counter-argument that seeks to demonstrate the ridiculous nature of its conclusion. Aquinas used this technique to show that infinite regress is illogical.
>
> **Infinite regress** refers to the idea of a chain or process of events going back forever without a beginning.

Arguments for God's Existence

In *Summa Theologica*, Aquinas presents five ways to God's existence, heavily influenced by the philosophy of Aristotle and rooted in **a posteriori** knowledge which he argues everyone has to accept – namely, natural facts about the world, or observable truths, from which we can reason back to God as the cause. Aquinas' five ways are **inductive**, and therefore are rational justifications arguing from probability rather than by logical proofs.

The first three ways are detailed formations of cosmological arguments. The fourth is an argument from morality which is not in the Board's specification, so will not be addressed here. The fifth way is a teleological argument.

The First and Second Ways

Aquinas' first and second ways are 'causal' arguments and follow a similar structure. They begin by noting observable traits in the universe, firstly motion, and secondly cause, that we all undeniably experience. By 'motion', Aquinas is referring to the philosophy of Aristotle concerning how things change from one state to another, moving from a **state of potentiality** to **actuality**. For example, wood has the potential to change state and become hot; an acorn has the potential to change state to an oak tree. Aquinas argues that something external is required to explain this motion, and whatever the external explanation is, this is itself actualised. For example, a human (actualised) needs to set the wood on fire to move the wood from a state of potentially hot to actually hot. An actual oak tree is required to produce the acorn that can then potentially be an actual oak tree in the future.

Similarly for cause, Aquinas notes how everything in the universe is an effect of a prior cause. Just as a marble statue cannot cause itself and requires an external explanation such as the sculptor, so the effects in the universe require a cause external to themselves.

Aquinas argues against the ancient Greek idea that the universe and its traits might have existed forever, by demonstrating this to be illogical through a philosophical technique known as **reductio ad absurdum**. Aquinas shows an **infinite regress** of motion and cause would be ridiculous because, if there were nothing first to bring motion and cause into existence, there would be no motion and cause at all. Therefore, the motion and cause that we experience in the world require an external explanation, something outside of the chain of motion and cause, so 'unmoved' and 'uncaused' itself. The only explanation for such an unmoved first mover and uncaused first cause, we call 'God'.

These two ways can be summarised as follows:

The first way: motion	The second way: cause
P1: We observe things in motion (a state of change).	P1: We observe a chain of cause and effect within the world.
P2: Nothing moves itself; an external mover is required.	P2: Nothing is the cause of itself; an external cause is required.
P3: We can imagine this chain going back in an infinite regress.	P3: We can imagine this chain going back in an infinite regress.
P4: An infinite regress is illogical as nothing comes from nothing – *reductio ad absurdum*.	P4: An infinite regress is illogical as nothing comes from nothing – *reductio ad absurdum*.
C: There must be a 'prime mover' (Aristotle's term) that is unmoved. This we call God.	C: There must be a first cause that is uncaused. This we call God.

The Third Way

Aquinas' third way differs from the first two ways, in that it is based on the **contingency** of the universe and argues that the universe is dependent on something for its existence, which itself is **necessary**. The notion of contingency is closely connected with the idea of dependency; that all contingent things depend upon something else for their existence, but also that contingent things might not have come to exist at all, and even where they do, they have a mortality and are not fixed.

For example, consider a specific sunflower. This specific sunflower is contingent (dependent) upon the previous generation producing the seed that went on to grow this one. However, that seed also required the right conditions to grow: soil, water and sunlight. Had any of those conditions not been met, this specific sunflower would not have existed. Further, if conditions change and our sunflower does not have continued exposure to adequate sunlight or water, our sunflower will die and cease to exist. So contingent things are impermanent (mortal).

> **ESSENTIAL!**
>
> **Contingency** is a form of existence that relies on/is dependent on other factors.
>
> **Necessary** here means a form of existence totally independent of everything, and dependent on nothing other than itself.

Aquinas argues that our universe is made up entirely of contingent things, which might, at some point, cease to exist. However, if ever there were nothing, nothing would exist: *ex nihilo nihil fit*. Yet we can clearly see that the contingent things making up our world *do* exist. Therefore, there must be something that doesn't exist in a contingent way to bring the world into existence, something that is permanent, on which all contingent things depend and are sustained. Aquinas concludes, this we call God.

The third way can be summarised as shown below:

> **ESSENTIAL!**
>
> Aquinas observed from the universe *ex nihilo nihil fit* – of nothing, nothing comes – thereby providing the a posteriori reasoning for why there *must* be something to start everything else off.

THE THIRD WAY: CONTINGENCY

P1: Everything in our universe is contingent.

P2: We can therefore imagine a time when everything passes out of existence and there is nothing.

P3: This is illogical as, if ever there was a time with nothing, nothing would exist now, as nothing comes from nothing – *reductio ad absurdum*.

C1: Therefore, there must be something not contingent, something *necessary* which contingent things depend upon.

P4: For something to be necessary, either it must be self-caused (not dependent on anything else), or if its cause is external to itself, it must be fixed and certain.

P5: We can imagine necessary things having external causes to themselves, and their existence being fixed.

P6: This is illogical, as then there would be no first cause of necessity and nothing would exist now – *reductio ad absurdum*.

C2: There must exist a necessary being who is self-caused, whose existence is permanent, and upon which all contingent things depend and are sustained. This we call God.

> **ESSENTIAL!**
>
> **Analogy** refers to the method of explaining something unfamiliar by drawing comparisons to something that is familiar.

> **INSIGHT**
>
> Aquinas is continuing to build on Aristotle's ideas of the four causes and everything moving from a state of potentiality to actuality in order to achieve the final cause or end goal (telos in Greek).

> **TIP**
>
> Aquinas' design argument should be understood as design qua (via) regularity, as it refers to everything working together in a sustained and ordered fashion to achieve an end goal.

> **ESSENTIAL!**
>
> **Univocal** language is where words have exactly the same meaning in every context, whereas **equivocal** language refers to words which have different meanings in different contexts.

> **ESSENTIAL!**
>
> **Anthropomorphism** means to give something not human human qualities or characteristics. For example, 'the hand of God' implies that God has a hand like humans.

The Fifth Way

Aquinas' fifth way for God's existence is a design argument, by **analogy**. Aquinas observes that things within the world appear to have a telos and so must be designed in such a way as to be able to achieve this in an ordered fashion. For example, the apple tree has a *telos* of producing apples and, if conditions are right, the potential to actually do so. The scent and colour of the springtime blossom attract the insects, which in turn pollinate the flowers, thereby producing the apples.

Aquinas then compares such natural orders within the world with a human activity: an archer firing an arrow towards a target. Just as the archer directs the arrow towards its end goal, something intelligent must likewise be directing these orders within the world towards their *telos*. An apple tree is no more able to direct the pollinator consciously to its flower than a target can direct an arrow.

Aquinas' design argument can be summarised as follows:

> **THE FIFTH WAY: *TELOS***
>
> P1: Living organisms lacking their own intelligence have a *telos*.
>
> P2: Such things cannot direct themselves; they must be directed towards that *telos* by something external which is intelligent.
>
> C: There must be some external intelligent being which directs all things towards their *telos*. This we call God.

Religious Language as Analogy

Due to Aquinas' belief that God is transcendent and our finite (limited) human minds are unable to comprehend God's nature, Aquinas had to address the way in which we can meaningfully talk about God.

Aquinas rejected the apophatic approach (*via negativa*) made popular by Jewish scholar Maimonides in the twelfth century, as he believed that speaking negatively about God and merely saying what God is not did not bring you any closer to saying anything about God directly. However, despite favouring the cataphatic approach (*via positiva*), Aquinas also rejected the traditional **univocal** and **equivocal** interpretations of language, arguing that univocal language failed to demonstrate the difference between God and human, and risked **anthropomorphising** God. To say 'God is good' univocally would be the same as saying a human being is good, thereby giving and limiting God to human qualities, whereas equivocal language would get us nowhere, as it would imply that God's goodness and the goodness of a human being are entirely different and there would be no basis from which to comprehend the statement.

Therefore, in *Summa Theologica*, Aquinas instead proposes his analogical approach as a middle way between the two. We can speak meaningfully about God and come closer to understanding his nature, but only if we recognise our language as analogical. That is, there is *some* similarity from which we can meaningfully discuss and understand God, but also we recognise that there is difference and therefore anything we do say has limitations.

Aquinas identifies two bases from which our language for God is analogical, which can be summarised as follows.

Analogy of attribution	Analogy of proportion
<ul><li>Despite the difference between God and humans, it is possible to work backwards from attributes in creation to say something about God's nature.</li><li>We observe goodness in humans, which we can attribute back to God as the *creator and source*.</li><li>Although our goodness will be different from God's goodness, as God's goodness is the cause of our own, some similarity can be drawn between them.</li><li>Aquinas gives the example of an ox's urine. If the urine is healthy, we can deduce that the ox is healthy, as the ox is the cause of the urine.</li></ul>	<ul><li>Things have qualities in proportion to their nature.</li><li>God's creations including humans may have qualities that are attributed to God, but they will be in proportion to (befitting) their status in comparison to God's.</li><li>God's nature will be infinite and beyond our comprehension according to his perfect and transcendent nature, but human nature will be a remote approximation (e.g. human goodness).</li><li>Aquinas uses the example of the strength of a lion and the strength of God. The strength of the lion is in proportion to the creation and God's strength will be infinitely greater.</li></ul>

However, this section warrants a note of caution. Aquinas is *not* intending, through his use of analogy, to say that God is similar to his creation. Rather, as God is the *source of creation*, we can use the similarities of our experiences and observations of creation to bring us closer to a *partial* understanding of the nature of God, and this in turn gives us a starting point for talking meaningfully about God.

This idea was further developed by John Hick in the twentieth century, who gives the example of the faithfulness of a dog compared to a human's faithfulness. The faithfulness is similar in concept but to a proportionate degree for the subject.

Aquinas' approach to religious language can therefore be understood as a cognitive approach because, as a thirteenth-century Christian, Aquinas believed that religious language described reality. The basis of Aquinas' analogical approach was the reality of God as the creator of the world. Saying 'God is good' analogically was still considered to be making a factual statement about the world, just taking into account analogy's limitations of attribution and proportion.

Furthermore, do not assume that Aquinas rejected the cataphatic approach just because he rejected both univocal and equivocal language. His analogical approach *is* cataphatic as it speaks about God in the positive.

INSIGHT

Aquinas relies on the truth of Genesis 1:26, 'Let us make mankind in our image, in our likeness', as a basis for his argument for religious language as analogical.

TIP

Be careful not to imply that God is a being like other beings within creation, only more perfect. Rather, *aspects* of God's nature can be like aspects within creation, but not God himself.

TIP

Define Aquinas' approach to religious language as cognitive, as he believes analogy does describe reality.

INSIGHT

See how Ian Ramsey (Chapter 30) developed Aquinas' ideas of religious language as analogy with reference to qualifiers and disclosures.

> **ESSENTIAL!**
>
> Aquinas defined a **miracle** as 'that which has a divine cause, not whose cause a human person fails to understand' (*Summa Contra Gentiles*).

> **ESSENTIAL!**
>
> **Realism** is the view that there are objective truths. Aquinas uses the term 'miracle' to refer to actual events, not subjective viewpoints.

> **ESSENTIAL!**
>
> **Anti-realism** is the view that only subjective truths (those based on personal interpretations or perspectives, not on objective facts) can be known. A miracle would be a matter of personal perspective, rather than an event in reality.

> **INSIGHT**
>
> Aquinas believed that when God created the world and the natural order, he included the potential for miracles to occur within that order.

Miracles

In line with his faith and cognitive approach to religious language, Aquinas holds a **realist** stance concerning miracles. He expands on St Augustine's definition of **miracles**: that miracles are not contrary to nature but contrary to our knowledge of nature. Aquinas clarifies that while miracles go beyond the normal observable order of nature, these events are not miraculous simply because humans do not understand their cause but because of their divine origin.

We can see the influence of Aristotle here. Both Aristotle and then Aquinas believed that everything that exists has a set nature. Consequently, any event which diverted from the typically observable nature of things was most definitely a real event but one which could only be explained by God. Aquinas is therefore opposed to the **anti-realist** view, for example, where the birth of a much-desired child could be considered as a 'miracle' by the parents, as the birth of a child is well within the typical nature of things.

Aquinas uses the example of a solar eclipse. An uneducated person might well think the eclipse of the sun is a miracle and express wonder at the event, but not the astronomer who understands the event to be one which occurs typically, though not frequently, within the natural order of things. For Aquinas, **miracles** are real events but their explanation is a total mystery to all, regardless of their knowledge and understanding of God's world. Yet as these events are caused by God, they are not contrary to God's plan for nature, but accounted for within that plan. The fact that humans cannot explain these events just magnifies the limited understanding humans have of God's created order.

With this definition of miracles in mind, Aquinas identifies and explains three ranks of miracles, using examples from the Bible to illustrate. A miracle is something done by God which:

- nature could never do – a physical impossibility: for example, stopping the sun (Joshua 10:13)
- nature could do but not in that sequence – nature could explain someone being alive, but not after they have died: for example, the resurrection of Lazarus (John 11:38–44)
- nature could do, but which occurred without the usual forces of nature: for example, turning water into wine (John 2:1–11). Nature *can* turn water into wine, but not instantly, and grapes, yeast, sugar and time are also required.

Understand Aquinas' Arguments

Aquinas' philosophical thoughts are guided by the following general convictions. Being aware of these will help you to explain and evaluate his approach in the areas we have already examined.

Philosophy as a tool that can be used to serve theology and the Church. Aquinas is sometimes misunderstood as having 'synthesised' Aristotelian philosophy with Christianity, implying he took the parts of Aristotle's work that were compatible with Christianity and, disregarding the rest, created a smooth blend. However, this is inaccurate. As a devout Dominican Catholic friar, Aquinas accepted the teachings of the Church as absolute, and believed that sacred teaching contained the most comprehensive account of God's nature. However, he also believed that, when properly understood, the teachings of Aristotle did not contradict Christian teaching, but that Christian beliefs could be rationally demonstrated through Aristotelian philosophy. As Aquinas famously wrote, 'if anything is found in the words of the philosophers that is contrary to the faith, this is not philosophy but rather an abuse of philosophy, due to a failure of reason'.

In order to account for a universal ability to reason fundamental truths about God's nature, Aquinas coherently developed Aristotle's teaching on knowledge gained through sense experience of the world and on the *hierarchy of souls*. Aquinas differentiated between the knowledge we gain through our sense experience of the world – knowledge based on sight, smell, taste, touch, hearing, etc. which we share with other living organisms (animals) – and the intellectual knowledge we generate through reason that goes beyond our sense experience. He believed that all our intellectual knowledge of the world came from this ability to reason (philosophy), which was unique to *all* human beings due to their being made *Imago Dei* (in the image and likeness of God): 'Let us make mankind in our image, in our likeness' (Genesis 1:26).

> **ESSENTIAL!**
>
> Aristotle's **hierarchy of souls** describes the soul or essential nature of all living organisms, but only humans have rational thought and they are the top of the hierarchy.

Therefore, all people could understand certain truths about the nature of God, even without knowledge of Church teaching and scripture. Aquinas recognised the great value of this to the Church and its mission, and the benefit that progress in philosophy could have for Christian faith, as arguments on the basis of reason could be understood by non-believers. Hence one of Aquinas' best-known works, *Summa Contra Gentiles*, was also titled *Book on the truth of the Catholic faith against the errors of the unbelievers*.

Therefore, when reading Aquinas' philosophical works, remember that he understood such philosophical reasoning as a *source* of spiritual truth, rather than as a separate methodology which leads to a separate type of knowledge, as is often the view of many modern-day atheist and agnostic philosophers. For Aquinas, as was common in the medieval worldview, 'philosophy was the handmaid of theology' and not superior to or separate from it. Aquinas understood all sciences as being in servitude to theology.

> **ESSENTIAL!**
>
> A **supernaturally revealed truth** is that which cannot be known through human efforts, but can only be known by direct revelation from God: for example, the concept of the Holy Trinity.

God as the cause, creator, source and sustainer of the world. The importance of this principle and worldview for Aquinas cannot be overstated. It underpins all aspects of his work. Writing in the scholastic method of the time, where objections concerning a line of thought are responded to logically, Aquinas responded to the objection that God's existence could not be demonstrated, as it was just an article faith, by asserting that God's existence was not a **supernaturally revealed truth**. Instead, God's existence was a fact able to be demonstrated a posteriori, which supernatural revealed truths presuppose.

From Aquinas' point of view, the reason that God's existence is so apparent in the a posteriori fashion, working back from evidence of an effect to its cause, is that the world and everything around us is by its very nature the effect of God. Therefore, the evidence can be logically traced back to God. This thought is evident in all aspects of his work, but primarily in his 'five ways' to God's existence and his analogical approach to religious language, as discussed in the 'Know Aquinas' Key Ideas' section above. Remembering this while considering Aquinas' ideas will enable you to see the thread that connects his philosophy and theology, but also to wonder, what would happen if this thread came loose? Aquinas' works can only be understood within the medieval Christian context, where God's existence was perceived as an irrefutable and undeniable fact, which is evidenced at every turn in the natural world. Where does this leave Aquinas' work today, when there is little such certainty?

> **TIP**
>
> Improve your evaluation by demonstrating a holistic understanding of the works of Aquinas and how his ideas link.

However, be careful not to assume that just because Aquinas accepts God as the creator, as taught in Church teaching and sacred scripture, this means he interprets the Bible and Genesis creation accounts literally. Aquinas argued that, although factual in terms of deeper religious truth, the Bible was written with metaphorical language in order to describe the indescribable for finite (limited) human minds, as illustrated through his religious language as analogy approach. Where the Bible states, 'The Lord is my shepherd' (Psalm 23), Aquinas does not believe that this is saying God is a literal shepherd; rather this analogy points to how God should be understood as a caring figure who watches over and guides his creation, as a shepherd does with his flock. Therefore, Aquinas maintains we can only *know* God through the material world, as that is how we as finite beings can know anything for ourselves. We depend on nature and the evidence around us to know truths, which in turn provides the building blocks for faith based on reason and rational thinking.

> **ESSENTIAL!**
>
> A **deductive** argument attempts to give a 100 per cent certain, absolute logical proof. If the premises are true, the conclusion necessarily follows.

God can only be known inductively due to the limitations of the human mind. In Part One of *Summa Theologica*, Aquinas spends some time addressing and refuting the notion that God's existence can be self-evident to humans and that, as St Anselm proposes, we are able to know God a priori, in a **deductive** fashion (see Chapter 7 for St Anselm's a priori and deductive argument for God's existence). Aquinas explains that demonstration of any truth could theoretically be made in two ways: a priori, which is to argue from what is known prior to any evidence of effect; or a posteriori, which is to argue from the evidence of effect back to the cause. Aquinas says that when an effect is better known to us than the cause, we must proceed in our knowledge from the evidence of effect back to the cause. In the case of God, Aquinas disagrees with Anselm, who claimed that all are capable of knowing and understanding the essence of God. Aquinas believed the existence of God can only be demonstrated inductively (that is, on grounds of probability) via the effects of God that are known to us: namely, through a posteriori knowledge of the natural world around us.

However, the fact that Aquinas' inductive and a posteriori cosmological and teleological ways for proving God's existence are so dominant in most A-level Religious Studies and Philosophy courses can be misleading, as in reality, this aspect of Aquinas' work was not itself central to his thought. Aquinas never set out to 'prove' that God exists. Nor did he aspire to the missionary life to convert non-believers personally. He believed the minds of non-Christians would not necessarily be open to the rational argument anyway. Instead, Aquinas sought to demonstrate God's existence as a rational proposition, based on the evidence within the natural world, which can then be studied scientifically through philosophy to demonstrate spiritual truths about the nature of God and our world. This approach has been said to maintain the parameters of what theologians can say is known about God, while recognising and upholding the mystery and **epistemic distance** between humans and God.

> **ESSENTIAL!**
>
> **Epistemic distance** is the phrase coined by John Hick to describe the gap between human knowledge and God. See Chapter 16 for more details on this.

WHAT DO YOU THINK?

One way to improve your ability to evaluate a scholar's ideas is to be aware of your own thoughts and reactions to the arguments you read.

Write these down in a notebook and revisit them shortly before the exam to see if your views have changed.

Read Aquinas for Yourself

The following passages are taken from *Summa Theologica* and illustrate some of Aquinas' arguments concerning God's existence, religious language and miracles.

Aquinas' Inductive Arguments for God's Existence

On the First Way

> The first and more manifest way is the argument from motion. It is certain, and evident to our senses, that in the world some things are in motion. Now whatever is in motion is put in motion by another … For motion is nothing else than the reduction of something from potentiality to actuality. But nothing can be reduced from potentiality to actuality, except by something in a state of actuality … It is therefore impossible that in the same respect and in the same way a thing should be both mover and moved, i.e. that it should move itself. Therefore, whatever is in motion must be put in motion by another. If that by which it is put in motion be itself put in motion, then this also must needs be put in motion by another, and that by another again. But this cannot go on to infinity, because then there would be no first mover, and, consequently, no other mover; seeing that subsequent movers move only inasmuch as they are put in motion by the first mover; as the staff moves only because it is put in motion by the hand. Therefore it is necessary to arrive at a first mover, put in motion by no other; and this everyone understands to be God.

TASK

Read Aquinas for yourself in the extracts below. The notes in the margin will help you to grasp his ideas.

- This is a reference to his a posteriori approach and underlying belief that we can know God through reason concerning our experience of his creation.

- Hence the need for an external explanation that moves things from one state to another.

- *Reductio ad absurdum* – *ex nihilo nihil fit*, of nothing, nothing comes, so if there were nothing originally there would be nothing now.

- The fact there is something demonstrates there must have been a first mover, so the unmoved mover, God, must exist.

On the Second Way

> This is a reference to Aristotelian philosophy and the four causes. The efficient cause for Aristotle was that which was ultimately responsible for things changing state or remaining stable.

> Aquinas is rejecting the notion of infinite regress.

> *Reductio ad absurdum* – *ex nihilo nihil fit*, of nothing, nothing comes, so if there were nothing originally, there would be nothing now.

> The fact that there is something demonstrates there must have been a first cause, so the uncaused cause, the efficient cause, God, must exist.

The second way is from the nature of the efficient cause. In the world of sense we find there is an order of efficient causes. There is no case known (neither is it, indeed, possible) in which a thing is found to be the efficient cause of itself; for so it would be prior to itself, which is impossible. Now in efficient causes it is not possible to go on to infinity, because in all efficient causes following in order, the first is the cause of the intermediate cause, and the intermediate is the cause of the ultimate cause, whether the intermediate cause be several, or only one. Now to take away the cause is to take away the effect. Therefore, if there be no first cause among efficient causes, there will be no ultimate, nor any intermediate cause. But if in efficient causes it is possible to go on to infinity, there will be no first efficient cause, neither will there be an ultimate effect, nor any intermediate efficient causes; all of which is plainly false. Therefore it is necessary to admit a first efficient cause, to which everyone gives the name of God.

On the Third Way

> Aquinas explains that the world is made up of contingent things and therefore there will be a time when they did not and will not exist.

> *Reductio ad absurdum* – Aquinas demonstrates that to have only a contingent thing is absurd because there would be a time when nothing existed, meaning that nothing could exist now, which is clearly false.

> Necessary – as in something that simply has to exist and is fixed, regardless of everything else.

> This is a reference to Aquinas' second way – the argument from cause.

> Aquinas means we can't help but think of something which is self-caused, the source of its own existence, not contingent on anything or any factor. It is the only logical conclusion in Aquinas' mind.

The third way is taken from possibility and necessity, and runs thus. We find in nature things that are possible to be and not to be, since they are found to be generated, and to corrupt, and consequently, they are possible to be and not to be. But it is impossible for these always to exist, for that which is possible not to be at some time is not. Therefore, if everything is possible not to be, then at one time there could have been nothing in existence. Now if this were true, even now there would be nothing in existence, because that which does not exist only begins to exist by something already existing. Therefore, if at one time nothing was in existence, it would have been impossible for anything to have begun to exist; and thus even now nothing would be in existence – which is absurd. Therefore, not all beings are merely possible, but there must exist something the existence of which is necessary. But every necessary thing either has its necessity caused by another, or not. Now it is impossible to go on to infinity in necessary things which have their necessity caused by another, as has been already proved in regard to efficient causes. Therefore we cannot but postulate the existence of some being having of itself its own necessity, and not receiving it from another, but rather causing in others their necessity. This all men speak of as God.

On the Fifth Way

Text	Annotation
The fifth way is taken from the governance of the world. We see that things which lack intelligence, such as natural bodies, act for an end, and this is evident from their acting always, or nearly always, in the same way, so as to obtain the best result. Hence it is plain that not fortuitously, but designedly, do they achieve their end. Now whatever lacks intelligence cannot move towards an end, unless it be directed by some being endowed with knowledge and intelligence; as the arrow is shot to its mark by the archer. Therefore some intelligent being exists by whom all natural things are directed to their end; and this being we call God.	How things appear to be regulated and sustained in an ordered fashion. Aquinas is referring to things such as the planets and stars, plants, trees and natural processes. To fulfil the *telos* (purpose) everything has. Aquinas allows for some unexpected actions due to his belief that God plans for occasional miracles to occur within the natural order. God is good and creation is good as revealed in the Bible, therefore naturally God's creation will function so as to achieve a good outcome. Aquinas refutes the Ancient Greek Epicurean idea that the world and its complexity could have come about by chance (see Chapter 5 for more detail on the Epicurean hypothesis). Building on Aristotelian philosophy and Aquinas' cosmological arguments, an external explanation that is itself actualised is required. For Aquinas this 'being' is God.

On Religious Language as Analogy

In this passage, Aquinas explains how humans can speak meaningfully about God and make positive affirmations about his nature, via analogy that is rooted in the Christian belief and sacred teaching, found in Genesis 1, that God is the creator and source of all.

Text	Annotation
Neither … are names applied to God and creatures in a purely equivocal sense … Because if that were so, it follows that from creatures nothing could be known or demonstrated about God at all; for the reasoning would always be exposed to the fallacy of equivocation. Such a view is against the philosophers, who proved many things about God, and also against what the Apostle says.	This is reference to the error of using ambiguous language that conceals the truth: for example, 'All beetles have six legs. John Lennon is a Beatle. John Lennon has six legs.' The Greek philosophers, such as Socrates, Plato and Aristotle. This reference demonstrates Aquinas' view that philosophical reasoning can be a tool to demonstrate truths about God. Reference to St Paul where in the Bible he says, 'For since the creation of the world God's invisible qualities – his eternal power and divine nature – have been clearly seen, being understood from what has been made, so that people are without excuse' (Romans 1:20).
… all names applied metaphorically to God, are applied to creatures primarily rather than to God, because when said of God they mean only similitudes to such creatures … so the name of 'lion' applied to God means only that God manifests strength in His works, as a lion in his.	Aquinas clarifies that we can only speak meaningfully about God in the cataphatic ('via positiva') tradition, if we can acknowledge we are using metaphors, by which he means analogies, where we build on the similarities between the creatures which are God's creation, and God himself. We have to acknowledge that the similarities can only take us so far, as each also have its own differences, as explained in his lion example.
But to other names not applied to God in a metaphorical sense, the same rule would apply if they were spoken of God as the cause only, as some have supposed. For when it is said, 'God is good,' it would then only mean 'God is the cause of the creature's goodness'; thus the term good applied to God would included in its meaning the creature's goodness.	The analogy of attribution, reflecting not just Aquinas' belief but that of the vast majority of western Europe at the time, that humans are made in the image and likeness of God (Genesis 1:26). However, by likeness, Aquinas does not mean physical likeness, but an intellectual one.
… For the words, 'God is good,' or 'wise,' signify not only that He is the cause of wisdom or goodness, but that these exist in Him in a more excellent way. Hence as regards what the name signifies, these names are applied primarily to God rather than to creatures, because these perfections flow from God to creatures …	The analogy of proportion. Aquinas is explaining that we have attributes of God as his creation, but to a lesser degree, as is befitting our status in relation to his, as the God of classical theism. Aquinas explains that he sees qualities such as goodness, wisdom, justice, reasoning – our virtues so to speak – as perfections that are attributed to God.

On Miracles

In this passage, Aquinas explains the finer details of what does and does not constitute a miracle, why they are not contrary to nature in an absolute sense and, of the miracles that have occurred, how they can be categorised in a hierarchy of three ranks.

Aquinas believes all things have a typical nature and order.	From each cause there results a certain order to its effects, since every cause is a principle … God cannot do anything against this order; for, if He did so, He would act against His foreknowledge, or His will, or His goodness. But if we consider the order of things depending on any secondary cause, thus God can do something outside such order; for He is not subject to the order of secondary causes; but, on the contrary, this order is subject to Him, as proceeding from Him, not by a natural necessity, but by the choice of His own will … Wherefore God can do something outside this order created by Him, when He chooses, for instance by producing the effects of secondary causes without them, or by producing certain effects to which secondary causes do not extend.
Aquinas explains that God would not, and indeed could not, cause a miracle to happen that was contrary to his own intended creation or nature. That would be illogical.	
By secondary causes, Aquinas means a part of nature that is not the full or primary cause of such an event, as that would be God's will. Hence miracles are potential within nature rather than contrary to it. This is an important distinction for Aquinas and should not be overlooked when discussing his work on miracles.	
Throughout his works, Aquinas refers to Aristotle as 'the Philosopher'.	… as the Philosopher says in the beginning of his Metaphysics … Now the cause of a manifest effect may be known to one, but unknown to others. Wherefore a thing is wonderful to one man, and not at all to others: as an eclipse is to a rustic, but not to an astronomer. Now a miracle is so called as being full of wonder; as having a cause absolutely hidden from all: and this cause is God.
An example very much of the era, illustrating that while an uneducated person might think of an eclipse as a miracle, as they do not know or understand the cause, an astronomer would, so it is not a miracle as the cause is not hidden to all. For Aquinas, a true miracle will not be known or understood by any human, as the event has to be outside of human observation of the natural order.	
This is clarification of Aquinas' realist stance. A miracle is an external event which has no known cause, regardless of what different people with their different knowledge make of it.	
Aquinas categorises and ranks miracles according to the degree to which the typical natural order is overturned.	… the more the power of nature is surpassed, the greater the miracle. Now the power of nature is surpassed in three ways: firstly, in the substance of the deed, for instance … if the sun goes backwards … such things nature is absolutely unable to do; and these hold the highest rank among miracles. Secondly, a thing surpasses the power of nature, not in the deed, but in that wherein it is done; as the raising of the dead … for nature can give life, but not to the dead; and such hold the second rank in miracles. Thirdly, a thing surpasses nature's power in the measure and order in which it is done … or the usual process of nature … as when the air is suddenly condensed into rain, by Divine power without a natural cause … and these hold the lowest place in miracles.

Know Criticisms of Aquinas

ESSENTIAL!

An **inductive leap** refers to the flaw in inductive arguments: as the conclusion does not necessarily follow on from the premise, the conclusion is not necessarily justified.

An underlying assumption which itself is not certain. As mentioned previously, any close inspection of Aquinas' ideas and works reveals his underlying belief that God is the creator, source and sustainer of the world and the natural order within it.

For Aquinas this is not an assumption but a truth that is also revealed through scripture and Church teaching. In terms of philosophy, this belief remains an assumption that could be criticised as an **inductive leap**. That is, it has no observable, empirical proof or certain experience to justify the conclusions drawn, which Aquinas ironically so favoured.

Sceptical empiricist David Hume highlighted this problem of induction and the **issue of causality**, arguing that we only ever experience effects of causes rather than causes themselves. Therefore, we have no grounds to make assumptions from past experiences, apply them to different or future situations and call that knowledge. With regard to Aquinas' assumption that God is the creator of the world, Hume would argue that Aquinas has no experience of the creation of the world and so he cannot assume to know the cause (see Chapter 5 for more details). In terms of how this affects and undermines Aquinas' works, some examples are below:

Underlying assumptions in cosmological arguments. These can be questioned in the following ways:

- Aquinas argues from observation of traits in the world, such as a series of motion, cause and contingency, to conclude that something external to the series must exist to initiate the series that results in the world existing today. However, considering Hume's issue of causality, we have only ever observed the effects within the series, so cannot then apply this experience to the cause of the series, which is beyond our experience.

- On what grounds or from what experience does Aquinas argue that the series of motion, cause and contingency cannot exist in an infinite regress? Hume argues that an infinite regress is possible. This idea has been supported by some twentieth-century scientific ideas, such as the Steady State theory, which suggested that the universe was eternal and constantly created matter to maintain the same consistent density as the universe expanded.

- Studies into quantum physics have also demonstrated that some sub-atomic particles are capable of inertia: that is, moving themselves from one state to another, therefore not requiring an external cause or mover. If some particles do not require a cause, we cannot rule out that the universe might not require a cause to bring it into existence. Aquinas is just assuming from his position of faith that God is the unmoved mover, uncaused cause and necessary first being, when in fact there may be none required. Hume argues that Aquinas has made the logical **fallacy of composition** here. What may be true of a part is not necessarily true of the whole.

- Furthermore, Aquinas seems to contradict his own logic by stating that everything in the world needs to be moved or caused by something external, or depends on something external, except for God who as a necessary being is exempt from requiring an external mover or cause. On what evidence or experience does Aquinas justify this inductive leap other than a priori faith in God as something totally other to and different from the matter that makes up the world? If, as Hume attempts to argue, an infinite regress is possible, then there are no grounds for why a necessary being must logically exist. If such a being as God does exist, if all experience tells us everything has an external cause, then it would be reasonable to ask what caused God before assuming God to be exempt from the norm.

- Even if we agree with Aquinas' logic in his first three ways for God's existence, that the motion, cause and contingency we observe in the world could not exist without something external, something necessary to bring them into existence, what observable evidence is there that this unmoved, uncaused, necessary first being is God and the God of classical theism? **Occam's razor** would support the notion that the universe itself could be the necessary being that is self-caused. There is no evidence or need to make the inductive leap that this being is God. Twentieth-century scholar Bertrand Russell developed this point in a radio debate about cosmological arguments in 1948, arguing that the universe could just be a brute fact and that is the end of it.

ESSENTIAL!

The **issue of causality** is the problem that we cannot be certain in our knowledge of causes because we only ever experience effects and rely on habit, guesswork and probability in terms of assuming a cause.

ESSENTIAL!

A **fallacy of composition** means that what is true of the part is not necessarily true of the whole. Arguments that make this assumption are guilty of this type of false logic.

ESSENTIAL!

Credited to William of Occam, **Occam's razor** is the law of parsimony: that is, that the simplest explanation is often the correct one.

Underlying assumptions in teleological arguments. Similar to the above, even if we agree with Aquinas that there is evidence of apparent design within the universe, what observable proof is there that the designer is the God of classical theism? Hume argued in his *Dialogues Concerning Natural Religion* (1779) that apparent design could be just that, and instead be a result of chance. Hume also makes the comparison with shipbuilding, where it would take a team of shipbuilders rather than an individual to create such a complex thing. These arguments illustrate that there is no more evidence for God as a designer over chance or a team of designers. Aquinas is making an inductive leap in assuming that there is a designer, who must be God, which cannot be justified.

On reflection of the criticisms above, Aquinas appears to fall prey to the trap of **circular logic** in his five ways. His philosophy develops on the basis that God exists and created the world, and thus his arguments go on to conclude that therefore God created, caused and designed the world and thus exists.

Underlying assumptions in religious language as analogy and miracles. These can be criticised in the following ways:

- If we remove the basis of God as creator, upon which Aquinas depends as a means to talk meaningfully about God, his approach to using language to speak about God in a meaningful way falls flat. If God is not the source of creation and therefore the source of our attributes, the connection and similarity does not stand and we cannot move from experience of these back to God, regardless of any difference in proportion.

- With regard to miracles, if we remove the assumption that God created the world and the natural order within it, there remain no grounds for God as the explanation and cause of all miracles. Occam's razor would simply suggest that if an event seems to go against the natural order, it is because we do not fully understand the natural order.

Limitations in what philosophy can conclude about the God of Christianity. In addition to the problem of Aquinas' underlying assumptions, the reliance on the causal basis of God's relationship with the world is problematic for many of Aquinas' ideas, as such a relationship would not logically have to be restricted to positive qualities and the characteristics of the God of classical theism. The following examples illustrate:

- **Limitations in Aquinas' inductive arguments.** Aquinas uses a posteriori forms of knowledge to move from natural orders and regularity apparent in the world, back to God, who in turn is understood as being powerful and intelligent enough to design such features, and loving and good enough to desire to have the will to design them. However, the same can be said in reverse – this is known as the **dysteleological argument**. This closely links with the problem of evil (see Chapters 12–16 for more) and David Hume's criticisms of the design argument (see Chapter 5).

- **Limitations in religious language as analogy.** Similarly, Aquinas traces the positive attributes found in creation back to God, and via the analogy of attribution says that goodness in humans can lead us to proclaim confidently that God is good, but in greater proportion. However, this logic can be applied the other way concerning negative attributes. Humans can just as often exhibit attributes such as anger, hate and jealousy as goodness, wisdom and justice. Does it therefore follow that God as the creator and source of our attributes is also angry, hateful and jealous, but to a greater proportion?

> **ESSENTIAL!**
>
> **Circular logic** refers to the fallacy (false logic) where an argument begins with what it goes on to conclude.

> **ESSENTIAL!**
>
> The **dysteleological argument** is a parody of the design argument. It argues that as there is evidence of bad design in the world, it could just as equally be argued that, if there is a designing God, such a God must in turn be malevolent.

- **Limitations in Aquinas' understanding of miracles.** Concerning miracles, Aquinas' understanding raises the issue that if God can and has intervened in the world to produce miracles for some individuals, why not for others? Maurice Wiles said in *God's Action in the World* (1986) that a God who arbitrarily intervened to help some individuals and not others – for example, the biblical resurrection of Lazarus and miraculous healings – would not be worthy of worship and could be rejected on moral grounds. Such a God who would not want to, or was not able to, help all who needed it would not be the traditional, omnibenevolent (all-loving), omnipotent (all-powerful) deity that is Aquinas' God. Therefore, the nature of Aquinas' definition of miracles, which he argued points to the Christian God with an omnipotent and omnibenevolent nature, is not necessarily persuasive.

Due to the points raised above, Aquinas' ideas can be criticised for being unreasonably biased towards conclusions that point to the existence of the God of classical theism and specifically the Christian God of Catholic thought and sacred teaching. His philosophy, despite widely recognised as being immense and on the whole coherent within his belief system, does not necessarily or successfully persuade everyone that we can have true knowledge of God and his nature as a result.

For example, despite being a Christian Immanuel Kant was a fideist, which means someone who believes that knowledge of God comes through faith or revelation alone. Kant argued that, due to the limitation of human knowledge, we simply could *not* know God's nature or existence through reason or argument from evidence. For Kant, knowledge of God came through faith and was not something that could be demonstrated (see Chapter 11 for more on this). For example, while Aquinas' philosophy might be considered successful in making the case for the probable existence of a necessary being as the first unmoved mover, uncaused cause, this philosophy does not demonstrate the Christian belief in God's nature as Trinitarian – God as a Holy Trinity of father, son and holy spirit. Nor does Aquinas' philosophy demonstrate the necessary truth of Jesus as the incarnation. And if further justification of this criticism of Aquinas' philosophy were needed, Aquinas himself noted that, after a direct supernatural religious experience and revelation of God, his words 'were as straw' and he could write no more.

Aquinas' use of analogy. Lastly, in many of Aquinas' ideas and works, he draws upon analogy as a means to explain his point. However, the success or failure of an analogy rests on how similar the two concepts are that are being compared. In addition, analogies are not neutral and can be biased.

To illustrate these points, consider the following analogies as a means to persuade someone either way on having surgery with either an experienced consultant or a trainee:

Analogy A	Analogy B
Consider cars. If you had the choice of a brand new car, with full warranty, recently checked before leaving the factory and passing its MOT with flying colours, you'd pick that, wouldn't you, over the vintage, classic car, which is old, will inevitably be worn out, and requires work and care on a regular basis?	Consider the situation where you needed work doing on your house. If you had the choice between a tradesperson with a long track record, established and verified clients and reviews, plenty of previous experience and therefore expertise, wouldn't you pick them over a new start-up, or apprentice tradesperson, with no track record, proven history of experience or client reviews?

Reading each example, it would be reasonable to agree in each specific circumstance, but what do the analogies actually offer in terms of what they are being compared to? Not a lot. Neither analogy is actually valid in this context because there are very few similarities, if any, that can be drawn between surgery and the analogies presented.

This point was made by Hume in relation to arguments from design. As Hume notes, an analogy is only as strong as the similarities between the two concepts being compared. If the similarity is weak, then the conclusion drawn will be weak. With regard to the success of Aquinas' design argument, how strong do you think the analogy between an archer firing an arrow at a target and the regularity of natural order within the world is?

A similar criticism can be made of Aquinas' approach to religious language as analogical. The strength of this approach rests on the comparison, and thus relation between, God and humans. Aquinas himself in the majority of his work defends the stance that God is not self- or directly evident to humans due to their finite minds, and humans are material and within space and time whereas Aquinas believed God is transcendent, outside space and time. Could a successful analogy between humans and our experiences within the created world ever be strong enough to enable us to talk confidently and meaningfully about God's nature?

Watch Out for Traps

Don't forget to use key terms. One way that students can improve answers is to use and define relevant key terms accurately. For Aquinas, these include terms such as *realist, cognitivist, inductive, a posteriori* and *necessary being*, as well as the opposite terms such as *anti-realist, non-cognitivist, deductive, a priori* and *contingency*. Correct application of such terms and understanding of the wider philosophical approach or specific concept they refer to will strengthen your exam responses across the specification.

Don't forget to use examples or biblical references. Make use of the examples to explain your answers, as it demonstrates that you understand the ideas. You could use the examples that Aquinas used, such as the following:

- The archer and the arrow – things lacking intelligence require direction from something intelligent.
- The ox and its urine – you can attribute qualities to God due to a causal relationship.
- The lion's strength and God's strength – creatures and God have metaphorical similarities in proportion to their status.
- An eclipse is not a true miracle despite uneducated people expressing awe and wonder at the event.

Add your own if you are confident.

There are also several biblical references that guided Aquinas' thinking, which you can use to explain and defend his ideas. Become familiar with these so that you can express them yourself. For example:

- Genesis 1:26, 'Let us make mankind in our image, in our likeness', as the basis for comparison, and as justification for philosophy and human reason as a source of truth
- Romans 1:20, 'For since the creation of the world God's invisible qualities – his eternal power and divine nature – have been clearly seen, being understood from what has been made, so that people are without excuse', as justification for an a posteriori approach to truth

- various biblical references to support supernatural revealed truths, such as Jesus as God's incarnation or God as Trinitarian
- biblical examples of miracles, such as John 11: 38–44, the resurrection of Lazarus.

Don't confuse Aquinas' notion of God as a necessary being with that of Anselm. Although Anselm and Aquinas both use the terms 'necessary' and 'being' in relation to their arguments for God's existence, they arrive at these points from different angles and therefore they have slightly different meanings. For Aquinas, God must be necessary because experience and reasoning point to something existing that never comes into existence and never goes out of existence, and which must therefore be eternal and fixed. Anselm arrives at God as the necessary being because by definition God, as that which nothing greater than can be conceived, cannot be contingent. For Anselm, God cannot be thought of as non-existent without resulting in a logical self-contradiction. However, for Aquinas it is the notion of an infinite regress of contingent things that is illogical (of nothing, nothing comes, *ex nihilo nihil fit*), so there must be a necessary being to begin and sustain everything.

Don't waste time. Don't waste valuable time writing about Aquinas' life, as it is his ideas and arguments that you need to be familiar with, not his biography. However, it helps to know that he was a medieval Christian who believed that the God of classical theism existed and was the creator of the world, and that sacred scripture revealed the full truth.

Describing criticisms is not evaluation. Remember that in part a) AO1 questions you could be asked to explain criticisms, challenges or objections to something. Therefore, merely describing criticisms of Aquinas' ideas is not AO2 analysis and evaluation. Analysis comes from identifying strengths and weaknesses in Aquinas' ideas, and evaluation develops from this analysis by then considering how successful or unsuccessful these are and weighing them up to reach a justified conclusion. It helps, for example, to consider whether the ideas or different aspects of the ideas are coherent, credible, persuasive or logical.

STRENGTHEN YOUR GRASP

1. Make a table for each of the ideas listed in the 'Know Aquinas' Key Ideas' section, with three columns: description, strengths and weaknesses. Fill each table with useful bullet point notes and information, including examples and the names of relevant scholars.
2. Write out a paragraph summarising why each of the ideas listed in the 'Know Aquinas' Key Ideas' section are either successful or unsuccessful. Use the tables you made for activity 1 to help you in deciding a line of argument and reaching a justified conclusion. After you have written your paragraphs, look over them all and try to spot any patterns. Do you think some of Aquinas' ideas are stronger than others? Are there common themes or reasons as to what you think are strengths or weaknesses? Being aware of these will help you to be able to evaluate and justify your point of view.

Exam Guidance AO1

For part a) AO1 knowledge and understanding questions, as Aquinas spans multiple themes within the specifications at both AS and A Level, you could be asked to outline (AS only), explain or examine any of his ideas, challenges to his ideas, or the wider theme and topic area where he is referred to in the Board's specification. To help you revise, ensure you read thoroughly the 'Know Aquinas' Key Ideas', 'Understand Aquinas' Arguments' and 'Know Criticisms of Aquinas' sections in this book, covering inductive arguments for God's existence, religious language as analogy, and miracles. The material covered in these sections would feed into AO1 discussion of the following:

- **Aquinas' three ways.** Depending on the specific question wording, you may need to focus on breadth or depth, or provide a mixture of the two. However, if you are discussing one of Aquinas' ideas in depth, ensure that you do not miss out any premises when explaining the argument, and use examples or biblical references where you can. If you are discussing Aquinas' ideas in breadth, you may wish to provide context and demonstrate insight into his wider philosophical approach and style: for example, his medieval Christian belief system. When responding to a broad question about the nature of inductive or a posteriori arguments, you may wish to use Aquinas' ideas to illustrate how inductive logic and a posteriori knowledge of motion, cause and contingency feature in his arguments.

- **Aquinas' fifth way.** Depending on the question focus, you could include key AO1 concepts that would demonstrate breadth, such as observable natural order, direction from an intelligent being and Aquinas' use of analogy. To demonstrate depth, in addition to the above you might also wish to refer to Aquinas' approach, philosophical method and underlying Christian assumption that God is the creator. When responding to a broad question about the nature of inductive or a posteriori arguments, you may wish to discuss Aquinas' rejection of the idea that the regularity we experience in the natural world to best fulfil the *telos* of things came about by sheer fortune or chance, and explain that he sought to demonstrate it was more rational to conclude there was a designer.

- **Aquinas on miracles.** Depending on the question asked, you could include in your response reference to Aquinas' understanding of what a miracle is, his realist stance in believing miracles to be real events that differ from the typical, rather than someone's perspective, his hierarchical ranking of miracles with biblical examples, and how he developed his view from Augustine to take into account the issue of hidden or known knowledge of the cause of such an event. Depending on the depth required, it might be beneficial to link back to Aquinas' view of God as the creator and sustainer of the world, and therefore Aquinas' belief that God planned for miracles to occur within the natural order. As such miracles cannot be events that go against nature, they just appear to do so to us because we do not understand the full picture of the natural order. This perspective enables Aquinas to maintain his understanding of God as immutable (unchanging) because to understand a miracle as an event that goes against nature as created by God in the first instance would imply that God has changed his plans, which raises questions and potential problems regarding God's omniscience (being all-knowing).

- **Religious language as analogy; attribution and proportion.** In this instance, depending on the question and the depth or breadth required, you might wish to include the context of Aquinas' solution to the problems of religious language, how he believed that religious language can be meaningful in a realist and cognitive way through *via positiva*, and the assumption of a causal link between the world and God underpinning Aquinas' ideas. Ensure you are able to explain effectively the different types of analogy and how they work with reference to Aquinas' examples. Depending on the wording of the question, you might want to refer to how Aquinas' ideas were developed by Ian Ramsey (see Chapter 30).

Exam Guidance AO2

For AO2 evaluation questions, you may be presented with a one-sided statement, regarding Aquinas' key ideas as identified in the specification, or a theme/topic to which his key ideas relate.

- **Aquinas' arguments for God's existence.** Depending on the question, you might want to refer to both the specific strengths and weaknesses of the different arguments in question as well as the wider strengths and weaknesses of Aquinas' inductive and a posteriori approach, analysing the overall success and impact of his argument. You might want to weigh up the success of these arguments in light of scientific discoveries, or specific criticisms, such as his use of analogy. You could also include comparisons to alternative arguments from different scholars in the same specification theme, and contrast their strengths and weaknesses to analyse how persuasive or convincing Aquinas is, within context. Remembering Aquinas' prior assumptions, starting point and approach will be beneficial in evaluating his ways for God's existence, especially when in contrast to challenges or alternatives. Remember, it could also be relevant to include an aspect of evaluation and analysis about Aquinas' inductive and a posteriori argument as a counter-argument in response to a statement concerning the success or failure of deductive and a priori arguments. Finally, you could refer to Aquinas' arguments for God's existence in response to a question about how different religious views on the nature of God impact on arguments for the existence of God, as Aquinas' arguments can be considered to be based on his Christian beliefs and possibly demonstrate circular logic as a result.

- **Aquinas on miracles.** Depending on the question, your response could include evaluating the success of Aquinas' definition, in that while he holds a cognitive and realist view of miracles as real events, he denies they are contrary to the laws of nature, which seems to clash with the common understanding of what a miracle is. Further, the logic of Aquinas' definition can be considered. Is it coherent and logical for Aquinas to claim that miracles are real events that appear to us to be contrary to the natural order, insofar as they are not typical events and the cause is completely hidden to us, yet at the same time to claim that such miracles are completely possible in accordance with the natural order, as planned by God? According to Aquinas' view, could not any rare event then be considered a miracle, provided humans did not understand the cause? This raises further issues regarding Aquinas' point that the cause of miracles must be hidden to us for an event to be considered a true miracle; in the twenty-first century, we have far more scientific understanding of rare natural events that previously Aquinas might have considered a miracle. Would Aquinas no longer consider the parting of the Red Sea in Exodus a miracle because we now understand about wind speed, tides, tsunamis and other factors that can cause water to part and rise up temporarily? You could also consider how agreeable his definition is for other theists in contrast to atheists and in light of objections.

- **Religious language as analogy; attribution and proportion.** Depending on the question, you might want to consider the problems that Aquinas identified in using *via negativa*, univocal and equivocal language to discuss God, and how successful his solution is. In terms of Aquinas' own logic and philosophical argument, his basis in the assumption that God created the world and that there is a causal link from which to justify an analogical approach, and the relevance this has for theists and atheists today, would be relevant. However, your response could also evaluate his solution in light of more modern problems of religious language, such as the challenge of falsification, and evaluate his cognitivist approach and how persuasive that is, in different contexts.

Evaluating Aquinas Today

In an exam, you could be asked to evaluate the adequacy or success of any of Aquinas' ideas as named in the specification. You can draw upon this section for ideas as you prepare, but note that Aquinas' theories cannot be addressed here in detail. You will be required to reach a judgement on the views that you present, but you do not need to reach the same conclusion as this reflection.

There are many thinkers who believe that, despite Aquinas' medieval Catholic worldview and subsequent underlying religious assumptions, he had tremendous impact on philosophical thought and actively contributed to the reshaping of Western philosophy and the Western approach to the natural sciences. As a vocal supporter of the a posteriori approach using observable sense experience and logical inductive reasoning, especially concerning his cosmological and teleological arguments, Aquinas has been credited with foreshadowing the scientific revolution and requirement for empirical evidence and falsification, which reflects an awareness that at best our theories are merely probable. Therefore, many might argue that Aquinas' inductive arguments for God's existence are by their nature more persuasive than deductive arguments, as they can rationally persuade us that God's existence is at least possible, if not probable, unlike ontological arguments, which can be considered to fail completely if the premises can be shown to be false.

In addition, Aquinas' arguments for God's existence are still incredibly relevant, and are considered by many to be compatible with modern-day scientific support due to their a posteriori use of evidence. For example, the evidence for the Big Bang theory supports and is compatible with Aquinas' cosmological arguments, and the mathematical probability of the universe developing in such a way as to be suitable for life to flourish supports, and is compatible with, Aquinas' teleological argument. The fact that there have since been modern developments of Aquinas' cosmological and teleological arguments in the Kalam, Anthropic and Aesthetic arguments also suggests that there was something of value to them in the first instance.

However, by modern-day standards, many of Aquinas' theories could be considered to fall short of satisfactory evidence due to the inductive leap he makes, going from where the premises might reasonably lead to the conclusion that the God of classical theism must therefore exist. While philosophical reasoning might go some way towards making the existence of a powerful being a rational proposition, there is no evidence to say that it is specifically an omnipotent, omnibenevolent, omniscient deity, who also happens to be God as understood as the God of Christian theism. Many of the objections to cosmological and teleological arguments raised by later scholars such as David Hume are widely considered to be successful, especially in terms of how the problem of evil can so effectively challenge the teleological argument, from both a logical and an evidential perspective.

In addition, Aquinas' reliance on a causal link between God and the world as an underpinning principle of multiple theories, such as religious language as analogical and his ideas on miracles, upon closer inspection can be considered to be unfounded, which in turn leaves many of his ideas with no legs to stand on. If we appreciate the extent to which Aquinas was certain that God was the creator of the world, his arguments begin to look more and more circular.

That said, Aquinas remains one of the greatest scholastic philosophers, responsible for reconciling Aristotelian philosophy with Christian thought, and his belief that human reason was universal to *all* fundamentally influenced ideas at the time about what truths could and could not be known, by whom, and by what means.

2. WILLIAM LANE CRAIG
GET INTO CRAIG'S WORLD

Quick Overview William Lane Craig (born 1949) is an American **Christian apologist** and philosopher, famous for proposing a contemporary cosmological argument. Craig revived and developed the Islamic **Kalam** argument, writing from a Christian perspective.

William Lane Craig is an American philosopher who became an evangelical Christian in his teens, and from an early age demonstrated a keen ability in debate, having won the Illinois state oratory championships. Craig studied Philosophy of Religion and cosmological arguments for God's existence under the supervision of John Hick at the University of Birmingham, before going on to study historical arguments for the resurrection of Jesus in Germany. With regard to the Kalam cosmological argument, Craig was studying in the second half of the twentieth century, following scientific discoveries such as Einstein's law of relativity, Hubble's red shift, and cosmic background radiation. All of these provided evidence of an expanding universe, therefore supporting the idea that the universe had a very definite beginning.

The Big Bang theory illustrates that the universe had a beginning, at which point space and time began. However, it is not known what caused the Big Bang to occur, only that it must have been something outside of space and time.

Up until this era of scientific discovery, there had been very little evidence that the universe had a beginning, and most of the scientific community had previously favoured notions of an eternal, infinite universe such as **Steady State theory**. However, for believers in the God of classical theism (omnipotent, omnibenevolent, omniscient and transcendent), it was hard to reconcile belief in an omnipotent creator God with a universe that had no beginning. This also posed contradictions for religious scripture: for example, Genesis categorically states that God created the universe by *creatio ex nihilo* (creation out of nothing). It was against the backdrop of this new scientific evidence and renewed interest in the origin of the universe that Craig revived medieval Islamic cosmological arguments from the likes of **Al-Ghazali**, and caught the interest of the West.

In the decades that followed, Craig went on to debate his arguments publicly with many notable atheists, and he continues to engage in debate regarding God's existence, leading to many developments of his original arguments.

TIP

Thinkers can never be separated from their times. Note some of the societal events and ideas that Craig was living through and to which he was responding.

ESSENTIAL!

A **Christian apologist** is someone who defends the truth of Christianity and Christian belief.

Kalam is an Arabic term for 'speech' which refers to the method of teaching and debate. It is much like the medieval Christian method of scholasticism.

INSIGHT

Evidence of an expanding universe is the basis for the Big Bang theory, which argues that the universe had a beginning, about 13.7 billion years ago.

ESSENTIAL!

Steady State theory proposed that the universe was eternal, and continuously created matter to ensure the density remained the same despite expansion.

INSIGHT

Al-Ghazali was an eleventh-century Islamic philosopher who proposed a cosmological argument for God's existence, rooted in the rejection of the concept of infinity.

Know Craig's Key Ideas

IMPROVE YOUR UNDERSTANDING

Make sure that you grasp how Craig's Kalam argument leads him to conclude that the cause of the universe is a personal creator.

The Kalam Cosmological Argument

Craig was inspired by the writings of Al-Ghazali, who argued that the idea of a universe without a beginning was absurd. Al-Ghazali said that the universe must have had a beginning, and as everything that has a beginning has a cause, the universe has a cause too. The only cause that could lead to the universe was a transcendent being. Therefore the cause of the universe was God.

Craig developed this idea, taking into account modern-day scientific evidence and using humour. Craig argued that something cannot come from nothing, and to claim such is 'worse than magic'. Craig continued with the magic analogy: 'When a magician pulls a rabbit out of a hat, at least you've got the magician, not to mention the hat!'

Craig refutes the modern objection that some things do in fact come from nothing, as Craig argues that this is referring to sub-atomic particles which are in fact caused by something else – a quantum decay process. This, he says, is therefore completely irrelevant to discussion about the cause of the universe, so we can proceed in confidence with the idea that a universe without a beginning would be absurd.

The first part of Craig's Kalam argument is deductive, meaning that if the premises are true, the conclusion necessarily follows. However, Craig's argument as presented here maintains an a posteriori nature due to reference to scientific evidence. His argument can be expressed in its simplest form in the following way:

> P1: Everything that has a beginning must have a cause.
>
> P2: The universe had a beginning.
>
> C1: The universe must have a cause.
>
> C2: Since no scientific law or explanation can account for the cause of the universe, the cause must be a personal cause, which is God.

INSIGHT

It is 'so intuitively obvious that I think scarcely anyone could sincerely believe it to be false' (William Lane Craig, *Reasonable Faith: Christian Truth and Apologetics*, 1994, on the subject of God as the cause of the universe).

Craig's argument as outlined above may look similar to Aquinas' second way, but his P1 avoids the pitfall of stating that '*everything* has a cause'. By clarifying that only things which *have a beginning* have a cause, Craig is appealing to our rational intuition, confirmed a posteriori.

Rejection of Actual Infinities

Craig went on to defend his P2 premise that the universe had a beginning in a further deductive but a priori (reason via logic, prior to experience) argument with reference to Al-Gazali's rejection of an infinite universe. Al-Ghazali argued that if the universe had always existed, there would be an infinite number of past events. Therefore we would never arrive at the present moment, which is absurd and contradicted by the very fact that we do. Therefore, this proved a priori that the universe could not be infinite, so therefore logically had to have a beginning.

Craig clarified this idea and argued:

> P1: An **actual infinite** cannot exist in reality as the concept is incoherent.
>
> P2: An infinite series of past temporal events would be an actual infinite.
>
> C: Therefore, the universe cannot be an actual infinite so must have a beginning and therefore a cause.

> **ESSENTIAL!**
>
> An **actual infinite** is an infinite series or regress of elements, which Craig argues is logically absurd.

Craig illustrated this with the theoretical example of a library. Imagine a library with an infinite number of books. This library consists of an infinite number of both red and black books. Together, there are an infinite number of red *and* black books, which is a contradiction. There cannot be the same number of *just* red books, as the number of red *and* black books combined. Similarly, if there were an infinite number of books, but one was loaned out, there would still remain an infinite number of books. We can continue: if there were an infinite number of books, but we added a further infinite number of books to the collection, there would still remain an infinite number and not a single one more. These examples demonstrate that there is no actual infinite in reality.

Craig responded to critics who argued that a **potential infinite** could exist, by arguing that a potential infinite just further demonstrates that the universe requires a beginning. A potential infinite occurs when something could in theory continue forever: for example, starting to count and continuing for infinity. We could always add more numbers. We can likewise imagine the universe continuing for infinity. However, to actually arrive at any present moment, which a moment ago would have been the future, requires the universe to have had a beginning. Otherwise we would never have arrived at the present moment, as with an actual infinite there would always be an infinite amount of time before arriving at a future moment. The past therefore cannot be infinite. A potential infinite is only possible when the past is finite.

> **ESSENTIAL!**
>
> A **potential infinite** is something with a beginning that can be added to and which goes on indefinitely.

The concept of a personal creator

Craig then adds an additional element to his Kalam argument, which is inductive (arguing from probability rather than logical proof). The cause of the universe must be a personal cause – or 'personal agent' – with self-awareness and free will: in other words, the God of classical theism. He argues that because the universe and everything within it is **temporal**, within time and temporary, the cause of the universe must be **transcendent**, outside of space and time, because nothing can come from nothing. There must have been something outside of and prior to the temporal matter to begin creation of the temporal matter which is our universe. The transcendent cause of the universe must also be **eternal**, otherwise we can ask what caused the cause, which is absurd. Therefore the transcendent and eternal cause of the universe is God.

> **ESSENTIAL!**
>
> **Temporal** means within time, and temporary.
>
> **Transcendent** means outside of space and time.
>
> **Eternal** means having no beginning or end.

Furthermore, as the cause of the universe must be outside of space and time and so cannot be physical or relate to matter, Craig argues that it must be either an abstract concept or a transcendent mind. Abstract concepts – for example, the number 7 – cannot cause anything. They also lack the ability to choose to act, so would not be able to account for a temporal effect (concerning matter, within time). Therefore, the cause of the universe must be the free choice, of a personal, transcendent mind: God.

■ **WHAT DO YOU THINK?**

Write down your thoughts about Craig's arguments in a notebook and revisit them shortly before the exam to see if your views have changed.

Read Craig for Yourself

The following passage is taken from *The Existence of God and the Beginning of the Universe* (1979), and illustrates why the cause of the universe must be a personal creator. The notes in the margin will help you to grasp the main ideas.

By 'personal Creator' Craig is referring to the God of classical theism – a personal God, whom he takes to be the Christian God.	I think that it can be plausibly argued that the cause of the universe must be a personal Creator. For how else could a temporal effect arise from an eternal cause? If the cause were simply a mechanically operating set of necessary and sufficient conditions existing from eternity, then why would not the effect also exist from eternity? For example, if the cause of water's being frozen is the temperature's being below zero degrees, then if the temperature were below zero degrees from eternity, then any water present would be frozen from eternity. The only way to have an eternal cause but a temporal effect would seem to be if the cause is a personal agent who freely chooses to create an effect in time. For example, a man sitting from eternity may will to stand up; hence, a temporal effect may arise from an eternally existing agent. Indeed, the agent may will from eternity to create a temporal effect, so that no change in the agent need be conceived. Thus, we are brought not merely to the first cause of the universe, but to its personal Creator.
Craig is highlighting this complex issue that requires an explanation. 'Temporal effect' refers to an effect concerning matter within space and time, such as the creation of the universe, which must be caused by something outside the universe which exists without end. If the cause of the universe is eternal, what explanation can be given for why an effect of this cause is temporal – that is, temporary – and within a specified time?	
Craig is referring to non-religious ideas surrounding what caused the Big Bang, such as nuclear forces.	
Craig's solution to why an eternal cause created a temporal effect is personal choice. A mechanical explanation that is also eternal due to being outside of space and time, such as nuclear forces, cannot explain why the universe was created in time.	
	[…]
Craig is highlighting how he has drawn from a priori and a posteriori sources of knowledge.	In conclusion, we have seen on the basis of both philosophical argument and scientific confirmation that it is plausible that the universe began to exist. Given the intuitively obvious principle that whatever begins to exist has a cause of its existence, we have been led to conclude that the universe has a cause of its existence. On the basis of our argument, this cause would have to be uncaused, eternal, changeless, timeless, and immaterial. Moreover, it would have to be a personal agent who freely elects to create an effect in time. Therefore, on the basis of the kalam cosmological argument, I conclude that it is rational to believe that God exists.
Craig is referring to his use of inductive argument.	
Craig is referring to a priori knowledge here.	
Due to evidence and experience from the world that Craig's cosmological argument relies upon, he considers his argument overall to be inductive rather than deductive, as a rational basis for faith rather than conclusive logical proof.	

Know Criticisms of Craig

Not necessarily the God of classical theism. Even if we accept Craig's points that the universe requires a cause, it does not necessarily mean that Craig has proved the cause must be God, who is omnibenevolent, omnipotent and omniscient, etc. It is still possible that the universe began as a result of chance, without any conscious personal choice, or that even if the cause was a personal agent choosing to create the world, it does not prove that the agent is a deity with the characteristics of classical theism. The aspect of Craig's Kalam argument where he argues that the cause must be a personal creator, which is God, is inductive and therefore makes an 'inductive leap'. The sceptical empiricist David Hume argued that inductive arguments for God's existence are flawed because we cannot be certain of the conclusion. Inductive arguments make leaps or assumptions based on our past experiences in very specific contexts, and we have no grounds from which to claim knowledge about future or unknown contexts, such as the creation of the world.

Occam's razor. Occam's razor states that the simplest principle is the most likely. To say that the universe is finite, but the cause (God) is infinite, is over-complicating things unnecessarily. Philosopher Bertrand Russell said that we should restrict our search for the cause of the universe to the universe itself. It is simpler to accept that the universe itself is necessary, rather than to make the leap to a necessary being for which we have no concrete evidence. Furthermore, new scientific discoveries are made all the time, and some scientists are now proposing that the Big Bang expansion may have been triggered by a previous contraction of a universe, and that this process could be an infinite regress of Big Bang and contraction cycles, meaning that the universe could in fact be infinite.

Philosophical fallacy. Craig's argument can be said to make the following philosophical fallacies of contradiction:

- Craig denies the reality of an actual infinite, but then relies on an actual infinite in the form of God's existence.
- Craig argues that everything that has a beginning has a cause because nothing comes from nothing, but then goes on to uphold the view that God created the world from nothing.

Watch Out for Traps

Don't forget that for Craig, God is a personal creator. Sometimes when explaining Craig's ideas, students stop at the universe requiring a cause, or jump straight to the idea that God must be the cause. To show deeper understanding of Craig's ideas, remember to develop his argument correctly and include his final conclusion. Explain why the cause of the universe must be a personal creator, with the free will to choose to cause the universe. Craig's example of the eternally sitting man who chooses to stand temporarily is helpful here.

Don't forget to use examples to illustrate why an actual infinite cannot exist in reality. There are many examples to choose from to illustrate this, such as Craig's library illustration outlined in the 'Know Craig's Key Ideas' section, Hilbert's Hotel Argument or older forms such as Zeno's paradox, which demonstrate that an actual infinite cannot traverse time and space, so the destination or present/future moment can never be arrived at.

Don't get lost in the detail. You are not expected to go into detail regarding evidence for the Big Bang theory or Craig's more complex concepts such as a potential infinite. Focus on ensuring that you can demonstrate an understanding of how Craig's Kalam argument is formulated and how it differs from Aquinas' cosmological arguments.

STRENGTHEN YOUR GRASP

1. The order of Craig's arguments is important. Go through the 'Know Craig's Key Ideas' section, chunking up his ideas into the following key points:
   - scientific evidence that the universe has a beginning
   - an actual infinite is incoherent and impossible
   - a possible infinite still requires a beginning
   - the cause of the universe must be a personal cause.
2. Go through the notes you made for activity 1, noting potential criticisms for each key point. Which ideas seem Craig's weakest? Which seem the strongest? You can use the 'Know Criticisms of Craig' section to help.

> **CREATE YOUR OWN QUESTION**
>
> Read this chapter and use command words such as 'explain' or 'examine' to create your own AO1 questions. For an AO2 question, make a one-sided statement about the success of cosmological arguments in the twenty-first century or in response to scientific challenges, put the statement between quotation marks and follow it with the phrase, 'Evaluate this view.'

Exam Guidance AO1

Depending on the question asked, to boost the depth of understanding in a part a) response you could show how the Kalam argument is a modern development of older cosmological forms, and moves from a deductive argument to an inductive argument, retaining an a posteriori nature. You might want to demonstrate how it differs from Aquinas' three ways in terms of its philosophical rejection of infinity and justification of a personal creator, making use of modern scientific evidence with examples such as red shift and cosmic background radiation.

Regarding the challenges to cosmological arguments, it could be beneficial to be able to describe how various ideas challenge aspects of the Kalam argument in addition to older forms. For example, Hume's empirical objections and critique of causes can still apply to Craig's argument, as the argument goes on to become inductive and so can still be said to make an inductive leap, going from the known (universe has a beginning/universe has a cause) to the unknown (the cause is a personal creator).

Exam Guidance AO2

When answering part b) evaluation questions on the Kalam argument, be mindful that although some general challenges to cosmological arguments will apply, there are specific criticisms of, and challenges and responses to, Craig's ideas, and you would need to refer to these to access the higher bands in the marking criteria. Read over the criticisms of Craig's argument above and in your course textbook and other resources to revise specific strengths and weaknesses of Craig's ideas and direct challenges. You should also consider the context of the twenty-first century and how modern scientific evidence such as the Big Bang theory can support the Kalam argument.

If evaluating a more general statement regarding inductive arguments for God's existence, you could prepare by making a table of all the different inductive arguments in one column, and the challenges to inductive arguments in another, and note down whether you think each argument is successful in light of each challenge.

3. WILLIAM PALEY
GET INTO PALEY'S WORLD

Quick Overview William Paley (1743–1805) was an English priest, famous in his time for his moral and political philosophy, and his work towards the abolition of slavery. However, Paley is most remembered today for his **Natural Theology**.

William Paley lived during a period of great change in Britain, including the **Enlightenment**, which emphasised reason over superstition, and the **industrial revolution**. Paley's works reflect the new scientific discoveries and understanding of mechanics and embrace the progressive political and moral ideas of the times, while remaining grounded in his Anglican Christian beliefs. As a Christian priest, Paley believed in the truth of Christian teachings and the God of classical theism – omniscient, omnipotent, omnibenevolent and transcendent. He believed that the study of the natural world revealed the nature of God. He understood religion and science to be in harmony, and he sought to demonstrate this through his *Natural Theology or Evidences of the Existence and Attributes of the Deity* (1802).

Know Paley's Key Ideas
The Teleological Argument

Paley's **teleological argument** sets out that, were we to discover a stone on the ground and an unintentionally dropped watch while walking, we would come to different conclusions about how they were formed. Unlike a stone, a watch is made up of complex intricate mechanisms for the purpose of telling time. Furthermore, the intricate mechanisms of the watch are put together in the perfect order to ensure everything works together to fulfil its purpose. Had the watch not been assembled in this precise fashion, it would not be able to tell time. These observations lead us to conclude that the watch is a product of intelligent design by a watchmaker rather than random chance.

Paley then refers to examples of complexity, purpose and order in nature, such as the eye, whose intricate mechanisms work together to fulfil the purpose of sight. Just as we inferred a watchmaker from the complexity, order and purpose of the watch, so we can infer an intelligent designer from the complexity and purpose in the natural world. Paley concludes that this designer is the God of Christianity.

> **ESSENTIAL!**
> **Natural Theology** is the study of the natural world as a means to discover truths about God.

> **ESSENTIAL!**
> The **Enlightenment** was a cultural movement that dominated the eighteenth century, sometimes known as 'the age of reason'.
>
> The **industrial revolution** is the term given to the period when Britain transitioned from producing goods by hand to using large-scale mechanical machines.

> **ESSENTIAL!**
> **Teleological arguments** are arguments from design. They look at evidence within the world to suggest design and therefore a designer, who must be God.

Understand Paley's Arguments

IMPROVE YOUR UNDERSTANDING

Make sure that you understand how Paley uses observations of the natural world to present an inductive argument to show that it is reasonable to believe God is the designer of the world.

> **ESSENTIAL!**
>
> **Qua** is Latin for 'by virtue of' or 'via'. An example is design via regularity.

WHAT DO YOU THINK?

Write down your thoughts on Paley's arguments and revisit them shortly before the exam to see if your views have changed.

Paley's design argument is often broken down into two forms:

- **Design qua purpose.** God as the intelligent designer designed the world and everything in it not only with a purpose, but with the ability to fulfil that purpose: for example, the way the different parts of an eye work together to enable sight.

- **Design qua regularity.** Paley notes how complex mechanisms within the natural world also function in a certain order with specific motion to fulfil their purpose. For example, the motion of the planets within the solar system occurs in such a way (enabling day and night and the seasons) that living things on the earth can thrive.

Paley's design argument is inductive, as the conclusion does not necessarily follow on from the premise. Paley is seeking to show that it is reasonable to believe God is the designer rather than other possible conclusions, by use of a posteriori knowledge. Paley uses observations of purpose and regularity in the world as evidence to support his argument.

Read Paley for Yourself

This passage is taken from Paley's *Natural Theology* (1802), and illustrates his argument. The notes in the margin will help you to grasp his ideas.

The purpose of telling time. >	When we come to inspect the watch, we perceive (what we could not discover in the stone) that its several parts are framed and put together for a purpose, e.g. that they are so formed and adjusted as to produce motion, and that motion so regulated as to point out the hour of the day.
Put together in the order required for correct function to fulfil the purpose of telling time. >	
	[...]
The inference is where Paley's analogy lies. Not in the watch itself, but in how one can infer a designer from a watch one can also infer a designer from the world. >	the inference ... is inevitable, that the watch must have had a maker: that there must have existed, at some time, and at some place or other, an artificer or artificers who formed it for the purpose which we find ... and designed its use.
	[...]
Paley is responding to Hume's criticism that because we have not experienced the creation of the universe we cannot speculate or assume there was a designer. >	Nor would it ... weaken the conclusion, that we had never seen a watch made; that we had never known an artist capable of making one ... Neither ... would it invalidate our conclusion, that the watch sometimes went wrong ... It is not necessary that a machine be perfect, in order to show with what design it was made.
Paley is responding to Hume's criticism from the problem of evil, for bad design indicating either a malevolent designer or no designer. >	

Know Criticisms of Paley

Paley makes an inductive leap. Many of the philosophical criticisms levelled at Paley's design argument were published in Hume's *Dialogues Concerning Natural Religion*, 22 years prior to Paley's argument. Although Paley attempted to respond to these, they are still considered by many to be successful, particularly those challenging the notion that if there is a designer, it is the God of classical theism. This is an inductive leap as Paley is leaping from knowledge gained through observations of the world to assumptions about the origin of the world. See Chapter 5 for more detail.

The theory of evolution. Darwin's theory of evolution, which was published 57 years after Paley's *Natural Theology*, is often considered to be the greatest challenge to Paley's argument. Evolution provides a scientific explanation for why complex mechanisms exist without reference to a designer, as a result of natural selection. Richard Dawkins, evolutionary biologist, wrote *The Blind Watchmaker* (1986) to argue that the universe is the product *not* of design, but of natural selection, which is entirely random.

Watch Out for Traps

Paley did not compare the world to a watch. While Paley's argument is often considered an argument from analogy, Paley did not say the world is like a watch. Rather, it was the inference that has similarities. Just as we infer a watchmaker from a watch, so we can infer a designer from the world.

> **STRENGTHEN YOUR GRASP**
> 1. Think of three examples from the natural world that could be used to demonstrate 'design qua purpose' and 'design qua regularity'. Explain them in a paragraph to illustrate Paley's argument. For example, you could use the water cycle.
> 2. Read Chapter 5 on Hume's objections to teleological arguments to help you identify weaknesses and challenges that can be applied to Paley's idea. Can you think of any responses to these to defend Paley's argument? Which is the stronger view?

Exam Guidance AO1

You could be asked about Paley's watchmaker and complex design argument, either along with another scholar from the specification or as a stand-alone, or as part of a wider question about teleological or inductive arguments.

When writing about Paley's watchmaker argument, don't forget to include his conclusion that the world therefore has a designer, which is God.

Exam Guidance AO2

You could be asked to evaluate ideas such as the effectiveness/persuasiveness of teleological arguments generally but also in the twenty-first century, the success of the challenges to teleological arguments, and whether scientific explanations for the universe outweigh philosophical ones. Paley's argument may just be one aspect of any response.

When revising Paley's argument, make a bullet-point list of the main challenges (philosophical and scientific) and note whether Paley is successful in overcoming these challenges, the strengths and weaknesses of Paley's argument, and its inductive nature.

4. F.R. TENNANT
GET INTO TENNANT'S WORLD

> **ESSENTIAL!**
>
> **Theistic evolution** is the understanding that God guides the process of evolution, acting through natural selection.

Quick Overview Scientist Frederick Robert Tennant (1866–1957) is perhaps best known for his theory of **theistic evolution** and contributions to modern design arguments for God's existence.

F.R. Tennant was a science teacher before hearing the 1889 Huxley lectures about how evolution challenged the evidence for a creator God. He then became interested in religion and trained to be a clergyman in the Church of England.

Tennant did not believe that Paley's argument of complex design could be justified in light of the theory of evolution. Rather he believed that the precise nature of evolution through natural selection, which not only allowed intelligent life to flourish but also sustained it, required an explanation that went beyond random chance. He was therefore an early advocate of theistic evolution, which aimed to harmonise Christian beliefs with evolutionary science, and neutralise the increased conflicts between religion and science that had developed in the decades following the publication of Darwin's *On the Origin of Species* (1859).

Know Tennant's Key Ideas

Anthropic Principle

> **ESSENTIAL!**
>
> **Anthropic** comes from the Greek *anthropos*, meaning human.

Despite not using the term, Tennant developed what is now recognised as the '**anthropic** principle'. His arguments are generally categorised as follows:

- The universe can be understood rationally, so it is rational to infer a designer.
- It is unlikely that the universe could be so perfectly conditioned to be able to sustain life by chance; it is more convincing to infer a designer who fine-tuned conditions.
- The fact that evolution led to intelligent life with self-awareness, consciousness and morality points to something more divine than just brute laws of nature as a guide.

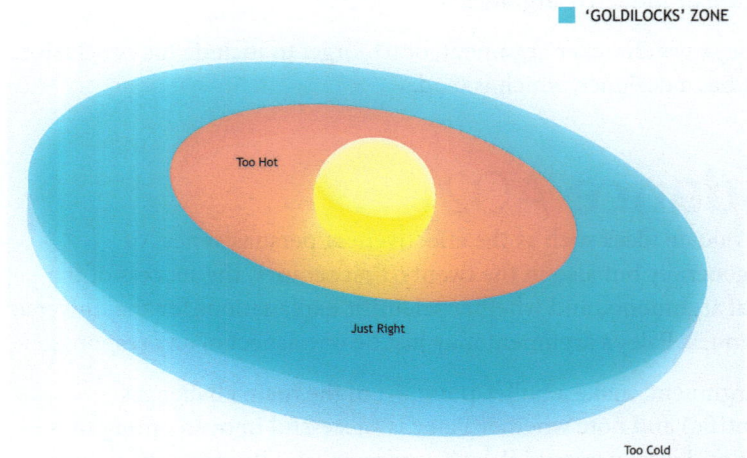

Evidence used to support Tennant's anthropic argument includes 'the Goldilocks zone'. Science has revealed that the precise location of planet earth in the solar system means life can survive – too close to the sun and it would be too hot, and further away from the sun it would be too cold. Earth is positioned *just right* for life to survive.

Aesthetic Principle

Tennant also argued that the fact that the world is beautiful, and that humankind is capable of recognising and appreciating this beauty, points to a benevolent designer. This is termed his 'aesthetic' principle'. Evolution could not account for such beauty or humankind's ability to appreciate it because these features do not contribute to survival. Therefore, Tennant believed the only reason we can appreciate the beauty and perfect conditions in the world is because it was designed *for us* with the intention that it would please us and we would be able to recognise this. For Tennant, the only explanation was a loving God who wanted his creation to enjoy living in his world.

> **ESSENTIAL!**
>
> **Aesthetic** refers to the appreciation of beauty.

> **INSIGHT**
>
> 'Nature is meaningless and valueless without God behind it and Man in front' (F.R. Tennant).

Understand Tennant's Arguments

IMPROVE YOUR UNDERSTANDING

Make sure that you know how Tennant responded to the challenge of evolution and used scientific knowledge to formulate two modern teleological arguments for God's existence.

Tennant intended his arguments not as logical proofs (deductive, a priori) but as arguments of probability. Tennant's arguments are inductive and a posteriori by nature, meaning they use external evidence to come to a conclusion that is, at best, probable. Therefore, Tennant's arguments are proposed as grounds for reasonable belief, not conclusive proof, as outlined below:

> P1: We can imagine a chaotic world, where conditions did not turn out so perfect for life or as beautiful as they have.
>
> P2: However, the world is not so. There is undeniable beauty and the perfect conditions for life to survive. There is order, and adaptations have occurred that have benefited life.
>
> P3: Further, humans are capable of recognising and appreciating the world as beautiful and beneficial for us.
>
> P4: Such factors cannot be a result of mere chance.
>
> C: Therefore it is entirely probable that all which has occurred has been part of a benevolent God's plan, for the purpose of sustaining and pleasing intelligent life.

WHAT DO YOU THINK?

Write down your thoughts on Tennant's arguments and revisit them shortly before the exam to see if your views have changed.

TASK

Read Tennant for yourself in the extracts below. The notes in the margin will help you to grasp his views.

Read Tennant for Yourself

The passages below are taken from Tennant's *Philosophical Theology*, Volume 2 (1930), and illustrate the following principles.

Anthropic

> Tennant is referring to the theory of evolution and natural selection.

The multitude of interwoven adaptations by which the world is constituted a theatre of life, intelligence, and morality, cannot reasonably be regarded as an outcome of mechanism, or of blind formative power, or aught but purposive intelligence.

Aesthetic

> Tennant is saying that the more science reveals about our world, the more beauty we see.

> By 'superfluous' he means having no practical value in terms of survival.

Nature is not just beautiful in places; it is saturated with beauty – on the telescopic and microscopic scale. Our scientific knowledge brings us no nearer to understanding the beauty of music. From an intelligibility point of view, beauty seems to be superfluous and to have little survival value.

[…]

> Tennant clarifies that his argument is not deductive but inductive in nature.

> Tennant is arguing that beauty and the ability to appreciate beauty are the ways in which God reveals himself.

The aesthetic argument for theism becomes more persuasive when it renounces all claims to proof and appeals to a logical probability. And it becomes stronger when it takes as the most significant fact … the saturation of nature with beauty … God reveals himself in many ways; and some men enter His temple by the Gate Beautiful.

Know Criticisms of Tennant

Tennant is criticised for being anthropocentric. Tennant's ideas put humans at the centre of everything. Where Tennant argued that the conditions of the world were evidence of a designer's plan for intelligent life, critics say it was the other way around. The laws of nature developed due to random chance, and life in turn adapted to them. Douglas Adams, author of *The Hitchhiker's Guide to the Galaxy* (1979), illustrated this point well: 'Imagine a puddle waking up one morning and thinking, "This is an interesting world I find myself in – an interesting hole I find myself in – fits me rather neatly, doesn't it? In fact it fits me staggeringly well, must have been made to have me in it!"'

EVALUATION SKILLS

An answer to an evaluative question about a scholar is always deepened by demonstrating awareness of how other thinkers have disagreed with their ideas.

Beauty is in the eye of the beholder. Tennant's aesthetic argument assumes that beauty is something objective. However, modern-day understanding sees beauty as a subjective response in the brain to external stimuli. Furthermore, appreciation of beauty could in fact help humankind to survive: for example, if humans are drawn to a beautiful location because it is calm and warm, and has luscious plants and clear water. We might find these things beautiful as a survival mechanism because such a location would seem safe from predators, have clean water for drinking, and lush foliage, indicating that food could grow sufficiently.

Watch Out for Traps

Be careful not to say that Tennant invented the anthropic principle. Tennant 'developed' the idea, which in turn has gathered momentum following further scientific discoveries.

Don't forget to give examples. Give detailed examples illustrating Tennant's ideas, such as the Goldilocks zone and how the position of earth is perfect for life to thrive, as support for the anthropic argument.

Don't forget the link between beauty and design. When discussing the aesthetic argument, remember to make the link between beauty and design, and explain how, for Tennant, beauty pointed to an intelligent and benevolent designer. God must have wanted humans to enjoy the world, so he created beauty and gave humankind the ability to perceive and appreciate that beauty.

STRENGTHEN YOUR GRASP

1. Challenge yourself to see how much you can write without looking at notes to explain Tennant's anthropic and aesthetic arguments. This will test how well you understand and can explain these ideas.
2. Write an AO2 paragraph, explaining which of Tennant's arguments you think is more successful and why. Ensure you refer to objections, criticisms and how aspects of Tennant's ideas (if any) can successfully respond to these.

Exam Guidance AO1

You could be asked about both or just one of Tennant's anthropic and aesthetic arguments, so be prepared to discuss the ideas separately, and give examples to illustrate. However, you could also be asked a broader question about teleological arguments, where it would be beneficial to include modern versions. In your revision, make a timeline of the different design arguments and note how they have developed over time.

Exam Guidance AO2

Depending on the question, it could be important to consider the context of the twenty-first century, or scientific challenges to teleological arguments. To help revise for this, make notes on the philosophical and scientific challenges to design, such as the criticisms of David Hume, evolution and the Big Bang, and note whether Tennant's ideas are able to overcome each of these.

5. DAVID HUME
GET INTO HUME'S WORLD

Quick Overview David Hume (1711–76) was educated at the University of Edinburgh during a time when the city was at the heart of the European Enlightenment. Hume is known as one of the major British empiricists and is now widely recognised to be one of the greatest philosophers who ever lived.

At the time of David Hume's birth, around the start of the European Enlightenment and British industrial revolution, the dominant topic in European philosophy concerned the nature of knowledge. Since Descartes' *Discourse on the Method* (1637), there had been renewed interest across Europe in **rationalism** – the notion that truth could only be known through reason, and that human rationality was what separated humans from other animals.

This was a time of great intellectual and societal change in Britain, due to new discoveries, the development of a new scientific method (see Chapter 8), mass urban migration and major progress in terms of engineering, and it was during this time that the **empiricist** movement took off. Great thinkers such as John Locke and later George Berkeley argued against rationalism, maintaining that knowledge can only be obtained via experience and perception. It was in this context that Hume emerged as one of the major British empiricists, dealing a blow to rationalism and creating a legacy that would shape much of nineteenth- and twentieth-century philosophy and scientific method.

From a young age, Hume had shown great academic promise; some accounts say that he began studying at the University of Edinburgh at the age of ten. Although destined for the family business of law, Hume did not want to take this route and he turned his attention briefly to business, before committing to academia and study. However, following a nervous breakdown in his early twenties due to the intensity of his studies, after a period of recovery Hume spent time in France writing his first major work, publishing *A Treatise of Human Nature* in 1739. It famously 'fell dead-born from the press' and failed to make an impact, presumably due to the radical nature of Hume's ideas and suspected atheism. This led Hume to rewrite it before he eventually turned away from philosophy.

He then took up the post of librarian at the Edinburgh Faculty, where he would write *The History of England* (1754), a bestseller that quickly became the standard text of the time, rendering Hume within his own lifetime famous as a historian rather than a philosopher. However, towards the end of his life he returned to philosophy, and wrote his most controversial works in secret, including *Dialogues Concerning Natural Religion* (1779). He left instructions for this to be published only after he died, due to his concern for his social standing and the impact further accusations of atheism might have on his social life and career.

INSIGHT
As an empiricist, Hume believed true knowledge could only be gained through sense experience. He was opposed to rationalism and any notion that humans could have knowledge prior to experience.

ESSENTIAL!
Rationalism is the principle that knowledge and truth can only be attained through reason and rational reflection.

Empiricism is the principle that knowledge and truth can only be attained by experience of the external world gained through the senses and direct observation.

INSIGHT
Hume spent some time working and living in France. During this period, he made a reputation for himself as a socialite and host, and became known as 'the good David' or *Le bon David*.

TIP
Thinkers can never be separated from their times. Note some of the societal issues, ideas and movements that Hume was living through and to which he was responding.

Know Hume's Key Ideas

IMPROVE YOUR UNDERSTANDING

Make sure you understand Hume's sceptical empiricism, so that you can grasp the basis of his arguments.

> **TIP**
>
> Hume lived before Paley and was not responding to Paley's design argument. Paley goes on to read Hume's *Dialogues*, though, and attempts to respond to them in his *Natural Theology* (1802).

It is very possible that Hume developed the following ideas at an early age and maintained them in some form throughout his entire life. We will never be sure because due to the radical nature of those views and his suspected atheism, he was to some degree censored by his friends and his own conscience. His objections to traditional arguments for God's existence remained unpublished until after his death, and his challenge to miracles was held back for later publication, due to concern for his societal standing. However, it is worth noting that, although today we may suspect that Hume was an atheist due to the nature of his arguments, he never categorically stated that he was so, and many re-readings of Hume now suggest he appears to adopt more of an agnostic stance. That is, he was open to the existence of God but not convinced of it. In either case, no categorisation of Hume will change the content and impact of his pivotal ideas, which are explained below.

Inductive Arguments for God's Existence

In *Dialogues Concerning Natural Religion* (1779), Hume discusses and refutes arguments for God's existence, including the teleological and cosmological arguments, via the perspective of three fictional characters:

- Philo, who is believed to represent Hume's scepticism
- Cleanthes, who argues for natural theology and a version of the teleological argument
- Demea, who defends the cosmological argument and supports fideism (the belief that faith should be independent of reason).

Criticisms of Teleological Arguments

After Cleanthes puts forward a design argument based on the comparison of the universe to a great machine and its designer (similar to Paley's later watchmaker argument), Philo responds with a list of objections that can be summarised in the following themes:

1. **Weak analogy**

    - The strength of any analogy relies on the level of similarity between the things being compared. The difference between a machine and the universe is too great. Therefore, the argument is one of **disanalogy** rather than analogy, and cannot be persuasive.

> **ESSENTIAL!**
>
> **Disanalogy** is a term used to describe when an analogy has failed. This is a criticism Hume levels at those who would compare the organic universe to a non-organic item such as a machine. Hume appears to be pre-empting arguments such as Paley's.

> **INSIGHT**
>
> William Paley poses a famous similar argument for design, but uses a watch and watchmaker as a basis for analogy with the universe (see Chapter 3).

    - The universe is more like an organic item and a machine is non-organic; any similarity drawn between the natural world and an artificial construct (that is, something that doesn't happen naturally) must be rejected. It would be better to compare the universe to an organic item such as a vegetable.

2. **An inductive leap**

    - We can only experience the universe in terms of its smaller and separate parts. Design arguments therefore make a fallacy of composition. Just because there is apparent design within parts of the universe does not mean the universe as a whole was designed.

- We have no experience of universe-making. As we have never experienced the formation of our universe, we cannot have knowledge of its cause or design. The universe might have arisen by chance, but we have no basis from which to know, either one way or another.

- The **Epicurean hypothesis**. Hume poses an idea that dates back to Epicurus, stating that in an infinite amount of time, the particles of a chaotic universe would be bound to come together at some point in such a way as to appear ordered and structured. No matter how unlikely or preposterous such a notion may seem, in an infinite amount of time it is guaranteed to occur.

3 **Not necessarily the God of classical theism**

- Even if the universe does have a designer, the evidence within the universe does not point to the conclusion that the designer has the qualities of classical theism.

- Like effects do not imply like causes. If we do accept that complex things within the world are a result of intelligent designers (humans) and then apply that to the universe itself, we end up with a designer who resembles human designers, an anthropomorphised God.

- The designer could be malevolent due to the apparent suffering we see in nature. A benevolent God would surely not make the world this cruel.

- Hume then compares the designer of the universe with shipbuilders, and notes that the designer of the universe might even be an apprentice designer, who has left behind them a series of 'botched and bungled designs' before arriving at the universe we find ourselves in today.

- There could also be a 'plurality of gods' (more than one). The designer could be part of a team of designers, as we observe in the case of the teams who build great masterpieces such as ships.

- The universe could even point towards a designer who has since moved on and abandoned his creation to its own devices, as do designers of ships and houses. All of this does not amount to the God of classical theism.

Criticisms of Cosmological Arguments

Within *Dialogues*, the character Demea defends a cosmological argument based on contingency and necessity, much like Aquinas' 'third way' (see Chapter 1). Both Cleanthes and Philo respond with a list of objections that can be summarised in the following themes:

> **ESSENTIAL!**
>
> The **Epicurean hypothesis** is the theory that, in an infinite amount of time, the particles of the universe would by random chance come to be arranged in an orderly form that appeared to be structured.

> **TIP**
>
> Short quotes can be beneficial to your essays when criticising the teleological argument. Hume writes, 'have worlds ever been formed under your eye …?'

> **INSIGHT**
>
> The 'dysteleological argument' – otherwise known as the argument from poor design – did not emerge as a phrase until the nineteenth century. But it seems that Hume pre-empted the idea with his reference to a poorly designed world pointing to a less than perfect deity (not the God of classical theism).

> **INSIGHT**
>
> David Hume said, 'Whatever we conceive as existent, we can also conceive as non-existent. There is no being, therefore, whose non-existence implies a contradiction.' See also Hume's criticism of Anselm (discussed in Chapter 7).

- **A necessary being.** Hume claims that the non-existence of any being, any concept, can be imagined. Therefore, there are no logical grounds for assuming there must be a necessary being. However, if we are to assume a necessary being, why not the universe itself? This also reflects the principle of Occam's razor (see Chapter 1), of accepting the simplest solution as the most likely. It is simpler and more principled to keep the search for the explanation of the universe to the universe itself or accept that there is no cause, otherwise we risk accepting the idea of an infinite regress or series of causes. This is a point later picked up by Bertrand Russell through his declaration that the universe is just a 'brute fact' (see page 21).

- **Causality.** There is an inductive leap. As we have no experience of universe-making, we can have no knowledge of the cause of the universe. We certainly couldn't know the cause to be the God of classical theism. We can also question the notion of cause and effect itself, as we do not empirically observe causation; we just see its effects. However, through custom and 'habit of mind' we form an idea about a natural law or principle for which we have no empirical grounds (no evidence). See the 'Understand Hume's Arguments' section (starting on page 47) for more on this.

- **An explanation of parts is sufficient.** Hume, through Cleanthes' character, gives the example of 20 coins. An explanation of where each individual coin came from is sufficient (one from a friend, one from a family member, and so on). After each coin has individually been accounted for, there is no extra value in asking: but where did the total collection of coins come from?

Key Ideas on Miracles

In Chapter 10 of his *Enquiry Concerning Human Understanding* (1748), Hume defines a miracle as a violation of a law of nature by a supernatural agent. To clarify, for Hume laws of nature are just generalisations we conceive due to past observations and our 'habit of mind'. Therefore, a miracle would be an event that contradicts or goes against our repeated experience of the world at the direction of an angel, demon or God. Despite this understanding of natural laws, which implies that they can in theory be broken, as they are not certain or objective truths in the first place, Hume argues that the evidence will always fall in favour of the natural law, so we will never have a basis from which to accept a miracle.

His objection can be expressed as follows:

- 'A wise man proportions his belief to the evidence' (*Essay Concerning Human Understanding*, Chapter 10). We have more evidence for natural laws than for miracles. There could never be enough witnesses or evidence to outweigh the evidence from past experience for upholding the natural law. Miracles are more improbable from the outset.

- The testimony and accounts of miracles cannot be considered as evidence because they tend to come from 'ignorant and barbarous nations' rather than the rational, scientific and well-educated (note the context being Hume's eighteenth-century British imperialist perspective). The witnesses may also lack integrity and may report such events for gain or to promote a cause. It is likely that a witness 'should either deceive or be deceived'.

- Humans are driven by passion and feeling, and have a natural tendency to look for the marvellous and supernatural. Reason is abandoned when they do so.

- All religions claim miracles but equally they contradict each other, thereby effectively cancelling each other out. Christian miracles illustrate the divinity of Jesus, Muslim miracles, Allah, and so on. They cannot all be genuine.

It is worth noting that Hume's views on miracles were not included in his first major work, *Treatise Concerning Human Nature*, and although they were included in his 1748 *Enquiry Concerning Human Understanding*, not all publishers at the time included the controversial Chapter 10 so as to avoid offending the religious sensibilities of people living in this period. Often, we only find the chapter on miracles in versions published from 1776 onwards, after Hume's death. Hume's suspected atheism and controversial critique of theistic philosophy had caused him to be excluded from some academic positions and aspects of society during his lifetime, and in 1761 all of his works appeared on the *Index Librorum Prohibitorum*, a list of heretical publications that Catholics were forbidden to read.

Understand Hume's Arguments

Hume's Scepticism

Although Hume is arguably the best-known British empiricist, empiricism has a far longer history and can be traced back to the works of Aristotle and possibly beyond. Hume's philosophy builds on the Enlightenment thinking of his time, but his arguments should be understood within the context of his empirical scepticism. While empiricists traditionally believe that knowledge derives from experience, Hume's view takes a more extreme turn when moving on to inductive inference (applying generalisations from one circumstance to another), which leads him to refute the logic of Aquinas and use of a posteriori, inductive arguments for God's existence. Aquinas believed we can look at the effects (observations from the universe) and then go back and infer the cause (God) (see Chapter 1). However, Hume attacks this reasoning, stating that we have no grounds to reason *from* rather than *to* our convictions. He developed this into what is now known as the problem of induction, or an inductive leap.

To illustrate, Hume refers to the following example:

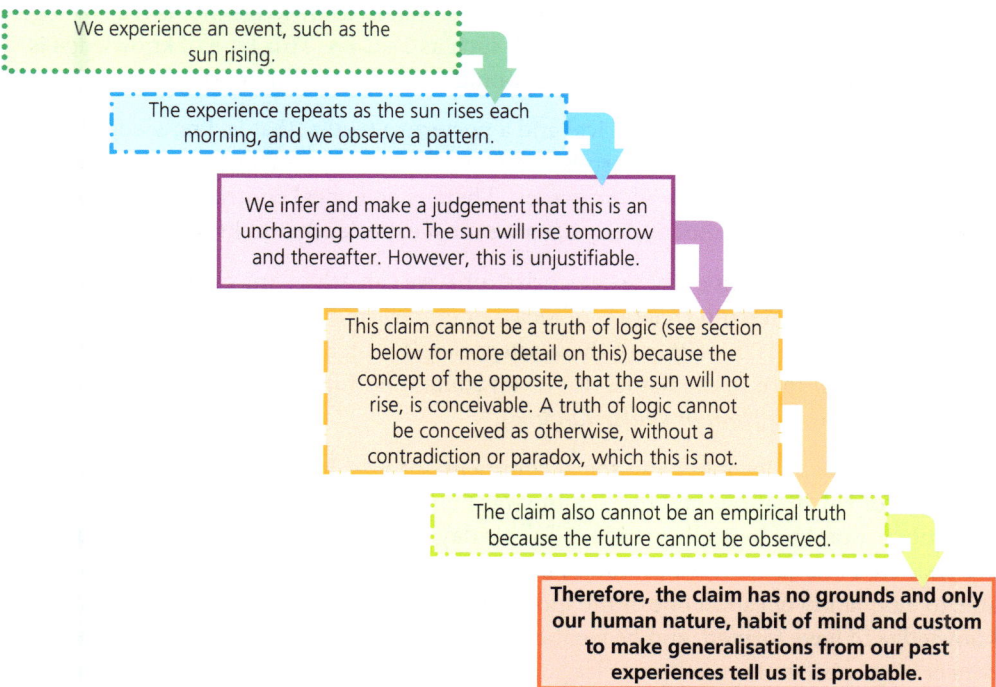

The problem of induction

We have experienced the sun rising every day, so we assume there is a fixed pattern and it will rise again tomorrow. However, this assumption is unjustified as we have no experience of tomorrow. Our minds are just spotting patterns and assuming them to be true.

Hume's Fork

Hume categorises knowledge into two kinds:

- **Relations of ideas.** These are developed from John Locke's intuitive and demonstrative proofs. These are a priori truths: that is, knowledge that is true by logic due to how the ideas involved are related, such as $2 + 2 = 4$. This type of knowledge is self-evident and necessary, as to deny it would involve a contradiction.

- **Matters of fact.** These are empirical and a posteriori truths: that is, knowledge that is not self-evident, but where the truth or falsity of it has to be experienced in order to be known, such as *the cat is in the garden*. There is no logical contradiction involved in the idea were we to accept or deny it, so we must experience it to know it.

Hume argues that in light of these categorisations, we can ask of any claim to knowledge, whether it is a logical truth (relation of ideas) or empirical truth (matter of fact). If any claim to knowledge is in neither of these categories, it is meaningless and no knowledge at all. 'Commit it then to the flames: for it can contain nothing but **sophistry** and illusion' (*Enquiry Concerning Human Understanding*).

Austrian-British philosopher and social commentator Karl Popper, widely considered the father of Falsification, said that 'Hume was perfectly right in pointing out that induction cannot be logically justified.' To this day, the problem of induction remains and is considered one of the most profound philosophical challenges imaginable. Hume was able to eloquently question one of the most fundamental ways in which we understood knowledge to have formed, and he went on to inspire numerous philosophical ideas concerning epistemology, religious language, moral philosophy, metaphysics (abstract concepts such as the origin of the universe) and scientific method. Philosopher Bertrand Russell famously commented that, if Hume's problem of induction cannot be resolved, 'there is no intellectual difference between sanity and insanity'.

> **INSIGHT**
>
> Immanuel Kant (see Chapter 11) later built upon Hume's fork and termed Hume's relations of ideas 'analytic truths', and his matters of fact 'synthetic truths'.

> **ESSENTIAL!**
>
> **Sophistry** is the use of false arguments, with intent to deceive.

Regarding the existence of God, Hume seeks to demonstrate that just as we have no grounds for knowing that the sun will rise tomorrow, so we have no grounds for knowing God exists. We cannot know a priori that God exists by definition, as we can conceive of his non-existence without contradiction, so it cannot be a logical truth. We also cannot conclude by experience that God exists as an empirical truth, as his objections demonstrate there are other possible and arguably more probable explanations for the apparent design or cause of the universe. Therefore, God's existence is also not an empirical truth, just one of many possible explanations. The claim that God exists is not knowledge at all and no argument that Hume refutes can be considered as successful.

So how does Hume account for the apparent knowledge that religious believers have about God and his nature? Hume cannot conclude that the knowledge is genuine, as for Hume all knowledge of either kind must derive from impressions, ultimately as a result of experience. This idea has since been coined Hume's 'copy principle', meaning that all ideas evolve or develop from initial experience; we cannot conceive of anything of which we have had no impression or experience. Hume considers that we must base our concept of God on some other notion for which we do have impression and experience, namely ourselves. He thus concludes something akin to the complete opposite of Aquinas' principles of attribution and proportion, and proposes what might be considered a forerunner for the likes of Freud (see Chapter 17) and Feuerbach's ideas of a deity as an embodiment of human wish fulfilment – God as a being consisting of qualities such as goodness, power and intelligence, forming a complex concept that is ultimately derived from reflection on our own human nature.

Hume on Causality

Hume applied the same issues identified in the problem of induction to the concept of causality (or causation), which in turn became a basis for objections to arguments for God's existence and to the possibility of miracles (see the 'Know Hume's Key Ideas' section above).

For example, although we may experience event A (labelled 'a cause') as preceding event B (labelled 'an effect'), this does not tell us categorically that event A was the cause of event B. There could be other explanations that we do not understand. All we see are events. For example, a cat jumps on a table and its tail knocks the newspaper, which falls onto the floor. However, imagine the table was outside and there was a strong gust of wind which blew the newspaper onto the ground, at the exact same moment the cat's tail made contact with it. The different causes do not make the effect appear any different.

Therefore, Hume argues that we are not actually observing causation. Instead, we observe a constant conjunction of events, and where these are repeated, we come to develop a feeling of anticipation. If the events are repeated enough, our custom and habitual way of thinking, our very human nature, will make generalisations from which we can assume, in order to go about our business and live our lives. These we call laws of nature. However, we cannot actually *know*. Therefore, any event that may be unexpected given past experiences, to the point we declare it is a miracle, may not be. It could just be a conjunction of events in specific circumstances which we have not previously experienced. Similarly in the cosmological argument, we cannot assume that the universe needs a cause and that this cause must be God. The error of causality, as Hume points out, means we have no grounds for such an assumption.

So profound were Hume's ideas that they left a lasting legacy on philosophy and inspired Immanuel Kant to 'awake from his dogmatic slumber' and reconsider the notion of cause and effect in his *Critique of Pure Reason* (1781).

> **WHAT DO YOU THINK?**
>
> Write down your thoughts on Hume's arguments and revisit them shortly before the exam to see if your views have changed.

Read Hume for Yourself

> **TASK**
>
> Read Hume for yourself in the extracts below. The notes in the margin will help you to grasp his ideas.

Inductive Arguments

This passage comes from *Dialogues Concerning Natural Religion* (1779). The first three paragraphs object to the teleological argument, and the final to the cosmological argument.

> *Hume undermines the notion that the designer is the god of classical theism, who as a perfect being – omniscient, omnipotent and benevolent – would not need to learn and develop, or permit the suffering of any creatures living within a less than perfect world.*

But were this world ever so perfect a production, it must still remain uncertain, whether all the excellencies of the work can justly be ascribed to the workman. If we survey a ship, what an exalted idea must we form of the ingenuity of the carpenter, who framed so complicated, useful and beautiful a machine? And what surprise must we feel, when we find him a stupid mechanic, who imitated others, and copied an art, which, through a long succession of ages, after multiplied trials, mistakes, corrections, deliberations, and controversies, had been gradually improving? Many worlds might have been botched and bungled, throughout an eternity, ere this system was struck out: much labour lost: many fruitless trials made: and a slow, but continued improvement carried on during infinite ages in the art of world-making …

[…]

> *Hume is pre-empting a response to his challenge here based on Occam's razor, that the simplest solution is most likely and sufficient. However, he responds by clarifying that in this particular case Occam's razor does not apply, as a team of designers sharing out the qualities of one great designer is simpler than imagining one designer to have all the necessary qualities.*

And what shadow of an argument … can you produce, from your hypothesis, to prove the unity of the Deity? A great number of men join in building a house or ship, in rearing a city, in framing a commonwealth: why may not several deities combine in contriving and framing a world? … To multiply causes, without necessity, is indeed contrary to true philosophy: but this principle applies not to the present case. Were one deity antecedently proved by your theory, who were possessed of every attribute, requisite to the production of the universe; it would be needless, I own (though not absurd) to suppose any other deity existent. But while it is still a question, whether all these attributes are united in one subject, or dispersed among several independent beings: by what phenomena in nature can we pretend to decide the controversy?

[…]

… What if I should revive the old Epicurean hypothesis? This is commonly and I believe justly, esteemed the most absurd system that has yet been proposed; yet I know not whether, with a few alterations, it might not be brought to bear a faint appearance of probability. Instead of supposing matter infinite, as EPICURUS did, let us suppose it finite. A finite number of particles is only susceptible of finite transpositions: and it must happen, in an eternal duration, that every possible order or position must be tried an infinite number of times. This world, therefore, with all its events, even the most minute, has before been produced and destroyed, and will again be produced and destroyed, without any bounds and limitations. No one, who has a conception of the powers of infinite, in comparison of finite, will ever scruple this determination.

> Hume argues that, although this idea might seem remote, the theory cannot be disregarded. From our perspective, we may see this idea as a precursor to the theory of evolution, as complexity, order and structure could be explained by a random natural principle such as adaptation through natural selection rather than a designer.

> Hume means 'infinite amount of time'.

> Hume means no one with insight would 'have trouble with this conclusion.'

[…]

Nothing, that is distinctly conceivable, implies a contradiction. Whatever we conceive as existent, we can also conceive as non-existent. There is no being, therefore, whose non-existence implies a contradiction. Consequently, there is no being, whose existence is demonstrable … It is pretended that the Deity is a necessarily existent being; and this necessity of his existence is attempted to be explained by asserting, that if we knew his whole essence or nature, we should perceive it to be as impossible for him not to exist, as for twice two not to be four. But it is evident that this can never happen, while our faculties remain the same as at present. It will still be possible for us, at any time, to conceive the non-existence of what we formerly conceived to exist; nor can the mind ever lie under a necessity of supposing any object to remain always in being; in the same manner as we lie under a necessity of always conceiving twice two to be four. The words, therefore, necessary existence, have no meaning; or, which is the same thing, none that is consistent.

> In response to the cosmological argument based on contingency, and the conclusion that a necessary being must be the first cause.

On Miracles

This passage comes from Chapter 10 in *An Enquiry Concerning Human Understanding* (1748).

A wise man, therefore, proportions his belief to the evidence … He considers which side is supported by the greater number of experiments: To that side he inclines, with doubt and hesitation … A hundred instances or experiments on one side, and fifty on another, afford a doubtful expectation of any event; though a hundred uniform experiments, with only one that is contradictory, reasonably beget a pretty strong degree of assurance.

> Hume means past experience.

> Meaning 'result in'.

[…]

Hume uses easy-to-grasp examples to illustrate how probable laws of nature are in contrast to the high improbability of miracles.

A miracle by definition must be something that goes against common laws of nature, so it cannot be an everyday affair or matter of improbability or well-timed luck.

Hume is referring to the Pentateuch (Christian name for the Torah).

Hume is referring to the stories from the Pentateuch, the fall of man (significant for much of St Augustine's theology in particular), the great flood, and the Hebrews' exodus from Egypt under the ten plagues.

A miracle is a violation of the laws of nature; and as a firm and unalterable experience has established these laws, the proof against a miracle, from the very nature of the fact, is as entire as any argument from experience can possibly be imagined. Why is it more than probable, that all men must die; that lead cannot … remain suspended in the air; that fire consumes wood, and is extinguished by water; unless it be, that these events are found agreeable to the laws of nature, and there is required a violation of these laws, or in other words, a miracle to prevent them? Nothing is esteemed a miracle, if it ever happen in the common course of nature … When anyone tells me, that he saw a dead man restored to life, I immediately consider with myself, whether it be more probable, that this person should either deceive or be deceived, or that the fact, which he relates, should really have happened. I weigh the one miracle against the other; and according to the superiority, which I discover, I pronounce my decision, and always reject the greater miracle.

[…]

Here then we are first to consider a book, presented to us by a barbarous and ignorant people, written in an age when they were still more barbarous, and in all probability long after the facts which it relates, corroborated by no concurring testimony, and resembling those fabulous accounts, which every nation gives of its origin. Upon reading this book, we find it full of prodigies and miracles. It gives an account of a state of the world and of human nature entirely different from the present: Of our fall from that state: Of the age of man, extended to near a thousand years: Of the destruction of the world by a deluge: Of the arbitrary choice of one people, as the favourites of heaven; and that people the countrymen of the author: Of their deliverance from bondage by prodigies the most astonishing imaginable: I desire any one to lay his hand upon his heart, and after a serious consideration declare, whether he thinks that the falsehood of such a book, supported by such a testimony, would be more extraordinary and miraculous than all the miracles it relates; which is, however, necessary to make it be received, according to the measures of probability above established.

Know Criticisms of Hume

The Verification Principle. Unfortunately for Hume, his underlying principles of sceptical empiricism are subject to the criticism of the twentieth-century Verification Principle, which his own ideas actually inspired. They fail to pass the criteria of Hume's fork. Hume's basis – that knowledge can ultimately be derived only from experience – cannot itself count as a relation of ideas (a demonstrative truth/analytical knowledge), or as a matter of fact (an empirical truth/synthetic knowledge). Therefore, any arguments Hume proposes based on these principles are undermined, including his arguments against inductive arguments for God's existence. If Hume were to follow his own advice on this, then he should 'Commit it then to the flames.'

Criticisms of Hume's argument against inductive arguments. With regard to Hume's objections to the cosmological and teleological arguments, more specific criticisms can be made, including the following:

- Hume's fallacy of composition can be counter-argued, as there is no true logical fallacy being made. The success or failure of this objection would depend upon the content of the argument. Sometimes what is true of the part *is* true of the whole: for example, the ingredients of a cake have been baked in the oven, therefore the cake has been baked in the oven.

- Where Hume states that a total explanation of the whole is not required in objection to the cosmological argument, the seventeenth-century philosopher Gottfried Wilhelm Leibniz would disagree via his principle of sufficient reason. Leibniz argued that partial explanations would only ever be partial, but that there must logically be a sufficient reason which accounts for everything.

- In objection to the teleological argument where Hume states that the nature of the world could point to a designer who is malevolent, there are countless defences of a benevolent God who for various reasons permits suffering for a purpose or greater plan (see Chapter 16 for potential solutions to the problem of evil).

Hume's objections to the above inductive arguments, while considered successful by many, have not necessarily proved that the arguments fail. Both the cosmological and teleological arguments continue to this day, and there are modern versions and scientific evidence that can serve in support. Further, it can be argued that as inductive arguments, they are not intended to provide proofs of God's existence per se, just that God's existence is reasonable, or at best probable. While Hume can demonstrate that there are other possible conclusions, this does not itself undermine the success of the arguments by their own nature.

However, overall it is widely considered that Hume's objections to the teleological argument are more successful than his objections to the cosmological argument. The main reason for this is that Hume has been criticised for misjudging the understanding of God's existence as 'necessary' and for lumping the ontological and cosmological argument together in his objections, therefore confusing the two and perhaps losing precision in his critique. We understand that when it is said that God's existence is necessary, this can refer not only to Aquinas' argument (see Chapter 1) that God cannot start or stop existing, but also, in a different manner, to Anselm's argument (see Chapter 7) that God cannot be thought of as not existing. Hume, however, rejects the concept of necessary existence for both arguments in one blow, by arguing that God *can* be thought of as not existing, therefore not sufficiently challenging Aquinas' use of the term in the cosmological argument.

Criticisms of Hume's argument against miracles. Hume's approach to miracles can be criticised on several points:

- Hume said belief in miracles was unreasonable, as there is never enough evidence to accept them. However, it is inevitable that miracles lack evidence, as the point of miracles is that they are one-off events and not frequently repeated. Further, Hume himself admitted that miracles are only improbable, not impossible, and as such this challenge is considered by many to be no challenge at all.

- Hume states that miracle accounts from witnesses are not believable, as it is likely that the witnesses were deceived or deliberately deceiving, ignorant of the natural explanation, or biased towards accepting miracle accounts due to being drawn to wonder. Richard Swinburne raises a specific response to this with his principles of testimony and credulity (see Chapter 25), arguing that it is in fact reasonable to accept witness accounts in specific situations.

- Hume argues that the miracles from different religions cancel each other out. However, various theories of religious pluralism and non-cognitive approaches demonstrate that this is not necessarily the case. For example, the moral of 'The Blind Men and the Elephant' poem teaches that human experience differs but multiple truths are possible, as one never has the perspective of the whole, only a part. It can also be argued that religions are not necessarily based on the occurrence of miracles, but miracle stories can help promote and spread religious teachings and wisdom. These miracle stories, while helpful and memorable, are not necessarily central to any religion.

- A criticism that offers a catastrophic blow to Hume's argument against miracles is that he contradicts his own sceptical stance. We saw in the 'Understanding Hume's Arguments' section that Hume is sceptical to the point of arguing that natural laws are just generalised notions based on past observations, and therefore cannot count as knowledge for what will occur in the future. We cannot *know* the sun will rise tomorrow; we can only anticipate it. Therefore, we cannot *know* that the sun will *not* rise tomorrow. Yet, in his argument against miracles, Hume does not permit that we cannot know that a person will not rise from the dead. Hume's scepticism allows the former, so why not the latter?

The accusation of solipsism. One final criticism of Hume is that his overall philosophical stance of sceptical empiricism can potentially lead to **solipsism**, which would undermine the empirical position he begins with, and result in the scenario where we cannot assume we have knowledge of anything at all regarding the world we inhabit outside of our own minds. By so challenging the notion of causality and induction – on which most human knowledge regarding the world we live in, and our understanding of how it works and will continue to work, is based – Hume inadvertently calls all science and knowledge gained through experience into question.

> **ESSENTIAL!**
>
> **Solipsism** is an extreme sceptical philosophical view, which holds that we cannot have true knowledge of anything other than our self. Knowledge of anything outside of our self is unsure, as it cannot be known directly.

Watch Out for Traps

Don't forget to use key terms. Appropriate key terms should be used alongside Hume's ideas, as noted in the specification. For example, Hume's challenges to cosmological and teleological arguments come under the 'inductive arguments' theme. Therefore, any answer concerning Hume's challenges to these arguments should refer to the nature of inductive arguments, issues of causality and Hume's challenge of the inductive leap.

Similarly, the specification refers to Hume's empirical objections, so showing awareness of Hume's empiricism is relevant. In the 'religious experience' theme, the specification refers to Hume's scepticism of miracles, so reference to the empirical origins of that scepticism and the issues of coherence within Hume's scepticism, which underpins his works, would be beneficial.

Don't confuse objections to the design argument with objections to the cosmological argument. When an exam question asks about Hume's challenges to cosmological or teleological arguments, you should ensure you refer specifically to Hume's objections to each argument: for example, weak analogy, random chance and 'not necessarily the God of classical theism' for teleological arguments; and the objection to a necessary being, problems of causality and an explanation of parts for cosmological arguments. You can include more general challenges from Hume relating to the nature of inductive arguments if relevant. However, you will not be able to access the higher bands if you are not able to demonstrate knowledge of the appropriate objections for the different arguments.

Ensure you understand the different objections as explained in the 'Know Hume's Key Ideas' section. And note, while the Big Bang theory and the theory of evolution are potential scientific challenges to cosmological and teleological arguments, they were not common knowledge until after Hume's lifetime, so they would not gain marks in answering a question about Hume's challenges specifically.

Merely listing Hume's objections is not good AO1 or AO2. Sometimes for revision purposes, students end up learning a long list of Hume's objections to various arguments or ideas, reducing these complex notions to bullet points or even catchphrases. Regardless of the question, don't just reel off Hume's ideas (about miracles, teleological or cosmological arguments) for either AO1 or AO2 questions. It is far better to be selective in which objections you include, and to demonstrate you are engaging with the ideas and understand them and how they fit into Hume's worldview and the topic on a deeper level. Hume's ideas have been discussed thematically in this chapter, to help you make sense of the connections between points and underpinning ideas. AO2 evaluation, in particular, requires critical analysis, which means showing that you have weighed up Hume's ideas against others and that, based on their strengths and weaknesses, how coherent, persuasive or logical the ideas are, can come to a judgement. For example, if asked an AO2 question evaluating the definitions of miracles, you would need to analyse how successful Hume's definition is in contrast to others, explaining any weaknesses and strengths.

STRENGTHEN YOUR GRASP

1. Make your own revision sheet for the key terms associated with Hume and his ideas. Define them in your own words. As an extra challenge, in a different colour add related scholars and arguments. Use the following key terms: empiricism, rationalism, inductive, a posteriori, fallacy of composition, inductive leap, disanalogy, the Epicurean hypothesis, the God of classical theism, necessary, contingent, causality, analytic, synthetic, realist.
2. Make a table of two columns. In the first column, list Hume's reasons for objecting to the teleological, cosmological, a priori and inductive arguments, and miracles. In the second column, write down whether you find each of Hume's objection a success or failure (and briefly why). Look over the table afterwards and identify any patterns. Do you think Hume is more successful in some topic areas than others? Consider why this might be.

CREATE YOUR OWN QUESTION

Read this chapter and use command words such as 'explain' or 'examine' with regard to Hume's definition of or challenge to miracles, and his challenges to inductive/a posteriori/teleological/cosmological arguments to create your own AO1 questions. For an AO2 question, make a one-sided statement about the success of inductive/deductive/cosmological/teleological arguments or the success of arguments against miracles. Put the statement between quotation marks and follow it with the phrase, 'Evaluate this view.'

Exam Guidance AO1

For an AO1 knowledge part a) question, you could be asked a variety of outline (AS only), explain, examine or, in the case of miracles, a compare question referring to Hume.

For the 'inductive arguments' theme, ensure you are able to refer to Hume's specific challenges to the cosmological and teleological arguments and try not to get these arguments muddled up. All of Hume's major objections to cosmological and teleological arguments are found in *Dialogues Concerning Natural Religion*, and are summarised in the 'Understand Hume's Key Ideas' section above. When revising, ensure you understand which objection challenges which argument and, ideally, which specific aspect of the argument. Note that Hume's objections pre-date Paley's watchmaker argument, the theory of evolution, the Big Bang theory, and the modern versions of teleological and cosmological arguments.

Depending on the question, it could also be beneficial to refer to Hume's challenges in addition to other relevant material – specifically, Hume's objection to the nature of inductive arguments and the problem of moving from past experience of events to future or different scenarios. You could also refer to his objections to the inductive logic of cosmological and teleological arguments as specific examples, such as the problem of causality in cosmological arguments, and the problem of making an inductive leap to the God of classical theism in teleological arguments. However, depending on the breadth of the question, Hume might only be one aspect of the answer. Therefore, in your revision you should make plans for a variety of questions you could be asked, and ensure you can effectively select the relevant material for the different questions.

For the 'religious experience' theme, if you were referring to Hume's definition of miracles you might want to break down his definition and clarify his understanding of natural laws, and what he meant by violation/transgression and by the will of a supernatural agent. You could include examples. Depending on the question and if it had a wider scope, you might want to include other definitions of miracles, and identify similarities or differences in approach, such as realist or anti-realist. In your revision, ensure you understand the different scholars' definitions as named on the Board's specification and can illustrate the views with examples.

Depending on the depth required for the question, you might want to explain Hume's four-part argument against the possibility of miracles in depth, with reference to examples. Including his empiricist and sceptical background could be beneficial, as grounds for favouring the weight of evidence of natural laws and past experiences over witness testimony. If referencing the contradiction of miracles in other religions, specific examples would be useful. For a question where you might contrast Hume's view with Swinburne's, aiming for an equal weight distribution across the two scholars would be helpful. In addition to discussing the two scholars' views, describing similarities/differences as part of a contrast question could improve the depth of your answer.

Exam Guidance AO2

For the 'inductive arguments' theme there are many statements you could be asked to evaluate where it would be relevant to refer to Hume. For example, the following taken from the specification:

1. Whether inductive arguments for God's existence are persuasive.
2. The effectiveness of the cosmological/teleological argument for God's existence.
3. Whether cosmological/teleological arguments for God's existence are persuasive in the twenty-first century.
4. The effectiveness of the challenges to the cosmological/teleological argument for God's existence.
5. Whether scientific explanations are more persuasive than philosophical explanations for the universe's existence.
6. The extent to which different religious views on the nature of God impact on arguments for the existence of God.

To approach any AO2 question, you will want to ensure that you can weigh up the strengths and weaknesses of the selected and relevant material. Don't just reel off or describe Hume's ideas. For example, with regard to 5, evaluating the success of philosophical or scientific explanations would require a different focus than that of 4, referring to the success of Hume's challenges. For the latter, a more specific approach to Hume's challenges, tackled separately by argument/point, could be a good strategy. However, for the former, Hume's challenges would provide better evaluation for philosophical or scientific explanations of the universe, if tackled thematically.

For 6, reference to cosmological, teleological and ontological arguments would be relevant, but particularly concerning the nature and definition of God on which the arguments are based. Hume could be relevant in this evaluation, as he questions religious views on the nature of God and the origin of these ideas. Hume would argue that traditional beliefs about the God of classical theism, as held by the monotheistic and Abrahamic religions, must originate from experience of human nature, as Hume's fork demonstrates there are no true grounds for knowledge of God (see the 'Understanding Hume's Key Ideas' section). These in turn form the basis of arguments for God's existence, resulting in an inductive leap for a posteriori arguments such as the cosmological and teleological arguments, which arrive at only one conclusion rather than any of the other logically plausible or possible conclusions. The ideas of God previously held therefore direct the arguments to biased conclusions, which are unjustified. However, for a question such as this, inclusion of wider material would be important. See the exam guidance in Chapter 7 on Anselm for more on this.

For the 'religious experience' theme, you could be asked something similar to the following examples listed in the specification, where Hume would be relevant:

1. The adequacy of different definitions of miracles.
2. How far different definitions of miracles can be considered as contradictory.
3. The effectiveness of the challenges to belief in miracles.
4. The extent to which Swinburne's responses to Hume can be accepted as valid.

> **TIP**
>
> To help with your revision, practise making AO2 essay plans for the above question themes. Use the Illuminate textbook and revision guide to ensure you select wider relevant material for each question.

Regarding any discussion about miracles, it could be beneficial to include the strengths and weaknesses of the different realist and anti-realist definitions of miracles. With regard to evaluating Hume's definition, the issue of a miracle as a violation of a natural law, which in turn contradicts his own sceptical understanding of natural laws and the fact that they are not fixed, would be relevant. Evaluation like this links to a focus like 3, as part of Hume's challenge to miracles is that the evidence always falls in favour of the natural law, but this does not demonstrate miracles to be impossible. According to Hume's own sceptical empiricism, we have no grounds for assuming the natural law will hold in the future, so how effective can his challenge really be when his own understanding would logically allow for miracles to occur? Further, Hume's challenge to the nature of witnesses and accounts of miracles can be considered biased, elitist and generally unjustified. Swinburne's response and principles of testimony and credulity serve as a powerful counter-argument and offer an opportunity for highly relevant evaluation – they could be the basis of a question focus in their own right, such as 4. To continue with the example of a question focus like 3, it would also be worth including how relevant Hume's challenge to miracles can be, if someone holds a different definition of miracles, such as R.F. Holland. If a miracle is not a violation of a natural law in the first place, does the rest of Hume's challenge collapse?

Evaluating Hume Today

In an exam, you could be asked to evaluate the adequacy/success of any of Hume's ideas and challenges as stated in the specification. You can draw upon this section for ideas as you prepare, but note that Hume's arguments cannot be addressed here in detail. You will be required to reach a judgement on the views that you present, but you do not need to reach the same conclusions as these reflections.

Regardless of whether you agree with Hume's conclusions or not, there is no doubt that he was one of the greatest philosophers who ever lived, and left a legacy that shaped not only multiple fields of philosophy but also scientific method – in particular, his problem of induction and scepticism of causality.

With regard to inductive arguments for God's existence, Hume can be credited with driving forward the debate in metaphysics, pre-empting analogical design arguments, and even the theory of evolution and the Big Bang with his revival of the Epicurean hypothesis. Paley went on to try to address Hume's objections to design arguments, but had to admit that his own watchmaker argument did not necessarily prove the existence of the Christian God in particular, only that it demonstrated the reasonableness of Christian belief. Hence Hume was quite correct in pointing out that design arguments did not necessarily point to the God of classical theism, and that arguments from analogy were only as strong as the similarities drawn between them. However, as the teleological argument is inductive in the first instance, Hume's objection to an inductive leap is not necessarily valid. Inductive arguments do not set out to be proofs of anything; rather they are arguments for what is possible, reasonable or probable at best. Hume's objections to the teleological argument do not show that it is impossible for the God of classical theism to be the designer of the world, only that to Hume there are other equally plausible alternatives, so there is still scope to persuade in any event, by nature of the argument.

Furthermore, it could be argued that Hume's philosophy, in particular his more sceptical principles, become incoherent and absurd. For example, the scepticism of causality would, if we all held true to Hume's logic, leave us with no concept of clear natural laws or expectations for how the world works. This in turn would undermine the basis of the scientific method as we understand it today, which is to repeat experiments until we observe a pattern, and identify a natural law that we can test to verify and falsify. Elizabeth Anscombe argues against Hume that we do often observe causation, and therefore have grounds rooted in experience, for knowledge concerning natural laws of cause and effect, which can therefore be applied to the future and in arguments such as the cosmological argument.

In terms of Hume's definition of and objection to miracles, although he is standing with religious tradition in accepting the realist notion of a miracle as an actual event that violates a natural law, it becomes apparent that he loses credibility. It appears that despite Hume's emphasis on empirical evidence, he is so averse to accepting potential evidence for a miracle – which by his own sceptical principle could in theory occur at any given moment, due to human inability to know things about the future, or different situations to those previously experienced – that he prefers to make sweeping judgements regarding witness accounts, without evidence and on what grounds? Swinburne's principles of credulity and testimony may in fact be more in keeping with Hume's sceptical empiricist principles than he would have wished to admit.

6. CHARLES DARWIN
GET INTO DARWIN'S WORLD

> **Quick Overview** Charles Darwin (1809–82) was a naturalist whose studies into natural history and biology led to the theory of evolution. This revolutionary discovery forever changed the way we understand the origin of species and fuelled controversy between religious and scientific thinkers.

> **ESSENTIAL!**
>
> **Natural selection** is the mechanism through which evolution occurs. Traits that gives species a survival advantage are inherited by offspring and over time this can lead to significant changes.

Charles Darwin was living in the post-Enlightenment world, where it was believed that humanity could be improved by new scientific discoveries and rational thought. While studying theology at the University of Cambridge, Darwin read William Paley's *Natural Theology* (1802) and developed a passion for natural history as a means by which to understand more about the world and its natural laws. This was a busy period for the discovery and study of fossils, and Darwin himself became a passionate collector. His collection and studies abroad eventually led him to develop his theory of evolution by means of **natural selection**.

Know Darwin's Key Ideas
On the Origin of Species

In 1859, Darwin published *On the Origin of Species*, which introduced the theory that the diversity and complexity we observe in nature is due to species evolving over generations through the process of natural selection. Darwin argued that, through survival of the fittest, only those individuals with characteristics best suited to the environment were able to reproduce and so pass on desirable characteristics. Over a very long period of time, this accounted for complexity, change and even entirely new species suited to survival in different environments.

When he travelled to the Galápagos Islands, Darwin studied the different species of finches found on the various islands. He observed that the differences between the finches reflected the different environments on each island, and their beaks in particular meant each species was perfectly suited to the food available on each island. Such evidence eventually convinced Darwin to publish his theory.

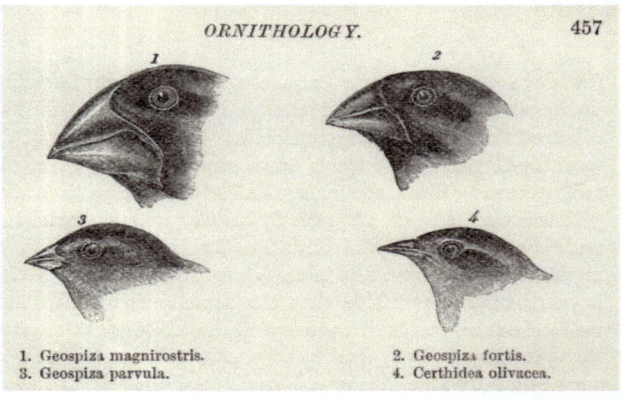

From his findings regarding the differences of individuals within a single species, Darwin went on to develop the concept of the tree of life, which explains how all species on earth are related and have evolved over time from a common ancestor. This idea also illustrates how species were closely or more distantly related. For example, humans and monkeys are all primates and therefore stem from the same 'branch' of the tree of life.

Understand Darwin's Arguments

IMPROVE YOUR UNDERSTANDING

Make sure that you know why Darwin's theory of evolution presents a challenge to teleological arguments.

> **ESSENTIAL!**
>
> **Beneficent** means kind, generous and resulting in good. It describes a lesser form of good than 'omnibenevolent'.

With the publication of Darwin's theory of evolution, he was not attempting to challenge natural theology and religion outright, but was contributing to an already established perspective which, using evidence of extinct fossils, challenged a literal interpretation of Genesis. Many scientists were already considering creation as a slow, unfolding progress rather than a single event. Although Darwin did see natural selection as a replacement for Paley's argument, he did not rule out the role of a guiding creator and **beneficent** God. However, in the years that followed, Darwin's theory fuelled debate and controversy between religious and scientific thinkers, such as Thomas Huxley and Samuel Wilberforce, bishop of Oxford, in 1860. Huxley used Darwin's theory as a means to challenge the authority of the clergy in England at the time.

> **TIP**
>
> Note that although Darwin, for the majority of his adult life, did not believe in the Christian God, he was *not* an outright atheist. His letters indicate that he believed it likely there was a divine first cause involved in creation.

Read Darwin for Yourself

This passage is taken from Darwin's autobiography (often published as an appendix to *On the Origin of Species*). The notes in the margin will help you to grasp his ideas.

Although I did not think much about the existence of a **personal deity** until a considerably later period of my life, I will here give the vague conclusions to which I have been driven. **The old argument of design in nature, as given by Paley ... fails, now that the law of natural selection has been discovered.** We can no longer argue that, for instance, the beautiful **hinge of a bivalve shell must have been made by an intelligent being, like the hinge of a door by man.** There seems to be no more design in the variability of organic beings and in the action of natural selection, than **in the course which the wind blows.** Everything in nature is the result of **fixed laws** ... But passing over the endless beautiful adaptations which we everywhere meet with, it may be asked how can the **generally beneficent arrangement of the world be accounted for?**	By 'personal deity' Darwin is referring to an interventionist God who responds to prayer, such as the Christian God. Darwin is specifically referring to Paley's teleological argument from complex design. As Paley made use of analogy, so too does Darwin. However, he argues, this reasoning is no longer justifiable. In Darwin's time there was no discernible pattern in wind behaviour to give the impression of 'design'. By 'fixed laws' Darwin is referring to natural selection. Darwin wondered what accounted for the overall beneficial arrangement of things in the world, which left room for belief in a guiding and benevolent God.

Know Criticisms of Darwin

Some religious groups continue to this day to oppose the theory of evolution. Creationists, neo-creationists and intelligent design advocates argue that the theory of evolution can be challenged for several reasons, including the following.

Lack of evidence. Creationists argue that evolution itself has not been empirically observed, and that there are large gaps in the fossil records, meaning significant changes in species are unaccounted for. This undermines the theory, as there could be other explanations.

> **INSIGHT**
>
> F.R. Tennant criticised evolution (see Chapter 4), arguing that natural selection cannot account for the beauty in the world or the human ability to appreciate such beauty.

> **INSIGHT**
>
> Many Christian denominations accept the theory of evolution in harmony with belief in a creator God, who initiated and guides the process.

> **EVALUATION SKILLS**
>
> An answer to an evaluative question about a scholar is always deepened by demonstrating awareness of how other thinkers have taken different positions.

Irreducible complexity. This is the argument that some organisms and biological systems could not function on a simpler level, so they could not have evolved from less complex systems over time. One example often referred to in support of irreducible complexity is the blood clotting cascade, which is a complex function in vertebrate species that causes blood to coagulate. In 1996, Michael Behe said that examples of irreducible complexity in this world demonstrate that evolution through natural selection alone is impossible.

Watch Out for Traps

Darwin was not an atheist. Darwin's theory of evolution was not intended as a direct challenge to God's existence. The theory has subsequently been used to challenge design arguments, but the success of this challenge depends on different religious interpretations: for example, a literal or metaphorical understanding of Genesis.

> **STRENGTHEN YOUR GRASP**
>
> 1. Explain in a paragraph how the scientific theory of evolution challenges teleological arguments for God's existence. To improve your answer, use examples and key vocabulary, including natural selection, adaptation, traits, environment, survival and reproduction.
> 2. Note down the strengths of evolution as an explanation for the complexity, order and purpose we see in the world around us. Then note down the strengths of the teleological argument. Which side is more persuasive? Can you counter-argue against any of these strengths at all? This will help with your AO2 evaluation.

Exam Guidance AO1

You could be asked to outline (AS only), explain or examine challenges to teleological arguments, which could include Darwin's theory of evolution. When revising this, it might help to note down, alongside key points of Darwin's theory, how they can challenge aspects of the design argument. For example:

- Adaptations to species over time – here God is not required as the designer of complex mechanisms.
- Natural selection – this means no role for a creator God, as it can be explained by random chance and the environment.

Exam Guidance AO2

You could be asked to evaluate the success of the teleological arguments or the challenges to design arguments. When referring to the theory of evolution, remember two crucial points:

- Merely referring to the theory of evolution is not evaluation. Evaluation comes from weighing up the strengths and weaknesses of ideas.
- While evolution may challenge Paley's watchmaker argument specifically, it does not necessarily contradict the conclusion of design arguments: that God exists.

7. ST ANSELM
GET INTO ANSELM'S WORLD

> **Quick Overview** St Anselm (1033–1109) was a Benedictine monk who became archbishop of Canterbury. Although not recognised as such in his own time, he is today credited as the originator of the ontological argument and considered to be the father of scholasticism.

St Anselm was born and grew up in Aosta, Italy, where it is reported that, as a child, he had a vision of God at the summit of the Becca di Nona peak in the Alps near his home. Anselm wanted to become a monk but his father would not permit it. However, Anselm's faith persevered and in his early twenties he left to study and train at the monastery of Bec. While at Bec, Anselm flourished, going on to become a monk and abbot of the monastery before becoming archbishop of Canterbury in England.

As a scholar, Anselm was heavily influenced by the rationalism of Plato and the logic of Aristotle, which he came across through the works of St Augustine and Boethius in particular. However, in keeping with many contemporaries of this era, he did not believe that faith should be based purely on reasoned thought or logic. During this period, medieval philosophers tended to be Christian monks of various orders who discussed theological issues, and many of them were interested in how far human reason could go to demonstrate what they believed to be true as revealed in scripture and God's revelation.

> **ESSENTIAL!**
> Knowledge is derived from reason. Religious knowledge must therefore be grounded in rational thought and valid arguments.

> **INSIGHT**
> Anselm was declared to be the *Doctor Magnificus* (Magnificent Doctor) by the Catholic Church due to his contributions to Christian thought and scholasticism.

Anselm did not distinguish between reason and revelation as different sources of truth, as later scholars like Aquinas did (see Chapter 1); instead he blended the two. He argued that Christian principles of faith could be rationally understood, but that faith is required for that rational understanding: 'unless I believe I shall not understand'. Faith preceded reason.

During his lifetime Anselm wrote many works on topics ranging from the Trinity and Incarnation to truth, logic and free will. However, he is most famous for his unique proof of God's existence, which became known as the ontological argument.

Know Anselm's Key Ideas

> **IMPROVE YOUR UNDERSTANDING**
> Make sure that you know why Anselm believes we can know God exists a priori.

> **INSIGHT**
> It was not Anselm but Kant (see Chapter 11) who coined the term 'ontological argument', in 1781. Ontology refers to the nature of 'being'.

In the preface to *Proslogion* (meaning 'Discourse'), Anselm wrote that he was seeking to demonstrate in a single, short argument God's existence and everything he understood about God's nature. He describes how the notion eluded him for some time, but came to him one night after praying. He considered naming this work 'Faith Seeking Understanding', before settling on *Proslogion*.

Proslogion (written in 1077–78) consisted of 26 chapters concerning God's existence and nature. The second and third chapters, known as Proslogion 2 and 3, contain his ontological arguments, which we will focus on here.

Anselm's First Ontological Argument

As Anselm wanted to put forward an argument that relied on nothing else for its evidence other than itself, his argument is a priori and relies on deductive logic concerning the definition of God, and is therefore analytical and seeks to prove that God by definition must exist. His first argument, found in Proslogion 2, can be expressed as follows:

> P1: We can think of a being who is 'that than which nothing greater can be conceived', which we call God.
>
> P2: Even the fool (atheist) understands that this being is God.
>
> P3: The fool says the greatest conceivable being exists only *in intellectu* (in the mind).
>
> P4: But it is greater to exist *in re* (in reality) than in the mind alone.
>
> C1: Therefore we can think of a being that exists in reality as well as the mind, but this being would therefore be greater than God (*reductio ad absurdum*).
>
> C2: This contradicts the definition of God (P1), so God cannot exist in the mind alone.
>
> C3: The greatest conceivable being, which is God, therefore must exist in both reality *and* the mind.
>
> (C4: The fool really is a fool to deny the existence of the greatest conceivable being, which by definition must exist.)

Although Anselm's first ontological argument is sometimes summarised without the elements relating to the fool, we included the fool here (in C4) because Anselm was not only attempting to prove the existence of God by definition, but also that it is the fool who is guilty of absurdity. Anselm does this by essentially posing two scenarios: one where the greatest conceivable being only exists in the mind, and another where the greatest conceivable being also exists in reality. He declares that it is the fool who is guilty of absurdity because, for him, the scenario with the greatest conceivable being is the one where such a being actually exists in reality, as that would be the greater quality. Yet the fool continues to conclude that something which so plainly must exist does not.

TIP

The Bible declares that a non-believer is a fool, but does not explain why. Anselm uses reason to understand why this is so.

INSIGHT

Psalm 14:1 and 53:1: 'The fool hath said in his heart, "There is no God".'

Anselm's Second Ontological Argument

Anselm received a quick objection to his first argument from Gaunilo, a fellow eleventh-century monk, living in Marmoutiers. Anselm was pleased by this objection as it gave him the chance to respond and further demonstrate the truth of his argument, so he included it in the appendix to *Proslogion*, and added his *Responsio* (response). Anselm drew upon the second version of his ontological argument to point out that Gaunilo had made a fatal error in his objection, and had misunderstood the unique nature of God. Anselm's second ontological argument appears in Proslogion 3, and centres on an extension to his definition of God, as that which 'cannot be conceived not to exist'.

Anselm's second argument can be expressed as follows:

> P1: We can think of a being who is 'that than which nothing greater can be conceived', which we call God.
>
> P2: A being that cannot be thought of as not existing, is greater than a being which can be thought of as not existing.
>
> P3: If the greatest conceivable being (God) is understood as not existing in reality, then this being (God) is not the greatest conceivable being (*reductio ad absurdum*).
>
> C1: A being that existed in reality would be greater, but this contradicts the definition of God (P1).
>
> C2: Therefore if God is the greatest conceivable being, and this notion exists *in intellectu* (in the mind), then God must exist *in re* (in reality).
>
> P4: The notion of God clearly does exist in the mind.
>
> C3: Therefore God clearly must exist in reality and his non-existence is absurd and an incoherent notion.

■ **INSIGHT**

See Chapter 10 for Gaunilo's 'Lost Island' objection to Anselm's first ontological argument.

■ **INSIGHT**

Anselm said P3 resulted in an 'irreconcilable contradiction'.

Understand Anselm's Arguments

Anselm's *first* argument centres on two crucial elements:

- P1: his definition of God as 'that than which nothing greater can be conceived'. By this, he means that God is the most excellent, perfect thing that anyone could imagine, and as such it would be impossible to imagine anything greater. Although this is not a strictly biblical definition of God, it is supported by scripture, Christian revelation and the usual understanding of the God of classical theism (omnipotent, benevolent and transcendent).

■ **TIP**

Anselm's understanding of God can be supported with scripture, such as Psalm 147:5, 'Great is our Lord, and abundant in power; his understanding is beyond measure.'

- P4: Anselm believes it is greater to exist in reality than in the mind alone. To illustrate this, he uses the analogy of a painter. Someone can conceive of a painting in their mind, but unless the painting existed in reality it would not be something of value, and you certainly would not call someone a painter unless they had actually painted something in reality. Therefore, for Anselm, existing in reality is the greater quality. From this perspective, we can understand Anselm's confidence in declaring that the non-believer is a fool.

Anselm used the analogy of a painter to illustrate his theory. A person would only be labelled a painter if they actually produced paintings. A painting is tangible and has value. An idea of a painting in the mind alone has no value and does not make someone an artist in reality.

With regard to Anselm's P1, there has been debate as to whether his first ontological argument is nothing more than wordplay, or sheer genius. For example, **superlatives** are adjectives or adverbs which describe something to the highest degree of a specific quality, for example the bravest soldier, the fiercest lion or the tallest building. By definition, these must exist in reality. At any one time, of all the buildings in the world, one *will* be the tallest. However, it may not always be the same building (at the time of writing, the world's tallest building is the Burj Kalifa in Dubai, but in 1923 it was the Woolworth building in New York City). Therefore, although the greatest possible being *will* exist, the question of whether that being is God is still very much debated.

Anselm's second argument was traditionally understood as expanding on the points made in his first argument. However, in the twentieth century, scholars such as Charles Hartshorne, Norman Malcolm and Alvin Plantinga started to argue that Anselm was making a very different point: not just that by definition God must exist, but that by definition God must *necessarily* exist. The technical term for necessary existence is **aseity**.

It appears, then, that in Proslogion 3 and in response to Gaunilo, Anselm was distinguishing between two types of existence: contingent existence and necessary existence. We have already explored these concepts in Chapter 1 with Aquinas, but they are relevant here in terms of their implications for what can be conceived or thought of. Anselm states that Gaunilo's island (see Chapter 10) can only have contingent existence. Every aspect of the island depends on other factors for existence. The trees depend upon what seeds took root and grew; the type of beach or coastline depends upon the geographic location and landscape. The very existence of the island depends on the sea level. We can easily imagine this island, however great, as not existing, or not existing in its greatest form, for a multitude of reasons. However, God has necessary existence. God does not rely on anything else for existence and this existence would not be affected by any change within the universe, otherwise our very understanding of God would be contradicted. God, then, cannot be thought of as not existing, unlike contingent things.

> **ESSENTIAL!**
>
> A **superlative** is a way of describing something to the highest degree or quality: for example, 'the bravest'.

> **INSIGHT**
>
> Schopenhauer famously called the ontological argument a 'sleight of hand trick'. The argument does sit well with most people, but it is very difficult to identify exactly why.

> **ESSENTIAL!**
>
> **Aseity** is the unique form of existence belonging to a being that is self-caused and self-sustained, which cannot *not* exist.

WHAT DO YOU THINK?

Write down your thoughts on Anselm's arguments and revisit them shortly before the exam to see if your views have changed.

TASK

Read Anselm for yourself in the extract below. The notes in the margin will help you to grasp his ideas.

Read Anselm for Yourself

The following passage is taken from *Proslogion*, and illustrates the way in which Anselm expressed his ideas, now recognised as a form of meditation or prayer.

Anselm is seeking an a priori argument, which requires no evidence other than its own deductive logic.	I began to ask myself whether there might be found a single argument which would require no other for its proof than itself alone; and alone would suffice to demonstrate that God truly exists …
Anselm is targeting the fool from Psalm 14:1 and 53:1 in the Bible. It is today understood that Anselm was seeking to understand, through reason, why the atheist was declared a fool in the Bible. Anselm believes he demonstrates here how absurd the atheist's logic is.	Truly there is a God, although the fool has said in his heart, there is no God … Even the fool is convinced that something exists in the understanding, at least, than which nothing greater can be conceived. For, when he hears of this, he understands it. And whatever is understood, exists in the understanding … Therefore, if that, than which nothing greater can be conceived, exists in the understanding alone, the very being, than which nothing greater can be conceived, is one, than which a greater can be conceived. But obviously this is impossible. Hence … there exists a being, than which nothing greater can be conceived, and it exists both in the understanding and in reality.
This is *reductio ad absurdum*.	
Anselm's wording suggests he is directing his work to God himself, hence it is today understood as a form of prayer or meditation.	God cannot be conceived not to exist … That which can be conceived not to exist is not God … So truly, therefore, do you exist, O Lord, my God, that you cannot be conceived not to exist; and rightly. For, if a mind could conceive of a being better than you, the creature would rise above the Creator; and this is most absurd. And, indeed, whatever else there is, except you alone, can be conceived not to exist. To you alone, therefore, it belongs to exist more truly than all other beings … Why, then, has the fool said in his heart, there is no God, since it is so evident, to a rational mind, that you do exist in the highest degree of all? Why, except that he is dull and a fool?
Everything apart from God has contingent existence and their non-existence can be contemplated.	
Anselm's use of reason has brought him to the same conclusion as revealed in scripture: that the atheist is a fool. This reinforces Anselm's belief that rationalism can, when pushed, support the truth as revealed by God.	
The root of criticisms that see this argument as a play on words. To describe something to the highest degree, in this case as 'the greatest', is to use an adjective. There will always be the greatest X (whatever X is …), but does the greatest being in reality necessarily have to be God?	

Know Criticisms of Anselm

Logic. The first criticism of Anselm's ontological argument came from Gaunilo. For more information about this subject and Gaunilo, see Chapter 10. Other criticisms are dealt with below. These criticisms are not mentioned in the specification but will provide you with further insight into different perspectives and help you to develop your own view.

A priori nature. In the thirteenth century, St Thomas Aquinas took an oppositional stance to Anselm's a priori argument despite his own belief in God, for two main reasons:

- We could never truly comprehend God's nature due to our limited and finite minds. Therefore the nature of God and God's existence could never be self-evident to humans, only to God.

- People clearly have different definitions of God, other than Anselm's 'that than which nothing greater can be conceived'. Non-believers, for example, do not by definition understand God to exist in reality, whereas Anselm did.

Consequently, Aquinas believed we could only have knowledge of God through revelation and a posteriori reasoning, and inductive logic (see Chapter 1), something more concrete and evidential than human deductive reasoning alone. Hence Aquinas' five ways, which were a posteriori, in his great work *Summa Theologica*. Aquinas was so influential during his lifetime and after that most Christian philosophers and theologians also rejected Anselm's argument, and it lay dormant until revived by René Descartes in the seventeenth century (see Chapter 8).

Necessary existence. David Hume was an eighteenth-century empiricist, meaning he believed that knowledge was derived from experience. He is most famously known today for developing Hume's fork, a method of identifying the nature of knowledge (see Chapter 5). Hume reasoned that God's existence was not knowledge obtained through analysis of the definition alone. Knowledge was only truly a priori if anything contrary would then be a logical contradiction. For example, $2+2=2$ is a contradiction of $2+2=4$, and a triangle having four sides is a contradiction of the definition of a triangle, which states that it has three sides. However, Hume argued that, whatever we can imagine as existing, we can also imagine as not existing, without contradiction, and this includes God. Therefore God *cannot* exist *necessarily*, as we can imagine a world where God does not exist. God's existence cannot therefore be known a priori and the argument fails.

> **INSIGHT**
>
> 'Whatever we conceive as existent, we can also conceive as non-existent. There is no being, therefore, whose non-existence implies a contradiction' (Hume, *Dialogues Concerning Natural Religion*, 1779).

Circular logic. As we have seen, medieval philosophers tended to be primarily concerned with matters of theology, and philosophy was a tool with which to confirm conclusions that they already believed. Anselm's ontological argument, in particular, can be criticised for using circular logic, as his very starting point is the definition of God, which according to Anselm entails the very existence that he goes on to conclude. The evidence of the argument is itself the very claim of the argument, and as philosopher Bertrand Russell noted, 'the finding of arguments given in advance is not philosophy'.

Wider criticisms. Not everyone would agree that things are greater in reality. Roman philosopher Seneca once stated, 'we suffer more often in imagination than in reality'. Our greatest fears, once we face them, do not seem as great as we imagined. But is this not also true of the positive? How often does the idea of something wonderful that we have been looking forward to prove to be greater than the experience in reality (for example, Christmas Day)? If Anselm is wrong to assume in his first argument (P4) that it is greater to exist in reality than in the mind alone, then the rest of his argument fails.

Watch Out for Traps

Don't skip steps. When writing an AO1 answer and explaining Anselm's ontological arguments, ensure you do not miss out any steps or premises in the argument. The conclusion is supposed to follow on logically from the premises, so if any are missing, the conclusion will not be justified. For example, with Anselm's first argument, you need to include the premise that it is greater to exist in reality than just in the mind, and in the second, you need to include that having necessary existence is greater than having contingent existence. Therefore, the greatest conceivable being must, by definition, have to exist necessarily, otherwise the conclusion cannot logically follow.

Commentary and analysis. When writing an AO2 answer and referring to strengths or weaknesses of Anselm's arguments, don't just list or describe them without analysis or evaluative commentary, as describing them alone would be an AO1 skill. You need to comment on how they are persuasive/successful/incoherent/weak and weigh up these points to demonstrate analysis and evaluation.

> **INSIGHT**
>
> Karl Barth (twentieth-century fideist philosopher) claimed that Anselm's arguments were a meditation on the nature of God and an account of his religious experience rather than a philosophical proof.

Proof or justification for faith. Remember, Anselm may not have intended his ontological argument as a form of proof for God's existence. *Proslogion* is written in the form of a personal meditation or prayer and appears at times to be written to God directly. It often contains passages stating things like 'to You, O Lord, my God', in which case it was perhaps never intended to function as a philosophical proof that can be evaluated as such. Perhaps it was instead intended to function as a support to faith, so its merit lies in whether it has value for religious believers in understanding or justifying their faith.

STRENGTHEN YOUR GRASP

1. Make a list of five superlatives that must exist: for example, 'the tallest human' and 'the highest building'. Can these statements define things into existence, or are they describing things that exist in reality already? Can you explain your answer? How does this link to Anselm's definition of God?
2. Was Anselm correct to believe that things are greater in reality than in our mind alone? Consider any of the following examples and note down whether you think the greater version is the one in reality or in the mind alone, and note your reasons why:
   - the most poetic, moving and inspiring speech
   - the greatest ending to a story
   - the scariest and most ferocious monster
   - the perfect partner
   - the animal version of events in the *Life of Pi*
   - Christmas Day.

   How might this idea challenge Anselm's argument?

Exam Guidance AO1

In part a) questions you could be asked to discuss Anselm's ontological arguments within an outline (AS only), explain or examine question, regarding ontological arguments/their development/deductive arguments/a priori arguments. As named scholars in the specification, Anselm, Descartes and Malcolm could be named in the question, or the question could simply be broader.

In any event, you will need to carefully select the relevant material that would best suit the nature of the question. For example, a question asking you to examine Anselm's ontological arguments will require far more depth and detail than a question asking you to outline the developments on ontological arguments, where reference to Anselm may form only a part of the answer, which would then go on to discuss Descartes and Malcolm.

Ensure you understand the different command words and what they entail.

Exam Guidance AO2

In part b) questions you could be asked to evaluate different kinds of one-sided statements. For example, the following taken from the specification:

1. The extent to which 'a priori' arguments for God's existence are persuasive.

2. The extent to which different religious views on the nature of God impact on arguments for the existence of God.

3. The effectiveness of the ontological argument for God's existence.

4. Whether the ontological argument is more persuasive than the cosmological/teleological arguments for God's existence.

5. The effectiveness of the challenges to the ontological argument for God's existence.

6. The extent to which objections to the ontological argument are persuasive.

In the case of something like 3, emphasis would best be placed on the strengths or weaknesses of specific ontological arguments or their challenges (for example, Gaunilo's objection), with regard to how successful the arguments are.

In the case of 1, 4 and 5, however, it could be better to keep linking back to the a priori or deductive nature of the argument and ensure that is the focus of your evaluation: for example, Aquinas and Hume's rejection that God's existence can be known a priori, and the issues raised by Gaunilo regarding the logic of Anselm's argument.

For 4, reference to ontological arguments would only be part of the answer as you would need to contrast the strengths and weaknesses of those with cosmological/teleological/a posteriori/inductive arguments. To help with your revision, make a table where you compare different aspects of these arguments and the nature of the arguments, noting their strengths and weaknesses.

With 2, reference to cosmological, teleological and ontological arguments will be relevant, but particularly concerning the nature and definition of God on which the arguments are based – in this case, Anselm's God as 'that than which nothing greater can be conceived', which entails necessary existence. To revise for this type of question focus, first make a note of the qualities of God that the cosmological, teleological and ontological arguments imply or require (for example, transcendence, omnipotence and omniscience). Then make a note of the similarities that different religions have in their understanding of what God is like and compare this with the God of classical theism. Now add in other views on the nature of God, such as deism or process theology, or concepts of a limited God, where logical issues may restrict God in some form. Then return to the arguments and the nature of God that they imply. Can you see anywhere where a different view of God would impact the argument?

8. RENÉ DESCARTES
GET INTO DESCARTES' WORLD

> **Quick Overview** René Descartes (1596–1650) was a mathematician, scientist and philosopher renowned for his methodological scepticism, which provided a blank canvas for modern Western philosophy. Through his rationalist method as the foundation for knowledge, Descartes posed an ontological argument for God's existence.

INSIGHT

Descartes is widely considered to be the father of modern philosophy.

René Descartes was born into a wealthy French family and was educated in the scholastic method under the Jesuits (an intellectual Catholic order, whose followers saw education and teaching as part of their mission). During his childhood, Descartes experienced ill health and had to spend much of his time lying in bed, where he developed a habit for meditating, a routine he maintained for the majority of his life. Family wealth meant that Descartes was never required to earn an income, so after completing his studies he volunteered for the military and spent many years travelling. It is recorded in his biography that, while in Germany with the military, Descartes experienced a series of visions and dreams that had a profound effect upon him. In one vision he saw the universe as a mathematical picture, which convinced him that the universe could be understood via mathematical principle. Descartes came to believe that these visions were a sign that he should seek truth through reason. However, many years passed before he turned his full attention to establishing his great philosophy. In fact, prior to this, Descartes became a leading figure in the world of mathematics.

INSIGHT

Descartes sought to bring the certainty of mathematics to philosophy, without referring to any religious authority, as had been the trend in previous eras.

TIP

Thinkers can never be separated from the time of their existence. Note some of the societal issues, ideas and movements that Descartes was living through and to which he was responding.

He also wrote on a great many subjects and his contributions to both science and philosophy left a lasting legacy. But he had to be cautious about what he published due to the dominance of the Catholic Church at the time, as scholars accused of heresy could be sentenced to house arrest or burnt at the stake. In fact, during Descartes' lifetime, Galileo was condemned as a heretic for publishing evidence for the Copernican system (which states the earth orbits the sun), causing Descartes to fully appreciate the potential implications of his own ideas and possible accusations of atheism or heresy that could come his way. To ensure he didn't go too far beyond what the Church could tolerate, Descartes would run his ideas and first drafts past his lifelong friend and ordained Catholic priest, Marin Mersenne. However, even this did not prevent the Catholic Church placing Descartes' works on the *Index Librorum Prohibitorum*, their list of banned books, and Descartes was forced to seek refuge in the Netherlands, a land known for its intellectual liberty and freedom of thought.

Know Descartes' Key Ideas

▌ IMPROVE YOUR UNDERSTANDING

Make sure that you grasp how Descartes defined God and why he thinks God therefore exists necessarily.

Descartes is widely regarded to be the Father of Modern Philosophy, as he was one of the first thinkers to abandon Scholastic-Aristotelian thought, leading him to reject the medieval approach of building on uncertain assumptions about the world. Instead, he sought to re-establish a foundation for knowledge of which we could be certain, and from here to build up step by step what could be known about the world.

Many of Descartes' key philosophical ideas are laid out in his *Meditations on First Philosophy* (1641), which prior to publication he sent out for critique, enabling him to include objections and reactions alongside his initial ideas. A summary of some of his key ideas as required by the Board's specification are detailed below.

Knowledge

As a result of his experiences in mathematics and morning meditations, Descartes had come to realise that much of the current knowledge of the time was based on uncertain belief systems. He used the metaphor of a shaky building, built on weak foundations. In the quest for certain, sure knowledge, Descartes sought to dismantle the shaky building and its weak foundations and start from scratch. He wanted to construct a strong building, brick by brick, on sure foundations. To do this, he developed a method of doubt, sometimes known as 'methodological scepticism' or 'hyperbolic doubt': in essence, an extreme form of doubt where he questioned all beliefs and apparent knowledge of the world, seeking to identify what could be undeniably and *indubitably* known.

> **ESSENTIAL!**
> **Indubitable knowledge** is knowledge that is impossible to doubt.

Descartes began by subjecting empirical knowledge and sense experience to doubt. He identified that the senses are able to deceive – he himself had been subjected to visions and illusions in previous years. So how, then, could we be certain that we were not dreaming now? When we dream, we often believe we are where we appear to be and are doing whatever it is we are doing in the dream, yet it is not so. If all experience we have in the world could be a dream, we have cause to doubt. Such knowledge is therefore not certain and cannot be a foundation for further ideas.

> ▌ INSIGHT
>
> Descartes' evil demon idea may sound far-fetched, but it has inspired modern versions which you may be more familiar with, including the 'brain in a vat' scenario, and films such as *The Matrix* and *Free Guy*.

Descartes goes on to introduce his most radical sceptical thought, and explores the notion that an evil demon could have fabricated every aspect of reality and all sense experience, including colour, taste, shape and sound. All external experiences could be traps to trick someone into believing the external world as they experienced it was true.

However, it was at this point that Descartes discovered the first certainty: that he could not doubt his own existence. This is because of his famous statement *cogito, ergo sum* – I think, therefore I am. By being able to doubt in the first place, he could be certain that he existed. He knew this to be true just by thinking. The truth of this certainty does not depend on any evidence other that itself. It is, therefore, an *innate idea*.

> **ESSENTIAL!**
> **Innate ideas** are concepts already held in the mind prior to experience.

▌ INSIGHT

Descartes was not the first to identify the 'I think, therefore I am' idea. Aristotle, in *Nicomachean Ethics*, stated that 'to be conscious that we are thinking, is to be conscious that we exist'.

God as an Innate Idea

Having identified that there was a priori knowledge (known truths), innate ideas, of which he could be certain, Descartes sought to identify what else could be known according to his new methodological doubt. Certain knowledge, he argued, had to be equally clear and distinct from knowledge that could be doubted, such as that derived from the senses. It must also be true and understood through reason, such as mathematics, geometry and logic. So, Descartes became a rationalist.

However, this still left the problem of the external world and how we could be sure of anything outside the mind, including sense experience. Descartes' solution was found in the religion of his upbringing, the Catholic faith. God could be the guarantor for the certainty of knowledge regarding the external world, but Descartes would need to prove that God exists a priori (for certain) first. Hence Descartes formulated his proofs for God's existence. The first, concerning God as an innate idea, is sometimes known as the 'trademark' argument:

> P1: I have in my mind the idea of God as infinite and perfect.
>
> P2: But as a human I am finite and imperfect.
>
> P3: I cannot be the cause of the idea of God, as the cause of anything must be at least as perfect as its effect.
>
> C1: Therefore only a perfect and infinite being can be the cause of my idea of God.
>
> C2: God must exist.

In other words, the concept of God is an innate idea, imprinted in the minds of humans, much like a trademark.

Ontological Proof

Having established the concept of God as an innate idea and proof of God's existence, Descartes went on to pose his own ontological proof of God's existence. It can be summarised as follows:

> P1: God is a supremely perfect being.
>
> P2: A supremely perfect being would possess all perfections.
>
> P3: Existence is a perfection (along with omnipotence, omniscience and omnibenevolence).
>
> C: God, the supremely perfect being, necessarily exists.

Like Anselm, Descartes relies upon his definition of God, making his argument analytic. As a supremely perfect being, God must be perfect in every way. Descartes develops what was assumed in Anselm's argument: that existence is an essence, or intrinsic property, of perfection – a predicate of a subject, in other words. Therefore 'God exists' is true by definition, a priori, as to state that God does not exist would be self-contradictory and absurd, demonstrating that God's existence is therefore necessary – a logical truth.

To illustrate this, Descartes uses the following two examples:

- The concept of a triangle entails the three sides and three internal angles adding up to 180 degrees.
- The concept of highlands (mountains) entails the lowlands (slopes of the valley).

INSIGHT

Descartes defines God as 'a supremely perfect being', having all perfections, including the perfection of existence.

TIP

Descartes made no mention of Anselm's argument, so we do not know if he was aware of the earlier proof.

INSIGHT

For Descartes, existence could not be separated from the essence of God any more than other attributes or perfections, such as omnipotence, omniscience and omnibenevolence, could.

WHAT DO YOU THINK?

Write down your thoughts on Descarte's arguments and revisit them shortly before the exam to see if your views have changed.

Read Descartes for Yourself

The following passage is taken from *Meditations on First Philosophy* (1641), and illustrates Descartes' deductive logic. The notes in the margin will help you to grasp his ideas.

Descartes considers that existence may not be an inherent quality of the concept of God, or 'predicate' as it was later termed, but goes on to reject this for the reasons outlined below.	The question 'What is the essence of triangles?' asks what it takes for something to qualify as a triangle. Answering this still leaves open the existence question, which asks whether there are any triangles. I can easily believe that in the case of God, also, existence can be separated from essence … so that God can be thought of as not existing. But on more careful reflection it becomes quite evident that, just as having-internal-angles-equal-to-180° can't be separated from the idea or essence of a triangle, and as the idea of highlands can't be separated from the idea of lowlands, so existence can't be separated from the essence of God. Just as it is self-contradictory to think of highlands in a world where there are no lowlands, so it is self-contradictory to think of God as not existing – that is, to think of a supremely perfect being as lacking a perfection, namely the perfection of existence.
Descartes' reference here to what is translated as highlands and lowlands has previously often been translated as mountains and valleys. However, more recent readings have instead suggested that Descartes' original French referred to foothills or the lower slopes of a higher mountain, therefore making more concrete the self-contradiction that he identifies.	
Descartes identifies what is later deemed as a 'relation of ideas' by Hume: a logical truth, evident because to deny it results in self-contradiction. However, unlike Hume, Descartes believes these truths to be innate knowledge, known prior to experience.	
	Here is a possible objection:
	… I can't think of God except as existing, just as I can't think of a river without banks. From the latter fact, though, it certainly doesn't follow that there are any rivers in the world; so why should it follow from the former fact that God exists? How things are in reality is not settled by my thought; … so I can attach existence to God in my thought even if no God exists. This involves false reasoning …
Descartes appears to pre-empt the criticism that Kant later posed, that if you accept the concept of a triangle, then you also accept that the concept entails three sides – although, just as you can reject the existence of a triangle and its three sides, you can also reject the existence of God and the existence it entails. Descartes argues that this is false reasoning.	I agree that I don't have to think about God at all; but whenever I do choose to think of him, bringing the idea of the first and supreme being out of my mind's store, I must attribute all perfections to him … This necessity in my thought guarantees that, when I later realize that existence is a perfection, I am right to conclude then that the first and supreme being exists. Similarly, I don't ever have to imagine a triangle; but whenever I do wish to consider a figure with straight sides and three angles, I must attribute to it properties from which it follows that its three angles equal no more than 180 …
It has been said of Descartes that he came dangerously close to solipsism (being self-centred) due to his methodological scepticism and belief that we could not be certain of any knowledge derived from sense experience. However, in *Meditations*, Descartes discovered rationalist grounds for knowledge that he believed to be a certainty, thereby avoiding solipsism.	Whatever method of proof I use … I am always brought back to the fact that nothing completely convinces me except what I vividly and clearly perceive … The supreme being exists; God, the only being whose essence includes existence, exists; what is more self-evident than that?

Know Criticisms of Descartes

Major criticism of Descartes' ontological argument came from Immanuel Kant. To discover more about Kant and his ideas, see Chapter 11. Other criticisms are discussed below (although these are not named directly in the Board's specification), and will provide you with further evaluation and insight into different perspectives, to help you develop your own view.

Descartes' ontological argument is incomplete. Gottfried Wilhelm Leibniz argued that Descartes' argument for God's existence failed because he had not taken the necessary steps to demonstrate that his concept, of God as perfect and infinite being, was coherent. It is possible that some of the perfections that Descartes identifies – omnibenevolence, omnipotence, omniscience, existence – are incompatible with each other: for example, omnibenevolence, omnipotence and existence resulting in the problem of evil, or omniscience, omnibenevolence and existence resulting in the problem of human free will and just judgement. Leibniz therefore proposed his own ontological argument, explaining that each perfection of God must be self-contained and cannot be defined by the negation (contradiction) of anything else.

The Cartesian Circle. Antoine Arnauld, fellow French philosopher, famously objected to the apparent circular nature of the logic in Descartes' *Meditations*. Descartes argues that we can rely on our clear and distinct ideas regarding the world because God guarantees we are not deceived (see 'Know Descartes' Key Ideas' above). However, his proof for this is that God exists because God is an innate, clear and distinct idea who must exist by definition. Arnauld points out the circular reasoning that, in order to show that God exists (as an innate, clear and distinct idea), Descartes assumes that God exists (as guarantor of innate, clear and distinct ideas). This became known as the Cartesian Circle.

The concept and definition of God are not innate. Both Descartes' trademark and ontological proofs of God can be challenged. As noted in Chapter 5 on Hume, empiricists believe that *all* ideas ultimately originate in some form of sense experience. Descartes' concept of God as a supremely perfect and infinite being can be explained as originating in human experience of relative virtues and qualities in people. Omnipotence can derive from experience of powerful people such as kings, omniscience can derive from experience of great scholarly works, and omnibenevolence can derive from experience of the great acts of love, kindness and bravery that people can demonstrate. Fuelled by desire and imagination, we can then go on to conceive ideas which are greater than the cause. For example, from experience of our finite existence we can imagine a being who is infinite. From experiences of our relative qualities, we can conceive of them to a greater degree in a more perfect being. Therefore, if our concept and definition of God are derived from experience, then they are *not* innate or a priori. If Descartes' arguments then rely on a posteriori experience, they do not serve as a priori proofs of God.

Watch Out for Traps

Don't forget to use examples. Remember to use examples to illustrate Descartes' ideas and what he means. Descartes refers to many examples, including the following:

- The essence of a triangle includes the intrinsic property of three sides and three internal angles, which add up to 180 degrees.
- By definition, the concept of a highland includes the inseparable concept of a lowland (the 'what goes up, must come down' theory).
- The concept of a river cannot be separated from the concept of the river banks between which it flows.

Don't forget that Descartes' concept of God is an innate idea. Descartes has two a priori arguments for God's existence, of which the ontological argument is his second. When examining Descartes' proofs for God's existence, it is worth ensuring you grasp his trademark argument and why he believed that God as a supremely perfect and infinite being, who necessarily exists, is an innate idea. It is pivotal for his starting point in his ontological proof, as the origin of this concept of God must be God himself.

EVALUATION SKILLS

An answer to an evaluative question about a scholar is always deepened by demonstrating awareness of how other thinkers have taken different positions.

INSIGHT

The incoherence of the nature and attributes of God has long been a focal point in the philosophy of religion because an incoherent concept results in a paradox, which cannot logically exist.

TIP

For further discussion on the problem of evil, see Chapters 12–16.

Anselm and Descartes do not have the same approach and argument. It is important to understand that, while Anselm and Descartes arrived at the same conclusion, that God must necessarily exist, they had very different starting points. Descartes' arguments arose from his methodological doubt and rationalist approach, in contrast to Anselm who came, in his own words, from a 'faith seeking understanding' approach. See the 'Know Descartes' Key Ideas' section for more on Descartes' original approach to knowledge.

> **STRENGTHEN YOUR GRASP**
>
> 1. The order of Descartes' arguments is just as important as his method, as he believed knowledge can only be built up one certain step at a time. Go through Descartes' ideas from this chapter, chunking them up into the following key points. Ensure you understand how each idea follows on from the previous one:
>   - methodological doubt
>   - rejection of empiricism
>   - *cogito, ergo sum*
>   - God as an innate idea
>   - his ontological argument.
>
> 2. Go through your notes for the above task, noting potential criticism for each key point. Which ideas seem to be Descartes' weakest areas? You can use ideas from Chapters 5 and 11, on Hume and Kant, in addition to this one.

Exam Guidance AO1

For a knowledge and understanding question, you could be asked to outline (AS only), explain or examine any aspect of the specification content, including the development of ontological arguments. When considering the development of ontological arguments, it will be important to demonstrate how Descartes' approach differed from Anselm's, and that he addressed the notion of existence as a property of perfection, which was assumed in Anselm's argument. It could also be worth including how Malcolm developed the argument from Descartes' approach (see Chapter 9). However, you could also be asked something about the challenges to ontological arguments, in which case it would be useful to refer to selected aspects of Descartes' argument, but only in so far as linking to specific challenges, such as those of Kant.

Exam Guidance AO2

Reference to Descartes' arguments would be relevant in an evaluation question concerning the success/effectiveness/persuasiveness of ontological arguments, a priori arguments or their challenges, especially concerning Descartes' methodological doubt and rationalist approach. You could also be asked to evaluate whether the cosmological or teleological argument is the more persuasive. Descartes would be relevant here because of his rejection of a posteriori arguments, due to being a rationalist and doubting knowledge that derived from experience. Finally, a possible question could require evaluation of the extent to which different religious views on the nature of God impact on arguments for the existence of God. Descartes' definition of God, its coherence and his subsequent a priori arguments could be evaluated alongside alternative ideas.

9. NORMAN MALCOLM

GET INTO MALCOLM'S WORLD

> **Quick Overview** Norman Malcolm (1911–90) was an American philosopher who studied at both Harvard and Cambridge universities, under Wittgenstein. Malcolm is known for reviving Anselm's ontological argument, and was instrumental in ensuring that Cornell University had one of the leading Philosophy departments in the USA.

Norman Malcolm was a committed Anglican who, through his studies in philosophy at Harvard and Cambridge universities, met and became lifelong friends with Ludwig Wittgenstein. Malcolm was also influenced by philosopher G.E. Moore, and developed an interest and specialism in analytical philosophy, which concerned the nature of mental concepts and knowledge. Malcolm contributed to philosophical psychology, which was concerned with how philosophical concepts and language are used in ordinary life.

Malcolm's philosophical interests were clearly influenced by Wittgenstein and Moore, and given his interest in mental concepts, it is no surprise that he ended up associated with the ontological argument, which argues for the existence of God via definition. However, as this was his first exploration of the specifically Christian philosophy of religion, Malcolm was met with some critique regarding his interpretation of Anselm.

Regardless of what people made of Malcolm's ontological argument, it is agreed that he was an important and influential figure who contributed greatly to philosophical methodology, particularly concerning language.

Know Malcolm's Key Ideas

> **IMPROVE YOUR UNDERSTANDING**
>
> Make sure that you grasp Malcolm's response to Immanuel Kant and why Malcolm believes God must exist necessarily.

During the 1960s there appears to have been a revival of discussion concerning Anselm's ontological arguments, and whether his Proslogion 2 argument was inherently connected to or different from that in Proslogion 3 (see Chapter 7 for more on Anselm's arguments). This discussion was fuelled by renewed interest in language and analytic philosophy, driven by the attentions of Charles Hartshorne and Norman Malcolm in particular.

Existence as a Predicate

Malcolm explained in an article published in 1960 that he accepted Kant's famous criticism (see Chapter 11) that existence is a not a **predicate**, but rejected Anselm's first ontological argument in Proslogion 2 and Descartes' argument in *Meditations* (1641) for failing to overcome this issue. However, Malcolm noted that Kant failed to demonstrate that **necessary existence** is not a predicate, and therefore went on to agree with and reformulate Anselm's second ontological argument, as presented in Proslogion 3, that God exists necessarily.

> **TIP**
>
> Thinkers can never be separated from the time of their existence. Consider some of the societal issues, ideas and movements happening during Malcolm's lifetime and how they might have affected his ideas.

> **ESSENTIAL!**
>
> A **predicate** is an intrinsic quality of something. For example, predicates of a triangle include three sides, three vertices and three internal angles that add up to 180 degrees.
>
> In this context, **necessary existence** is where something exists necessarily. It cannot be imagined to not exist, as it would then result in a self-contradiction, which would be absurd.

Malcolm argued that to say 'God exists' and 'God exists necessarily' is not the same. Where the likes of Kant and Bertrand Russell identified that statements like 'God exists' do not tell us anything about the concept of God, to say 'God necessarily exists' does. For Malcolm, qualifying the nature of God's existence as necessary unpacks the concept and contributes something to our understanding of it.

Malcolm also noted that Kant made an error, in accepting that the concept of God as the greatest possible being includes the idea that this being would exist necessarily, but he concluded that all this points to is that, *if* God exists, he exists necessarily. Kant argued that we can reject the concept of God along with any understanding of God's necessary existence. However, Malcolm argued that this was an error in logic, as Kant is then seeing 'God exists necessarily' as compatible with the possibility that 'God does not exist', which is a contradiction. Therefore, Malcolm went on to claim that, 'God exists necessarily' *is* something which can be known through reason, rather than experience, as Kant had concluded. In essence, Malcolm argues that not all forms of existence mean the same thing, and the concept of something with necessary existence will differ from the concept of something with **contingent existence**. This rules out what Kant supposed: that it is possible for God, as a concept entailing necessary existence, to not exist.

> **ESSENTIAL!**
>
> **Contingent existence** is where something's existence relies upon other factors to bring it into existence and sustain it. Contingent things can easily be imagined to not exist.

> **ESSENTIAL!**
>
> **Analytic** is Kant's terminology for Hume's relation of ideas: a statement which can be known to be true by logic concerning its definition, a priori. In contrast, 'synthetic' is Kant's terminology for Hume's matter of fact: a statement which can be known to be true or false by experience, a posteriori.

INSIGHT

Malcolm agreed with Kant that contingent existence is not a predicate, but he argued that necessary existence *is* a predicate.

He used the example of 'a square has four sides' as a logically necessary truth and argued that 'God necessarily exists' is true in the same manner.

Having established that necessary existence is a predicate and therefore part of the **analytic** concept of God, Malcolm agreed with Anselm's Proslogion 3 and argued that it is successful in evading Kant's criticism. Malcolm accepted Anselm's definition of God as 'that than which nothing greater can be conceived', but understood this to mean a being who could be described as unlimited. Malcolm therefore concluded that God is 'an unlimited being' and, consequently, one that would be worthy of worship, if he actually existed. The argument can be summarised as follows:

> P1: An unlimited being must be understood to be unlimited in terms of existence as well as any other qualities.
>
> P2: An unlimited being would be limited if such a being depended on anything else for its existence (contingent).
>
> C1: An unlimited being must therefore be understood as having necessary existence.
>
> C2: Hence God's existence is either necessary or impossible.

INSIGHT

Malcolm understands necessary existence as a property of God in the same way that omnipotence and omniscience are traditionally understood as necessary properties of God.

Modes of Existence

Having agreed in principle with Anselm's second form of the ontological argument, Malcom went on to reformulate it using **modal logic**. Malcolm identified three different modes of existence, and argued that the nature of God's existence must be qualified in terms of one mode exclusively.

> **ESSENTIAL!**
>
> **Modal logic** is a system of mathematical formal logic concerned with different modes of existence.

> **MALCOLM'S THREE MODES OF EXISTENCE**
>
> - **Necessary existence**: any being with the properties of God cannot logically be thought of as not existing.
> - **Contingent existence**: it is logically possible that a being with the properties of God could exist but also could not exist.
> - **Impossible existence** (sometimes termed necessarily false existence): any being with the properties of God logically cannot exist.

According to Malcolm, the statement 'God exists', when explored through his modal argument, therefore tells us that 'God necessarily exists'.

Malcolm's argument can be summarised as follows:

> P1: We can understand the concept of God as referring to 'an unlimited being'.
>
> P2: If such a being does not exist, this being cannot then at some point begin to exist.
>
> P3: To begin to exist requires a cause (contingent) or chance (merely possible), and this is a limitation inconsistent with an unlimited being.
>
> C1: Therefore God's existence is either impossible or necessary.
>
> P4: God's existence is not impossible: the only way he could be impossible is if he were logically absurd or paradoxical, which he is not.
>
> C2: Therefore God exists necessarily.

To illustrate, we can unpack Malcolm's argument in more detail. If we accept that God is, by definition, truly unlimited, then God cannot be caused to exist by anything or be caused to cease to exist by anything. God's non-existence is therefore inconceivable (unimaginable), as it would be logically absurd. Therefore *if* God exists, God exists necessarily. If God does not exist, his existence would be impossible, as there is nothing that could cause God to exist without limiting his unlimited nature, which is a contradiction and absurd. Therefore God's existence *cannot* be impossible. So, by proof of logical contradiction, God must exist and therefore exist necessarily, as demonstrated by logical reasoning.

With his formulation here, it appears that Malcolm has flipped the traditional notion of burden of proof on its head. Rather than it be the theist who has to prove God's existence, Malcolm's argument now requires the atheist to prove that God's existence is impossible, rather than just unlikely. If God's existence is still possible, however unlikely, then Malcolm's modal ontological argument demonstrates that God must then exist necessarily.

> **TIP**
>
> Malcolm used the same *reductio ad absurdum* technique as Anselm, or proof by contradiction, as he terms it. See more on this in Chapters 1 and 7.

WHAT DO YOU THINK?

Write down your thoughts on Malcolm's arguments and revisit them shortly before the exam to see if your views have changed.

Read Malcolm for Yourself

> **TASK**

Read Malcolm for yourself in the extract below. The notes in the margin will help you to grasp his ideas.

The following passage is taken from Malcolm's article 'Anselm's Ontological Arguments' (1960), and illustrates his development and reformulation of Anselm's Proslogion 3.

Malcolm accepts Anselm's definition but reframes it as 'an unlimited being'. >	Let me summarize the proof. If God, a being a greater than which cannot be conceived, does not exist then He cannot come into existence. For if He did He would either have been caused to come into existence or have happened to come into existence, and in either case He would be a limited being, which by our conception of Him He is not. Since He cannot come into existence, if He does not exist His existence is impossible. If He does exist He cannot have come into existence (for the reasons given), nor can He cease to exist, for nothing could cause Him to cease to exist nor could it just happen that he ceased to exist. So if God exists His existence is necessary. Thus God's existence is either impossible or necessary. It can be the former only if the concept of such a being is self-contradictory or in some way logically absurd. Assuming that this is not so, it follows that He necessarily exists.'
This would make God's existence contingent. >	
This would make God's existence only possible and reliant on some other factor, also rendering his existence contingent. >	
Malcolm uses proof by contradiction, to demonstrate that this line of enquiry would result in logical contradiction so must be rejected. >	
Rendering this a truth by logic, analytic in Kant's terms, or a relation of ideas according to Hume's fork. >	

Know Criticisms of Malcolm

> **EVALUATION SKILLS**

An answer to an evaluative question about a scholar is always deepened by demonstrating awareness of how other thinkers have taken different positions.

His argument is open to parody. Just as Anselm's ontological argument was open to parody via Gaunilo with his 'Lost Island' objection (see Chapter 10), Malcolm's argument also does not escape such ridicule. Let us take Malcolm's argument but substitute for God some other concept of which necessary existence is essential: for example, a necessarily existing Atlantis. If it is possible for this necessarily existing Atlantis to exist, and it would be a self-contradiction and absurd if it were considered to be impossible, then this necessarily existing Atlantis must necessarily exist. Yet it does not. Again, we find ourselves back at the original critique that keeps returning: *we cannot simply define something into existence, regardless of the concept or the type of existence the concept entails*. The defence also remains the same: there is something about God that is unique, meaning that the logic works for God but not for other concepts.

Not necessarily the God of classical theism. Malcolm's modal argument (see 'Know Malcolm's Key Ideas' above) that God must necessarily exist relies on the idea that God's existence is not impossible (P4 in the argument on modes of existence). Malcolm supported this with two theories:

- that God's existence as impossible contradicts the definition of God, and
- that the only way in which God's existence could be impossible is if the concept of God is itself incoherent, absurd or paradoxical, which Malcolm claims it is not.

However, as we have seen elsewhere in this book, there are many concerns regarding the coherence of the traditional attributes of the God of classical theism, and Malcolm does not address these concerns in his argument. American philosopher (and fellow believer of the modal ontological argument) Alvin Plantinga stated that Malcolm's argument did not go far enough to demonstrate that the God of classical theism (that is to say, possessing omnibenevolence, omnipotence and omniscience) exists in the actual world. He concluded that all Malcolm had proved was that there necessarily exists a being of maximal greatness. Plantinga then went on to reformulate Malcolm's argument with his own version that you can read about online if interested.

INSIGHT

'In 1960 ... Norman Malcom dropped his bombshell' – Plantinga's description of the publication of Malcolm's ontological argument.

Malcolm's understanding of 'necessary' changes within his argument. Malcolm has been criticised for seeming to change his use of the term 'necessary' within his argument, which invalidates his logic. In the argument on existence as a predicate, we can see that when Malcolm refers to 'necessary existence', he means it as a predicate, an intrinsic property or quality (a required part of something) that adds to the understanding of the concept and its essence – something which can be 'had' or 'lacking'. However, by his conclusion in the argument on modes of existence, Malcom is talking about necessary existence not in the sense of a predicate, but as a necessary or logical truth. This is not the same thing. We return to Kant's original criticism: we can accept that *if* God exists, he has the predicate of necessary existence, but this does not automatically entail that God's existence is a logical truth. We are still able to understand the concept or definition of God and also reject the necessary truth of God's existence in the actual world.

Watch Out for Traps

Don't waste time describing Anselm's argument. This is an easy trap to fall into, given how well students tend to know Anselm's argument compared to such modern modal forms as these. However, if a part a) AO1 question has named Malcolm's ontological argument, then this is what you need to demonstrate knowledge and understanding of. It would be relevant to comment on the origins of Malcolm's argument, in that he rejected Anselm's Proslogion 2 and believed that Proslogion 3 was making an altogether different type of argument, which remained valid despite Kant's criticism that existence was not a predicate. However, you certainly would not need to describe both of Anselm's arguments in full. It would be more relevant, for a question focused on Malcolm, to explain Malcolm's logic and how he moves from agreeing that contingent existence is not a predicate, hence the rejection of Proslogion 2, to believing that necessary existence is a predicate, hence agreeing with Proslogion 3, but reformulating it using modal logic and simplifying the definition of God to 'an unlimited being'. Then describe how Malcolm uses proof of contradiction to rule out the possible and impossible modes of existence, arriving at his conclusion that God must exist necessarily, by definition.

Don't forget the modal element. Too often when Malcolm is named in an AO1 question, he is left till the end and only occupies a few short sentences or a paragraph if he is lucky. When revising, ensure you go over the 'Know Malcolm's Key Ideas' section, and can explain both the modal aspect of his argument as well as his assertion that necessary existence is a predicate. Malcolm's attempt to demonstrate that the notion that

God's existence as impossible is self-contradictory is a vital part of his conclusion, and is open to criticism given the issues surrounding the coherence of the concept of God (see 'Know Criticisms of Malcolm' above), so omitting mention of this in an AO2 question would be to miss an opportunity.

Don't forget the context: Malcolm is responding to Kant's criticism. It can be easy to muddle up different scholars' ontological arguments and which version different criticisms were aimed at. When you revise, ensure that you grasp the chronological order of each argument and what (if any) criticism they were responding to. Malcolm was responding to Kant's criticism, which had been picked up by another philosopher, Bertrand Russell, during Malcolm's own lifetime. However, Malcolm did go back and revive Anselm's arguments in light of the criticisms that Kant had made in response to Descartes' argument. Malcolm also shows insight into Hume's fork (see Chapter 5), and his argument can be seen as an attempt to place God's existence as a relation of ideas and logical truth within Hume's fork. Yet he does not expressly say so. Remember, no philosopher lived and wrote in isolation. They are all influenced by what came before and what was happening during their lifetimes.

> **INSIGHT**
>
> Remember that all scholars in the Board's specification who proposed ontological arguments were Christian, and had faith in God's existence prior to composing their arguments.

STRENGTHEN YOUR GRASP

1. Make a timeline showing the development of the ontological arguments referred to in the Board's specification. Ensure you include the challenges to ontological arguments too, so you can see how the ideas were developed and responded to over time. As an extra challenge, label the scholars and their contexts: rationalist, empiricist, medieval scholasticism, Enlightenment, methodological doubt, etc.

2. Malcolm goes further than simply concluding that God must necessarily exist, claiming that this unlimited being is the Christian God (omnipotent, omnibenevolent and omniscient) and one worthy of worship. Make a list and explain any issues of compatibility or problems with the coherence of the traditional Christian attributes of God, such as the problem of evil and the problem of free will. If the concept of the Christian God is problematic or logically incoherent, does it result in problems for Malcolm's argument? Being able to analyse the different steps including the conclusion of Malcolm's argument will improve your AO2 evaluation.

Exam Guidance AO1

For part a) questions, you could be asked to outline (AS only), explain or examine any aspect of the specification content. An outline question requires an answer containing more breadth than an examine question, which would require more depth. You therefore need to be selective of which material you choose to include, depending on the question. For example, a question asking you to examine anything concerning Malcolm's ontological argument would require more detail concerning his analytic approach and use of modal logic, in contrast to a broader question requiring you to outline aspects concerning ontological arguments. In the latter case, covering the different approaches, starting points, definitions of God and examples from the different named scholars would be more relevant.

The specification also makes it clear you could also be asked something about the development of ontological arguments. If discussing Malcolm, it would be worth explaining how Malcolm agreed with Kant's criticism that existence was not a predicate, but that he believed Kant had failed to demonstrate that necessary existence was not a predicate. Therefore, although rejecting Anselm's Proslogion 2 argument, Malcolm revived Anselm's Proslogion 3 argument and reformulated it in his own modal form, concluding that necessary existence was a predicate of God and therefore that God exists necessarily. It would be beneficial to ensure you explain Malcolm's logic with regard to the different modes of existence he identifies, and why God's existence cannot be impossible, so God must therefore exist necessarily.

Exam Guidance AO2

For part b) questions, reference to Malcolm's argument could be relevant in an evaluation question concerning ontological arguments, a priori arguments or their challenges. Specifically, you could evaluate how successful Malcolm's response to Kant is: that while contingent existence is not a predicate, necessary existence is. It could also be beneficial to weigh up whether Malcolm's modal argument can overcome the criticism that, regardless of modes, one cannot simply define something into existence. It could also be worth considering that all supporters of the ontological argument, including Malcolm, began with a Christian faith. Therefore, can their arguments ever be separated from an underlying assumption that God exists in the first place, which points to circular logic?

Finally, the specification makes clear you could be asked about the extent to which different religious views on the nature of God impact on arguments for the existence of God. Malcolm's definition of God and whether it is coherent and successfully points to the God of classical theism can be evaluated alongside alternative views.

10. GAUNILO OF MARMOUTIERS

GET INTO GAUNILO'S WORLD

> **Quick Overview** Gaunilo of Marmoutiers was an eleventh-century French Benedictine monk and contemporary of St Anselm. Little is known about Gaunilo beyond his famous and influential 'Lost Island' parody, which was formulated in response to Anselm's ontological argument.

Gaunilo lived in a period following the early Middle Ages, during the high medieval scholastic movement, when the works of Plato and Aristotle were being rediscovered and studied. Plato provided a justification for the rational argument for the existence of God and an immortal soul, and consequently much of the medieval philosophy of the time was underpinned by Platonic thinking. Gaunilo is known to us because he joined the debate regarding this philosophical concern. He was an empiricist and disagreed that God could be known through rational thought. In an early response to Anselm's first ontological argument (Proslogion 2), he set out his parody of the Lost Island.

Know Gaunilo's Key Ideas

■ **IMPROVE YOUR UNDERSTANDING**

Make sure that you grasp how Gaunilo uses an analogy to challenge the logic of Anselm's first ontological argument.

Gaunilo's Parody of the Lost Island

Outside of *Proslogion*, there is very little mention of Gaunilo, although what we can see is that Gaunilo did not just respond with the Lost Island parody. He wrote a treatise titled *Liber Pro Insipiente* (On Behalf of the Fool) from the perspective of a non-believer, the 'fool who says there is no God'. The final section praises the remainder of *Proslogion* and is written from Gaunilo's own faith stance.

■ **INSIGHT**

The title of Gaunilo's treatise, 'On Behalf of the Fool', refers to the fact that Anselm directed his ontological argument at the fool from Psalms 14 and 53, who denies the existence of God.

Gaunilo's Lost Island argument can be summarised as follows:

> P1: There exists a lost island than which no greater can be conceived. It is the greatest possible island.
>
> P2: The greatest possible island exists in the mind, but not in reality (*reductio ad absurdum*).
>
> P3: Existence in reality is greater than existence in the mind alone.
>
> C: Therefore this lost, greatest possible island must exist in reality.

Gaunilo used this parody to demonstrate how absurd Anselm's logic was. By replacing the term 'God' with the 'greatest possible island', the use of *reductio ad absurdum* shows that to deny the existence of the island is a logical absurdity. If the argument can be used to define anything into existence, which is clearly absurd, the argument must be faulty.

Understand Gaunilo's Arguments

Gaunilo was not objecting to Anselm's conclusion that God must exist in reality, as Gaunilo was a Christian and believed in God. However, as an empiricist, Gaunilo objected to the use of a priori knowledge and deductive logic to try to prove God's existence. By highlighting that Anselm's argument just appeared to define something into existence, which all evidence can disprove, Gaunilo was able to show that there was a fault with the logic. Therefore, the whole argument is invalid as a proof of God's existence. Gaunilo's response intended to show the following:

> P1: If Anselm's argument were sound, it could prove the existence of other things that are the greatest that could be conceived.
>
> P2: However, Anselm's argument was unable to prove the existence of the greatest possible conceivable island.
>
> C: Therefore, Anselm's argument is not sound.

Gaunilo wrote that we would require evidence of such an island – 'real and indubitable fact' that this greatest possible island exists. Merely describing something as superlative (of the highest possible degree or quality) does not prove it exists.

 **WHAT** DO YOU **THINK?**

Write down your thoughts on Gaunilo's arguments and revisit them shortly before the exam to see if your views have changed.

TASK

Read Gaunilo for yourself in the extract below. The notes in the margin will help you to grasp his views.

Read Gaunilo for Yourself

This passage is from Gaunilo's response published in the appendix to Anselm's *Proslogion*.

> … it is said that somewhere in the ocean is an island … the lost island. And they say that this island has an inestimable wealth of all manner of riches and delicacies in greater abundance than is told of the Islands of the Blest … it is more excellent than all other countries.
>
> Now if some one should tell me that there is such an island, I should easily understand his words, in which there is no difficulty. But suppose that he went on to say, as if by a logical inference: 'You can no longer doubt that this island which is more excellent than all lands exists somewhere … since it is more excellent not to be in the understanding alone, but to exist both in the understanding and in reality, for this reason it must exist. For if it does not exist, any land which really exists will be more excellent than it; and so the island already understood by you to be more excellent will not be more excellent.'
>
> If a man should try to prove to me by such reasoning that this island truly exists, and that its existence should no longer be doubted, either I should believe that he was jesting, or I know not which I ought to regard as the greater fool: myself, supposing that I should allow this proof; or him, if he should suppose that he had established with any certainty the existence of this island.

Gaunilo uses the same reductio ad absurdum technique as Anselm to demonstrate how illogical the argument is.

Continuing Anselm's reference to 'the fool', Gaunilo defends the fool and says it would be more foolish to be taken in by this faulty logic, or even to be such a fool as to believe this logic was successful in the first place.

EVALUATION SKILLS

An answer to an evaluative question about a scholar is always deepened by demonstrating awareness of how other thinkers have taken different positions.

ESSENTIAL!

Disanalogy is a term used to describe when an analogy has failed. It is a criticism often levelled at Gaunilo.

Know Criticisms of Gaunilo

Disanalogy. Anselm responds, arguing there is a **disanalogy** between God and Gaunilo's island. A comparison cannot be made. This is because islands are contingent, relying on multiple geographical factors for their existence. How they are defined at one point in time cannot prove they exist in reality. In contrast, God's existence is necessary – God is unique and unlike contingent things. Therefore the logic of Anselm's argument is valid for God's existence, as it is a logical necessity and self-evident, but the logic is invalid for contingent things such as islands.

Islands can't have intrinsic maximums. Twentieth-century philosopher Alvin Plantinga develops Anselm's response by pointing out that islands can change. Their features are not fixed; we can always add to the concept – for example, more golden sand or wildlife. If the greatest possible island can be improved, then it was not the greatest possible island in the first place. Islands have no intrinsic maximum. Therefore, the concept of the most excellent, greatest possible island is incoherent and cannot be conceived in reality, unlike the concept of God, who as a necessary being does have an intrinsic maximum and can be conceived in reality.

Watch Out for Traps

Lack of precision and depth. Don't forget to use key terminology and avoid just describing Gaunilo's argument rather than showing *how* it challenges Anselm's argument. Try to be clear that, in Gaunilo's rejection of Anselm's argument to prove that God exists *a priori*, he used the same *reductio ad absurdum* technique with the *analogy* of the Lost Island to show that Anselm's *logic* fails. We cannot just *define* something into existence. The emphasis needs to be on Gaunilo's reasoning, which is also a priori.

> **STRENGTHEN YOUR GRASP**
>
> 1. To help understand Gaunilo's parody, create your own. Pick anything, such as the greatest possible chocolate bar or guitar. Go through the stages of Gaunilo's objection but replace 'island' with your example (see 'Understand Gaunilo's Arguments' above). You will still arrive at the same conclusion; the logic must be faulty because sadly your greatest possible 'X' does not exist in reality.
> 2. Make a list of the qualities of the God of classical theism and consider whether each of these qualities could be improved. Consider some of the problems and possible limitations of God's qualities (see also Chapter 13). Is it possible for God to be more loving or more powerful? If so, then Plantinga's criticism fails. Write down your response to this activity and whether you think Plantinga's criticism is successful or not, and why.

Exam Guidance A01

Part a) questions might require discussion involving challenges to the ontological argument, and Gaunilo might be specified. When explaining Gaunilo's objection, it would be important to detail how Gaunilo challenged the logic of Anselm's argument, rather than just describing it.

Exam Guidance A02

Gaunilo would be relevant in part b) questions concerning ontological arguments, a priori and deductive arguments, and challenges to ontological arguments. However, it is important to remember that explaining challenges to ontological arguments is not the same as evaluating them. With regard to Gaunilo, counter-arguments (such as those of Plantinga and Anselm) would need to be weighed up alongside Gaunilo's objection, and their strengths, weaknesses and persuasiveness considered.

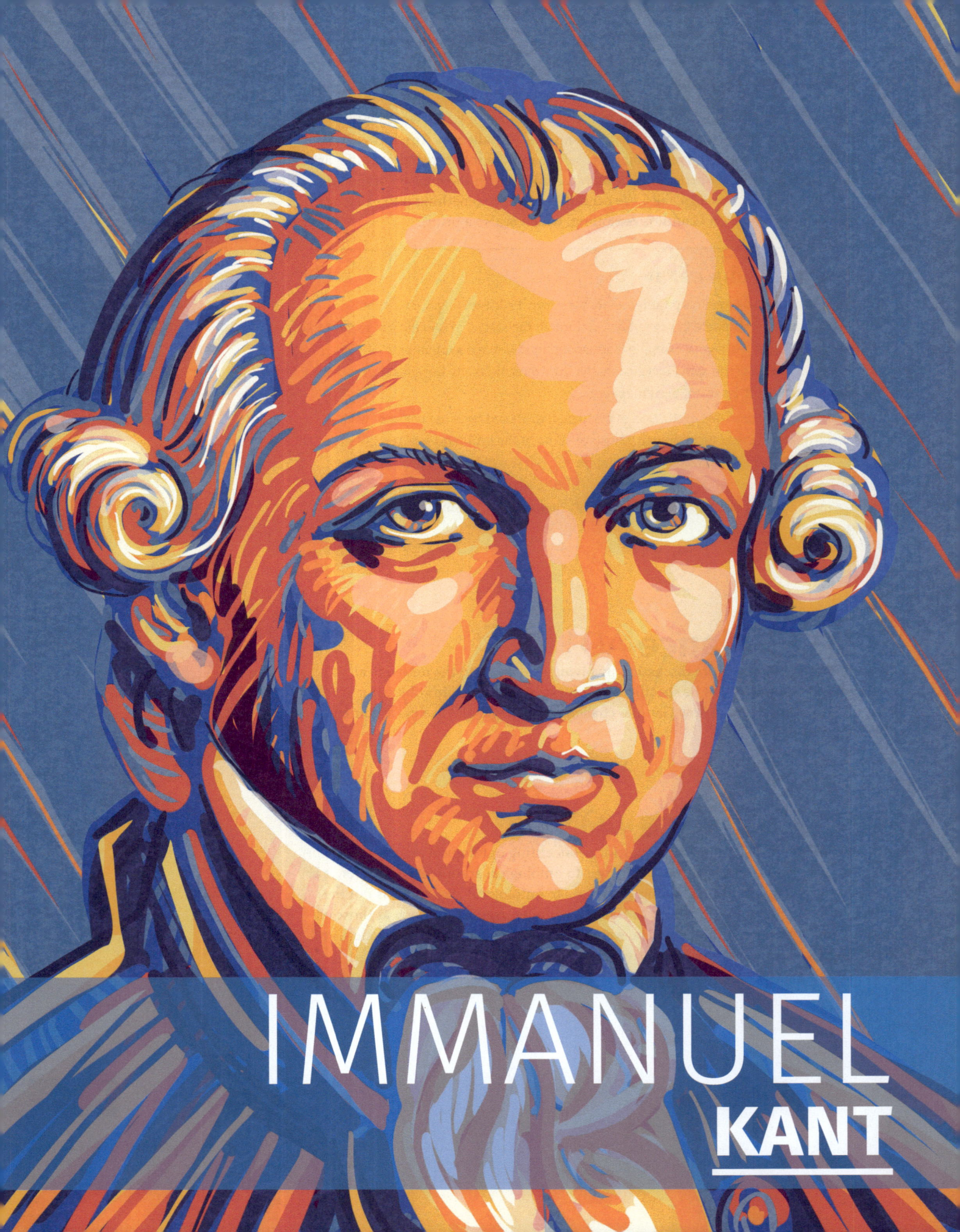

11. IMMANUEL KANT
GET INTO KANT'S WORLD

> **Quick Overview** Immanuel Kant (1724–1804) was a German philosopher and is widely considered to be the last of the great Enlightenment thinkers. Kant wrote on almost every aspect of philosophy, but he is particularly known for his thoughts on idealism and his synthesis of rationalist and empiricist theories of knowledge.

Unlike many other philosophers of his time, Immanuel Kant was born to a relatively poor family in Prussia (now Kaliningrad, Russia). However, he went on to study and then teach at the local university for the vast majority of his career, never travelling far from home. Kant's academic interests were extremely broad, and he lectured on subjects ranging from mathematics and philosophy to anthropology and geography. It was during his later years that he found fame as a philosopher, having been greatly inspired by re-reading the work of empiricist David Hume.

Kant developed scepticism for the limitations of rationalism, such as that which Descartes had proposed regarding knowledge of the external world. He was also aware of the problems concerning knowledge as a result of inductive leap and causality, as expressed through Hume's scepticism (see Chapter 5). As a result, Kant spent more than a decade trying to solve the dilemma concerning knowledge, which led to his most original idea and formed the basis of many other philosophical arguments – his 'Copernican Revolution'. Just as Copernicus had changed perspective by proving that the earth orbits the sun rather than the other way round, so Kant sought to prove that philosophical answers would be found via the method of using mental faculties (the mind) regarding sense experience (perception via use of senses) rather than by direct experience. This was due to his theory of transcendental idealism, which stated that external reality (the noumena) could only be experienced through a sense experience that our minds then organised and processed (the phenomena). We therefore never experienced or grasped the world as it directly was, without the filter of our mind. This idea underpinned all aspects of Kant's later works (known as his critical period), and left a lasting legacy that shaped modern Western philosophy for the subsequent centuries.

> **ESSENTIAL!**
> **Noumena** is the ultimate reality, which we cannot directly access.
> **Phenomena** is our experience of the world, which comes from mental processing of sense experience.

Know Kant's Key Ideas

INSIGHT

Kant credited Hume with waking him from a 'dogmatic slumber' and inspiring him to question the established principles of religion and knowledge.

IMPROVE YOUR UNDERSTANDING

Make sure that you grasp why Kant believes the existence of anything is a synthetic claim and cannot be a predicate.

Following Kant's awakening from his 'dogmatic slumber', he embarked on what is known as his critical period, when he wrote his most monumental works, essentially combining the approaches of empiricism and rationalism by arguing that knowledge derives from both experiences and ideas. For the purposes of the Board's specification, however, we are primarily concerned with Kant's *Critique of Pure Reason* (1781), where he expressed his objections to ontological arguments.

Kant made several objections, but they can broadly be understood in the two ways explained below. However, before discussing these objections, we need to be reminded of how Kant defined the relevant key concepts. Inspired by the categorisation of knowledge in Hume's fork (see Chapter 5), Kant categorises the *source* of knowledge as either:

- a priori – independent of experience and sense impression, or
- a posteriori – derived from sense experience, empirical.

Kant went on to categorise the *form* of knowledge as either:

- analytic – the predicate (property) is intrinsic, i.e. already contained within the concept of the subject, or
- synthetic – the predicate (property) is not contained within the concept of the subject, so can only be formed via experience.

ESSENTIAL!

Synthetic a priori is Kant's terminology for categorising a priori knowledge such as 'a bachelor is an unmarried man', which is formed via our experience of the term 'bachelor' and what it relates to in the external world.

Kant went on to oppose the traditional understanding that a priori knowledge is paired with analytic form (the focus of rationalism), while a posteriori knowledge is paired with synthetic form (the focus of empiricism). Instead he argued that these were not the only modes of knowledge, and there was in fact knowledge that could be known **synthetic a priori**: that is, there could be concepts that, through experience, we learn are absolute and universal, the truth of which could be demonstrated by proof of contradiction. These include mathematical knowledge. Kant gives the example of $7 + 5 = 12$. The truth of such a claim does not lie in the concept, so this knowledge cannot be analytic in form. The truth of the claim lies in our experience of the concepts and the addition.

It is through this introduction of a possible third mode of knowledge that Kant goes on to question what philosophers had previously argued we can know, including that God exists by definition.

INSIGHT

See the chapters on Anselm (Chapter 7), Descartes (Chapter 8) and Gaunilo (Chapter 10) for more details regarding their contributions or objections to ontological argument.

'God Exists' Is Not Analytic

It is clear that Kant is responding to Descartes' ontological argument, and he began initially by provisionally accepting Descartes' premise that the concept of God as a supremely perfect being entails the property of existence. However, where Descartes argued that to reject God's existence would, by definition, produce a logical contradiction, therefore God must exist necessarily, Kant clarifies that this will only be true *if* one accepts that God actually exists in the first place. If we deny the existence of God, we also deny the property of existence, therefore there is no logical contradiction. Kant takes Descartes' example of a triangle and argues that, while we cannot accept the triangle and reject its property of three angles without resulting in logical contradiction, we can reject the triangle along with its properties.

Therefore, the most that we can conclude, if we accept Descartes' argument, is that *if* God exists, then God exists necessarily. Kant is arguing that we cannot progress from concepts and definitions to reality (analytic propositions), which seems to reflect the essence of Gaunilo's objection to Anselm's ontological argument: we cannot simply define something into existence. For Kant, the claim that 'God exists' or anything at all exists, for that matter, is therefore a synthetic proposition, and one which would require some evidence in order fully to accept the a priori concept.

Existence Is Not a Predicate

> **INSIGHT**
>
> Kant believed that all arguments for God's existence would fail because any proofs belong to the noumenal world, which we cannot access as we only experience the phenomenal world.

Kant then goes on to question Descartes' premise that the concept or definition of God includes existence as an intrinsic property. Kant argues that existence is 'evidently not a real predicate' (that is, a property or quality that is intrinsic or vital in a subject). Predicates, Kant argues, are properties that add to our understanding of the concept. For example, 'horn' is a predicate of a unicorn, and 'oval' is a predicate of a rugby ball. Kant argues that adding 'it exists' does not alter our understanding of the concept in any way. Instead, we just mean that this idea can be verified in the actual world. Kant illustrates this with an example of 100 coins. We can add to our understanding of the concept of these coins with real predicates: for example, they are round in shape and gold coloured. However, saying 'they exist' does not alter or add to our understanding of the concept in any way. It only says that the coins that exist can be verified in the actual world.

This idea can be taken further, with a paradox to demonstrate how existence isn't a real predicate. Consider the following:

- There is a coat which is red.
- There is a coat which is not red.

Compare this to:

- There is a God who exists.
- There is a God who does not exist.

The first pair of statements make sense because 'red' is a predicate that something can have or lack. However, the second pair does not make sense because the inverse of 'exists' creates a paradox where it is said that there is a God but also that this God does not exist. Real predicates can be lacked, and no paradox or contradiction arises.

> **INSIGHT**
>
> Philosopher Bertrand Russell supported Kant's view. He stated that when we say something exists, we are claiming it can be instantiated: that is, there are real instances of it in the world.

WHAT DO YOU THINK?

Write down your thoughts on Kant's arguments and revisit them shortly before the exam to see if your views have changed.

Read Kant for Yourself

The following passage is taken from Kant's *Critique of Pure Reason* (1781) and illustrates his main objections to Descartes' ontological argument. The notes in the margin will help you to grasp his ideas.

> It is evident from what has been said that the conception of an absolutely necessary being is a mere idea, the objective reality of which is far from being established …
>
> Philosophers have always talked of an absolutely necessary being, and have nevertheless declined to take the trouble of conceiving whether … its existence is actually demonstrable. A verbal definition of the conception is certainly easy enough: it is something the non-existence of which is impossible. But does this definition throw any light upon the conditions which render it impossible to cogitate the non-existence of a thing … a triangle has three angles – it was said, is absolutely necessary … The proposition above-mentioned does not enounce that three angles necessarily exist, but, upon condition that a triangle exists, three angles must necessarily exist – in it. And thus this logical necessity has been the source of the greatest delusions. Having formed an a priori conception of a thing, the content of which was made to embrace existence, we believed ourselves safe in concluding … existence belongs necessarily to the object of the conception …
>
> I annihilate the predicate in thought, and retain the subject, a contradiction is the result; and hence I say, the former belongs necessarily to the latter. But … to suppose the existence of a triangle and not that of its three angles, is self-contradictory; but to suppose the non-existence of both triangle and angles is perfectly admissible. And so is it with the conception of an absolutely necessary being. Annihilate its existence in thought, and you annihilate the thing itself with all its predicates; how then can there be any room for contradiction? …
>
> Being is evidently not a real predicate … The proposition, God is omnipotent, contains two conceptions, which have a certain object or content; the word is, is no additional predicate – it merely indicates the relation of the predicate to the subject. Now, if I take the subject (God) with all its predicates (omnipotence being one), and say: God is, or, There is a God, I add no new predicate to the conception of God, I merely posit or affirm the existence of the subject with all its predicates – I posit the object in relation to my conception. The content of both is the same; and there is no addition made to the conception … Thus the real contains no more than the possible. A hundred real dollars contain no more than a hundred possible dollars.

Margin notes:

- Kant means that philosophers have not taken the time to explore fully whether such a being's existence is capable of being logically proven.
- Kant grasps the analytical point that, by definition, the concept of such a being cannot be thought of as non-existent.
- 'Cogitate' means to think deeply, reflect, or meditate, which could be a subtle reference to Descartes' *Meditations on First Philosophy*.
- An explicit reference to Descartes' example of a triangle and how its essence entails three internal angles that add up to 180 degrees.
- By 'annihilate', Kant means deny or reject – not to consider the predicate in his mind at all.
- Another reference to Descartes' argument here. While you cannot reject the predicate of its three angles if you accept the concept of the triangle, there is no contradiction in rejecting both the concept and its predicates.
- Kant uses the example of money to illustrate that because existence does not add anything to a concept, it therefore cannot be a true property of the concept. In terms of God, he accepts omnipotence as a predicate as it adds some understanding, but rejects existence because it does not.

Know Criticisms of Kant

Twentieth-century philosopher Norman Malcolm (see Chapter 9) rejected Kant's criticisms of ontological arguments on two counts:

- Malcolm asserted that necessary existence *is* a predicate.

- He argued that Kant was mistaken to claim 'God exists' is synthetic.

These and other criticisms detailed below will help you to build an evaluation of Kant's objections.

Existence is a predicate. Philosopher Stephen T. Davis also argued that Kant was mistaken when he claimed existence is not a predicate. Davis argued that existence can be a property that adds to a concept, and he used Kant's own example to illustrate this. Where Kant said that existence did not add to the concept of the 100 coins at all, Davis pointed out that the coins that exist consequently have 'purchasing power', and can therefore result in direct action and exchange within the actual world. Therefore, there are relevant differences between concepts which have a predicate of existence and those that do not. The fact that this response to Kant does not show that the concept of God must entail the predicate of existence is not a problem because Davis has arguably managed to show that existence can be a predicate in some cases, so Kant's objection can be challenged.

God's existence as a synthetic claim. Another philosopher, Willard Van Orman Quine, objected to many of Kant's arguments, including his challenges to ontological arguments, on the basis of Kant's acceptance of experience in the formation of knowledge. On what grounds did Kant justify his claim that knowledge concerning existence was synthetic and therefore real? Kant's underlying wider philosophy (known as his idealism) can be questioned here. Kant argued that we gain information about the world via sense experience, known as phenomena. We then use reason (our mind) to make sense of these phenomena. Underneath and behind the phenomena, though, are the 'noumena', which we can never experience directly. Hence the role of experience is very important in Kant's philosophy, and why he believed God's existence to be a synthetic claim. But what proof did Kant have for granting such significance to experience in the formation of knowledge? If Quine is correct and the role of experience can be questioned, on what basis can Kant argue that claims to existence can only be known via experience?

Incoherence in Kant's philosophy. In his *Critique of Pure Reason*, Kant rejects a priori arguments for God's existence, as he believes existence is a synthetic claim rather than a logical one. However, in his moral philosophy, which is often known as Kantian ethics, Kant argued that God is one of the necessary postulates, something assumed to be true as a basis of reasoning, that must be accepted as a rational basis for the moral law, which can then be known a priori. But on what grounds does Kant reject ontological claims that God's existence can be known rationally, while arguing that the moral law can be known rationally due to God's existence? Kant appears to be using the very logic that he rejects in ontological arguments to justify his moral philosophy. If Kant's philosophy as a whole can be shown to be incoherent, then the validity of his challenges to ontological arguments can be questioned.

Watch Out for Traps

Don't lump Kant's objections together. If you are asked a question specifically about Kant's challenges to ontological arguments, then you should go into more depth regarding his different objections. In Kant's first objection, he provisionally accepted Descartes' premise that the concept of God includes existence, in order then to reject both the concept and any properties. This differs greatly from Kant's second objection, where he categorically stated that existence is not something that can be included in the property of a concept. If you can demonstrate that you fully grasp the difference between Kant's criticisms and how they work, you will be able to demonstrate the knowledge and understanding required for higher bands.

Don't forget to use examples. When discussing Kant's ideas, illustrate with the examples Kant used and your own, to better demonstrate your knowledge and understanding. Kant used Descartes' example of a triangle and its three angles to demonstrate that, while you cannot reject the concept of a triangle without the angles, you can reject the triangle along with its three angles. Similarly, Kant used the example of 100 coins to illustrate how the concept of 100 coins in the mind and in real life does not change if we add existence. Examples can also help with your evaluation, such as Davis referring to the 'purchasing power' of 100 coins that actually exist compared to 100 coins that do not exist.

Don't think Kant believed that God's existence can actually be proven synthetically. Kant argued that God's existence was a synthetic claim, because he believed that knowledge of the world must derive from sense experiences (phenomena) that the mind later organises through reason. Kant believed that the existence of anything, generally, could only be known synthetically. He believed that faith (belief in God) was independent of reason, and that we can never directly know the external reality outside of our minds, as we cannot directly access the noumena.

STRENGTHEN YOUR GRASP

1. Divide a page into two columns. Read through 'Know Kant's Key Ideas' and make notes in the left column about each of his criticisms of ontological arguments. In the right-hand column, note down which parts of different ontological arguments Kant's criticism can be applied to. Add details about how someone might defend any aspects of the ontological arguments that are challenged.
2. Write a paragraph to summarise what Kant meant by 'existence is not a real predicate'. Then write down one justification and one objection to his view. Finally, come up with your own conclusion as to which is the stronger view – the justification or the criticism – and why. This will help you to respond to an AO2 question in this area.

CREATE YOUR OWN QUESTION

Read this chapter and use command words such as 'explain' or 'examine' to create your own AO1 questions. For an AO2 question, make a one-sided statement about the success of ontological arguments or the challenges to them, put the statement between quotation marks and follow it with the phrase, 'Evaluate this view.'

Exam Guidance AO1

You could be asked to outline (AS only), explain or examine any aspect of the specification. An outline question requires an answer containing more breadth than an examine question, which would require more depth. For example, an examine question concerning Kant's challenges to the ontological argument would require more detail regarding his different criticisms, in contrast to a broader outline question concerning challenges more generally to ontological arguments. In the latter case, it would be more concise to cover his rejection of a priori and analytic arguments in a more thematic way, among other challenges.

You could also be asked about the development of ontological arguments. Here it would only be relevant to refer to Kant in relation to how Malcolm developed the ontological argument from Descartes and Anselm in response to Kant's criticisms, as he believed Kant had failed to demonstrate that necessary existence was not a predicate. However, you will need to be selective of material that is relevant to the specific question being asked.

Exam Guidance AO2

Reference to Kant's challenges to the ontological argument would be relevant in an evaluation question concerning ontological arguments, a priori or deductive arguments, or their challenges. Depending on the question, you could evaluate how successful Kant's criticisms of Descartes' argument are and the wider implications of these criticisms for a priori and deductive arguments. You could weigh up these successes against Malcolm's response to Kant and whether or not Malcolm successfully sidesteps these criticisms with his modal argument. Further, was Malcolm correct to say that Kant made an error in stating that he could reject the concept of God along with the notion that the concept entails necessary existence? Did Kant fail to show that necessary existence is not a predicate? And was Kant successful in stating that 'God exists' was an analytic statement rather than a synthetic statement as Malcolm argued?

Also consider that Kant is often thought of as someone who did not believe that God's existence can or should be demonstrated through reasoned argument at all. What bias might that provide to his views on ontological arguments?

12. EPICURUS
GET INTO EPICURUS' WORLD

> **Quick Overview** Epicurus (341–270BCE) was an Ancient Greek philosopher and the founder of Epicureanism. Very little remains of his work except reference to him in the writings of others. The earliest form of 'the problem of evil' is attributed to him.

INSIGHT

Epicurus is known to have been a prolific writer. However, sadly very little of his work survived due to the loss of his texts and subsequent Christian hostility towards his ideas, which were often perceived as thinly veiled atheism.

TIP

Thinkers can never be separated from the time of their existence. As an Ancient Greek, Epicurus was living in a time prior to Christianity, and he did not write about the God of classical theism.

ESSENTIAL!

Epicurus' argument takes the form of a **trilemma**, meaning a difficult choice between three options, all of which are unacceptable in this case.

Epicurus was the founder of a secular (non-religious) philosophical movement known as Epicureanism. As an empiricist, Epicurus was an atomic materialist and understood the world through an entirely mechanistic model. He believed that everything within the world – including the human soul – was made up of small particles called atoms. As a result, Epicurus did not believe in the immortality of the soul or any form of afterlife, or that the gods could in any way intervene in human affairs. Therefore, for Epicurus, religious beliefs were irrelevant and unnecessary. Instead his philosophy focused on how humans should live and achieve happiness within their lives.

Know Epicurus' Key Ideas

IMPROVE YOUR UNDERSTANDING

Make sure that you grasp how Epicurus' three questions can be used to challenge the existence of the God of classical theism.

The Classical Problem of Evil

In his *Dialogues Concerning Natural Religion* (1779), David Hume attributes the earliest and classical form of the problem of evil to Epicurus. However, no record of it is evident in what little remains of Epicurus' writings. Hume also relies on the writings of Christian apologist Lactantius (a third-century Christian scholar) for this attribution.

Epicurus' problem of evil is often termed 'the Epicurean paradox', and was summarised as a logical **trilemma** in the following way by Hume:

> Epicurus' old questions are yet unanswered.
> 1. Is he (God) willing to prevent evil, but not able? Then is he impotent.
> 2. Is he able, but not willing? Then is he malevolent.
> 3. Is he both able and willing? Whence then is evil?

As previously mentioned, Hume uses Epicurus' argument to create a deductive and a priori logical argument against the existence of the God of classical theism with the associated attributes of omnipotence (all-powerful) and omnibenevolence (all-loving). Hume does not state the conclusion, but through deduction we arrive at the following: therefore God cannot exist with the qualities that have been supposed.

Understand Epicurus' Arguments

What we do know from Epicurus' writings is that he said that gods did exist, but in a different aspect of the cosmos, in an eternal state of tranquillity, and they were totally unaware of us and our suffering. In this context, his argument could be understood as challenging superstitious and religious beliefs of his lifetime, that the gods intervened in the world, should be flattered through worship, and their wrath feared.

Even during Epicurus' lifetime, critics doubted the sincerity of his views on the nature of the gods, and many saw them as a smokescreen behind which to hide his atheism. For example, given his materialist approach to the world, the notion of any immortal beings would be incoherent. Therefore, a more literal interpretation of his problem of evil may be accurate.

What is clear, however, is that Hume uses Epicurus' argument not to argue outright that God does not exist, but as evidence with which to challenge the design argument. Hume then concludes that belief in a designer God can be supported, but not the omnibenevolent (all-loving) God of classical theism.

Read Epicurus for Yourself

The following passage is taken from Lactantius' *On the Anger of God*, and illustrates the problem of evil as attributed to Epicurus. The notes in the margin will help you to grasp his ideas.

> God, he says, either wishes to take away evils, and is unable; or He is able, and is unwilling; or He is neither willing nor able, or He is both willing and able. If He is willing and is unable, He is feeble, which is not in accordance with the character of God; if He is able and unwilling, He is envious, which is equally at variance with God; if He is neither willing nor able, He is both envious and feeble, and therefore not God; if He is both willing and able, which alone is suitable to God, from what source then are evils? Or why does He not remove them?

> By 'he', Lactantius means Epicurus. But remember, it is Lactantius who is applying Epicurus' argument to the God of classical theism.

> By 'feeble', Lactantius means lacking power, therefore not omnipotent.

> By 'envious', Lactantius means not willing good for others, therefore not omnibenevolent.

Know Criticisms of Epicurus

As a logical paradox (self-contradictory statement) that relies on deductive reasoning, Epicurus' argument can be considered too simplistic, and easily refuted. For example, consider Epicurus' three questions.

Is God willing to prevent evil, but not able? Then Lactantius' On the Anger of God impotent. This is not necessarily true because perhaps it is not logically possible for good to exist without evil, so while God is unable to prevent evil, this need not limit his omnipotence. Richard Swinburne argues that God's omnipotence should be understood as limited by the realms of what is logically possible.

Is God able, but not willing? Then is he malevolent. This is not necessarily true because God could have good reasons for permitting evil. For example, arguments in defence of God have been posed by St Irenaeus and John Hick (see Chapter 16).

> **INSIGHT**
>
> The logical problem of evil is *a priori* because it uses reason rather than evidence, and *deductive* because the conclusion logically follows on from the premises.

> **INSIGHT**
>
> It is sometimes assumed that Epicurus' argument, at least in Hume's account, is an argument against the existence of God (or gods), but this is not necessarily so.

> **EVALUATION SKILLS**
>
> An answer to an evaluative question about a scholar is always deepened by demonstrating awareness of how other thinkers have taken different positions.

Is God both able and willing? Whence then is evil? This can be refuted in many different ways. For example, in Mahayana Buddhism, suffering is considered to be an illusion, and in the defence of God from St Augustine, he argues that evil is not a real thing but a privation (lack of) goodness.

As a deductive argument, if any of Epicurus' questions (which Hume presents as premises) can be refuted, then the conclusion fails.

Watch Out for Traps

Don't get Epicurus confused with J.L. Mackie (see Chapter 13). Mackie did develop Epicurus' classical problem of evil, and emphasised the deductive and a priori nature of it from Hume's account. However, Epicurus' form is understood mainly to be challenging the religious belief that God/gods are motivated to intervene in the world, and are powerful enough to do so. Hume's account of Epicurus' argument notes the extent of suffering that humans experience, not just at the hands of each other (moral evil) but also at the hands of the supposed designer (natural evil). Therefore, the classical problem of evil is presented as an argument against design arguments for God's existence.

> **STRENGTHEN YOUR GRASP**
>
> 1. Write your own account of Epicurus' classical form of the problem of evil. Ensure you define key terms and give the context for how his argument was later applied to the God of classical theism by Hume.
> 2. Design a table with three columns. In the first column, note down the three questions that make up Epicurus' trilemma. In the middle column, note down possible responses to each of the questions. In the final column, write down what you think. Can Epicurus be defended or are the responses more persuasive?

Exam Guidance AO1

In a part a) question you could be asked to write about the problem of evil, either generally or specifically with regard to Epicurus' classical form of the problem. Depending on the depth required for the question, it might be beneficial to give an account of Epicurus' trilemma as presented by Hume, and how the implications of each of his questions, if accepted, lead to the logical conclusion that a god with the qualities of omnipotence and omnibenevolence cannot exist to intervene in the world.

Exam Guidance AO2

In a part b) evaluation question concerning the classical form of the problem of evil, it might be beneficial to respond thematically, weighing up how successfully different responses and theodicies (defences of God) can refute Epicurus' three questions, which in turn would undermine the deductive and logical nature of the argument. It is also worth remembering, as the argument is a priori and revolves around the understanding of God's attributes and the apparent paradox this creates, that the problem of evil is not a problem if someone does not believe in God.

13. J.L. MACKIE
GET INTO MACKIE'S WORLD

> **Quick Overview** John Leslie Mackie (1917–81) was an Australian philosopher who studied at Oriel College, Oxford, before becoming a professor himself. Mackie is known for his contributions to ethics and the philosophy of religion, and his staunch defence of atheism.

Following his graduation from Oriel College, J.L. Mackie served in the British Army during the Second World War. Upon his return, he went back to academia with a prominent atheism that became evident in all aspects of his philosophy. By 1955, Mackie had become a professor, and after a few years in New Zealand and Australia he settled in the UK, where he remained until he died. In addition to his contribution on philosophical topics such as the problem of evil, Mackie is particularly known for his moral scepticism and rejection of any objective moral values.

Know Mackie's Key Ideas

IMPROVE YOUR UNDERSTANDING

Make sure that you understand how Mackie uses the inconsistent triad to demonstrate that belief in the God of classical theism is irrational.

The Problem of Evil

In an article written in 1955, Mackie reformulated Epicurus' trilemma problem of evil (see Chapter 12) as 'the inconsistent triad', which he showed in the following way:

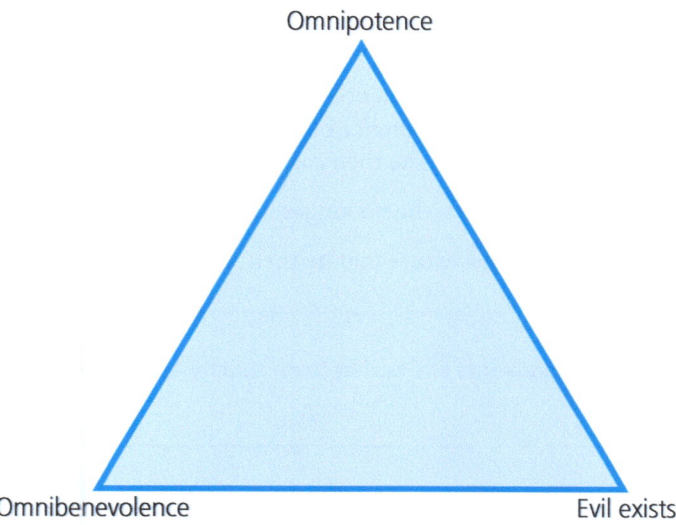

The inconsistent triad

> **INSIGHT**
>
> Mackie's argument is deductive and a priori, as his conclusion logically follows from his premises, using reasoning concerning the ideas only.

Each corner of the triangle is making a statement, which Mackie argued could not all be believed to be true. Logical contradiction would otherwise be the end result.

- God is omnipotent.
- God is wholly good (omnibenevolent).
- Evil exists.

If God were omnipotent, and by that Mackie meant having the power to do absolutely anything, God could have created the world without evil in it. If God were wholly good, he would want to prevent evil. Yet evil is undeniable in reality. Therefore, God cannot be both omnipotent and omnibenevolent. The triad is inconsistent.

Understand Mackie's Arguments

Mackie explained that to evade his problem of evil, one of the triad statements must be deemed false and removed. Unlike Epicurus and David Hume, Mackie then explored and responded to potential defences of the God of classical theism. However, he concluded that these 'false solutions' are all invalid because, ultimately, they only *appear* to disprove the problem. In reality they *do* abandon one of the points of the triad. For example:

Defence: evil serves a greater and more loving purpose.

Mackie's response: if evil is a necessary cause for a loving effect – for example, an opportunity to develop moral character – then God as the omnipotent creator created this causal order and is not wholly good, or God is restricted by pre-established causal order and cannot change it, therefore he is not omnipotent.

> **TIP**
>
> For more detail on the defence of God, see Chapter 16.

> **ESSENTIAL!**
>
> The **fallacy of false dilemma** is where only two options are presented, but in reality there is at least one other that has gone unstated.

And again:

Defence: evil is not caused by God but by human free will, which is more loving than a world without free will.

Mackie's response: this is a **fallacy of false dilemma**. Many individuals, due to their God-given character, make good choices on many occasions, so why could God, with his omnipotence, not ensure all humans have the ability to make good choices freely all of the time?

Mackie concludes by highlighting how many of the defences of God expose the inconsistency of omnipotence. That is, God's omnipotence becomes incoherent, as God ends up being limited by creating something which he then cannot control:

- God creates humans but gives them free will, so he no longer has power over them.
- God creates the world with laws of logic and nature that he then, in turn, is bound by.

> **INSIGHT**
>
> The approach that views human free will as compatible with belief in a God who has divine knowledge of the future (omniscience) is known as 'theological compatibilism'.

> **WHAT DO YOU THINK?**
>
> Write down your thoughts on Mackie's arguments and revisit them shortly before the exam to see if your views have changed.

Read Mackie for Yourself

The following passage is taken from Mackie's article 'Evil and Omnipotence' (1955).

> Here it can be shown, not that religious beliefs lack rational support, but that they are positively irrational … the theologian … must now be prepared to believe, not merely what cannot be proved, but what can be disproved from other beliefs that he also holds …
>
> The problem of evil … is a problem only for someone who believes that there is a God who is both omnipotent and wholly good. And it is a logical problem … it is not a scientific problem that might be solved by further observations …
>
> In its simplest form the problem is this: God is omnipotent; God is wholly good; and yet evil exists. There seems to be some contradiction between these three propositions, so that if any two of them were true the third would be false …
>
> It is clear that it can be solved … if one gives up at least one of the propositions that constitute it. If you are prepared to say that God is not wholly good, or not quite omnipotent, or that evil does not exist … or that there are limits to what an omnipotent thing can do, then the problem of evil will not arise for you …
>
> Of the proposed solutions of the problem of evil which we have examined, none has stood up to criticism.

TASK

Read Mackie for yourself in the extract below. The notes in the margin will help you to grasp his ideas.

- Hence Mackie's argument is a priori and deductive, as it only concerns reasoning from the points stated.
- Mackie's problem of evil is *only* a problem for a believer who defends God's omnipotence and omnibenevolence.
- Deductive and a priori. Mackie's argument tries to show that it is not just unlikely that an omnipotent and omnibenevolent God exists, but logically impossible.
- You can see how this is developed from Epicurus' trilemma as presented by Hume.
- The only way to solve the problem is to remove one of the points of the triad.
- Mackie explores many possible solutions, a few of which are addressed in this chapter. You can read more in Mackie's own article, which is freely available online.

Know Criticisms of Mackie

EVALUATION SKILLS

An answer to an evaluative question about a scholar is always deepened by demonstrating awareness of how other thinkers have taken different positions.

Omnipotence is not unlimited. It has long been understood by theists that God's omnipotence does not mean the ability to do the logically impossible, as there is no such thing in reality. Aquinas, for example, understood God's omnipotence to mean that God could do anything, so anything possible, which is restricted to what is logically possible. If it is not logically possible for God to prevent evil, for whatever reason, then Mackie's triad fails.

Free will cannot be determined. American philosopher Alvin Plantinga argued that Mackie was mistaken when he claimed that God could have created humans who freely chose good over evil at every opportunity. Plantinga said this would be logically impossible because, if God determined the character and therefore moral actions of humans, they consequently would not have genuine free will.

Watch Out for Traps

Don't confuse 'evil' for 'omniscience' in Mackie's triad. Sometimes students incorrectly explain Mackie's triad, labelling the three points as omnipotence, omnibenevolence and 'omniscience' rather than 'evil'. However, this proves problematic, as the inconsistency of the triad cannot be successfully demonstrated, nor the solution of removing one point made clear. Mackie did not need to include omniscience as a separate point, as the concept of divine foreknowledge is assumed within the concept of omnipotence.

> **STRENGTHEN YOUR GRASP**
>
> 1. Write an explanation of Mackie's development of the problem of evil. You should be able to explain *why* only two of the three points in the triad can stand. To improve your AO1 depth, explain how Mackie rejects some of the possible solutions to the problem.
> 2. To improve your AO2 evaluation, for each part of Mackie's triad, note down possible solutions and defences of an omnipotent and omnibenevolent God. Which views are strongest, and why? Colour code or use ticks and crosses to see visually which side you think has the more successful argument.

CREATE YOUR OWN QUESTION

Read this chapter and use command words such as 'explain' or 'examine' to create your own AO1 questions. For an AO2 question, make a one-sided statement about the success or failure of modern development of the problem of evil, put the statement between quotation marks and follow it with the phrase, 'Evaluate this view.'

Exam Guidance AO1

In a part a) question you could be asked about the problem of evil generally or with regard to Mackie specifically, and his modern development of the problem. Depending on the depth required for the question, it might be beneficial to give an account of how Mackie explores and rejects potential solutions to the problem, in addition to explaining how his inconsistent triad works and challenges the attributes of the God of classical theism.

Exam Guidance AO2

Depending on the question, it might be beneficial to approach an evaluation question about the problem of evil thematically, weighing up how successfully different responses and theodicies (defences of God) can solve Mackie's modern development of the problem of evil, which in turn could undermine the deductive and logical nature of the argument.

14. WILLIAM ROWE

GET INTO ROWE'S WORLD

> **Quick Overview** William Rowe (1931–2015) was an American philosopher and professor at Purdue University, USA. He is best known for his formulation of the evidential problem of evil and for work on the theology and philosophy of Paul Tillich.

As a young man, William Rowe was a fundamentalist evangelical Christian. However, over the course of his studies he experienced a gradual conversion to atheism, hence his formulation of the problem of evil. Rowe is credited with coining the term 'friendly atheist', which he considered himself to be, meaning a person who accepts that some theists have a rational basis for belief in God, even if they are not convinced themselves. He is therefore known for writing in support of some theistic arguments despite disagreeing with the conclusions.

Know Rowe's Key Ideas

■ IMPROVE YOUR UNDERSTANDING

Make sure that you grasp how intense suffering serves as evidence that the God of classical theism *probably* does not exist.

Intense Human and Animal Suffering

Rowe rejected the logical problem of evil as he recognised that there are grounds on which the premises could be challenged and that therefore as a deductive argument it fails (see Chapters 12 and 13). Rowe considered that it was possible that God is justified in permitting *some* evil for a greater good, although that evil would still be an **intrinsic evil** as it remains bad in and of itself. However, he argued that if we look to the world, there is evidence of pointless and unnecessary evil, such as intense human and animal suffering that 'occurs daily and in great plenitude', which can therefore suggest that the God of classical theism *probably* does not exist.

■ INSIGHT

As an evidential argument, Rowe only provides evidence to suggest that an omnipotent and omnibenevolent God *probably* does not exist.

> **ESSENTIAL!**
>
> By **intrinsic evil**, Rowe meant evil which is justifiable because it leads to a greater good, but as evil it still causes suffering so remains intrinsically bad in and of itself.

Rowe used examples to illustrate his evidential argument, including the following:

- **Human suffering.** A five-year-old girl is severely beaten and strangled to death by her mother's boyfriend. Whatever good that could have possibly occurred as a result of this evil surely could have been achieved with just the quick death of the little girl.

- **Animal suffering.** A fawn, trapped in a forest fire, is severely burned and lies in agony for days before dying. Any possible good that could have resulted from the fawn's death could surely still have occurred if the fawn had died quickly rather than suffering for a prolonged period.

Understand Rowe's Arguments

A crucial element of Rowe's argument is that the intensity of such human and animal suffering, as mentioned in the above examples, appears **pointless**, as it does not lead to any greater good, and **unnecessary**, as any greater good could have been achieved with less intensity of suffering. Ensure that you understand the difference here and are able to explain these ideas.

Rowe's argument can be summarised as follows:

> P1: Pointless evil contradicts the qualities of an all-loving and all-powerful God.
>
> P2: Pointless evil exists in our world and is evident on a daily basis.
>
> C: Therefore, evidence suggests that an all-loving, all-powerful God is a contradiction and does not exist.

ESSENTIAL!

By **pointless suffering**, Rowe meant that which does not seem to lead to any greater good.

By **unnecessary suffering**, Rowe meant that which could have achieved the same level of greater good if it had been restricted to a lesser degree.

WHAT DO YOU THINK?

Write down your thoughts on Rowe's arguments and revisit them shortly before the exam to see if your views have changed.

Read Rowe for Yourself

The following passage is taken from *The Problem of Evil and Some Varieties of Atheism* (1979) and illustrates Rowe's example of animal suffering.

> Suppose in some distant forest lightning strikes a dead tree, resulting in a forest fire. In the fire a fawn is trapped, horribly burned, and lies in terrible agony for several days before death relieves its suffering. So far as we can see, the fawn's intense suffering is pointless. For there does not appear to be any greater good … Could an omnipotent, omniscient being have prevented the fawn's apparently pointless suffering? The answer is obvious, as even the theist will insist. An omnipotent, omniscient being could have easily prevented the fawn from being horribly burned, or, given the burning, could have spared the fawn the intense suffering by quickly ending its life, rather than allowing the fawn to lie in terrible agony for several days. Since the fawn's intense suffering was preventable and, so far as we can see, pointless, doesn't it appear … that there do exist instances of intense suffering which an omnipotent, omniscient being could have prevented without thereby losing some greater good or permitting some evil equally bad or worse[?]

- An omnibenevolent God would wish to minimise suffering to the absolute minimum required for any greater good.
- Rowe acknowledges this is our perspective, but our perspective counts when concerning our own beliefs.
- Rowe as a 'friendly atheist' treats religious beliefs as rational.
- Reference to the idea that this world could be the best possible world with optimum conditions.

Know Criticisms of Rowe

Sceptical theism argues that we cannot understand God's reasons. Philosopher Daniel Howard-Snyder, writing about Rowe's argument in 1999, responded with a criticism that builds on Aquinas' view of the problem of evil. Aquinas said that we cannot know the mind of God and therefore any problem of evil is not actually a problem because, being human, we cannot correctly perceive or understand God and God's nature in the first place. Howard-Snyder writes, 'the idea that God may well permit **gratuitous evil** is absurd. After all, if God can get what he wants without permitting a particular horror, why on earth would he permit it?'

Howard-Snyder argues that Rowe's argument is based only on how things appear to us. It only seems to us that suffering such as the examples Rowe uses is pointless and unnecessary, as we are unable to see the full picture. The fact that God does ultimately permit such evil and suffering means that it cannot be pointless or unnecessary, as that contradicts God's nature. There will be a greater good and justifiable reason for such evil and suffering.

Howard-Snyder's criticism can be expressed simply as follows:

> P1: If pointless evil as Rowe describes it exists, then God does not exist.
> P2: But those of faith remain assured that such a God does exist.
> C: Therefore, pointless evil as Rowe describes it does not exist.

ESSENTIAL!

Sceptical theism is the view that God exists but that humans should be sceptical of their ability to understand God's reasons for anything.

By **gratuitous evil**, Howard-Snyder means evil that serves no purpose and has no reason.

INSIGHT

Biblical verses such as the following support the view of sceptical theism: 'Who has known the mind of God?' (Romans 11:34).

Watch Out for Traps

Don't just describe the fawn's suffering. Sometimes candidates discussing Rowe just describe the death of the fawn and go on to say that this shows that God cannot exist. However, for AO1 questions you should explain key points in Rowe's argument, such as his acceptance of intrinsic evil that serves a greater good, and both pointless and unnecessary suffering. Stronger responses also apply the issues raised from examples to the nature of God and are able to explain how Rowe's argument challenges the existence of the God of classical theism.

> ### STRENGTHEN YOUR GRASP
> 1. Write out the key terms for this topic area along with definitions in your own words. You should include the following: evidential, inductive, a posteriori, intrinsic evil, human suffering, animal suffering, pointless suffering, unnecessary suffering.
> 2. Make a list of reasons why Rowe's ideas are persuasive and successful. Then make a list of reasons why Rowe's ideas are not successful. Read over your lists and identify which has the stronger case and why. This will help with your AO2 evaluation.

Exam Guidance AO1

In a part a) question you could be asked about the problem of evil generally with regard to modern developments of the problem, or about Rowe's argument specifically. It would be beneficial to explain the nature of Rowe's evidential argument and how it only argues for the probability of God not existing, rather than serving as a proof. Depending on the depth required for the question, it could also be beneficial to explain the key ideas in Rowe's argument and how these challenge the existence of the God of classical theism.

Exam Guidance AO2

Rowe could be relevant in a variety of part b) evaluation questions concerning the problem of evil as a challenge to belief in the God of classical theism. It could be beneficial to weigh up the success of Rowe against criticisms, for example, as an evidential argument it provides no actual proof. In addition, Aquinas' and Howard-Snyder's criticisms from sceptical theism are potentially very successful. Finally, who is to judge when evil and suffering exceed a justifiable degree for the greater good which occurs?

15. GREGORY S. PAUL

GET INTO PAUL'S WORLD

> **Quick Overview** Gregory S. Paul (born 1954) is a freelance researcher and palaeontologist. Within the world of philosophy, he is known for his statistical argument that challenges the existence of a loving God.

Gregory S. Paul has no formal qualifications in philosophy. However, his argument is unique and has contributed significantly to modern discussions concerning the problem of evil and the existence of an omnibenevolent deity.

Paul's understanding of human evolution led him to question why the suffering of innocent young humans had been so neglected. He felt driven to bring attention to this fact and justified his emphasis on statistical evidence:

> Statistics matter, to the degree that it is not possible to wholly assess the moral nature of a ruler without quantitatively measuring the results of his management. That a modern statistical analysis of God's dominion over earth has not been conducted is a major failing of the ... debate that has prevented definitive conclusions.
>
> (Paul, 'Theodicy's Problem: A Statistical Look at the Holocaust of the Children and the Implications of Natural Evil for the Free Will and Best of All Worlds Hypothesis', 2007)

> **INSIGHT**
> Paul's argument isn't limited to a specific time period. His statistical evidence spans 10,000 generations of *Homo sapiens*.

Know Paul's Key Ideas

Innocent Suffering and Premature Deaths

Paul states that across 10,000 generations of humans (about 300,000 years), the deaths of a very large number of children, and premature deaths of conceptions that never made it to birth, challenge the existence of an omnibenevolent God. He uses statistical evidence to back up his argument:

> P1: Over 50 billion children have died from natural evil before reaching maturity.
>
> P2: Approximately 300 billion human conceptions have died before making it to birth.
>
> C1: The extent of the damage to human young could hardly be worse without permanently damaging the survival chances of the human race.
>
> P3: All these premature deaths are of innocent young humans, who never had the chance to develop free will.
>
> P4: An omnipotent and omnibenevolent God would not permit such suffering.
>
> C2: Such suffering exists, so clearly the God of classical theism does not.

> **INSIGHT**
> As a statistical argument, Paul only provides evidence to *suggest* that an omnipotent and omnibenevolent God doesn't exist.

INSIGHT

Paul refers only to *Homo sapiens*. He does not include statistics concerning the innocent deaths of the other human species. Therefore, the statistics would be even greater if we took all other human species into account.

Understand Paul's Arguments

Paul's arguments are a response to two traditional defences of God.

The Free-Will Defence

This is a development of St Irenaeus' theodicy (see Chapter 16), often attributed to philosopher Alvin Plantinga. The free-will defence argues that God is justified in permitting evil because it ensures that humans can act with 'morally significant free will'. Humans are completely free to make moral choices, which is far more valuable than a world of robotic humans who always act as programmed.

However, Paul's argument highlights that approximately 350 billion humans died before reaching an age to develop free will. Their suffering, weighed against the 50 billion who made it to adulthood to experience free will, is unjust.

The Best Possible World Hypothesis

Attributed to the seventeenth-century philosopher Gottfried-Wilhelm Leibniz, 'the best possible world hypothesis' argues that God is justified in permitting evil because the existing world is the best that could have possibly been created.

However, Paul argues that the human race would not have been able to survive had the premature deaths been any greater. In addition, the fact that humans have, in the last century especially, been able to dramatically improve the survival rate of children suggests that there was always the option for a better possible world. God is not justified in permitting our ancestors to suffer so much more than we do today.

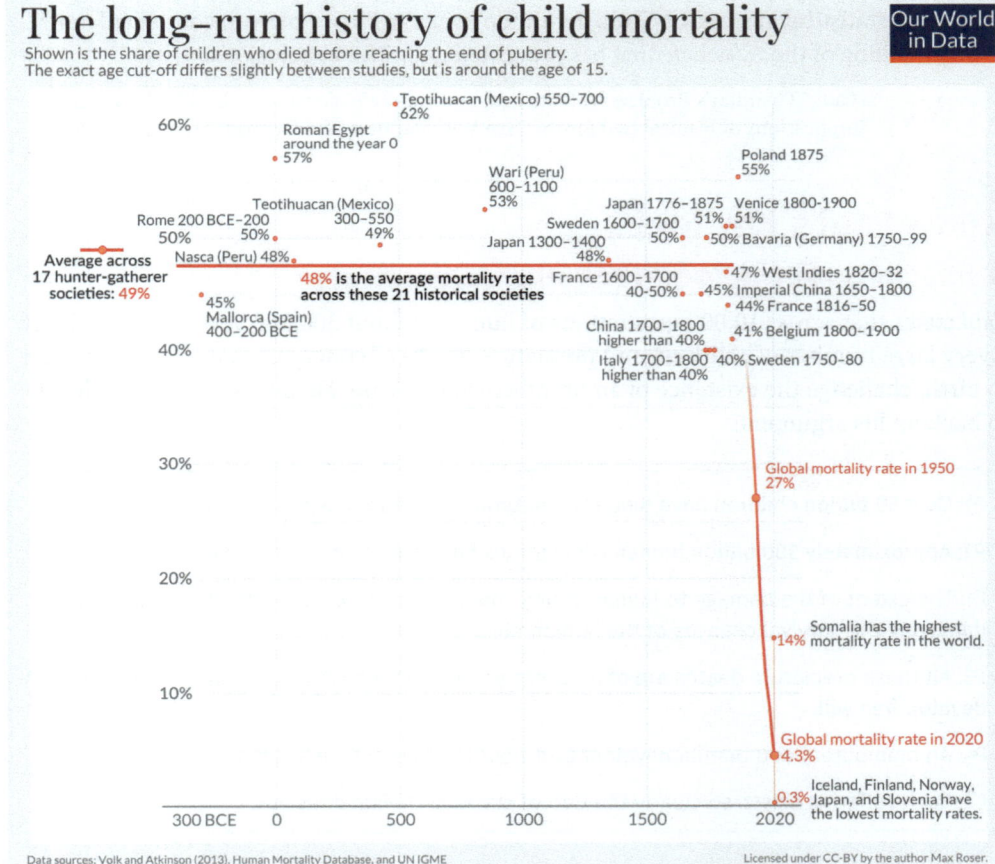

Read Paul for Yourself

The following passage is taken from Paul's article 'Theodicy's Problem: A Statistical Look at the Holocaust of the Children and the Implications of Natural Evil for the Free Will and Best of All Worlds Hypothesis' (2007). The notes in the margin will help you to grasp his ideas.

The Holocaust of the Children is so large in scale and depth that it poses such insurmountable problems for the classic Christian free will and best of all worlds hypotheses that they are falsified. If the Christian creator of this vast universe exists, then he has allowed the immature to dwell in such an oddly tiny and brutal habitat that it is a death trap … It is patently impossible to correctly assert that the PSCI gives humans free will when a large or major portion of humans never becomes old enough to make mature decisions, nor is it possible to accurately assert that the PSCI has produced the best habitat when humans have proven more willing than the creator to protect almost all children from serious disease and death without apparently seriously degrading the ability of humans to become suitable inhabitants of paradise … Because the PSCI is much more callous and negligent than its imperfect creations, the creator cannot be perfect … Because the difficulties that stem from the Holocaust of the Children are so numerous and intractable, it follows that the Christian theory of a perfect God with a perfect plan is so overwhelmed by the real world that it is falsified.	Paul's terminology for the combined approximate figure of 350 billion innocent deaths of young and unborn humans. Paul is specifically responding to Christian defences against the logical problem of evil. Paul refers to God as 'the proposed powerful supernatural creator intelligence' or 'PSCI'. This challenges the free-will defence. This challenges the best possible world hypothesis.

Know Criticisms of Paul

A transcendent God. The point of sceptical theism can be raised here (see Chapter 14). The God of classical theism is not just omnibenevolent and omnipotent, but also transcendent (existing outside of space and time). It is therefore entirely plausible that a transcendent and wholly good God, concerned with the long-term development and survival of the human race, designed the world with an inbuilt system to prevent overbreeding and population increase, and the inevitable evils that this would lead to. We do not have the full perspective that God does. So, we cannot say that the statistics taken from a snapshot of human history outweigh the greater good which we do not understand.

Modern-day crises. Modern-day evils resulting from human population increase, such as environmental crises, species extinction, pollution, shortage of resources, war and social injustice, all serve as evidence that God, in his infinite wisdom and all-loving nature, was justified in permitting a natural system to keep population numbers down to a level that ensured the best possible world, where all creation thrived and flourished.

Watch Out for Traps

It is not about God's non-existence. When discussing Paul or any of the problems of evil and their responses, remember that it is not simply about proving that God does not exist. The problem of evil is about whether the concept of God is coherent. If God is not a coherent concept, then such a God cannot exist. Therefore, when discussing Paul's argument, ensure that you make the link from his statistical evidence to the point that this challenges the omnibenevolent nature of God.

EVALUATION SKILLS

An answer to an evaluative question about a scholar is always deepened by demonstrating awareness of how other thinkers have taken different positions.

INSIGHT

Paul does not argue against the existence of any God, but against the existence of an omnibenevolent God.

STRENGTHEN YOUR GRASP

1. In your own words, describe Paul's statistical argument and how it challenges the existence of God. Use examples of human conceptions that never survived to birth and the number of children who died before maturity. This will help you to develop your AO1 skill.

2. Outline the free-will defence and best possible world hypothesis. Then outline Paul's evidence and reasoning in rejecting these defences. Which do you think is the stronger argument in each case, and why? This will help with AO2 evaluation of Paul's argument.

CREATE YOUR OWN QUESTION

Read this chapter and use command words such as 'explain' or 'examine' to create your own AO1 questions. For an AO2 question, make a one-sided statement about the extent to which modern forms of the problem of evil are successful in proving that God does not exist. Put the statement between quotation marks and follow it with the phrase, 'Evaluate this view.'

TIP

This book focuses solely on the scholars in the Board's specification. Use the Illuminate textbook and revision guide as part of your full revision process.

Exam Guidance AO1

Paul would be relevant in a part a) question on the problem of evil. If discussing Paul, it would be beneficial to explain the nature of Paul's statistical argument as an evidential problem of evil. Depending on the depth required for the question, it might also be useful to discuss how, for Paul, the number of premature deaths challenges both the free-will defence and best possible world hypothesis, pointing to the conclusion that an all-loving God does not exist.

Exam Guidance AO2

Depending on the question, if you refer to Paul in a part b) evaluation question it could be beneficial to weigh up the success of Paul in his rejection of the free-will defence and the existence of an all-loving God against the defences of God and weaknesses in his argument. For example, his argument is evidential (based on evidence), meaning it is not actual proof. Moreover, how can we know the mind of God? It is possible that this world is the best possible world and premature deaths did serve some purpose which we do not understand.

16. JOHN HICK ON AUGUSTINE AND IRENAEUS

GET INTO THE WORLD OF HICK, AUGUSTINE AND IRENAEUS

ESSENTIAL!

Theodicy means 'in defence of God', as it the name given for arguments that defend the attributes and existence of the God of classical theism against the challenge of the problem of evil.

Quick Overview John Hick, St Augustine and St Irenaeus are often considered to be the great defenders of God. Hick has been instrumental in our understanding of Augustinian and Irenaean **theodicies** (defences of God), having collated their ideas into coherent arguments in *Evil and the God of Love*.

Hick's World

John Hick (1922–2012) is considered by some to be the greatest philosopher of the twentieth century. After serving in the Second World War, he went on to complete his studies at the universities of Oxford and Edinburgh. Having attended a Quaker school as a child, Hick spent the majority of his adult life as an evangelical Christian before developing a religious pluralist stance following his experience of other faiths while teaching in Birmingham. Hick eventually became a Quaker in the years before he died.

Hick's philosophy has been influential in many areas, including ethics and moral relativism, religious pluralism, the problem of evil, the nature of faith and religious epistemology (theory of knowledge). With regard to the problem of evil, Hick is credited with collating the teachings of St Augustine and formulating them into a coherent theodicy in his book *Evil and the God of Love* (1966). Within this text Hick goes on to disagree with Augustine and instead supports the ideas of St Irenaeus, which he formulates as the Irenaean theodicy, and develops them with his own ideas in response to the problem of evil, as raised by Mackie (see Chapter 13) the decade before.

Augustine's World

St Augustine of Hippo (354–430CE) is widely considered to be the first of the great Christian philosophers. He was one of the most important early Church fathers (prominent Christian thinkers from the first to the eighth centuries who contributed to the development of the doctrinal foundations of the Catholic Church) and went on to have a profound impact on Christian thought and medieval philosophy.

As a young man, Augustine lived a hedonist lifestyle, rejecting Christianity and pursuing the pleasures of the flesh. However, at the age of 33, he converted to Christianity. His youthful sexual exploits are described in his *Confessions*, but the overriding themes of guilt and regret are prominent.

Influenced by the philosophical works of Plato in particular, Augustine sought to align the philosophy of the Greeks with Church teaching. Augustine was especially concerned with the potential that philosophy offered to make sense of the world and provide rational justification for Christian beliefs that he held to be true.

During Augustine's lifetime, Christianity became the official religion of the Roman Empire (from 380CE). Many Christians, Augustine included, dedicated themselves to working to spread the message of Christianity. It was at this point that Augustine wrote his most influential works. The Roman Empire, however, had entered a period of decline, and it descended into total collapse in western Europe during the fifth century, leading to a power vacuum that the Church of Rome rose to fill, becoming the dominant authority in western Europe for the next 1,200 years.

Irenaeus' World

St Irenaeus of Lyons (130–202CE) was an early Christian bishop, originally from Asia Minor (present-day Turkey). Irenaeus is said to have heard the preaching of the early Christian martyr Polycarp, bishop of Smyrna, when he was just a child. As Polycarp is said to have known St John the Evangelist when he was younger, this puts Irenaeus at just three degrees of separation and three generations from the Apostles of Jesus.

Irenaeus was living in a turbulent time, when Christianity was made up of different sects and factions. These sects, while disagreeing among themselves, also faced sporadic persecution from the Roman Empire. At the end of the second century, the historian Tertullian reported that the Romans had blamed Christians for all disasters and diseases, believing that the tendency of Christians to turn their back on the gods of their fathers and their refusal to pay respect to the gods of Rome had brought retribution and wrath from the gods. The suffering of Christians in the form of persecution and martyrdom was widely questioned, and could be said to have shaped Irenaeus' views regarding evil.

Irenaeus is best known today for his *Against Heresies* text, and is honoured by many Christian denominations not only for his services to the Church as a missionary who spread Christianity, but also as a mediator between different Christian factions.

> **INSIGHT**
>
> Irenaeus only narrowly escaped imprisonment and possible martyrdom due to being away from Lyons when the Christians there were persecuted. When Irenaeus returned, he became the bishop of Lyons as the previous bishop had been killed.

Know the Key Ideas of Augustinian-Type Theodicies

IMPROVE YOUR UNDERSTANDING

Make sure that you grasp how Augustine's views on creation led him to argue that God could not have created evil.

Evil as a Privation

Why an all-powerful and all-loving God permitted evil to occur was just as much of a concern for early Christians as it is today. Augustine, inspired by Platonic thinking in addition to his historical reading of Genesis, believed that God could not be considered the creator of evil because evil was not a thing in and of itself, rather an absence or lack of something.

> **INSIGHT**
>
> Plato had previously argued that evil was not a thing in itself, but an absence of a thing, in his *Gorgias* (around 400BCE).

Just as darkness is a privation of light, and the suffering of a blind man is due to a privation of sight, Augustine believed that evil was a privation of good, *privatio boni*. God could not be the creator or source of evil because the Bible teaches that God is Good, and the world as created by God was perfect: 'God saw all that he had made, and it was very good' (Genesis 1:31).

> **INSIGHT**
>
> 'For evil has no positive nature; but the loss of good has received the name evil' (Augustine's *City of God*, Book XI, Chapter 9).

Augustine believe the corruption that resulted from the angels and Adam and Eve turning away from God was what accounted for both natural and moral evil in the world. The plight of Adam and Eve has been a subject of much religious artwork over the centuries.

> **INSIGHT**
>
> The idea of seminal presence should not be written off without some consideration. From Augustine's perspective, the corruption of humankind's nature was inherited and passed down from ancestor to descendant, much like our modern understanding of genes.

> **INSIGHT**
>
> 'All evil is either sin or the punishment for sin' (Augustine).

Therefore Augustine accounts for evil, or the lack of goodness, as something that occurred *after* God created the world in a perfect state, via angels and humans misusing their free will and deliberately turning away from God. As part of the created order, which was varied and diverse, angels and humans were mutable (capable of change and corruption), so they had the ability to turn away from God, who is immutable (incapable of change and corruption). This turning away was a deliberate moral choice, and the result of absolute free will. The turning away was therefore what led to a lack of goodness in the world – evil – which subsequently caused an imbalance of the harmony in the created order. Ultimately, this led to both moral evil and natural evil (see below for more on this).

Seminal Presence

According to Augustine's allegorical interpretation of Genesis, the first evil in the world came from the fall of the angels as a result of their turning away from God. Satan, chief of the fallen angels, then takes the form of a serpent and tempts Adam and Eve to turn away from God by disobeying God's instructions. Adam and Eve freely choose to eat the forbidden fruit from the tree of knowledge of good and evil, and just as the angels had, they caused a lack of goodness within themselves and further contributed to the imbalance and corruption in the created order. Augustine identified this act as the 'original sin'.

> **INSIGHT**
>
> Note that Augustine's theodicy rests on both a historical and an allegorical interpretation of Genesis. The fall of the angels and the idea that the serpent is Satan is not mentioned in the Bible – these were Augustine's interpretations.

Adam and Eve freely chose to sin, so they were held morally responsible for their action and its consequences. Furthermore, because Augustine believed that all humans were descendants of Adam and Eve, he understood all humankind to be 'seminally present' in Adam at the time of the original sin. Therefore, Adam and Eve's sin passed evil into all of humankind and corrupted human nature. Consequently, Augustine believed that all evil and suffering experienced in the world was the fully deserved and just consequence of human sin and humankind's wicked nature.

Augustine distinguished between two types of evil:

- **Moral evil.** This is the consequence of human free will and a wicked, corrupted nature. Humankind has brought it upon themselves through original sin, and humans continue to make wrong choices, leading to further suffering.
- **Natural evil.** This is the consequence of both angels and humans corrupting the natural created order through their turning away from God. Adam and Eve were cast out of Eden just as the fallen angels were cast out of heaven. Genesis 3 describes how, in just punishment for their original sin, the land where Adam and Eve were banished to was cursed, humans would have to toil and struggle to grow enough food, and there would be hostility between different species. Humans would also experience pain, suffering and death.

Felix Culpa (the Happy Mistake)

One might wonder why a wholly good God, who being omniscient would know that evil would be brought into the world through his creation, continued to proceed with creation in this way. Augustine explains that the answer is simple: because 'God judged it better to bring good out of evil than to not permit any evil to exist.' God's perspective is not our perspective. Augustine uses the following examples to illustrate.

- The colour black on its own is not considered to be beautiful, but in the context of a painting, the colour black is purposeful and contributes to the beauty and good of the painting as a whole. If we live our life in the blackness, we do not appreciate its necessity for the bigger picture.

- Silence on its own is nothing remarkable, but carefully thought-out and well-timed pauses and moments of silence in a piece of music are purposeful and contribute to the beauty of the piece. If we lived our whole life in silence, we would not appreciate its necessity for the overall melody.

Therefore, God chose to create angels and humans despite knowing the consequences, because from his infinite perspective he judged it to be the greater good. This concept became known as the happy mistake, *felix culpa*, as it resulted in the redemption of humankind (being saved from sin) through the sacrifice of Jesus Christ.

For Augustine, this confirmed God's nature as omnibenevolent. The just punishment for humankind's wicked nature and state of sin was hell. However, through the grace of God (undeserved love and mercy), some of those who freely chose to follow Jesus would be saved and gain a place in heaven.

> **INSIGHT**
>
> Augustine believed humans were so fundamentally wicked that they could not save themselves from sin, regardless of good deeds or faith. Humans could only be saved by the grace of God.

Understand Augustinian-Type Arguments

There are many underlying assumptions of Augustine's theodicy, including the following, which will help you to understand and evaluate his ideas.

Evil cannot be caused by God because the Bible tells us creation was 'very good'. Augustine reads the Bible both literally in a historical sense, and also allegorically. From Genesis, Augustine interprets creation as *creatio ex nihilo* (creation out of nothing). Created matter is not eternal, and was brought into existence and order by a creative act of God. Creation is therefore able to change: although it was perfect at the point of God's creation, it was not fixed and could slide into chaos and corruption.

God is justified in permitting evil by the happy mistake, *felix culpa*. Augustine's theodicy has been termed **soul-deciding** on two counts:

- Due to human free will, Adam and Eve decided to turn away from God. Subsequent generations of humans also get to decide for themselves how to act and whether to accept Jesus. Therefore, through free will and moral responsibility for their choices, humans get to decide their eternal fate for themselves.

- Through God's omniscience, God knew what every individual through their free will would choose to do. He decided to create them anyway and decided their eternal fate at the point of their creation. This is known as predestination. Augustine believed this to be perfectly just, and *felix culpa*, the option of some receiving salvation, served as proof of God's loving and merciful nature.

> **ESSENTIAL!**
>
> Augustinian-type theodicies are known as **soul-deciding** because free-willed souls *decided* to sin and bring evil into the world, and God through his omnipotence and divine foreknowledge *decided* the eternal fate of all souls at creation.

Therefore, Augustinian-type theodicies render the 'problem of evil' not as a problem, but as a matter of perspective. While for humans evil appears real due to suffering on a day-to-day basis, for God there is no reality of evil – there is just a lack of goodness in some aspects as a result of the changeable nature of creation, which functions to magnify the goodness of creation as a whole.

For Augustine, God is therefore justified in his omnipotence as he was capable of creating a perfect world which was 'very good'. God is also justified in his omnibenevolence, as he did not create evil. After permitting creation to exist with free will and the evil that consequentially arose through sin, he provided an opportunity for redemption. God is also justified in his omniscience, as by proceeding with creation he foreknew everything that would happen and knew that the corruption of creation would only serve to glorify the greater goodness.

Know the Key Ideas of Irenaean-Type Theodicies

IMPROVE YOUR UNDERSTANDING

Make sure that you grasp how God is justified in creating evil to serve a greater purpose.

Irenaean-type theodicies developed from the writings of St Irenaeus, who attempted to explain why God permitted evil and suffering in the world as a deliberate act for a greater good. His argument is based on his interpretation of Genesis 1:26: 'Then God said, "Let us make mankind in our image, according to our likeness".'

Human Development

Irenaeus believed that when God made humans, he made them in his image (*imago Dei* – the image of God). They were not perfect and needed to grow in God's likeness. This means that humans have free will, because to be in God's image means to be moral agents, capable of making free choices, and being morally responsible for these choices. In order to grow into the likeness of God, humans have to mature and develop. Humans move from possessing the *potential* qualities of God to *actualising* the qualities of God. This moral development occurs through overcoming trials and tribulations. Therefore, evil is a necessary fact of creation to enable human moral development.

Irenaeus argued that, without evil, we would not be able to appreciate good. Good is therefore a qualitative judgement and can be understood comparatively. We have to experience things that are less good to appreciate fully how good other things are. He uses several examples to illustrate this:

- We would not appreciate sight unless we understood what it meant to be blind.
- We would not appreciate good health unless we understood what it was to be ill.
- We would not appreciate light unless we had experience of darkness.
- We would not appreciate life unless we had knowledge of death.

Irenaeus argued that our experiences of evil and suffering helped to mould and shape us into the likeness of God.

Humans had to learn to overcome difficulties and resist temptations to do evil, in order to grow. Irenaeus believed that good in humankind, such as the virtues of perseverance, patience and courage, could only develop if humans were given the opportunities in the first place. You cannot be courageous if there is no situation in which there is first fear. You cannot develop patience unless at first you experience frustration. Goodness develops in response to adversity. Therefore, Irenaeus believed that Adam and Eve were cast out from the Garden of Eden as they were immature and needed to develop morally.

Irenaeus uses an analogy of a craftsman to illustrate how God uses the evils in the world to mould and shape humankind to perfection.

Irenaeus went on to say that the only human who was truly in God's likeness was Jesus Christ. Therefore, by studying the life of Jesus and trying to live up to Jesus, someone could grow enough to fulfil their potential to be in the likeness of God.

Eschatological Justification

Why did God not make humans perfect from the beginning? Irenaeus explains that, just as a newborn baby is not yet ready to cope with solid food, humankind is not yet capable of being perfect and in the likeness of God. Enduring and overcoming suffering gives humankind the opportunity to grow in God's likeness, but humans will not be able to actualise this potential fully until after death. This is known as the **eschatological justification** for suffering.

Irenaeus wrote that those who rejected God, by continually turning away from good to evil, were unable to develop moral characters in this life and would be punished in the afterlife. However, in God's love and mercy, he would allow these individuals to continue to grow in his likeness in the afterlife, and they too can morally develop and come to actualise their potential and gain entrance to heaven.

God, in his wholly good and all-loving nature, accounts for what appears to us to be inequality in the extent to which some humans suffer compared to others. By having the moral development process continue in the afterlife, those who do not undergo enough suffering in this life or reject the opportunities to develop can continue to do so after death.

Furthermore, humans can take comfort in knowing that, regardless of whether we can see and understand the goodness and development that comes out of suffering, we should trust that it is necessary, and ultimately brings humankind closer to God.

> **ESSENTIAL!**
>
> **Eschatological justification** means 'justified after death'. In this case, being reconciled with God in heaven will justify the suffering that was endured to achieve this goal.

Hick's Second-Order Goods

Hick agreed with Irenaeus that God had made humankind 'unfinished'. Hick aligns Irenaeus' ideas with modern-day science, and describes humans as the pinnacle of evolution, which was a long process guided by God, leading to the development (including moral development) of humankind.

Hick said that the goal, *telos*, of humans was to have a personal relationship with God, but this could only be achieved through free will and in response to experience of good and evil in the world. He uses the terminology from Mackie to describe humankind's experiences and the potential development we can make in this world:

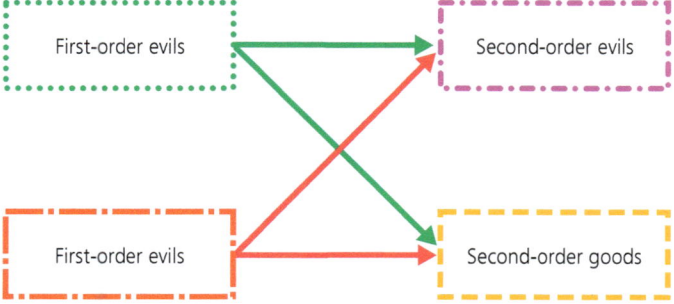

The relationship between first-order and second-order goods and evils

First-order events can be good or evil. They are the experiences or opportunities we have in life, to which we can then respond with our free will. Our responses can either be second-order goods or second-order evils. Where we freely choose to respond with good, it is a second-order good as we can morally grow and develop the virtues to which Irenaeus refers. For example, when faced with a first-order evil such as a natural disaster, we can respond with the second-order good of developing compassion, charity and kindness. However, due to being morally free, we can also choose to respond with a second-order evil, developing negative qualities such as bitterness or selfishness.

Hick admits that, although it is apparent that God is responsible for first-order evils in the world, it is out of perfect love for the greater good, and for free development of moral character. Hick describes humans as growing into 'children of God', through having the freedom to learn and develop their own moral character, which is infinitely more valuable than any virtues and moral character that could have been placed within them at the beginning, as if they were pre-programmed robots.

INSIGHT

Hick said this world was not a paradise of pets but one where humans have genuine free will to become children of God.

Understand Irenaean Arguments

Hick argued that the following two principles are central to the success of Irenaean-type theodicies. Understanding these ideas and being able to evaluate them will help you in your exam answers.

Epistemic distance. Hick develops the role of faith and free moral choice in Irenaeus' ideas, and argues that in order to preserve free will, God had to create humans at an epistemic distance from himself. This means that humans cannot be certain of God's existence and do not directly feel his imminent presence. This distance ensures that humans can act completely freely. If humans were aware of God overlooking their every move, they would obey and make the right choices not out of genuine and morally valuable free will, but out of obedience, which has no developmental value.

In order to preserve the epistemic distance and thus true free will, Hick developed Irenaeus' point that God had to make the world according to a predictable system. For Hick, this also meant limiting direct interventions that would reveal him, such as miracles. We experience natural evils that are unequally distributed, not because they are maliciously designed, but because the world functions in accordance to a predictable system of natural laws, created to provide opportunity for first-order goods and evils.

INSIGHT

Look up Kierkegaard's Parable of the King and the Peasant Girl. Write a short summary explaining how it can be used to illustrate Hick's epistemic distance.

ESSENTIAL!

Epistemic distance is not a time or spatial distance but a distance in terms of knowledge. It refers to the gap between humans' knowledge and God.

Eschatological justification. Hick agrees with and develops Irenaeus' eschatological justification, explaining his stance as a universalist – someone who believes all souls will eventually gain entrance to heaven, regardless of what they did in their life. With a modern-day perspective, Hick acknowledges that many humans who commit evils and cause suffering to others are themselves often victims and therefore cannot be held totally responsible for their actions. It is also apparent that suffering is unequally distributed, and not all suffering leads to all humans becoming morally developed within their lifetime. Some die prematurely while others live their life turning away from good. Therefore, as God is perfectly just and all-loving, the moral development process must continue in the afterlife and heaven is ultimately open to *all*. Subsequently, Hick described Irenaean-type theodicies as **soul-making**, reflecting the belief that evil serves the purpose of making one's soul ready for heaven.

> **INSIGHT**
>
> Hick described Irenaean-type theodicies as soul-making in reference to the poet John Keats, who described this world as more 'vale of soul-making' than vale of tears.

Hick defends this stance by arguing that only a supreme good such as reconciliation for all with God in heaven could justify the extent of suffering in this world. Furthermore, as God is omnibenevolent, he would never permit the eternal suffering of someone in hell when he could instead provide more opportunity for growth. For Hick, to imagine that a creation of God could reject goodness to such an extent as to separate themselves from God eternally would undermine God's power.

Therefore, Irenaean-type theodicies conclude that:

- God's omnibenevolence is justified because it is loving to allow humans to develop morally with genuine free will to gain a place in heaven. You cannot have a greater good without lesser goods also.
- God's omnipotence is justified because God was able to create a world to serve as a 'vale of soul-making', with opportunities enough in both life and death that all can be united with God in heaven eventually.
- Natural evil can be explained as part of the epistemic distance and as a first-order evil from which second-order goods can generate.
- Moral evil can be explained as the result of human free will, which in turn can serve as an opportunity to provoke second-order goods in others.

> **WHAT DO YOU THINK?**
>
> Write down your thoughts on Augustine's arguments and revisit them shortly before the exam to see if your views have changed.

Read Hick on Augustine for Yourself

The following passage is taken from Hick's *Evil and the God of Love* (1966) and illustrates some key parts of Augustine's theodicy. The notes in the margin will help you to grasp his ideas.

Lack of goodness, *privatio boni*. It is more loving of God to grant humans free will, and permit the subsequent evils that free will can cause, than not to permit evil and therefore not permit free will in the first place.	Augustine first asks, what is evil? Meaning, what is it metaphysically? ... Evil is not an entity in its own right but rather a **privation of good** ... Augustine next asks, Whence come evil? His response to this question is the so-called **free-will defence**, which explains, for him, both the moral evil of sin and, derivatively, human suffering in its many forms- physical pain, fear, anxiety, etc. [...]
Augustine is referring to Genesis 3, in which Adam and Eve disobeyed God. Augustine terms this the fall of man, which forms the basis of the Catholic Church's 'Doctrine of the Fall'. By 'mutably good' Augustine means humans are good but can change, or turn away from God, which he describes as the 'Good which is immutable', meaning the good to the highest degree, which cannot change or become less good. For Augustine, it wasn't the specific act of Adam and Eve which was sinful, but the fact that in their hearts they had the will to turn away from God and disobey in the first place. Augustine believed that due to seminal presence all humans were corrupt and inherently wicked, and had an intrinsic will to turn away from God regardless of how faithful and good they were in life. Therefore, God was justified in permitting the natural consequence of their sinful nature to persist.	Augustine attributes all evil, both moral and natural, directly or indirectly to the **wrong choices of free rational beings**. 'An evil will [improba voluntas], therefore, is the cause of all evils'. Again, 'the cause of evil is the defection of the will of a being who is **mutably good from the Good which is immutable**.' ... Here then is the heart of Augustine's theodicy ... The primary sin, which makes angels and men evil and brings upon them the further punitive evils of pain and sorrow is ... a wilful turning of the self in desire from the highest good, which is God Himself, to some lesser good. 'For when the will abandons what is above itself, and turns to what is lower, it becomes evil- not because that is evil to which it turns, but because **the turning itself is wicked**. It is this that occurred both in ... the primeval fall of man, and **this is the continuing nature of man's sinfulness today**. [...]
Augustine believed humans were not worthy of salvation and could not achieve it on their own merit in any instance. Salvation could only be granted by the grace of God.	The sin of Adam was at the same time the sin of all his descendants, who were 'seminally present' in Adam's loins. Thus all mankind is from birth in a state of guilt and condemnation, and there would be **perfect justice in the consignment of the entire human race to the eternal torments of hell**. [...]
This forms the basis of the classic free-will defence. It is more loving to permit evil for the sake of the goodness that such free will leads to, than not to have free will and the subsequent evil in the first place. In defence against the claim that a loving God would not have created the world if he had known of the evil that would enter it, Augustine argued that God did in fact know humankind would sin, but in his infinite wisdom he also knew that the opportunity for good would arise.	In what has become one of the key sentences in the whole literature of the theodicy, Augustine says, '**God judged it better to bring good out of evil, than to suffer no evil to exist**.' Again, '**For God would never have created any ... man, whose future wickedness He foreknew, unless He had equally known to what uses in behalf of the good He could turn him ...**'

Read Irenaeus for Yourself

The following passage is taken from *Against Heresies*, and illustrates many of Irenaeus' ideas. The notes in the margin will help you to grasp his ideas.

For, when strength was made perfect in weakness … it showed the kindness and transcendent power of God. For as He patiently suffered Jonah to be swallowed by the whale, not that he should be swallowed up and perish altogether, but that, having been cast out again, he might be the more subject to God, and might glorify Him the more who had conferred upon him such an unhoped-for deliverance, and might bring the Ninevites to a lasting repentance, so that they should be converted to the Lord, who would deliver them from death. […] because God made man a free [agent] from the beginning, possessing his own power, even as he does his own soul, to obey … God voluntarily, and not by compulsion of God. For there is no coercion with God, but a good will [towards us] is present with Him continually. […] And the harder we strive, so much is it the more valuable; while so much the more valuable it is, so much the more should we esteem it … the faculty of seeing would not appear to be so desirable, unless we had known what a loss it were to be devoid of sight; and health, too, is rendered all the more estimable by an acquaintance with disease; light, also, by contrasting it with darkness; and life with death. Just in the same way is the heavenly kingdom honourable to those who have known the earthly one. But in proportion as it is more honourable, so much the more do we prize it; and if we have prized it more, we shall be the more glorious in the presence of God. […] If, however, any one say, What then? Could not God have exhibited man as perfect from beginning? Let him know that … created things must be inferior to Him who created them … they come short of the perfect … so are they infantile; so are they unaccustomed to, and unexercised in, perfect discipline. For as it certainly is in the power of a mother to give strong food to her infant, [but she does not do so], as the child is not yet able to receive more substantial nourishment; so also it was possible for God Himself to have made man perfect from the first, but man could not receive this [perfection], being as yet an infant.	Irenaeus uses the Old Testament book of Jonah to illustrate that God used the suffering he inflicted upon Jonah to bring about greater good, for both Jonah and the Ninevites. Jonah previously disobeyed God and showed cowardice by trying to run away from God and the mission he had been given. However, after God had sent the whale to swallow Jonah for three days, Jonah accepted God and his mission, and the Ninevites went on to listen to Jonah and benefited, as Jonah brought them to God. This idea influenced Hick's epistemic distance. For humankind to have genuine freedom in how it responds to God, God's existence must be uncertain. Hence Hick's soul-making perspective. The harder the challenges, the more evil we face and overcome, the more we develop morally and the sooner we can be united with God in heaven. Those who do not develop as much in this life will have to undergo the process in the afterlife. Irenaeus is saying that goodness is understood comparatively. We will only truly understand the goodness of heaven, and thus be ready for it, if we have understood the lesser good and experienced opportunities to grow morally. Irenaeus pre-empts the question, why couldn't God have created humans already perfect, with moral development already actualised? Irenaeus responds that, as God is the ultimate superior and perfect, any creation will be inferior, and as such, humans are not ready-made to handle perfection. Like all living creations, they have to grow.

> [...]
> but man making progress day by day, and ascending towards the perfect ... Now it was necessary that man should in the first instance be created; and having been created, should receive growth; and having received growth, should be strengthened; and having been strengthened, should abound; and having abounded, should recover [from the disease of sin]; and having recovered, should be glorified; and being glorified, should see his Lord.

Irenaeus stresses that overcoming trials and tribulations is beneficial for the soul and will ultimately result in being with God in heaven, and so God's omnibenevolence is justified.

Know Criticisms of Augustinian-Type Theodicies

Many criticisms have been made of Augustinian-type theodicies, some of which can be categorised into the following themes.

Logical Problems

- Friedrich Schleiermacher argued that a truly perfect creation could not have been corrupted – this would be incoherent. If something is truly perfect, it will not corrupt. If something is capable of corrupting, it is not perfect.

- God's omnipotence can be considered indefensible because, if God had created angels and humans perfectly, they would have had the moral character to ensure that even with free will, they never chose to turn away from God. As Mackie later argued (see Chapter 13), if God can create humans with the moral character freely to choose good over evil on any occasion, he could have created humans with such a character that they *always* choose good over evil. Yet he did not create humans with such a character, suggesting that he could not, and so is not omnipotent.

- God's omnibenevolence can be considered indefensible because the sheer extent of evil and suffering outweighs the greater good as identified by Augustine – that a small number of humans are able to be redeemed and gain salvation. Further, the fact that God created hell as part of creation, and still proceeded with creation despite knowing that the vast majority of humans would be predestined for hell, suggests he is not all-loving.

- Pelagius, a contemporary of Augustine, considered the idea that humankind could be punished for the sins of another as unjust and not in keeping with the wholly good nature of God.

- God's omniscience means he had foreknowledge of the fall of angels and humankind, yet he proceeded with creation regardless. In this case, God *does* have a role in the creation of evil, as he permitted it to occur in full knowledge that it would. Hick compares this to a manufacturer that would be held responsible if they were later discovered to have knowingly produced a faulty product. Either God is responsible for evil, as he had foreknowledge of it and continued to proceed, or he is not omniscient, as he did not know it would occur.

- The soul-deciding aspect of Augustine's theodicy can be considered incoherent and unjust. If God is omniscient and foreknows what humans will do, then how can humans have true free will? If their choices are fixed because God already knows what they will do, then those choices cannot be truly free. In that case, predestination is unjust, as humans have no control over where God has destined them.

Evidential Problems

- Evidential problems of evil (see also Chapters 14 and 15, on Rowe and Paul) highlight the disproportionate and unequal scale of suffering in the world. This suggests that evil is in fact a real thing and not just a lack of goodness.

- Evidence suggests that natural evils such as disasters, diseases, carnivorous animals and poisonous plants all pre-dated human species by millions or billions of years. Therefore, natural evils cannot have been caused by the corruption of creation as a result of the fall of man.

- Scientific evidence, such as the Big Bang theory, supports the idea that the universe is 13.8 billion years old and developed in a sudden expansion from the singularity which contained all matter, and that it was at this point that space and time began. There is no evidence of a Prelapsarian world (a world before the fall), without death, disease or suffering. All evidence supports the theory of evolution, which argues that all life on earth evolved through adaptation by means of natural selection, because of death and disease. Such scientific evidence challenges any historical validity of the Genesis accounts on which Augustinian-type theodicies are based.

- Anthropological evidence has identified that there have been a variety of other ancient human species, of which *Homo sapiens* are only one. This therefore disproves Augustine's belief that all humans were descended from and seminally present in the first humans described in Genesis, Adam and Eve, so the consequence of original sin affecting all humankind cannot be justified.

- Geological evidence supports the view that the world was initially a place of chaos which only became suitable for life to inhabit after a long period of slow adjustment and change. This undermines the idea of a perfect world suddenly becoming corrupted.

Know Criticisms of Irenaean-Type Theodicies

Unscientific

- The theory of evolution describes how the human species evolved from primates, who in turn evolved from other animals over a very long period of time. At what point were humans made in the image of God? And were all human species made in the image of God, or just *Homo sapiens*? The theodicy as it currently stands can be said to be invalid, as it does not make sense alongside scientific understanding of the world.

Universal Salvation

- The idea that everyone will enter heaven contradicts traditional Christian teaching. Therefore, many Christians reject the theodicy which relies on this belief. Judgement, heaven and hell are all clearly described in the Bible.

- The point that those who cause immense suffering will also achieve moral development and grow into the likeness of God, being received in heaven alongside their victims, does not seem just. What would be the motivation for making moral choices and developing in this life if everyone gained salvation eventually anyway? It could be said that universal salvation undermines everything the Bible and Jesus taught.

- Universal salvation can also be said to undermine genuine free will. If everyone will eventually grow into the likeness of God regardless of their moral choices, it suggests that free will to reject God and decline moral development is limited.

Evil as a Tool

- Evil as a means of soul-making contradicts Christian teaching about salvation. It places salvation in the hands of humankind and its choices rather than in the hands of God and atonement through Jesus.

- The evidential problem of evil raises the question of immense suffering. No reward or greater good could ever justify the scale of suffering experienced by some, especially given that suffering is unequally distributed, and everyone will achieve salvation in the end anyway.

- Irenaean-type theodicies can be called 'soul-breaking' rather than 'soul-making'. This idea is supported by modern scientific understanding of trauma and its effects on the brain. Surviving a traumatic event does not in fact make us stronger, but changes how our brain and body function. Surviving trauma can cause lifelong problems in those who have gone through adverse experience, especially at an early age.

- It is well documented that suffering is not distributed equally. Therefore, it seems unjust for a loving God to mould and test some people more than others. It highlights a dilemma: whether some suffering is pointless and beyond what is required, which would contradict a loving God, or whether the maldistribution is intentional, which challenges the notion of a loving God even more. This has become a poignant topic. In *Is God a White Racist? A Preamble to Black Theology* (1973), William Jones writes that evil and suffering have, on the whole, been confined to a specific minority ethnic group, which raises the question of divine racism.

- It can be argued that epistemic distance does not successfully account for pointless suffering as a result of natural evils. For example, what opportunity for second-order goods did the sudden eruption of Vesuvius offer the citizens of Pompeii? There was no opportunity for a charitable response from others as the city became blanketed in volcanic matter so quickly, and little opportunity for virtues such as courage to develop due to the poisonous gases that were released, which killed the citizens in a relatively short space of time.

- It can be questioned why animals suffer if, in accordance with Christian teaching, they do not have souls that can morally develop. Hick's response that animal suffering can serve as an opportunity to develop second-order goods in humans seems unjust, especially given how many animals suffer and die without humans being aware – for example, in natural disasters.

Watch Out for Traps
Augustinian-Type Theodicies

Don't just rule out Augustine's ideas because of his historical reading of Genesis. Otherwise you will limit the depth of knowledge and understanding of Augustinian-type theodicies that you could demonstrate. Augustine's ideas are built on a complex system of biblical teaching, allegorical interpretation and Platonic philosophical reasoning. Augustine identified what later became known as the classic free-will defence, and influenced the Church for a millennium with his ideas. For many, he successfully defends God's existence and nature in light of the problem of evil. Augustine's theodicy should be understood in the context in which it was written, but note that some aspects can be considered compatible with scientific understanding today: for example, seminal presence and genes, and Y-chromosomal Adam and mitochondrial Eve DNA. You do not have to agree with Augustinian-type theodicies by any means, but be cautious in your criticism and show awareness of the success and value of his ideas for Christianity.

Irenaean-Type Theodicies

Don't forget the role of free will in Irenaean-type theodicies. It is easy to get carried away with the point that God deliberately created an imperfect world with natural evils in it, and forget to include that moral evil is actually down to human free will. So *both* Augustinian- and Irenaean-type theodicies involve a free-will defence. In the case of Hick's development of Irenaeus' ideas, human free will is crucial as the means by which humans can develop second-order goods or evils, and thus humankind is responsible for many of the very worst evils in the world, such as slavery and the Holocaust, but also our own moral development or lack of it. God cannot intervene because of epistemic distance and the need to uphold our genuine free will. For Hick, then, the coherence of Irenaean-type theodicies hangs on epistemic distance and human free will.

STRENGTHEN YOUR GRASP

1. Make a series of mind maps with the following at the centre: moral evil, natural evil, God's omnipotence, God's omnibenevolence. Divide the space around each heading into two. On one side note down how Augustinian-type theodicies can explain or defend each heading. On the other side, do the same for Irenaean-type theodicies. This will help ensure you can adapt your knowledge of the theodicies to the different types of questions you could be asked.

2. Using a different colour, add to the mind maps from activity 1. For each heading, note down the relevant strengths, counter-arguments and criticisms. Then make a decision: can the theodicies successfully explain or defend these headings in light of objections? On a separate sheet of paper, explain your view. This will help you to develop your analysis and evaluation skills for AO2 questions.

CREATE YOUR OWN QUESTION

Read this chapter and use command words such as 'explain' or 'examine' to create your own AO1 questions. For an AO2 question, make a one-sided statement about the success of Irenaean- or Augustinian-type theodicies, put the statement between quotation marks and follow it with the phrase, 'Evaluate this view.'

Exam Guidance for Augustinian-type Theodicies AO1

When answering a part a) knowledge and understanding question, it is important to tailor your knowledge to the exact question being asked. In your revision, read back over the 'Know Key Ideas' and 'Understand Arguments' sections in this chapter, and ensure you can explain *how* Augustinian-type theodicies can respond to the problem of evil, try to defend the characteristics of the God of classical theism, and try to explain and justify natural and moral evil, and the general objections and challenges to them. Depending on the depth required for the question, it could be helpful to use examples to illustrate your points.

Exam Guidance for Augustinian-type Theodicies AO2

Issues for analysis and evaluation will be drawn from any aspect of the specification, which could include:

1. Whether Augustinian-type theodicies are relevant in the twenty-first century.

2. The extent to which Augustine's theodicy succeeds as a defence of the God of classical theism.

For 1, it would be important to link your evaluation to the question context of the twenty-first century. Don't just evaluate Augustinian-type theodicies generally. It would be worthwhile to read back over the 'Know Criticisms of Augustinian-type Theodicies' section and make a note of criticisms relevant to the twenty-first century, such as scientific, geological and anthropological evidence, and use examples of immense suffering that have occurred within recent history. However, it is also worth remembering that the logical issues with Augustinian theodicies are timeless and so could be relevant, but this depends on how well you think they point to the twenty-first century. The success of logical issues depends on the beliefs held about God and creation. For example, many twenty-first century believers, such as Swinburne, believe that God's omnipotence *is* limited to what is logically possible, therefore undermining the criticism that an omnipotent God should have been able to create humans with the character always to do good.

With 2, remember that for an AO2 question you should *not* explain the theodicy or how it works. Instead, it could be beneficial to approach a question like this thematically, analysing and evaluating how successfully Augustinian-type theodicies try to defend each characteristic of the God of classical theism in light of evil and suffering, in turn. It could be helpful to read over Chapter 13, which refers to Mackie's inconsistent triad, noting down how Augustinian-type theodicies can potentially overcome his challenge and justify each of God's attributes, and why these may be successful or not. Other more general strengths or weaknesses of Augustinian-type theodicies could also be relevant if you can link them to a point regarding the defence of a characteristic of God. For example, seminal presence and punishing humans for the sins of their ancestors is not necessarily in keeping with the concept of God as all-loving.

Exam Guidance for Irenaean-type Theodicies AO1

When answering a part a) knowledge and understanding question, it is important to tailor your knowledge to the exact question being asked. In your revision, read back over the 'Know Key Ideas' and 'Understand Arguments' sections in this chapter, and ensure you can explain *how* Irenaean-type theodicies can respond to the problem of evil, try to defend the characteristics of the God of classical theism, try to explain and justify natural and moral evil, and the general objections and challenges to them. Depending on the depth required for the question, it would be helpful to use examples to illustrate your points.

Exam Guidance for Irenaean-type Theodicies AO2

Issues for analysis and evaluation will be drawn from any aspect of the specification, which could include:

1. Whether Irenaean-type theodicies are credible in the twenty-first century.

2. The extent to which Irenaeus' theodicy succeeds as a defence of the God of classical theism.

For 1, it is important to link your evaluation to the question context of the twenty-first century rather than just evaluating Irenaean-type theodicies generally. It would be worthwhile to read back over the 'Know Criticisms of Irenaean-type Theodicies' section and make a note of criticisms relevant to the twenty-first century, such as the theory of evolution, the injustice of disproportionate and potentially racially motivated suffering, the evidence for pointless animal suffering, and the evidence that trauma is 'soul-breaking' rather than 'soul-making'. Consider whether you think Irenaean-type theodicies can successfully overcome each of these or not, and why. However, as many Christians in the twenty-first century also adhere to the traditional teachings, it could also be relevant to refer to the ways that Irenaean-type theodicies differ from traditional teaching, such as undermining the role of God's grace and atonement through Jesus Christ. It could be worth arguing that other theodicies are more credible in the twenty-first century.

With 2, remember that for an AO2 question you should *not* explain the theodicy or how it works, as that would be demonstrating AO1 knowledge and understanding and waste valuable time. Instead, focus on demonstrating evaluation and analysis skills. For example, it could be beneficial to approach this question thematically, weighing up how successful Irenaean-type theodicies are in trying to defend each characteristic of the God of classical theism in light of evil and suffering in turn. It could be helpful to read over Chapter 13, which refers to Mackie's inconsistent triad, noting down how Irenaean-type theodicies can potentially overcome his challenge and justify each of God's attributes, and why these may be successful, or not. Other more general strengths or weaknesses of Irenaean-type theodicies could also be relevant if you can link them to a point regarding the defence of a characteristic of God. For example, universal salvation can potentially contradict the notion of an omnibenevolent God, as it doesn't seem particularly just to victims if the people who chose to harm them also ultimately receive the same salvation as they do.

Evaluating Hick, Augustine and Irenaeus Today

In an exam, you could be asked to evaluate the adequacy/success of religious responses to the problem of evil generally, or Augustinian- and Irenaean-type theodicies and their ideas specifically, as stated in the Board's specification. You can draw upon this section for ideas as you prepare, but note that the arguments cannot be addressed here in detail. You will be required to reach a judgement on the views that you present, but you do not need to reach the same conclusions as these reflections.

Regardless of whether you disagree with Augustinian-type theodicies today due to lack of scientific evidence and issues of invalidity, the fact is that they were considered highly successful and influential within the Church and Christian thought for over a millennium. If a believer holds the same beliefs about the nature of God and humankind as Augustine did, then Augustinian-type theodicies make the logical problem of evil redundant, explain both moral and natural evil in the world, and defend the characteristics of a wholly good and powerful God. However, to hold the beliefs required to make this theodicy successful in the twenty-first century is a big ask, and many believers today feel that the theodicy fails. While the free-will defence on the whole is considered by many to be a plausible defence of moral evil, Augustine's reliance on Genesis to account for natural evil causes insurmountable problems, especially now we have evidence to contradict any historical accuracy, and textual analysis of the Bible texts to question the reliability of any allegorical relevance. Additionally, society and Christian thought more generally have moved away from Augustinian pessimism regarding humankind and predestination, instead embracing more soul-making ideas than soul-breaking. Hence, there is renewed interest in more Irenaean-type theodicies in recent decades.

With regard to Irenaean-type theodicies, they are considered by some to be more successful than Augustinian-type theodicies in responding to the problem of evil, explaining moral and natural evil, and defending the God of classical theism. The soul-making outlook speaks to a more optimistic Christian perspective, seeking to understand the purpose of suffering and its widespread prevalence in a way that can empower and inspire humans to make the most of opportunities, be resilient, and develop themselves to have the best moral character they can. However, recent scientific discoveries concerning the extent of species extinction, animal suffering and immense moral injustices that are highly unequally distributed, such as slavery and genocide, call into question whether such evil and suffering can ever be worth the greater good, and whether God really is justified in permitting this experience. The fact that Irenaean-type theodicies do hold God directly responsible for natural evil means that, for some, these ideas cannot be considered as a theodicy at all, as the point of a theodicy would be to defend God against the accusation of not being omnibenevolent. The explanation of natural evil as a feature required to uphold epistemic distance and provide opportunity for a second-order good can further be challenged with the evidence of natural disasters that caused mass suffering for species which existed prior to humans, such as the extinction event and the dinosaurs. Humans did not then exist, so for what purpose did these animals suffer?

It is apparent that the logical and evidential problems of evil remain quite a challenge to Augustinian- and Irenaean-type theodicies, as presented by Hick. The success of these theodicies remains subjective and depends entirely on the religious beliefs and understanding of creation, God and humankind held by believers. As for the atheist, it is, as Mackie said, no problem.

17. SIGMUND FREUD
GET INTO FREUD'S WORLD

> **Quick Overview** Sigmund Freud (1856–1939) was the founder of psychoanalysis and radically changed how people viewed the workings of the human mind. Within the field of philosophy, he developed several theories of how religion and God are of human design, and a method of exerting some control over the universe as well as our own inner conflicts.

Sigmund Freud was writing in Vienna, a cosmopolitan city that, at the time, had flourished as the capital of the Austro-Hungarian Empire. He was acutely aware of the developments in scientific thought that came from Charles Darwin's theory of evolution and had also translated the works of philosophers and ethicists such as John Stuart Mill. Early twentieth-century Vienna was a hub for many significant thinkers of the time, who were standing on the verge of great discoveries about humankind and the natural world, making the city a melting pot for new ideas.

INSIGHT

Freud found that through talking about memories, desires and fears, the mental health of his patients improved.

At the end of the nineteenth century, Vienna found its wealth decreasing and Freud himself saw his own father go from a wealthy and influential position to an impoverished one. Viennese society withdrew into strict codes of social conduct, particularly around attitudes towards sex and sexuality. Many people felt judged by their peers and family regarding what Freud saw as natural sexual desires, and this caused people to repress their thoughts, feelings and 'shameful' memories.

Freud witnessed evidence in his patients that religious belief could, on the one hand, contribute to them feeling that their memories and thoughts were shameful, as the religion did not allow them. This meant that believers would repress and push these thoughts into their subconscious. On the other hand, religion offered a solution for these negative feelings, as it provided mechanisms to help people deal with guilt and find forgiveness from 'God'. In Freud's view, the religious mechanisms were really enabling the patients to forgive themselves. In this way, religion was both the cause of and the solution to these negative, guilty feelings.

While Freud's theories of the mind have been widely discredited and criticised in the development of psychoanalysis, many of his ideas around the human need for religion and a God-like figure are still influential. It is undeniable that a belief in God gives people comfort and a way to manage their desires in a socially acceptable way. What is debatable, however, is whether we have created this idea of God ourselves, or whether God is an objective, external reality that exists beyond our minds.

Know Freud's Key Ideas

IMPROVE YOUR UNDERSTANDING

Make sure that you know what Freud means by calling religion 'an illusion', and how this links with wish fulfilment.

The Tripartite Mind

Freud stated that there are three specific elements of the mind that together make up our personalities: the Id, the Ego, and the Super Ego. Not unlike Plato's understanding of the soul, with the charioteer steering two horses, the Ego must manage the urges of the Id and the expectations of the Super Ego to guide us successfully through life. The Id represents our most basic and natural wants and desires. This is most clearly seen in babies who impatiently scream for what they want and need without consideration for others. Concern for what is right in our society is provided by the Super Ego; this has internalised rewards and punishments that have been given to us (primarily by our parents) as we grow up. As Freud explains, 'Where the Id is there shall Ego be.' The Ego, therefore, has a difficult job of balancing the needs of the Id with the expectations of the Super Ego. For Freud, the conscience is part of this process, and this is where the idea of God, as an exalted father figure, fits in – watching and judging our every thought and action.

INSIGHT

The ancient philosopher Plato described the soul as having three parts: reason, appetites and *thumos* ('spiritedness').

INSIGHT

Mental stress and neuroses stem from the conflict within our mind between what we want (the Id) and what we think society expects of us (the Super Ego).

The Ego must manage these conflicting positions. At times it can be overwhelmed by the battle between them.

Religion as a Product of the Human Mind

Freud's view of the human mind is often illustrated in the form of an iceberg. The top of an iceberg can be seen above the water, but the majority of the iceberg is submerged under water. In the same way, the human mind has some elements that we are aware of, can think about and know, but most of the mind is hidden and unknown.

The conscious mind is like the tip of the iceberg, representing our immediate thoughts and awareness. The unconscious mind, on the other hand, is like the submerged part of the iceberg, containing hidden desires, memories and emotions that influence our behaviour without us being aware of them. We push, or repress, the thoughts, feelings and memories we are most ashamed of into our unconscious mind. While we are no longer aware of them, they continue to have a great influence on us.

INSIGHT

For Freud, religion is a symptom of a battle between attempting to control our desires and dealing with the guilt that comes from having them. It is not an 'illness' in itself but a symptom of the collective illness (neurosis) about the guilt and shame we feel.

Religion plays a role in what we deem as acceptable memories, thoughts and desires, and in what is therefore repressed into the unconscious mind. Religion and the idea of God are not real but imagined, and are used as a tool of the mind to perform certain functions for us. In Freud's view, religion is a mechanism that we have created to enable us to judge what is or is not acceptable in society. Religion's many rituals can help us to cope with the effects of our repressed and shameful emotions.

> **INSIGHT**
>
> For Freud, while religion and the idea of God have a great influence on our minds, they are not an external or objective reality. In this respect, Freud differed from his contemporary, Carl Jung (see Chapter 18).

Religion as Wish Fulfilment

Freud's view on religion can be summarised in his claim that it is 'mere illusion derived from human wishes'. Freud argues that religion, like a wish, is simply something we desperately want to be true – so desperately, in fact, that we put rationality and critical thinking to one side. However, calling something an illusion does not mean that it cannot ever be true; it just means we really want it to be true. For example, many people may dream of going to space, or winning the lottery. While this may not happen for the majority of people, it will for some.

Religion is a reaction against our feelings of helplessness. We fear death and the elements of nature as well as our own lack of control of our unconscious mind. An omnipotent God has the power to control those things that we fear we cannot, and so helps us against feelings of helplessness. God fulfils our wish for there to be some order, control and sense in the universe.

Religion can also fulfil wishes for us in other ways. For example, humans have ultimate questions that religion can answer. What happens when we die? What is the purpose of life in the first place? How can we manage the conflict between what we want and what we think we should have? By attempting to answer these questions, religion comforts us, much like a child will be comforted by a parent. As Freud states: 'It would be very nice if there were a God who created the world and was a benevolent providence, and if there were a moral order in the universe and an afterlife.'

> **INSIGHT**
>
> According to Freud, illusions are not necessarily false. What matters is that people desperately want them to be true. Therefore, the truth or falsity of the belief does not actually matter.

> **INSIGHT**
>
> While Freud viewed religion as an illusion, he also recognised that religion performs a function for society in protecting the weak from the strong: for example, with rules such as 'Do not kill'.

Freud believed that religion keeps believers in an infantile state of mind.

Understand Freud's Arguments
The Primal Horde

In 1913, Freud published his first book, *Totem and Taboo*, which explored the origin of religion through anthropological studies of cultures that practised ancient forms of religion and Totemism. In Totemistic religious practice, the Totem animal is worshipped and feared; it is a power that controls the lives of the community. Freud believed that this idolisation echoed the admiration and fear that primates felt towards the alpha male in their pack. Building on Darwin's theory of the primal horde, Freud hypothesised that, just as the young males of a family of large primates must kill their father to have sexual access to the women of the group, so early humans might have acted similarly within a primal horde.

In a Totemistic religion, the followers are often recorded as killing and consuming the animal they worshipped, in order to consume the power that they believe the animal has over their lives. Freud suggests that the guilt from this action is carried through to future generations. For Freud, the Christian rite of The Eucharist is an echo of this terrible act from the primordial horde – by symbolically consuming the body of Christ, believers are able to access the power that God has over them.

> **INSIGHT**
>
> 'Religion('s) ... doctrines carry with them the stamp of the times in which they originated' (Freud in *Moses and Monotheism*, 1938).

> **ESSENTIAL!**
>
> The primal horde was the earliest stage of human civilisation, in which one older male had access to all the females. He was then murdered and eaten by his sons, the young males, in order to gain access to the females.

> **TIP**
>
> Remember that Freud built on Darwin's theory of evolution in order to develop his theory of religion. In particular, the theory of the primal horde was first proposed by Darwin.

The Oedipus Complex

In later works, such as *The Future of an Illusion* (1927), Freud links religion to his most famous theory, the Oedipus complex. Oedipus is a figure in Greek mythology who killed his father and married his mother. Freud uses a case study of one of his patients ('Little Hans') to support his theory that male children have a forbidden and incestuous desire for their mothers. This leads to repression of those desires, a sense of guilt and a rivalry with the father of the family. He links this back to the theory of the primal horde.

Freud also put forward an equivalent for female children – the Electra complex – where girls have a desire for their fathers and a conflict with their mothers. For the genetic success of a community, incest must be a great taboo. In fact, in some societies Freud studied, it was the only taboo, necessary to ensure the continuation of the community.

Religion as a Collective Neurosis

For Freud, we are not aware that we have even had or thought of such feelings as the Oedipus or Electra complex, but religion manifests as a way for us to deal with, and control, these unwanted remnants in our psyche. According to Freud, religion is the symptom of the disease, rather than the cause or the disease itself. When we feel helpless in the face of natural forces that seem to control our lives, it is comforting to believe that there is an omnipotent, omnibenevolent God who will protect and care for us. In the same way, we are helpless in the face of the internal turbulence caused by the desires we have, but know that we should not have. Religion manifests again as a way to control these desires and help cleanse us from this 'sin'.

> **INSIGHT**
>
> Freud's patient 'Little Hans' was a small boy who had developed a fear of horses. Freud interpreted this fear as a manifestation of unresolved psychological conflicts related to his Oedipus complex and unconscious desires.

> **INSIGHT**
>
> Freud understood religion to be a collective neurosis. It is similar to individual neurosis, which is a mental illness, but it is something held across cultures and times as a symptom of our inability to deal with the guilt and feelings associated with the Oedipus complex.

> **WHAT DO YOU THINK?**
>
> Write down your thoughts on Freud's arguments and revisit them shortly before the exam to see if your views have changed.

TASK

Read Freud for yourself in the extract below. The notes in the margin will help you to grasp his views.

Read Freud for Yourself

In this passage from *The Future of an Illusion* (1927), Freud explains how religion fulfils our wishes for protection and comfort in a world over which we have little control.

> A term used when someone has love and hatred towards the same object, at the same time.
>
> Freud sees all religions as having the same root, as all of humanity stems from the primal horde. Therefore, all manifestations of religion have similar patterns relating to guilt and its removal.
>
> The anthropomorphic study of Totemistic religions in which Freud saw the ceremonial killing and consumption of the totem animal as the earliest form of religion.
>
> Just as a child looks to their parents to protect them, so religion keeps humans in a child-like state as they look to 'God' to save them from danger.
>
> To gain the favour of a God or gods by doing something that pleases them.
>
> Freud believed that religion keeps believers in a childish state, and he hoped for a world where humanity would progress beyond needing this 'illusion'.

In this function [of protection] the mother is soon replaced by the stronger father, who retains that position for the rest of childhood. But the child's attitude to its father is coloured by a peculiar ambivalence. The father himself constitutes a danger for the child, perhaps because of its earlier relation to its mother. Thus, it fears him no less than it longs for him and admires him. The indications of this ambivalence in the attitude to the father are deeply imprinted in every religion, as was shown in *Totem and Taboo*. When the growing individual finds that he is destined to remain a child for ever, that he can never do without protection against strange superior powers, he lends those powers the features belonging to the figure of his father; he creates for himself the gods whom he dreads, whom he seeks to propitiate, and whom he nevertheless entrusts with his own protection. Thus, his longing for a father is a motive identical with his need for protection against the consequences of his human weakness. The defence against childish helplessness is what lends its characteristic features to the adult's reaction to the helplessness which he has to acknowledge – a reaction which is precisely the formation of religion.

EVALUATION SKILLS

An answer to an evaluative question about a scholar is always deepened by demonstrating awareness of how other thinkers have disagreed.

Know Criticisms of Freud

Religion is a positive force. Freud struck up a professional friendship with Carl Jung, a contemporary Swiss psychiatrist, who he hoped would be his heir as the leading thinker of psychoanalysis. They agreed on many things while Jung developed his own analytic psychology. However, their thinking differed on the subject of the usefulness and necessity of religion for the human mind. This difference in views caused a rift to grow between them. While Freud viewed religion as an unnecessary illusion, Jung believed it was essential in helping humanity find harmony and balance. Jung's theory of religion is covered in more detail in Chapter 18, but his main criticism of Freud is that religion is a positive force for individuals and necessary for their personal growth, not something that needs to be removed in order for humanity to flourish fully.

Criticism of the Oedipus complex. Much of Freud's theorising in the realms of psychology and religion is based on his theory of the Oedipus complex. For this theory, he only provides one piece of evidence, that of the case study of 'Little Hans' – the rest remains simply a theory. The theory also only really applies to religions with a male deity (for example, the Judeo-Christian God), so it is not applicable to all religions. The Polish-British sociologist Bronislaw Malinowski criticises Freud's view of the Oedipus complex through the evidence that the family is not the same in all societies – for example, in matrilineal families the father has nothing to do with the upbringing of the children.

Lack of evidence. By their very nature Freud's theories of the mind, the primal horde, the Oedipus complex and religion in general are not empirically verifiable. As English philosopher Michael Palmer wrote: 'Almost all of the evidence that Freud presented has been discredited in some way or another' (*Freud and Jung on Religion*, 1997). The theory of the primal horde is based on the ideas of Darwin and Freud and we do not have physical evidence of this happening, nor that it was the only type of primitive society. Not all tribes had totem animals, for example, and very little evidence is put forward to support the Oedipus complex.

Watch Out for Traps

Not all religious believers dispute Freud's views. While Freud's view of religion seems negative, it is not rejected by all believers. John Hick (see Chapter 16) welcomes some of Freud's ideas, particularly the idea of God being a father figure as a way for us to understand more about how God has revealed himself to humankind, as well as how we are comforted and supported by that idea. In addition, religious concepts such as the fall of man and original sin could be seen to support the idea that we have an inner conflict between what we want to do and what we should do, and that we reach out to religion to help us control this conflict.

Freud's views are generally not still supported in psychology. While the impact that Freud as the father of psychoanalysis had on the understanding of the human mind cannot be overstated, many of his theories, particularly those around children and the Oedipus complex, have been rejected due to the lack of empirical evidence.

Don't confuse the ideas of Freud and Jung. Freud and Jung both saw religion as a construct of the human mind. Jung, however, viewed this as a positive force for society and necessary for personal growth. For Freud, religion should be removed for humanity to mature. Both thinkers saw the mind as having several parts, but for Freud we have a personal unconscious along with our Ego, whereas for Jung there is a collective unconscious that all of humanity shares.

> **INSIGHT**
>
> Freud saw his views as more scientifically valid than those of Jung. However, key thinkers such as Richard Dawkins debate the methods by which Freud reached his conclusions. While Dawkins accepts psychoanalysis as an important scientific endeavour, he views Freud's theories as based too much on subjective interpretations to be empirically viable.

STRENGTHEN YOUR GRASP

1. Close your books and notes and create a mind map of the following ideas of Freud on religion: religion as an illusion; the primal horde; the Oedipus complex; and religion as a collective neurosis. Explain how each point relates to the mind and religion. Now open your books and notes and add any extra information and examples in a different colour to remind you to revise this more thoroughly. This will help you with AO1 questions that focus on Freud's view of religion.

2. Create a table showing the strengths and weaknesses of Freud's explanation of religious belief. Use the 'Understanding Freud's Arguments' and 'Know Criticisms of Freud' sections for ideas. Which side of the table do you find the more convincing? Considering the points you have on each side of the table, write a paragraph explaining how adequate you find his explanation of religious belief to be. This will strengthen your AO2 answers relating to Freud's critique of religion.

> **CREATE YOUR OWN QUESTION**
>
> Read this chapter and use command words such as 'examine', 'explain' or 'compare' to create your own AO1 question. For an AO2 question, make a one-sided statement about Freud's views, put the statement between quotation marks and follow it with the phrase, 'Evaluate this view.'

Exam Guidance AO1

There are four main areas that you could be asked about in exam questions to demonstrate your knowledge and understanding of Freud's theory on religion. These are all related to his view that religion is a neurosis stemming from human needs and desires:

1. religion as an illusion
2. religion as a collective neurosis
3. the link between the primal horde and religions today
4. the link between the Oedipus complex and religion.

Use the 'Know Freud's Key Ideas' and 'Understand Freud's Arguments' sections in this chapter to make notes on each of these four aspects of his theory. Take a quote from the 'Read Freud for Yourself' section and show how this relates to the different aspects of his theory. You may also be asked to outline some of the strengths and weaknesses of his theory, without making your own personal judgement, as part of an AO1 question. Questions may also be more general, concerning the relationship between psychology and religion, so making comparative notes between Freud's theory and Jung's theory will be useful.

Exam Guidance AO2

You may be asked an evaluative question specific to Freud and his theories, but you may also be asked about how Freud's and Jung's views on religion compare, or perhaps even more generally about the relationship between psychology and religion. Strengths of Freud's theory include his appeal to empirical evidence and how religion acts as a crutch for those who fear death or feel hopeless in the face of the natural elements. He builds on the ideas of previous thinkers, such as Darwin and the theory of evolution. The 'Know Criticisms of Freud' section will help you with the weaknesses of his theory, and you may be asked to assess how successful those criticisms are.

18. CARL JUNG
GET INTO JUNG'S WORLD

> **Quick Overview** Carl Gustav Jung (1875–1961) was a Swiss psychiatrist and psychoanalyst who, like Freud, believed that religion is a creation of our minds. However, unlike Freud, he believed that religious belief is helpful and indeed necessary for personal growth.

During his upbringing, Carl Jung experienced various events that would later shape his interest in both psychoanalysis and religion, and the broader spiritual life of humans. After considering becoming a pastor or an archaeologist, Jung settled on studying medicine at the University of Basel. During his studies he became particularly interested in the new field of psychiatry that was just emerging in Europe.

Psychiatry allowed for discussions around the importance of balance, spirituality and life experiences, while helping people who suffered from mental health conditions (as Jung had witnessed first-hand with his own mother). Like his contemporary, Freud, Jung found that religion and spirituality were significant to many of his patients. Unlike Freud, however, he did not see this as an issue to be resolved or removed, but rather as something which could be utilised to make the person whole and balanced once more.

Freud saw Jung as his heir as the father of psychology, and they corresponded for some time. However, disagreements over their theories of the mind eventually led to their separation: Jung felt that Freud's theory was grounded in empiricism, while Freud thought Jung was too accepting and respecting of a spiritual realm. Jung viewed religion as a necessary part of the human experience, whereas Freud believed there was no need for this 'illusion'. For Jung, the objective existence of God did not matter as much as the process of **individuation**, where we achieve balance and harmony within ourselves. When pressed on the question of God's existence, Jung famously said, 'I don't believe there is a God – I know.'

ESSENTIAL!

Individuation is the process by which a person balances their Ego and personal unconscious with the collective unconscious, and the Self is actualised (balance and harmony within the person are realised). This involves becoming more aware of and balancing the opposing forces within oneself, and achieving psychological wholeness.

INSIGHT

Jung described individuation as 'the wearisome but indispensable business of coming to terms with the unconscious components of the personality' ('On the Nature of the Psyche', 1954).

INSIGHT

'I think that the friendliness of Jung presents a far more serious and radical challenge to religion as we know it than ever did the hostility of Freud' (Father Victor White, an English priest who collaborated with Jung).

INSIGHT

Freud viewed religion and religious belief as illusion – something that we want so desperately to be true that we believe it is, regardless of the evidence. In contrast, Jung viewed religion as a necessary part of life. To lead a full and harmonious life, an individual needed to access the religious dimension rather than deny it.

Know Jung's Key Ideas
Collective Unconscious

For Jung, the mind is made of three parts:

- the Ego – what we are aware of
- our conscious mind
- the unconscious.

In contrast to Freud's view, however, Jung believed there is a deeper and greater unconscious surrounding our own individual unconsciousness. In his 1916 essay 'The Structure of the Unconscious', Jung set out his theory that the collective unconscious is shared across all of humanity. Jung believed this could be evidenced through anthropology, archaeology and all disciplines that study human behaviour. As humans, we have the same themes, thoughts and stories repeating themselves throughout time and, for Jung, this was proof that we have a kind of shared soul as part of the legacy of evolution, which he named the collective unconscious. Neither benevolent nor malevolent, the collective unconscious can terrify the individual as well as heal them. For Jung, the collective unconscious is the source of all religion.

> **ESSENTIAL!**
>
> The Ego is the part of the human personality that is experienced as 'me' or 'I' – we are conscious and aware of it.

> **ESSENTIAL!**
>
> The collective unconscious (the part of the deep unconscious mind that is genetically inherited and not created by life experience) is an imprint left on the human psyche as a result of our shared evolution. It contains the archetypes, such as the Persona, the Shadow, the Anima/Animus, and the Self (see page 143 for more examples).

> **INSIGHT**
>
> Jung believed that personal unconscious comprises 'all the acquisitions of personal life, everything forgotten, repressed, subliminally perceived, thought, [and] felt' (Jung, 'Definitions', 1976).

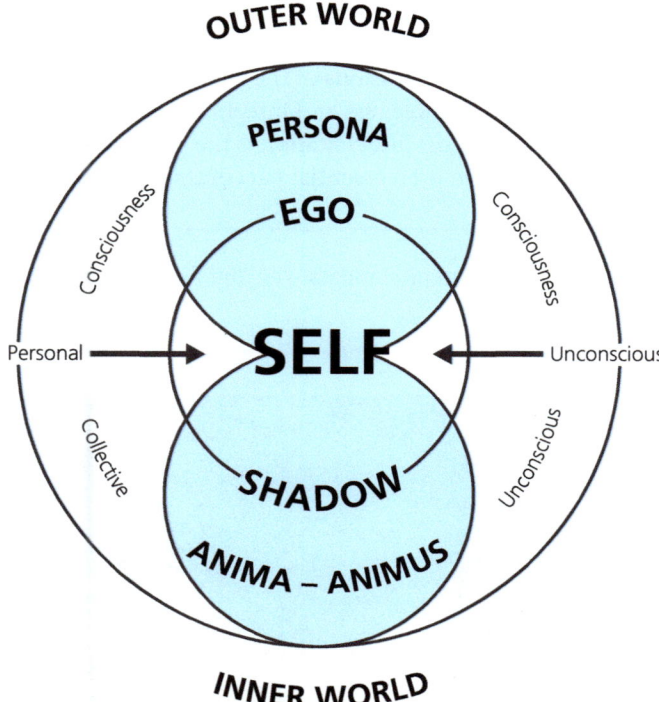

Jung's model of the psyche

> **INSIGHT**
>
> Jung on the collective unconscious: 'there is good reason for supposing that the archetypes are the unconscious images of the instincts themselves, in other words, that they are patterns of instinctual behaviour' (*The Archetypes and the Collective Unconscious*, 1969).

> **ESSENTIAL!**
>
> **Archetypes** are patterns, stories and symbols that are seen and understood by people across time and cultures as a consequence of the collective unconscious.

> **INSIGHT**
>
> Immanuel Kant (see Chapter 11) developed an understanding of reality that distinguished between what we can see and experience in the world around us, the phenomena, and the 'things in themselves', the noumena. We cannot access the noumena directly, as we only access the phenomena around us. This influenced Jung's view of the archetypes, which we cannot access in themselves but only through our experiences of the world around us.

> **ESSENTIAL!**
>
> **Mandala** is the Sanskrit word for 'circle'. Mandalas are geometric designs used especially in Hindu and Buddhist cultures. Jung saw these as a tool for emotional healing and the process of individuation.

> **INSIGHT**
>
> Jung on the God Within: 'The way is within us, but not in Gods, nor in teachings, nor in laws. Within us is the way, the truth, and the life' (*Liber Novus*, published as *The Red Book*, 2009).

The Archetypes

Within the collective unconscious are the archetypes, which are universally recognised patterns of life and thought that are understood regardless of the era, culture or language of the individual. Influenced by the Kantian understanding of the realms of the noumena and phenomena (see Chapter 11), Jung explains that we cannot experience the archetypes directly, but that we encounter them through experiences in our own lives. The themes between these encounters are similar enough to understand that there is a common archetype being accessed through these experiences. We can see that archetypes exist as common storylines, characters and personality types, manifesting in varying ways across cultures. Jung refers to these as 'imprints' on the human mind, as a legacy of evolution that lies beyond the human chronology; it is a blueprint for the mind just as natural selection is a blueprint for the body.

To illustrate this point, we can consider the kind of stories that families may have told one another round the fire thousands of years ago, of some great hero who saved their people from a terrible ordeal. This is different, of course, to families in the present day going together to see the latest superhero film at the cinema, but in many ways the themes of the story will be the same.

Individuation and the God Within

According to Jung, we can achieve good mental health through the process of individuation. This is when we balance our conscious mind (Ego) with the unconscious, both personal and collective. Religious ideas and expressions of the God Within archetype show this balance through symbols of wholeness and integration, such as mandalas, rangoli patterns and Celtic cross designs. Individuation is the process by which we become our own self. For Jung, religion is an essential part of this process.

> **INSIGHT**
>
> The Self archetype is often shown as a circle, square or mandala. The Self manifests as a result of the process of individuation.

This is a Tibetan Buddhist monk creating a sand mandala, a shape which represents the universe. The image is temporary and its creation and destruction form an important ritual in the tradition.

Understand Jung's Arguments

IMPROVE YOUR UNDERSTANDING

Make sure that you know why Jung thought religion was beneficial for individuals and society.

The Archetypes and Individuation

We can never know the exact number of archetypes (Jung gives 12 as examples but states that there may be more) or the precise delineation between them, but there are common archetypes that we can see throughout religions, cultures and artistic expressions. Some examples are listed below:

The Archetype	Explanation
The Mask	The persona or person we wish the world to see – what we think is respectable and proper in a given situation.
The Shadow	The side we do not want the world to see – the things we are ashamed of, the memories we would rather not have, and the desires we think are not acceptable.
The Hero	The deep desire to make the world a better place, often shown by strength and overcoming adversity.
The Anima/Animus	For Jung there are two distinct genders but within men there is a feminine side (anima), and within women there is a masculine side (animus).
The God Within	This is expressed through religious and spiritual ideas and beings, and represents the desire and drive within us to become better and more whole.
The Self	What we can achieve through individuation when our conscious and unconscious mind are in balance.

Religion and God Have a Psychological Explanation

According to Jung, religion is an essential part of the human psyche; it is necessary for the process of individuation and is beneficial to humankind. Religion for Jung represents humankind's yearning for meaning in life, purpose, direction and help. Jung's theory takes into consideration any expressions of religion – in fact, he acknowledges atheism as a form of religion. While religion is a product of the human mind, this does not mean either that there is or is not an objective reality of God or gods. Jung did not see the purpose of psychology to show whether there is or is not a God, and indeed if there is a God, which version of God is real. Jung is not particularly interested in 'proving' that either way. What he does state is that religion is a source of comfort, and a positive force for humanity, in contrast to his contemporary, Freud.

TIP

Remember that Jung, in contrast to Freud, viewed religion as a positive force, for both individuals and society as a whole. It should not be withdrawn from people but encouraged.

ESSENTIAL!

The Mask, or persona, is the version of ourselves we present to the world, 'designed … to make a definite impression on others and … to conceal the true nature of the individual' (Jung, *Two Essays on Analytical Psychology*, 1953).

The Shadow contains the desires, weaknesses and instincts that we think are unacceptable to society – these are often related to ideas around sex.

The Hero is an important archetype who saves society against the odds, through acts of extraordinary strength and self-sacrifice.

INSIGHT

Step 2 of the 12-step Alcoholics Anonymous programme uses Jung's ideas of needing a 'power greater than yourself' to find the strength to recover from addictive behaviours.

The Importance of Religion for Mental Health

For Jung, while the Self is related to religious ideas, it is in no way intended to replace God. Jung's patients were suffering from great mental distress and often found that religious ideas and rituals were a way of coping with this anguish. Drawing on a strength beyond the individual could bring them back to balance. A modern example of this is the number of people who embark on the 12-step programme for addiction; they rely upon a 'greater power' to be able to do this. For Jung, it is important to remember that this strength is drawn from integration and interaction with the collective unconscious rather than just from the individual. Between the ages of 39 and 45, Jung himself suffered a series of intense crises, including the loss of his father, the loss of his friendship with Freud, and a world seemingly on the brink of collapse due to war. He resigned his teaching post at the University of Zurich and travelled the world, researching different expressions of religion. He found that mandalas that appear across numerous cultures and eras helped him to integrate with the collective unconscious and find balance once more.

WHAT DO YOU THINK?

Write down your thoughts on Jung's arguments and revisit them shortly before the exam to see if your views have changed.

Read Jung for Yourself

This passage is taken from Jung's *Memories, Dreams and Reflections* (1961). The notes in the margin will help you to grasp his ideas.

Religion is a psychological construct; the idea of God has some impact on us but it is from within the psyche. >	It is only through the psyche that we can establish that God acts upon us, but we are unable to distinguish whether these actions emanate from God or from the unconscious. Strictly speaking, the God-image does not coincide with the unconscious as such, but with a special content of it – the Self. It is this archetype from which we can no longer distinguish the God-image empirically … The religious need longs for wholeness, and therefore lays hold of the images of wholeness offered by the unconscious, which, independently of our conscious mind, rise up from the depths of our psychic nature.
We cannot see objectively if there is a God or not, and if so, which understanding of God, from which religion. >	
The Self archetype is intertwined with the God Within. Jung did not say that the Self and the God Within are the same thing, but that the Self is an expression or image of the God Within. >	
The process of individuation is how we can achieve wholeness. Religion can play a large part in this and is why many people turn to it for help. >	
For Jung, it is not just our own individual unconscious that is important, but a deeper, collective unconscious. >	

Know Criticisms of Jung

Lack of evidence. Jung's views are often challenged for not being empirically proven. They are not able to be tested and verified through observation or experience. His views are often accused of being vague and lacking in any scientific basis. The archetypes and collective unconscious by definition cannot be observed, which makes them hard to prove or disprove. This was a point of disagreement between Jung and Freud; Freud was aiming to present psychoanalysis to the world as a science, while Jung was taking his analytic psychology down a more mystical route. Jung based a large amount of his theory on his personal experiences and thoughts, along with those of his patients, but it can be argued that this is not enough to base a whole theory of humankind upon.

Cultural explanations. Jung's evidence that themes and images occur across time and cultures could be explained through human experiences being similar – the stories, dreams and images have similarities. This does not mean that there is some greater collective unconscious, but that individuals have similar life experiences, leading to similarities in their own individual unconscious. Take, for example, the archetype of the Hero: war, conflict and battles between wrong and right have always been part of human culture and societies. It is to be expected, therefore, that similar stories are told of heroes who save the day. This does not point to a collective unconscious but to similar experiences leading to similar stories, myths and legends.

Happy and healthy non-religious people. The fact that many people live happy and healthy lives, and feel fulfilled and whole, without religion shows that we do not need the God Within, individuation or the collective unconscious. Jung seems to have considered atheism as a form of religion and was very dismissive of negative atheist claims. For example, he stated that atheists are exhibiting a contradiction, because in saying they don't believe in 'God', they are acknowledging that there is something called 'God' for them not to believe in. This could be seen as patronising towards atheists and would not be accepted by those in the **New Atheist movement**.

Additionally, many believe that Jung's experience with patients was based solely on extreme cases of mental imbalance: for example, people suffering psychosis and personality disorders. The fact is that most people in the world do not experience these issues and manage to maintain balance and good mental health without the religious ideas Jung believes are necessary.

Watch Out for Traps

Not all religious believers support Jung's views. With such a positive take on what religion can provide for humans and society, it is easy to make the false assumption that religious believers will necessarily support Jung's views. Jung's views may allow for **religious pluralism**, but that may not be how the majority of religious believers see and understand their own religion. Jung is accused by many of having a **reductionist** view of religion, meaning that he gave non-religious causes of religious phenomena – this is something many religious believers will not accept.

Jung did not argue that the God Within proves the existence of God. Jung was not interested in proving the existence of God or any other deities. When asked later in life about the question of God's existence, he said that it was not a matter of belief but that he knew God, and that his own experience of God was enough for knowledge. Jung did not see the role of psychology as answering the question of God's existence either way; rather, he was interested in how religious ideas and symbols could help people to connect to a deeper meaning for their life in the process of individuation.

> **INSIGHT**
>
> The lack of empirical evidence for Jung's views led scholars such as the logical positivists to reject his theories on religion and the mind. For example, Rudolph Carnap, a prominent thinker in the Vienna circle, viewed Jung's theories as metaphysics which did not stand up to the scrutiny of the Verification Principle.

> **INSIGHT**
>
> 'It is an admission of God when you call yourself an atheist, because whether you assert a thing or deny it, you confirm that it is: you cannot deny a thing without giving it a certain existence' (Jung, 'Zarathustra Seminar', 1934)

> **ESSENTIAL!**
>
> The **New Atheist movement** is characterised by the view that religion and superstition should be open to criticism and challenge by rational arguments.
>
> **Religious pluralism** defines the situation where all religions are recognised as equally valid and can co-exist in society. This contrasts with religious exclusivism, where one particular religion is seen as holding the truth and the others are not.
>
> A **reductionist** view of religion is where religious experiences and teachings are explained with non-religious reasons.

> **INSIGHT**
>
> Nietzsche famously said, 'God is dead, and we have killed him'. Nietzsche, was writing after the Enlightenment, at a time when many significant challenges to the Judeo-Christian idea of God had been raised.

Don't forget that Jung included atheists in his theory. Jung read the work of German philosopher Friedrich Nietzsche, who famously said that 'God is dead'. In response to this, Jung replied that atheism is its own form of religion. He included atheists as holding in their minds an idea of God, in order to say that God does not exist.

> **STRENGTHEN YOUR GRASP**
>
> 1. Write your own explanation of Jung's view of religion as a creation of the human mind. Include the following: the collective unconscious, the archetypes, individuation and the God Within. Cover up your notes and see what you can remember of those four areas. This will help you prepare for an 'explain' question in the exam.
> 2. Make a list of the strengths and weaknesses of Jung's view of religion. Ensure you consider how religious believers may view his ideas, particularly on the existence or not of God. Give a ranking out of five for each of these strengths and weaknesses to help you select the evidence that you think will make the strongest points in an essay. This will help you prepare for an 'evaluate' question in the exam.

Exam Guidance AO1

There are four main areas in AO1 that require your knowledge and understanding of Jung's theory on religion. These are all related to his view that religion is necessary for personal growth: the collective unconscious, individuation, the archetypes and the God Within. Use the 'Know Jung's Key Ideas' and 'Understand Jung's Arguments' sections in this chapter to make notes on each of these four aspects of his theory. Take a quote from the 'Read Jung for Yourself' section and show how this relates to the different aspects of his theory. You may also be asked to outline some of the strengths and weaknesses of his theory, without making your own personal judgement, as part of an AO1 question. Questions may be more general, concerning the relationship between psychology and religion, so making comparative notes between Freud's theory (see Chapter 17) and Jung's theory will be useful.

Exam Guidance AO2

You may be asked an evaluative question specific to Jung and his theories, but you may also be asked about how Jung's and Freud's views on religion compare, or perhaps even more generally about the relationship between psychology and religion as a whole. Strengths of Jung's theory include the fact that he recognised religion as a source of comfort and appreciated the importance of religion in developing positive personal and social mindsets for individuals and communities. The 'Know Criticisms of Jung' section in this chapter will help you with the weaknesses of his theory, and you may be asked to assess how successful those criticisms are.

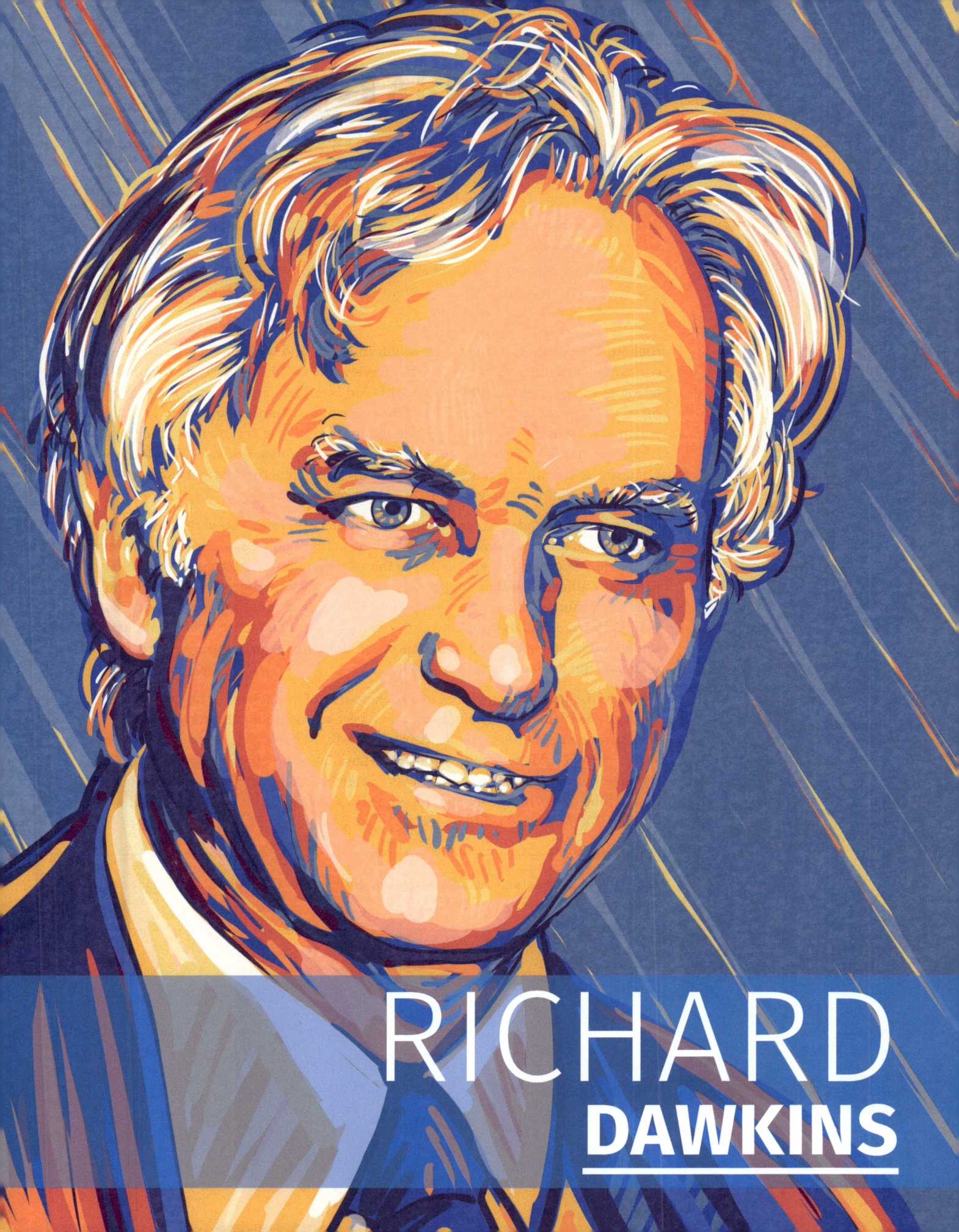

19. RICHARD DAWKINS
GET INTO DAWKINS' WORLD

> **Quick Overview** Richard Dawkins (born 1941) is an evolutionary biologist and a well-known critic of religious belief. He is known as one of the 'Four Horsemen' of New Atheism and regularly engages with key Christian apologist Richard Swinburne on the topic of theism.

Richard Dawkins was born into an Anglican family and was both baptised and confirmed into the faith as a child. In interviews he has said that William Paley's teleological argument for the existence of God (see Chapter 3) was the most convincing for him. However, as a teenager Dawkins encountered Darwin's theory of evolution, which – to Dawkins – acted as a better and more complete argument for the variety of life on earth. It was in the second year of his undergraduate studies at the University of Oxford that Dawkins began to understand the significance of Darwin's ideas, and the theory of evolution more generally, as part of his Zoology degree.

Throughout his academic career as an evolutionary biologist, Dawkins has played an active role in society, speaking out and taking action against activities he feels are morally wrong. For example, he participated in the anti-Vietnam War protests of the 1960s while living in California, and he supported a court case against a former Roman Catholic Pope over sexual abuse claims. The 11 September 2001 attacks on the World Trade Center in New York were a catalyst for Dawkins to start speaking out more publicly about what he understood as the dangers of religious belief, not only the extreme terrorist actions in that case, but the idea of religion itself.

> **TIP**
> By stating that 'God exists' theists are making a scientific claim, which leaves itself open to scrutiny and challenge from rational arguments.

Dawkins has become something of a spokesperson for atheism in the modern age through the Richard Dawkins Foundation, best-selling books about religion, TV programme presentations, public debates with theist apologists, and a strong social media presence. Many religious apologists have taken up his challenge to faith and rebutted his arguments. Most notable is Alister McGrath, who replied to one of Dawkins' best-selling books on the topic of religion, *The God Delusion* (2006), with his own book entitled *The Dawkins Delusion* (2007).

> **INSIGHT**
>
> *The God Delusion* sets out many of Dawkins' criticisms of the Judeo-Christian idea of God, which he calls 'The God Hypothesis'.

Know Dawkins' Key Ideas

IMPROVE YOUR UNDERSTANDING

Make sure that you know how McGrath challenges Dawkins' views.

The God Hypothesis

In *The God Delusion*, Dawkins sets out his reasoning for why it is rational and sensible not to believe in a God. For Dawkins, faith is irrational ('the great cop-out'), contrary to the evidence, and a cultural remnant of our evolutionary journey that we no longer need.

In *The God Delusion*, Dawkins attempts to prove the 'God Hypothesis' wrong. He characterises the God Hypothesis as a statement that 'There exists a superhuman, supernatural intelligence who deliberately designed and created the universe and everything in it, including us.'

This 'God' is believed to be an interventionist God, meaning that he (or she) must be capable of receiving millions of messages (that is, prayers) from millions of people, and sending replies of some form to all of them simultaneously. This would have to be an 'incredibly complex being'. As we know from evolutionary theory that things in this universe move from being less complex to more complex through their evolutionary stages, it is more probable that the universe started with an inanimate and simple starting point rather than something as complex as the God Hypothesis puts forward.

INSIGHT

'We are all atheists about most of the gods that societies have ever believed in. Some of us just go one god further' (Richard Dawkins, *The God Delusion*, 2006).

The Relationship between Science and Religion

Different attempts have been made by philosophers and scientists to set out the nature of the relationship between religion and science. Dawkins rejects palaeontologist Stephen Jay Gould's view known as NOMA (non-overlapping *magisterium*). As an *empiricist*, Dawkins argues that we only need science to have knowledge of our universe. McGrath, a key critic of Dawkins, rebuts this assertion by putting forward his POMA (partially overlapping magisterium) approach to the relationship between religion and science.

These different positions are summarised in the table below.

ESSENTIAL!

The 'God Hypothesis' is Dawkins' term for the claim made by theists that there is a supernatural, superhuman, intelligent being that created the world with intent.

ESSENTIAL!

Magisterium is a term meaning the authority of the teachings of the Catholic Church. In this context, it refers to an area of authority that religion and/or science has.

Empiricism is the idea that our knowledge of the world is based on our experiences, particularly of the senses.

INSIGHT

For Dawkins, science and religion are not compatible. They do not provide different but equally valid answers (the NOMA approach), nor do they provide overlapping answers (the POMA approach). Rather, science is the only approach needed to gain knowledge about the world.

	NOMA: non-overlapping magisterium	Science is the only magisterium	POMA: partially overlapping magisterium
Key thinker	Gould	Dawkins	McGrath
What is the approach?	Religion and science are asking different questions, and are different modes of inquiry about the world. There is no conflict between the two.	Science is the only method of inquiry needed, and religion cannot make scientific claims without being scrutinised as such.	Religion and science can interact and both mutually benefit through inquiries and discoveries about the universe.

Religion Unnecessary to Explain Things

As our scientific knowledge of the physical universe has increased, our need for spiritual or non-physical explanations, known as 'God of the Gaps', has decreased. This is particularly important for Dawkins' criticism of the 'design' or 'teleological' argument. Dawkins' specialism of evolutionary biology shows that life on earth was not created, or intelligently designed, but brought about by the process of evolution.

> **TIP**
>
> William Paley's teleological or design argument is criticised by Dawkins, who asks, 'Who designed the designer?'

> **INSIGHT**
>
> 'If you don't understand how something works, never mind: just give up and say God did it. You don't know how the nerve impulse works? Good! You don't understand how memories are laid down in the brain? Excellent! Is photosynthesis a bafflingly complex process? Wonderful! Please don't go to work on the problem, just give up, and appeal to God' (Dawkins, *The God Delusion*).

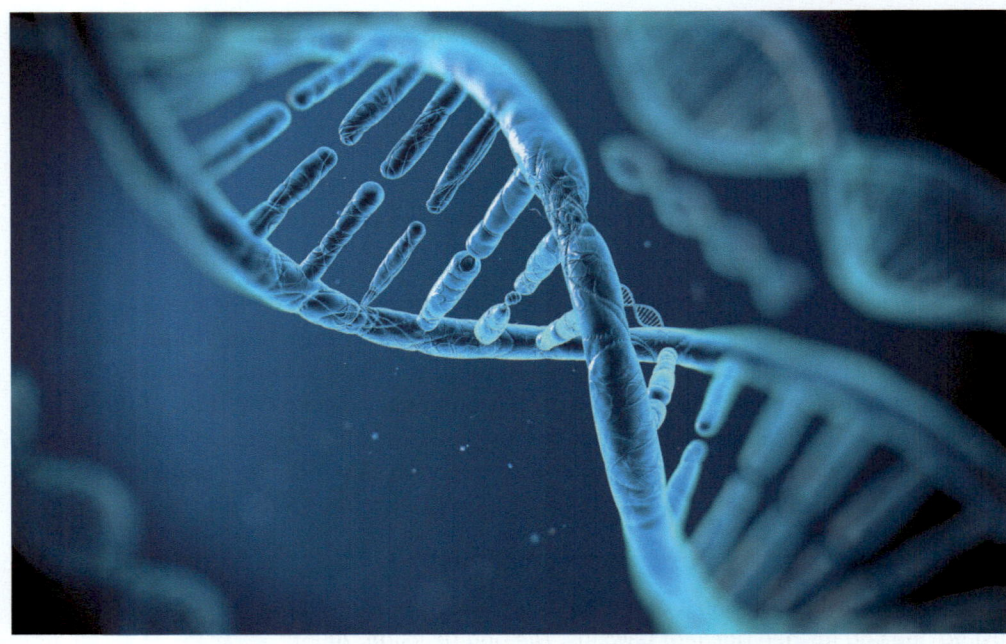

> **INSIGHT**
>
> 'God of the Gaps' refers to religious beliefs answering the questions for which there are not yet physical answers. As we learn more about the physical world through science, we are able to answer more of these questions, and therefore our need for 'God' diminishes.

> **ESSENTIAL!**
>
> **Memes** are similar to genes in that they replicate through generations, but they are cultural ideas rather than biological features.
>
> **Natural selection** is how all living organisms have adapted and changed to suit their environments. The successful adaptations are then able to pass on via reproduction.

In addition, any claimed religious experience or miracle will always have a natural cause, according to Dawkins. Even if we do not know it at first, there will be some natural reason which does not need a supernatural agent. In his UK television documentary *The Root of all Evil*, Dawkins investigated the miracles that are said to have happened at Lourdes, a place of pilgrimage for many Christians, who believe that the Virgin Mary appeared to St Bernadette there and that its waters have healing properties. All of the miracles, he concluded, could have had natural causes instead of being an act of God. Nobody has ever grown a limb back, for example.

Understand Dawkins' Arguments

Religion and religious ideas are products of how our minds have evolved. Not everyone has evolved to be religious, but the ways in which our minds have evolved have led to ideas of religion for many people. Religions have not come from a supernatural source but through giving some an evolutionary advantage; they are cultural **memes** passed on through **natural selection**. As these beliefs continue through the passage of time, they are seen to have more authority and to be more believable. This is compounded by the power of institutions that have an interest in continuing people's belief in their core statements. We have wrongly given supernatural and non-physical explanations for natural phenomena that we can now account for through science.

TIP

Remember that Dawkins accepts that at times, religious beliefs have given humans an evolutionary advantage. This is why they have been passed on as memes within human culture.

Dawkins uses the example of a moth flying into a flame. We could look at this behaviour and think the moth is suicidal, fed up with life, but we know that the behaviour takes places because the moth instinctually flies towards the light, even though the flame will kill it.

The God Hypothesis is a scientific claim and should be scrutinised as such. Some thinkers, such as Gould, argue that a NOMA understanding of the relationship between science and religion means that they do not overlap, in either their questions or where they source their answers. However, Dawkins insists that by stating the God Hypothesis – making the claim that there is a God in existence, a supernatural with superhuman intelligence, who has designed the universe with purpose – the theists are making a scientific claim. For Dawkins, this does not work as a claim because it cannot be empirically verified. Dawkins is in line with **logical positivists** such as A.J. Ayer with the Verification Principle, and Karl Popper and Antony Flew with the **Falsification** Principle when he states this. Something is scientific either when it is able to be empirically verified or, more importantly, when it can be shown how it can be falsified. Often, we see that theories are falsified and, rather than make changes to the hypothesis presented, the scientist will discount the theory and move on. The God Hypothesis should therefore be scrutinised as any scientific theory would be, due to the fact that it is stating a fact about the universe.

ESSENTIAL!

Logical positivism was a philosophical movement from the early twentieth century that viewed scientific knowledge as the only kind of factual knowledge.

Falsification is the ability for a statement or hypothesis to be proven wrong.

INSIGHT

A.J. Ayer was a prominent logical positivist in the UK, although later in life he dismissed those claims as mostly false.

Religion is an aberration and is anti-intellectual by nature. Religion for Dawkins is a 'mental virus', a deficiency in thinking. In particular, Dawkins highlights **religious fundamentalism** as a form of this affliction. To raise children within the faith and introduce them as 'a Christian child', for example, is wrong, particularly when there are vivid descriptions and threats of hell and torment if a child does not believe. This, he believes, is a form of child abuse.

INSIGHT

Dawkins views religion as anti-intellectual and an aberration or illness of the mind; atheists, in contrast, have healthy and rational minds. This is a view that other atheists, such as Owen Jones, would not support and contrasts with Carl Jung and John Randall, who both view religion as necessary for healthy minds.

ESSENTIAL!

An **aberration** in this context is a 'mental virus' – a deficiency or problem with how people are thinking and reasoning.

Religious fundamentalism is characterised by a strict and literal interpretation of religious texts and teachings.

Dawkins also refutes the idea that raising children to be unquestioning in their faith is a virtue. The pseudo-science of Intelligent Design will impede scientific progress, keeping more people in the infantile state of religious belief. To Dawkins, religion is 'nothing more than a useless, and sometimes dangerous evolutionary accident'.

TIP

Dawkins can be used as a challenge to the argument from religious experience. He accepts that people may have strong convictions that they have experienced God – but then so do people with mental health conditions who believe Napoleon has spoken to them, for example.

WHAT DO YOU THINK?

Write down your thoughts on Dawkins' arguments and revisit them shortly before the exam to see if your views have changed.

Read Dawkins for Yourself

TASK

Read Dawkins for yourself in the extracts below. The notes in the margin will help you to grasp his views.

The following passage is taken from Dawkins' *The God Delusion* (2006).

> Linking to Freud (see Chapter 17), Dawkins relates religious belief to a childlike need for a 'God' being a reason why people are theists.
>
> Dawkins does not argue that human life has no meaning, but that we don't need to find that meaning from the existence of God.
>
> There will always be physical explanations for this universe and we do not need to blame or thank a supernatural being or 'agent' that is acting upon our life.

There is something infantile in the presumption that somebody else (parents in the case of children, God in the case of adults) has a responsibility to give your life meaning and point … Somebody else must be responsible for my well-being, and somebody else must be to blame if I am hurt. Is it a similar infantilism that really lies behind the 'need' for a God?

This passage is from Richard Dawkins.net, which is the website of Dawkin's Foundation for Reason and Science. Here Dawkins publishes articles and events in order to help foster a secular, scientific worldview.

> After arguing that there is no need for an intelligent designer due to our understanding of evolution, Dawkins wonders what kind of God we need to believe in, if any.
>
> This links to Dawkins' view that it is more probable that there is an inanimate cause for the universe which must be much simpler than the universe itself. Evolution happens and the theistic God would not need to take part.

There is a temptation to argue that, although God may not be needed to explain the evolution of complex order once the universe, with its fundamental laws of physics, had begun, we do need a God to explain the origin of all things. This idea doesn't leave God with very much to do: just set off the big bang, then sit back and wait for everything to happen.

This is another passage from *The God Delusion*.

> This is the statement put forward by theists that there is an intelligent being that intentionally designed this universe.
>
> This is a famous criticism by Dawkins of the design or teleological argument.
>
> Dawkins is not stating that there is definitely no God, but that it is highly statistically improbable.

The temptation [to attribute the appearance of design to actual design itself] is a false one, because the designer hypothesis immediately raises the larger problem of who designed the designer. The whole problem we started out with was the problem of explaining statistical improbability. It is obviously no solution to postulate something even more improbable.

INSIGHT

Dawkins states that the God Hypothesis is statistically improbable as it is more probable that intelligent life evolved from inanimate matter than from an intelligent being.

Know Criticisms of Dawkins

A key critic of Richard Dawkins is Alister McGrath (born 1953). McGrath is a Christian apologist who has held teaching positions at the universities of Oxford and Cambridge. He aims to show how theism, and specifically Christianity, can stand up to the criticisms of New Atheism generally, and of Dawkins in particular. He sets out these arguments most famously in his book *The Dawkins Delusion* (2007).

New Atheism is defined by what it is not, rather than by what it is. McGrath criticises New Atheism as a whole for being defined by what it is not. He states that Dawkins provides very little evidence for the claims he makes, and characterises Dawkins himself as a fundamentalist clinging to his own faith, atheism.

> **INSIGHT**
>
> 'One of the most melancholy aspects of *The God Delusion* is how its author appears to have made the transition from a scientist with a passionate concern for truth to a crude anti-religious propagandist who shows a disregard for evidence' (McGrath, *The Dawkins Delusion*).

There can be a POMA. In addition, McGrath criticises Dawkins' outright rejection of Gould's NOMA approach to the relationship between religion and science by suggesting a third possibility (POMA), which for McGrath is 'a realization that science and religion offer possibilities of cross-fertilization on account of the interpenetration of their subjects and methods'. He builds on the ideas of other evolutionary biologists such as Francis Collins to support his view. Collins argues that there is 'a richly satisfying harmony between the scientific and spiritual worldviews'.

Owen Jones rejects Dawkins' extreme attitude. Criticism has also come from other non-religious people, such as the journalist Owen Jones. Jones, who does not have a belief in God, has distanced himself from the New Atheist movement, and Dawkins in particular. He argued in *The Independent* newspaper that Dawkins' views, particularly those put out on social media regarding Islam and Muslims, are bigoted and Islamophobic. While he argues for the values of secularism, and for religious belief to be scrutinised, he feels he cannot take part in these discussions 'because atheism in public life has become so dominated by a particular breed that ends up dressing bigotry as non-belief'. Dawkins, for Jones, is part of that 'breed'.

Watch Out for Traps

Dawkins does not say that life has no meaning or point. Critics of Dawkins suggest he sees no meaning or purpose in life, but he refutes this: 'The truly adult view, by contrast, is that our life is as meaningful, as full and as wonderful as we choose to make it. And we can make it very wonderful indeed' (*The God Delusion*).

Dawkins does not condone selfish behaviour. Dawkins' best-selling book *The Selfish Gene* (1976) has been dubbed the most influential science book of all time. Dawkins has since admitted that the title of this book can mislead people into thinking he believes nature and all creatures within it have to be selfish to survive, and that he therefore views the world in a pessimistic way. But it is the gene that is 'selfish': if it is an evolutionary advantage to evolve selfish behaviours, this is what will happen; if, however, altruism will lead to survival, this is what will evolve.

> **INSIGHT**
>
> *The Selfish Gene* accounts for the altruism and kindness that humans show in evolutionary terms.

ESSENTIAL!

New Atheism holds that religious belief should not simply be tolerated but actively criticised and challenged by rational argument.

TIP

Dawkins is an example of a thinker within New Atheism who believes that religion should be open to rational scrutiny, just as all scientific hypotheses should be.

ESSENTIAL!

Secularism is the belief that religion should be separate from institutions in society. People can be religious, but religions cannot hold positions of power and influence across all citizens in that society.

INSIGHT

Dawkins is in line with the logical positivists with his views on the meaningless of religious language. Both Dawkins and the logical positivists see metaphysical claims as 'nonsense' because they are statements that are seen to be unexplainable by science and therefore appealing to emotion or the spiritual/supernatural realm, which cannot be verified.

Don't lose focus on the relationship between religion and science. Remember to bring your points back to the precise question in an exam setting. While an understanding of Dawkins' views on religion and the key ideas he holds around the God Hypothesis, memes and religion as an aberration are important, make sure you can write about Dawkins' view of the relationship between religion and science more generally. Ensure you know how this may differ from other thinkers mentioned in this chapter.

> ### STRENGTHEN YOUR GRASP
> 1. Write your own explanation of Dawkins' view of religion as a by-product of evolution. Include the following: the God Hypothesis, memes and single magisterium. Cover your notes and see what you can remember about those four areas. This will help you prepare for an 'explain' question in the exam.
> 2. Make a list of the strengths and weaknesses of Dawkins' view of religion. Pay particular attention to McGrath's criticisms and his rebuttal, *The Dawkins Delusion*. Give a ranking out of five for each of these strengths and weaknesses to help you select the evidence that you think will make the strongest points in an essay. This will help you prepare for an 'evaluate' question in the exam.

Exam Guidance AO1

You may be asked in the exam to show knowledge and understanding of what Dawkins' view of religion is. You should be aware of his criticisms of religion as well as those who criticise him. Pay particular attention to his approach to the relationship between religion and science, as this is a significant part of the specification. Be aware of how Dawkins' view differs from other views on this. You may also be able to use Dawkins in answers on other topics where you are asked to explain challenges to religious experiences, miracles and the design argument.

Exam Guidance AO2

You may be asked to evaluate and come to a judgement on Dawkins' view of religion. It is particularly important for you to know the work of McGrath as a key critic of Dawkins and you may need to evaluate how successful McGrath is in his rebuttal of Dawkins and therefore his defence of theism. You may also need to evaluate different positions held on the relationship between religion and science, so knowing the strengths and weaknesses of these approaches will help you with an AO2-style question on that content. Finally, you may be able to use Dawkins' arguments in an evaluation of religious experiences, miracles and the design argument, so having a list of strengths and weaknesses of his approach to these topics will aid you in an evaluation question on this.

20. TERESA OF AVILA
GET INTO TERESA OF AVILA'S WORLD

> **Quick Overview** Teresa of Avila (1515–82) was a Spanish Carmelite nun who wrote vividly about her religious experiences. She also wrote more broadly on the topics of mysticism, prayer and living a Christian life during the Counter-Reformation of the sixteenth century. After founding the Barefoot Carmelites, Teresa wrote *The Way of Perfection* in the 1560s. Forty years after her death, she was canonised (made a saint).

Teresa of Avila lived in medieval Spain, in a region influenced by the mystical branches of both Islam (Sufism) and Judaism (Kabbalah). As a young child, she suffered the loss of her mother and was sent to a Catholic convent school, which belonged to a particular order called 'The Carmelites'. Its founders were Crusaders who became hermits and lived segregated lives in Mount Carmel, Israel, and the order followed these same principles of living a simple life removed from society. Eventually the order spread west into Europe, but over time, its members came to value wealth and property rather than disowning them.

It is in this context that Teresa joined the order. As a teenager she was popular and, in her own words, 'worldly', but she later developed a practice of prayer and contemplation when she suffered a serious illness and was bedbound. Teresa was disheartened by the growing wealth and status she witnessed around her in an order that had been founded on opposing principles. She wished for a simpler way of living.

Much later in life, Teresa began to have intense religious experiences. At 40, she suddenly felt overwhelmed by the love of God in a way she'd never experienced before. Later, Teresa became a central figure in discussions around religious experiences (for example, in the writing of William James – see Chapter 21) due to her detailed record-keeping of these events.

Through reading the works of the Catholic saints who lived before her, Teresa found a deeper and more meaningful faith. She was influenced greatly by St Augustine's writings on his own conversion, as he too had left behind a life of sin and turned away from all worldly desires. This inspired Teresa to reform the Carmelite order, and she founded the Barefoot Carmelites in 1560, which returned to the central principles of living a life of poverty and simplicity.

> **INSIGHT**
>
> The Counter-Reformation came about in an effort to oppose the Protestant Reformation and grew out of criticism about the corruption and worldliness of the Catholic Church at the time.

> **ESSENTIAL!**
>
> **'Sola Scriptura'** is the principle that the Bible is enough for any Christian to ground their faith on, in contrast to Teresa's emphasis on religious experiences.

> **ESSENTIAL!**
>
> **Mystical experiences** are when someone has direct communication with or experience of God, often in a state of spiritual ecstasy.
>
> **Transverbiation** is the term Teresa uses to describe her most intense experiences. They are experienced as a 'dart' piercing the heart, with an overwhelming sense of love and the presence of God.

Teresa was writing during a crucial time for Catholicism, as the challenge posed by the Protestant Reformation had caused a 'Counter-Reformation' in the Catholic Church. One significant challenged posed by the Protestant Reformation was that it argued that all a Christian needed to have faith was the words of scripture. It was no longer necessary for an intermediary to translate and interpret the scriptures, nor was there a need to follow traditions that were not found in the Bible. This became known as the principle of **'Sola Scriptura'**, and Teresa's emphasis on direct religious experiences of God should be understood within this theological context.

Teresa continued to have **mystical experiences** and described them as **transverbiations** of her heart. Her descriptions of her experiences are considered by people of the Catholic faith to be relatable and understandable, and they show an intimate relationship between herself and her Lord, which is exemplified in her final words, 'My Lord, it is time to move on. Well then, may your will be done. O my Lord and my Spouse, the hour that I have longed for has come. It is time to meet one another.'

> **TIP**
>
> Teresa of Avila's writings show the great impact of religious experiences on belief. Through her own first-hand evidence of a divine presence, her faith was deepened, showing the power of these experiences to reinforce belief.

Know Teresa of Avila's Key Ideas

IMPROVE YOUR UNDERSTANDING

Make sure that you know how Teresa's stages of prayer relate to mystical experiences.

Mystical Experiences as a Process

Like other medieval mystic writers, Teresa defined her mystical experiences as a process rather than a product, which is in contrast to other understandings from scholars such as William James and Rudolf Otto (see Chapters 21 and 22). While these scholars were concerned with the impact of the experience on the believer – for example, the change in their life and outlook – Teresa was concerned with how one can achieve such an experience, and what steps could be taken to ensure this union with God. Teresa was aware that not all believers would experience God in the same way through prayer, but she thought that it was beneficial to have a structure or guide to follow which aligned with Christian theology and practice.

Central to Teresa's understanding of mystical experiences was her belief that these experiences were possible through God's love for humanity and through his grace. While Teresa was not particularly concerned with the argument for God's existence through religious experiences, she did offer a way to check whether or not these experiences were truly from God. She had two tests which could be given to each experience:

- Did the experience fit in with Christian teachings?
- After the experience, did the individual feel at peace?

Using these tests could demonstrate if the experience was from God, or a malevolent force (that is, the Devil).

The Stages of Prayer

In Teresa's first two books, her autobiography *The Life of Teresa* (1565) and her manual for prayer *The Way of Perfection* (1583), she guides the reader from being a beginner at prayer, using words alone, to the pinnacle of complete union with God.

Using the metaphor and symbolism of water in a garden, she shows how nine stages of prayer can help the believer to detach from worldly desires and thoughts, and become more disciplined in their faith and more able to manage temptations. The waters in the garden show how the stages of prayer give sustenance and life to the believer, and help them to draw on the love of God more fully.

Water stage	Garden metaphor	Represents
The First Water	Collecting water from a well	Active nature of prayer
The Second Water	Using a water wheel	Prayer bringing greater clarity
The Third Water	The water comes from a stream or a brook	Jesus Christ's input to prayer
The Fourth Water	When the garden is watered by heavy rain	Requires no human effort as God is in total control

INSIGHT

Teresa wanted people to remove worldly desires and thoughts, and to be less concerned with material values and ordinary life. She wanted more focus on spiritual matters. Love was at the centre of all stages of prayer, 'for prayer is nothing else than being on terms of friendship with God'.

TIP

Teresa uses the metaphor of a garden being watered to show how discipline in prayer can lead to nourishment at different levels. The efforts from the believer are great at the lower levels, leading to God taking total control at the highest level.

The Way of Perfection sets out nine stages of prayer:

1. **Vocal prayer:** words said aloud.
2. **Meditation:** for example, with a rosary.
3. **Affective prayer:** love dominates the mind.
4. **Prayer of simplicity:** prayer while observing something holy.
5. **Infused contemplation:** granted by God's grace an entrance of the Holy Spirit.
6. **Prayer of quiet:** the soul is lacking nothing, and wishes to do nothing but love.
7. **Prayer of union:** the mind and will are totally absorbed into God and God's will.
8. **Prayer of ecstatic union:** all the interior thoughts are fully centred on God and external senses are feeling a closeness to God and God's will.
9. **Prayer of transforming union:** the self is completely forgotten, and God is known fully in all things; this is the most intimate union with God that is possible.

> **INSIGHT**
>
> *The Interior Castle* was written by Teresa in 1577 and is said to have influenced Descartes' *Meditations on First Philosophy* (1641) (see Chapter 8).

> **INSIGHT**
>
> Teresa used the metaphor of the Diamond Castle to show how the discipline of prayer can lead the believer to discover God within them, in the 'deepest room'. 'We need no wings to go in search of Him, but have only to look upon Him present within us.'

> **ESSENTIAL!**
>
> The **'Dark Night of the Soul'** is when the believer may feel a loss of meaning or purpose in their life, which leads to a spiritual purification; it allows a rebirth and deeper mystical union with God.
>
> **St John of the Cross** was a mentee of Teresa who set up a male version of her Carmelite order. He experienced the 'Dark Night of the Soul' and wrote about this in poetry.

The Interior Castle

Teresa's third book, *The Interior Castle*, was written under the orders of her superiors in the Carmelite order at the height of the controversy surrounding her reforms to the order and her experiences. She wrote it towards the end of her life, after she had received a vision from Jesus Christ, where she saw 'the soul as if it were a castle made of a single diamond or of a very clear crystal, in which there are many rooms, just as in Heaven there are many mansions'.

Teresa used a large used spacious castle to represent the soul. The castle is beautiful and made in the image of God. Within this 'castle' are many rooms and 'mansions', with the closest one to God being the deepest within, at the centre. Different prayers and spiritual experiences are attached to each mansion, which people move between during their lives. Teresa encouraged the reader to find God within themselves as they journeyed through the mansions: 'The Lord is within us and we should be there with Him.'

Stage of mansions	Nature of the mansions	Practices associated
Mansions 1–3	Our spiritual efforts benefit our soul here.	Prayer, reading the Bible, learning from spiritual people.
Mansions 4–5	Here the soul is nourished and makes a commitment to God, like a silkworm's cocoon nourishing what is within and that has not yet been reborn.	The soul may have mystical experiences, which must be evaluated to see if the experiences come from God or the Devil.
Mansions 6–7	Some suffering and trials will occur, perhaps a **'Dark Night of the Soul'** (similar to **St John of the Cross**'s experiences) as the soul travels between the final two mansions.	Intense mystical experiences may occur, such as visions, feeling the presence of God, raptures and 'The Dart'.

> **INSIGHT**
>
> Teresa outlines seven stages of prayer in her book *The Interior Castle*. The stages are: recollection, quiet, union, ecstasy, dark night, betrothal to marriage. However, each person's journey is unique and may not follow this order.

> **WHAT DO YOU THINK?**
>
> Write down your thoughts on Avila's arguments and revisit them shortly before the exam to see if your views have changed.

Read Teresa of Avila for Yourself

In this passage from *The Life of Teresa* (1565), Teresa of Avila describes her sensations while having an intense religious experience. The notes in the margin will help you to grasp her ideas.

> He appeared to me to be thrusting it at times into my heart and to pierce my very entrails; when he drew it out, he seemed to draw them out also, and to leave me all on fire with a great love of God. The pain was so great, that it made me moan; and yet so surpassing was the sweetness of this excessive pain, that I could not wish to be rid of it. The soul is satisfied now with nothing less than God. The pain is not bodily, but spiritual; though the body has its share in it, even a large one. It is a caressing of love so sweet which now takes place between the soul and God.

< The phrase 'appeared to be me' indicates that it is not 'real' but a vision acknowledged by Teresa. In *The Interior Castle*, Teresa refers to this experience as 'The Dart', which may be experienced when the seventh and final mansion is entered. Other saints such as St John of the Cross experienced this as part of their mystical experiences.

< The experience is in many ways ineffable (extreme) and beyond usual descriptions. Suffering and pain are seen as part of the journey through prayer to the union with God and are welcomed.

< This relates to the final stages of prayer for Teresa, where the soul has union with God in the mind and the heart.

In this passage from *The Interior Castle* (1577), Teresa discusses visions.

> Now we come to treat of imaginary visions, whereby it is held that the devil is more liable to deceive people than by the other visions I have already described. This is probably true. Yet when imaginary visions are divine, they seem, in a certain manner, more profitable for us than the others, as being more suited to our nature – with the exception of the visions sent by our Lord in the seventh mansion which far surpass all others.

< Notice the differentiation between intellectual visions and imaginary visions.

< Here Teresa is addressing her critics who said the Devil was giving her these visions, and others who said she was making them up.

< This is how Teresa is judging the validity of the experiences – is it for the good of the person i.e. matching with God's omnibenevolence. This links to William James' pragmatic approach (see Chapter 21).

Know Criticisms of Teresa of Avila

Teresa's experiences were sexual dreams or excitement. At the time, Teresa was criticised for what could be construed as graphic descriptions of love, ecstasy and the sexual allusion of a plunging spear entering her. She, however, disputed this by stating that she would not have felt goodness, love or benevolence from something sinful, such as was being suggested. Using her two criteria for testing whether or not an experience was from God, she concluded that it was.

A focus on experience over scripture. Writing at the time of the Protestant Reformation and the Catholic Counter-Reformation, the relative importance of experience and scripture was a significant element of theological discussions. The Protestant churches were formed under the rallying cry that scripture was enough. The Bible, containing the 'Word of God', would provide all the teaching and insight that a Christian needed. This was in conflict with Teresa's claim to have experienced a direct union with God.

Physiological explanations. Recent discoveries in the field of neurotheology have shown us how certain brain injuries and conditions can lead to sensations similar to those Teresa experienced. For example, neuroscientist V.S. Ramachandran found that some individuals with damaged temporal lobes, or suffering from **temporal lobe epilepsy**, have powerful and intense experiences similar to religious ones. They may feel a presence with them, hear words, have visions of heavenly places or experience feelings of terror. The link between the brain and religious experiences has also been explored through the work of scientists Andrew Newberg and Michael Persinger. This could bring into question the validity of Teresa's experiences. If a physical explanation could suffice, were her experiences actually from God? However, Ramachandran does not state that his research proves there is no God.

EVALUATION SKILLS

An answer to an evaluative question about a scholar is always deepened by demonstrating awareness of how other thinkers may disagree.

ESSENTIAL!

Temporal lobe epilepsy is a disease that causes some people to have sensations similar to religious experiences.

INSIGHT

Ramachandran presents some evidence to show there may be material, physical causes for religious experiences and that Teresa's experiences might have been caused by some physical impact on her brain.

ESSENTIAL!

Heresy is when a belief is said to be against accepted or correct beliefs – in Teresa's time, it would have been treated as a crime against God.

Instead, certain brain conditions could be God's way of programming some brains to be able to communicate with him more easily than others.

Watch Out for Traps

Don't focus only on Teresa's life history and personal mystical experiences when you write about her. Consider also her approach to prayer and mystical experiences in general. When using the metaphors of watering the garden, and the Interior Castle, ensure you can illustrate how they relate to prayer, the nature of those prayers and when such mystical experiences may occur.

Don't assume that Teresa was accepted by the Catholic Church during her lifetime. Some people were suspicious of the reforms she was making to the Carmelite order, and she was instructed to retire. Her writings were unmediated (there was no intervention) by the Pope at the time, and this was likened to **heresy**, and it was not until 1970 that Teresa was appointed a Doctor of the Church (the first woman to hold this title).

Teresa's experiences don't fit neatly into other writers' categories of religious experience. William James (see Chapter 21) refers to Teresa as an example of someone writing about religious experiences. However, she does not fit into the 'passive' category he gives to mystical experiences, as she shows that these come with discipline and training on the part of the believer.

STRENGTHEN YOUR GRASP

1. Write your own explanation of Teresa of Avila's views of religious experiences. Include the following: types of prayer, the stages of prayer, and the impact of religious experiences on belief. Cover your notes and see what you can remember of those three areas. This will help you prepare for an 'explain' question in the exam.
2. Make a list of the strengths and weaknesses of Teresa of Avila's understanding of religious experiences. Give a ranking out of five for each of these strengths and weaknesses to help you select the evidence that you think will make the strongest points in an essay. This will help you prepare for an 'evaluate' question in the exam.

Exam Guidance AO1

You may be asked in the exam to show knowledge and understanding of what religious experiences are, and Teresa of Avila would be an excellent case study to use to illustrate your points. You could discuss her conversion experience and also her continued mystical experiences. You may also be asked about the nature of mystical experiences. Teresa of Avila's explanations of the stages of prayer can be compared with the understandings of mystical experiences held by other religious thinkers, such as William James and Rudolf Otto (see Chapters 21 and 22).

Exam Guidance AO2

You may be asked to evaluate and come to a judgement on how far religious experiences can be used as proof of God's existence, and Teresa's rebuttal of those who doubted her experiences could be useful for such a debate. You may also find it helpful to put Teresa's experiences (from 500 years ago) up to the scrutiny of modern science and New Atheist explanations of such phenomena. Finally, you may find it useful to prepare a judgement on the different scholars of religious experience in this book regarding who has the most useful and appropriate understanding of mystical experiences, and why.

21. WILLIAM JAMES
GET INTO JAMES' WORLD

> **Quick Overview** William James (1842–1910) was an American psychologist who popularised pragmatism as an approach to discussions around truth within philosophy, where what is 'true' is seen to be what is useful, practical and helpful. James wrote perhaps the most influential book on religious experiences. His characteristics of mystical experiences have been extremely influential in philosophy.

William James was born in the mid-nineteenth century into a wealthy family that embraced science and religion. At this time there was a growing interest in scientific materialism, where physical and scientific explanations were being sought as a means of understanding the universe. This was an alternative to religious and mythical explanations.

During this time, core Christian scriptures were being closely scrutinised due to the emerging discipline of Higher Biblical Criticism. This questioned key truth claims found in the Bible.

James' father suffered bouts of poor mental health and found solace in a Church that sought to embrace scientific progress as well as retain spirituality. This influenced James' interest in religious experiences that occur across religious traditions.

Like his father, episodes of poor health fed into James' keen interest in how religious experiences help individuals, as well as how religion can help believers cope with the darker side of human existence. His understanding was that the most 'complete' religions are those that account for, rather than shy away from, the pessimistic side of human experiences, 'rather than just embracing the optimistic'.

In opposition to Realism, which was popular in Europe at the time, James was a key thinker in the development of **pragmatism**. This approach argued that what is practical, useful and helpful is what is truthful. For James, it was the *effects* of religious experiences on an individual that matter when considering their truthfulness, as opposed to whether the claims of a religious experience could be proven to be true in 'reality'. James sought to understand these experiences through the tools of the social sciences, while incorporating the personal element of how these experiences impact on people's lives.

> **TIP**
> It is impossible to exaggerate James' influence. He is viewed as the father of American psychology, inspiring many others in the philosophy of religion, including Ludwig Wittgenstein (see Chapter 33).

> **ESSENTIAL!**
> **Pragmatism** is a philosophical approach that considers the usefulness of ideas when judging if they are true or not.

Know James' Key Ideas

> **IMPROVE YOUR UNDERSTANDING**
> Make sure that you know what James' four characteristics of mystical experiences are, and that you are able to give examples of each.

The Will to Believe and Pragmatism

James' lecture 'The Will to Believe' outlined his reasons for why people have a right to believe in something religious or spiritual, even when the evidence for this may be lacking or inconclusive. Certain religious beliefs can have powerful and transformative effects, even if they cannot be 'proved'. As long as there is a positive impact from that belief, then people have the right to choose to believe it.

▬ **INSIGHT**

James' approach offers a way for religious belief and accounts of religious experience to stand up to the criticisms of key thinkers in the social sciences during his time. Sigmund Freud (see Chapter 17) called religion a 'collective neurosis' and an 'illusion' that must be removed for society to progress. James, in contrast, emphasised the positive impact that a religious experience and attitude can have on individuals, and therefore society as a whole.

ESSENTIAL!

The **'sick-souled'** believer is one who grapples with the dark side of existence, as James himself did.

▬ **INSIGHT**

James built on his ideas in lectures such as 'The Will to Believe'. He viewed religious experiences as being at the heart of religions, with teachings and institutions as secondary.

James lectured on his beliefs during a time when scientific enquiry was bringing into question many of the key truth claims in the world's religious traditions. For James, the truth of a claim or belief did not stem from an objective reality that could be discovered purely through empirical testing, as the Realists were claiming. Instead, truth could be found in the impact the belief or experience had on a person.

James is a key thinker in the pragmatic approach to understanding truth, which was popular among philosophers in the USA at the time and later gained support in Europe. This may be summarised as 'fruits over roots' – what matters when we claim that something is true is the impact it has on the person who believes it. James' approach relied very much on the individual who experienced or believed something. Although James saw merit in studying these individuals using the social sciences, he did not want the personal and subjective nature of the 'truth' to be lost.

Within religion there are people with optimistic outlooks, whom James called the 'healthy minded' – they appear untouched by the ideas of evil in the world, or doom in their future. Conversely, there are those who are preoccupied with the darkness they experience or see around them. These **'sick souls'** are more likely to have religious experiences. The impact these experiences have on believers is positive and often life transforming, and this is why James considered their accounts to be true.

▬ **INSIGHT**

Conversion experiences show a profound change in the person. The experiences may be sudden or gradual, but they also have an element of self-surrender.

The Varieties of Religious Experience

Like Rudolf Otto (see Chapter 22), James viewed religious experiences as an important part of human life, and having enduring and powerful effects on humanity. He classed them as among the 'most important biological functions of mankind' (*The Varieties of Religious Experience*, 1902). His exploration of religious experiences was not confined to one religious tradition, and he drew from examples in literature, history, first-hand accounts, religious texts and psychological analysis as well as through attending religious services himself.

James first categorises religious experiences into conversions, visions and mystical experiences, and then goes on to discuss the characteristics of mystical experiences in more depth. These are summarised below.

Conversions	Visions	Mystical experiences
These occur when someone makes a profound and lasting change to their life, values, beliefs and behaviour. They are often related to a deeper religious commitment (e.g. Malcom X experienced two conversions, one to Islam while in prison and a second conversion to a full rejection of racism while on Hajj, the Muslim pilgrimage to Mecca).	These are vivid 'sights' of something divine or supernatural. They may be something seen externally (e.g. Bernadette seeing the Virgin Mary at Lourdes), or an internal vision (e.g. Teresa of Avila's vision of the Interior Castle).	These are deep and powerful states of mind where the individual feels connected to something greater than themselves, such as God, or something divine. They go beyond human understanding and language, and they completely change how someone sees the world. Otto classed these as 'numinous' experiences.

The Characteristics of Mystical Experiences

INSIGHT

Mystical experiences are religious experiences where the individual believes themselves to be 'lost' in union with God or another form of the Divine or ultimate reality. Examples of mystical religious experiences are Teresa of Avila's transverbiations (see Chapter 20).

TIP

Remember that, as well as categorising religious experiences into conversions, visions and mystical experiences, James stated that mystical experiences have four characteristics: ineffable, noetic, transient and passive.

James was concerned with descriptions of religious experiences rather than evaluations of these experiences. In his book *The Varieties of Religious Experience*, he set out his four categories of 'mystical experiences'.

Characteristic	Explanation	Quotation	Examples
Passive	The person having the experience is not in control of it.	'The Mystic feels as if his own will were in abeyance [temporarily stopped], and indeed sometimes as if he were grasped and held by a superior power.'	The Prophet Mohammed is told to 'recite' by Jibreel, although he is illiterate.
Ineffable	It is impossible to put into words and language what the experience was or how it felt.	'No one can make clear to another who has never had a certain feeling, in what the quality or worth of it consists.'	Teresa of Avila found it 'impossible' to describe her experiences fully.
Noetic	The experience brings new personal and intuitive knowledge and understanding.	'Mystical states seem to those experiencing them to be also states of knowledge.'	St Paul gained knowledge of the true nature of Jesus Christ through his conversion experience on the road to Damascus.
Transient	The experience is temporary; it does not last.	'Mystical states cannot be sustained for long. Except in rare instances, half an hour or at most an hour or two seems to be the limit beyond which they fade into the light of common day.'	The Buddha could not remain in his Enlightened state; he had to return to the 'normal' world to pass on teachings.

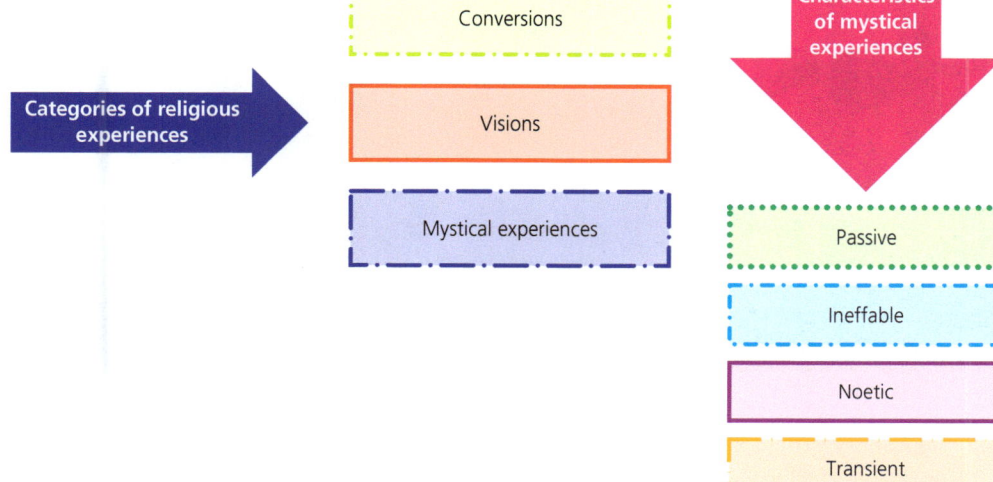

Mind map showing the categories and characteristics of mystical experiences

WHAT DO YOU THINK?

Write down your thoughts on James' arguments and revisit them shortly before the exam to see if your views have changed.

TASK

Read James for yourself in the extracts below. The notes in the margin will help you to grasp his views.

Read James for Yourself

In these passages from *The Varieties of Religious Experience* (1902), James discusses religious and mystical experiences. The notes in the margin will help you to grasp his ideas.

The pragmatic approach: we are judging by the effects the experience has on the experient (the person experiencing it).	'We must judge the tree by its fruit. The best fruits of the religious experience are the best things history has to offer. The highest flights of charity, devotion, trust, patience, and bravery to which the wings of human nature have spread themselves, have all been flown for religious ideals.
The influence of religious experiences on human history.	
The good things that have come from these religious experiences; for James, this means the experience first, and the institution second.	[...]
Mystical experiences are noetic: they reveal some deeper truth to the person who experiences them.	They are states of insight into depths of truth unplumbed by the discursive intellect. They are illuminations, revelations, full of significance and importance, all inarticulate though they remain; and as a rule they carry with them a curious sense of authority for after-time.'
Mystical experiences cannot be fully understood or explained by logical thinking or reasoning.	
Mystical experiences cannot be articulated or explained to those who have not had one.	
Mystical experiences are transient: they do not last, but their effects do.	

INSIGHT

James' pragmatic approach means that he judges the truthfulness of the claims of a mystical experience by the outcome for the experient – fruits over roots.

Know Criticisms of James

Religious experiences, especially mystical experiences, could have other explanations than God or a divine being. Specific challenges are posed from both a psychological and materialistic approach. Freud argues, using the psychological explanations for religious experiences, that they are induced by the experient as a form of wish fulfilment and are a symptom of religion as a collective neurosis. The individual longs for an omnipotent and omnibenevolent being to exist and communicate with them, and thus the experience occurs.

Materialistic explanations that religious experiences are due to activity in the brain can also be given. This accounts for why people have such a strong sense that they have experienced something greater than themselves – 'God' or something 'divine'. Tools such as Persinger's Helmet can be used to show that 'religious experiences' can be induced by stimulating certain areas of the brain. This brings into question James' understanding that religious experiences are from God.

INSIGHT

Michael Persinger (1945–2018) was a neurologist who conducted experiments to show that by stimulating the temporal lobes of the brain, religious experiences could be felt. This is supported by V.S. Ramachandran's work around temporal lobe epilepsy and religious experiences (see Chapter 20).

Not all experiences fit neatly into the categories that James presents. Teresa of Avila (see Chapter 20), whom James referenced in *The Varieties of Religious Experience*, could be seen as a believer in active rather than passive religious experiences. She believed that the experience came with great discipline and training, rather than being something that 'happened' to the passive experient.

The huge variety of religious experiences. A major criticism of religious experiences being proof of a God or divine being is their huge variety, with often conflicting claims about that God or being. A Charismatic Christian may experience the Holy Spirit as part of God understood as a Trinity, whereas a Sufi Muslim may experience the Tawhid or undivided one-ness of Allah through their worship. How can we know which one is true, as they seem to conflict? James' pragmatic approach would encourage us to look at the effects of those experiences on the individuals rather than an objective 'truth'.

Antony Flew (see Chapter 27) argued that religious experiences seem 'to depend on the interests, background and expectation of those who have them rather than on anything separate and autonomous'. If there really is an objective reality of God, why is there such a variety of religious experiences, some of which contradict one another?

INSIGHT

Antony Flew was a British philosopher who applied the Falsification Principle to discussions around the meaning of religious language. Claims of religious experiences would be seen as an example of religious language.

INSIGHT

Psychological and materialistic explanations of religious experiences include Freud's criticisms of religious experiences.

Freud (Chapter 17) challenged religious experiences as part of the illusion of religion and the mind's wishes for an omnipotent, omnibenevolent father figure.

Dawkins (Chapter 19) challenges religious experiences by stating that all religious experiences will have a materialistic cause not a supernatural one.

TIP

C.F. Davis (see Chapter 23) offers a rebuttal of this criticism.

Watch Out for Traps

Two common errors are made while writing essays on James' understanding of religious experiences. These are: first, listing numerous experiences without showing how they are characterised by James and how they exemplify his passive, ineffable, noetic and transient characteristics; and second, listing his four characteristics without exemplifying. Ensure that you link the characteristics with examples when writing an essay on James and religious experience.

The misconception that because a religious experience cannot be described, it is not valid. While it is integral to James' understandings of religious experience (and Otto's as well) that these experiences are not explainable, he never used that as a judgement on their accuracy. Due to James' pragmatic approach to philosophy and his 'fruits over roots' approach, for him it is the change in the experient that shows the truthfulness of the claim of an experience.

James' characteristics do not only apply to Christian religious experiences or experiences of the Christian God. While the vast majority of the experiences he addresses in *The Varieties of Religious Experience* are drawn from Christian traditions (for example, Teresa of Avila), James did not want his characteristics to be limited to one religious tradition.

James used Christian ideas (such as God as 'the Father') and alluded to Jesus' quote, 'My father's mansion has many rooms' (John 14:2–3). However, he had a pluralistic approach towards other religions and was therefore open to the validity of claims of religious experiences from them.

> ### INSIGHT
> 'The subject of it immediately says that it defies expression, that no adequate report of its contents can be given in words. It follows from this that its quality must be directly experienced; it cannot be imparted or transferred to others' (James, *The Varieties of Religious Experience*).

> ### INSIGHT
> 'In our Father's house are many mansions, and each of us must discover for himself the kind of religion and the amount of saintship which best comports with what he believes to be his powers and feels to be his truest mission and vocation' (James, *The Varieties of Religious Experience*).

STRENGTHEN YOUR GRASP

1. Write your own explanation of James' characteristics of mystical experiences. Include the following: passive, noetic, ineffable and transient. Have examples for each of these characteristics and make sure you link them to James' ideas. Cover your notes and see what you can remember of those four areas. This will help you prepare for an 'explain' question in the exam.

2. Make a list of the strengths and weaknesses of James' characteristics of mystical experiences. Ensure you consider how other philosophers might view his characteristics. How do his characteristics compare and contrast with those of Otto and Avila? Give a ranking out of five for each of these strengths and weaknesses to help you select the evidence that you think will make the strongest points in an essay. This will help you prepare for an 'evaluate' question in the exam.

CREATE YOUR OWN QUESTION

Read this chapter and use command words such as 'examine', 'explain' or 'compare' to create your own AO1 question. For an AO2 question, make a one-sided statement about James' views, put the statement between quotation marks and follow it with the phrase, 'Evaluate this view.'

Exam Guidance AO1

Ensure that you can explain James' pragmatic approach to the truth claims of a religious experience. Make notes on the phrase 'fruits over roots' and apply that to discussions of the validity of claims of religious experiences.

You should have an understanding of what mystical experiences are, and how James' view relates to that of other scholars such as Rudolf Otto (see Chapter 22). You may find it useful to have an understanding of how mystical experiences are related to other experiences, such as visions, dreams and conversions. It is essential that you know James' characteristics of mystical experiences as passive, ineffable, noetic and transient. Be prepared to explain and exemplify each of these characteristics. In an 'explain' question, you could be asked about the importance and validity of religious experiences in general, but also about the characteristics and understanding of James more specifically.

Exam Guidance AO2

Consider the strengths and weaknesses of James' approach to religious experiences. You may be asked to evaluate how adequate his characteristics of mystical experiences are. On the one hand, he offers a system that can be applied to all mystical experiences and allows us to study them as a human phenomenon without being too preoccupied with what it means to say whether the experience is 'true' or not. On the other hand, other ways of understanding experiences may be more adequate, such as Teresa of Avila and her approach of disciplined prayer, or Otto's characterisation of the numinous as an experience of something wholly other that is both terrifying and compelling. How does James compare to these interpretations? Perhaps it depends what you are using the characteristics for, as regards how adequate they will be.

Another way to evaluate James is to consider alternative explanations for the experience, other than a 'God'. Do the challenges from psychology or from scientific materialism prove that these experiences are not real? By seeming to accept the truthfulness of a claim of a 'God', is James being too naïve in his characteristics? This was perhaps the limit of these characteristics during the time James was working, and modern advances in neuroscience and other approaches now provide alternatives.

22. RUDOLF OTTO
GET INTO OTTO'S WORLD

> **Quick Overview** Rudolf Otto (1869–1937) was a German Protestant theologian and philosopher who categorised religious experiences as 'numinous' (that is, they are filled with a holy presence). He believed these are at the core of all religions and allow the believer to have a direct experience of God without the need of an intermediary such as the institution of the Church.

Towards the end of the nineteenth century and the start of the twentieth century, much Christian writing focused on defending Christianity against what was seen as an onslaught of scientific challenges on religious faith. This meant that much of the discussion centred on how Christian faith could still be seen as logical, reasonable and 'true'. This is known as 'Christian apologetics'. At this time, Protestant Christian Rudolf Otto saw the gulf widening between religion and science, and he aimed to create a kind of 'science of religion', building on the ideas of Immanuel Kant (see Chapter 11) on rationality and how we interpret the world we experience. He also admired the ideas of Friedrich Schleiermacher, who saw 'the religious' as an awareness distinct from simply rational and ethical understandings.

At this time, the nature of academic discussions regarding religion was changing. The dominant approach had been to focus on the theological claims within a religion, perhaps with an assumption that their truth claims were true or at least important. But a new approach, where religions were compared to one another, and studied in a more sociological and cultural way, was emerging. Modern scholars have noted that Otto was writing just before this shift, which may explain why his ideas have had a lasting influence on the study of religions.

Otto speaks of a distinctly religious experience – the **numinous** – that all humans have a capacity for, but which only some experience. During the First World War, he wrote *The Idea of the Holy* (1917), in which he coined the term 'numinous' to help explain these mystical experiences. The book was a sensational success, and within 12 years it had been translated into seven different languages including Japanese and Dutch.

He later applied his ideas of 'The Holy' within the Judeo-Christian context to the wider experiences at the heart of other world religions, reflecting the wider shift in focus of the academic study of religion from the theological to comparative religious studies. Otto's idea of the numinous had a lasting influence not only on key thinkers of the twentieth century, such as Karl Jung (Chapter 18), Paul Tillich (Chapter 32) and C.S. Lewis, but also on popular culture through novelist Aldous Huxley and rock band Pink Floyd, and, most recently, in the writings of academic and broadcaster Reza Aslan and neurotheologist Andrew Newburg.

> **ESSENTIAL!**
> The **numinous** is Otto's term for the feelings that experients have during a religious experience; the experience itself is beyond rational discussion.

Know Otto's Key Ideas

IMPROVE YOUR UNDERSTANDING

Make sure that you grasp how Otto defined numinous religious experiences.

Religious Experiences as Numinous

The literal meaning of 'numinous' is 'denoting or relating to a numen', which is a description of a great presence, great power or an awareness of the Divine. Otto coined this term when describing the feelings induced by a religious experience. Drawing on the work of philosopher and theologian Friedrich Schleiermacher, Otto states that religious experiences are not like other experiences that can be rationalised, or understood through reason alone. Although they may have some similarities to other human experiences – for example, a creeping fear in a forest in the dark that something is with you – they are experiences completely distinct, according to Otto, and deserve their own category away from any psychological or social understandings. As these experiences are ineffable (too extreme and intense to describe through language), it is very hard to explain to someone else what they are and how they feel.

A numinous experience is a 'non-rational, non-sensory experience or feeling whose primary or immediate object is outside the self'. Although religious experiences are extremely hard to put into words and ultimately beyond the realms of rational thought, we can see how they make people feel, and so Otto focuses on these *feelings* in his discussion of religious experiences.

A Fearful and Fascinating Mystery

Otto clarifies that numinous experiences are made up of three parts, or components, encompassed in the Latin phrase *Mysterium tremendum et fascinans*. By taking each term in the phrase, we can unpack Otto's components of a numinous experience.

Mysterium: majesty	*Tremendum*: an awesome encounter	*Fascinans*: fascination
The encounter is with something wholly 'other'. The German title of Otto's book translates as *The Holy*, not, as it often appears in English translations, *The Idea of the Holy*. For Otto, people encounter an objective reality, not just an idea. This emphasises the transcendent 'otherness' of God.	The experient feels full of awe, terror and dread that God or the Divine is unapproachable, and there is a sense of the 'wrath' of God. The experient is reminded of their own nothingness and powerlessness in comparison. They may have a sense of urgency, vitality and will due to the strength of the power in the moment.	Though terrified, the experient is drawn to this presence and encounter; they are curious and attracted towards it in spite of the power they are in awe of. They also feel a great love from and towards God or the Divine.

TIP

Remember that numinous experiences are both terrifying and compelling, as the experient feels a combination of fear, love, awe and compassion in the presence of 'God' or the Divine.

INSIGHT

Otto observes in his book, *The Idea of The Holy*: 'The reader is invited to direct his mind to a moment of deeply-felt religious experience … Whoever cannot do this, whoever knows no such moments in his experience, is requested to read no farther.' Otto believes that there is a human predisposition for religious experience, although not all humans will have one.

INSIGHT

According to Otto, all religions have numinous experiences at their core, and their teachings, institutions and beliefs are secondary. Numinous experiences give the experient an overwhelming sense of being in the presence of something wholly other than themselves; they then feel powerless and humbled by the power of the Divine.

ESSENTIAL!

Mysterium tremendum et fascinans is a Latin phrase meaning 'a terrifying and fascinating mystery'.

Numinous Experiences and the Abrahamic Faiths

In 1911, Otto was in Muslim Morocco at a Jewish synagogue on Yom Kippur (The Day of Atonement). Here he witnessed the mesmeric chanting of the words from Isaiah, 'Holy, Holy, Holy is the Lord of Hosts', and the powerful encounter that the experients had with something wholly other than themselves. This inspired him to write *The Idea of the Holy*. Otto's understanding of religious experiences fits particularly well with Abrahamic interpretations of the Divine, in which fear and awe (a compelling feeling to draw near, and a trembling at the thought) are often set together in scripture.

Consider the experience of Moses and the burning bush as described in Exodus 3:

> ¹Now Moses was tending the flock of Jethro his father-in-law, the priest of Midian, and he led the flock to the far side of the wilderness and came to Horeb, the mountain of God. ²There the angel of the Lord appeared to him in flames of fire from within a bush. Moses saw that though the bush was on fire it did not burn up. ³So Moses thought, 'I will go over and see this strange sight – why the bush does not burn up.'
>
> ⁴When the Lord saw that he had gone over to look, God called to him from within the bush, 'Moses! Moses!' And Moses said, 'Here I am.'
>
> ⁵'Do not come any closer,' God said. 'Take off your sandals, for the place where you are standing is holy ground.' ⁶Then he said, 'I am the God of your father, the God of Abraham, the God of Isaac and the God of Jacob.' At this, Moses hid his face, because he was afraid to look at God.
>
> (The Bible, New International Version)

Here Moses is drawn to the bush, and yet afraid to look at God.

Similarly, the Prophet Mohammed experienced the sensations of awe and fear during the first revelations of the Qur'an:

> The angel came and said, 'Read!' The Messenger of Allaah SAWS (peace and blessings of Allaah be upon him) said, 'I am not a reader.' He said, Then he took hold of me and squeezed me until I could not bear it any more then he released me and said, 'Read!' I said, 'I am not a reader.' He took hold of me and squeezed me a second time until I could not bear it any more, then he released me and said, 'Read!' I said, 'I am not a reader.' He took hold of me and squeezed me a third time until I could not bear it any more, then he released me and said,
>
> 'Read! In the Name of your Lord Who has created (all that exists).
>
> He has created man from a clot (a piece of thick coagulated blood).
>
> Read! And your Lord is the Most Generous.
>
> Who has taught (the writing) by the pen.
>
> He has taught man that which he knew not.'
>
> Then the Messenger of Allaah went back with his heart beating wildly, until he came to Khadeejah and said, 'Cover me! Cover me!' They covered him till his fear went away. Then he said to Khadeejah, 'O Khadeejah, I fear for myself.'
>
> (Hadith – Bukhari and Islam)

For Otto, these experiences are at the heart of all religions and come first, before religious doctrines and traditions. The scriptures of all three Abrahamic faiths include instructions such as 'Fear of the Lord is the beginning of wisdom' (Proverbs 9:10), 'Fear Allah … Allah is ever watchful of you' (Surah 4:1) and St Paul 'Work out your salvation with fear and trembling' (Philippians 2). This also chimes well with the experiences of Teresa of Avila (see Chapter 20) and contemporary Sufi worship within Islam. To Otto, these experiences are at the heart of all religions and span cultures and times. All humans are predisposed to being able to experience this feeling – although not all do.

> **INSIGHT**
>
> For Otto, all religions have numinous experiences at their core, and the teachings and traditions are secondary. Religious experiences cannot be rationally understood, so Otto focuses on what people feel when they have them.

WHAT DO YOU THINK?

Write down your thoughts on Otto's arguments and revisit them shortly before the exam to see if your views have changed.

Read Otto for Yourself

In this passage from *The Idea of the Holy* (1917), Otto explains what he means by the *mysterium tremendum*. The notes in the margin will help you to grasp his ideas.

> We are dealing with something for which there is only one appropriate expression, '*mysterium tremendum*'. The feeling of it may at times come sweeping like a gentle tide, pervading the mind with a tranquil mood of deepest worship. It may pass over into a more set and lasting attitude of the soul, continuing, as it were, thrillingly vibrant and resonant, until at last it dies away and the soul resumes its 'profane', non-religious mood of everyday experience. It may burst in sudden eruption up from the depths of the soul with spasms and convulsions, or lead to the strangest excitements, to intoxicated frenzy, to transport, and to ecstasy. It has its wild and demonic forms and can sink to an almost gristly horror and shuddering. It has its crude, barbaric antecedents and early manifestations, and again it may be developed into something beautiful and pure and glorious. It may become the hushed, trembling, and speechless humility of the creature in the presence of – whom or what? In the presence of that which is a mystery inexpressible and above all creatures.

- Otto's term for a mysterious experience that leaves us fearful but also in awe and wonder.
- It is distinct from normal life; we know we have encountered something sacred and of the Divine.
- The onlooker/observer may not understand what is happening, much like those who witnessed Pentecost assumed the Apostles were drunk.
- Otto is showing that these experiences are ineffable and cannot be expressed in words.

Know Criticisms of Otto

Pluralism of religious experiences. By accepting all numinous experiences across cultures and times as equally valid, and from the same source, Otto is in opposition to much Christian thought, as well as views within the other world religions that he speaks of. If the religions themselves teach there is one objective reality of God, then how do we know which one is right if all are equally valid? Many of Otto's Christian contemporaries found his views too open to other religions outside of the Christian domain, while others, such as Scottish philosopher Ninian Smart, found them too vague and woolly, and not detailed enough.

> **ESSENTIAL!**
>
> **Religious pluralism** is the idea that all religions have equal truth within them.

> **INSIGHT**
>
> Ninian Smart was a Scottish philosopher who pioneered the secular study of religions, according to which religions are studied from a non-religious viewpoint.

Other explanations for numinous feelings. It can be argued that Otto's understanding of the numinous is just a feeling which can be explained through other means. The creeping feeling of something following you in the dark of the forest can easily be explained through evolution: caution towards lurking predators is advisable. Likewise, there may be evolutionary explanations for all numinous feelings, and evolutionary biologists such as Richard Dawkins (see Chapter 19) would agree with this. There may also be physical explanations for the feelings: for example, the effects of temporal lobe epilepsy that V.S. Ramachandran and Michael Persinger have shown.

> **INSIGHT**
>
> Dawkins is an evolutionary biologist who would argue that all religious experiences have a physical cause and are a remnant of our evolution.
>
> Neuroscientist V.S. Ramachandran argues that a neurological 'cause' of religious experience does not prove it is not God; it could be a way of God allowing us to contact him.
>
> American professor of psychology Michael Persinger has induced religious experiences through his experiment 'The God Helmet'.

Generalising all religious experiences from Christian examples. Some of Otto's critics argue that he has taken an idea about religious experiences that best fits Christianity and imposed it on all other faiths, by claiming that all religions at their base have a numinous experience. While there may be examples within the Judeo-Christian religions, as Otto himself witnessed in Morocco, other religions such as Buddhism do not emphasise fear of the Divine. Instead, Buddhists experience feelings of overwhelming calmness and serenity when Enlightenment is attained. Likewise, this can be said of experiences during meditation within the Dharmic traditions of, for example, Hinduism, Buddhism and Sikhism.

Watch Out for Traps

Otto does not expect all religious believers to have a numinous experience. He does not say that every religious believer will have an encounter with 'God' or the Divine. Rather, he argues that all humans have the potential for this, but they will not necessarily see this potential fulfilled – a fact he admits at the start of his book *The Idea of the Holy*.

The English translation of Otto's book title is misleading. The title *The Idea of the Holy* is somewhat misleading because he was writing not about merely an idea of 'the Holy' but about an actual encounter with some objective essence that is wholly other than ourselves. That we can't express this outside of our own schema (our plan or theory) and understanding of the world does not mean that there is not an objective 'God' that we are encountering.

Otto does not mean that social and cultural ideas can explain away religious experiences. This can account for why a Muslim is less likely to see the face of Jesus than a Christian, and why a Catholic Christian is more likely to see Mary in a vision than a Jew. For Otto, this did not stand as a criticism, as it is precisely our social and cultural ideas and schema that help us to process and make sense of the encounter with 'God'. Building on Kant's ideas, Otto believed that we can only make sense of such an encounter through our own view of the world.

STRENGTHEN YOUR GRASP

1. Write your own explanation of Otto's view of the numinous, focusing on his description of these experiences as *mysterium tremendum*. Once you have read the chapters on Teresa of Avila, William James and Caroline Franks Davis (Chapters 20, 21 and 23), compare notes between them. What is similar about them? What is different? Cover your notes and see what you can remember of Otto's views and how these compare and contrast with the other scholars. This will help you prepare for an 'explain' question in the exam.

2. Make a list of the strengths and weaknesses of Otto's view of religious experiences. Make sure you consider how different questions may raise different evaluations. Consider how useful his view would be for defending the existence of God, compared to how useful it is as an understanding of religious experiences without a discussion around God's existence. Give a ranking out of five for each of the strengths and weaknesses you have listed, to help you select the evidence that you think will make the strongest points in an essay. This will help you prepare for an 'evaluate' question in the exam.

Exam Guidance AO1

You may be asked how Otto understands religious experiences, and how this compares and contrasts with the understandings of William James and Teresa of Avila. You may be asked specifically about his ideas around numinous religious experiences. You will need to know what the term 'numinous' means and be able to exemplify this with religious practices and figures. You will also need to know the three parts to Otto's idea: *mysterium*, *tremendum* and *fascinans*. You may be asked a more general question on the argument for the existence of God from religious experience, in which case you will find Otto's defence of an objective reality 'God' useful.

Exam Guidance AO2

An evaluation question could ask you to weigh up the strengths and weaknesses of Otto's understanding of the numinous, or the strengths and weaknesses of the argument for the existence of God from religious experience more generally. A strength of Otto's view could be that it is a helpful categorisation which distinguishes religious experiences from other experiences in life. With its focus on feelings, it is centred on what matters to the believer, and we can take the comparative religious approach of considering the similarities across different traditions without necessarily needing to argue the existence of God. The 'Know Criticisms of Otto' section of this chapter will help you to consider the weaknesses. You should come to your own evaluation as to how helpful or adequate his view is.

23. CAROLINE FRANKS DAVIS

GET INTO DAVIS' WORLD

Quick Overview Caroline Franks Davis is a key contributor to discussions around the argument for the existence of God from religious experience. She wrote the key text *The Evidential Force of Religious Experience* as her PhD thesis and published it as a book in 1987 while at the University of Oxford. She now works as a researcher at Saskatchewan University, Canada.

Caroline Franks Davis wrote *The Evidential Force of Religious Experience* while completing her PhD under the supervision of Basil Mitchell (see Chapter 29) at the University of Oxford. She was writing at a time when discussions around the nature of religious language and the truth claims of religions were being scrutinised and faced the specific challenges brought up by New Atheism.

INSIGHT

New Atheism is a movement that encourages scrutiny and criticism of religious ideas, rather than simply tolerance of them. See Chapter 19 on Richard Dawkins for more on this.

While at Oxford, Davis studied under such key thinkers as Richard Swinburne (see Chapter 25) an , of course, Basil Mitchell. Both thinkers were instrumental in aiding Christians in the discussions around reason, faith and belief at a time when the 'Four Horsemen of New Atheism' and others were pushing for closer scrutiny of faith claims and religions. A key element of Swinburne's writing that influenced Davis is his principles of testimony and credulity when applied to someone who claims to have had a religious experience.

> **INSIGHT**
>
> In *The Existence of God* (2004), Swinburne wrote: 'It is a principle of rationality that (in the absence of special considerations) if it seems (epistemically) to a subject that χ is present, then probably χ is present; what one seems to perceive is probably so.'
>
> Davis refers to this in her book *The Evidential Force of Religious Experience*: 'These principles of credulity and testimony are ultimate principles of rationality which ally to all types of perceptual experience.'

It is in this setting that Davis presents her influential book on the interpretation of religious experiences as being from God. In her book she relays the common criticisms of religious experiences as proof of the existence of God and then proceeds to rebut them by showing how they can, in fact, add to arguments for why God does indeed exist.

> **INSIGHT**
>
> In *The Evidential Force of Religious Experience*, Davis outlines the key criticisms made of the argument from religious experience and explains how each of them can be countered. She takes the approach that, taken together with other evidence, they contribute to a cumulative argument for God's existence (see below).

Throughout her writing Davis draws on ideas from other contemporary writers of philosophical theology:

- Janet Martin Soskice and her approach of **critical realism**, a branch of philosophy which tried to take a middle ground between empiricism and social constructionism. Soskice influences Davis' emphasis on the importance of our interpretations of events as religious experiences.
- Margaret Yees' writing on the validity of theology, particularly her defence of the claims of theology as having meaning and the ability to withstand an empirico-critical scrutiny. Engagement with the physical and social sciences, and showing how religious experiences can still be valid in the face of such scrutiny, are central to Davis' work.

> **ESSENTIAL!**
>
> **Critical realism** is a branch of philosophy that sees a distinct difference between the 'real' and the 'observable' world.

Know Davis' Key Ideas

> **IMPROVE YOUR UNDERSTANDING**
>
> Make sure that you know what description-related, subject-related and object-related challenges are to religious experiences and how Davis overcomes these.

A Critical Realist Approach

Davis writes very much in the tradition of Richard Swinburne, who supervised the end of her PhD writing. She seeks to defend a realist view of religion and religious experiences from the attacks of logical positivism, as well as to offer an alternative view to the purely symbolic understandings of scholars such as John Randall (see Chapter 31).

> **INSIGHT**
>
> Randall, in contrast to Davis, viewed religious language as symbolic and mythological.

Davis takes a critical realist approach, which can be seen as a mid-point between the logical positivist interpretation of religious experiences and that of the purely symbolic and interpretive.

Logical positivist	Critical realist	Symbolic/interpretive
All talk of religious experiences is meaningless as they cannot be empirically verified.	Talk of religious experiences should be open to critical inquiry, but not dismissed as meaningless.	All talk of religious experiences is symbolic. They cannot be understood in any other way.
That someone has 'experienced God' cannot be shown to be true through our senses, as God is 'beyond' our senses. Therefore, religious experiences cannot have any evidential force.	Someone speaking of 'experiencing God' might have had a truly transformational experience with great significance for them and their community – but this it not taken at face value and the social, psychological and cultural contexts of the experience are also considered.	Someone speaking of 'experiencing God' is using the term 'God' as a symbol for something that cannot be expressed fully in words. This cannot have any evidential force beyond individual and subjective interpretation.
Religious experiences and talk of them are not **cognitive**. This means that they do not have meaningful content.		

> **ESSENTIAL!**
>
> To interpret religious language as **cognitive** is to say that it should be taken literally as true or false. To interpret religious language non-cognitively is to say that it is neither true nor false but may have some other meaning.

INSIGHT

'In order for an investigation of religious experience as evidence for something beyond purely autobiographical claims to get off the ground we must defend the proposition that religious experience and religious utterances can and ought to be treated as capable of having cognitive content' (Davis, *The Evidential Force of Religious Experience*).

Three Types of Challenge to the Claim of Religious Experience

As part of her argument, Davis identifies three types of challenge to the claim that someone has had a religious experience.

Type of challenge	Explanation
Description-related challenges	These criticisms focus on how the description of the religious event could be doubted: for example, when the description is not coherent or logically consistent. There may be inconsistencies between what was said to have been experienced, and how the experient then goes on to behave, which may not be in the way we would expect after such an experience. The experient may also be known as a liar and therefore not able to be trusted to provide a valid account. The experient may not have remembered the experience correctly, or may have misunderstood the experience.
Subject-related challenges	These criticisms focus on how the person claiming the religious experience may be doubted as a reliable source. For example, dreams, visions and hallucinations are not generally regarded as reliable. Different religious experiences also make different claims about God, the Ultimate Reality or the Divine that are often in conflict, leading to the question of how they can all be valid. Finally, challenges are posed regarding the state of the person when they had their experience – were they lacking in sleep or on hallucinogenic drugs? It is here that Freud's psychological challenges to religious experiences are obvious – did the experient have a strong desire or wish that was being fulfilled?
Object-related challenges	These criticisms focus on the claim of religious experience in general and how this can be doubted. First, it is argued that God, the Ultimate Reality or the Divine is unlikely to exist and is improbable. This may be a challenge to the type of God in the experience – for example, a God commanding someone to harm another – or a more general criticism that God does not exist and therefore cannot be experienced. Second, it is argued that other people present at the event may not have seen or perceived anything, meaning that the occurrence itself is brought into question.

INSIGHT

Freud understood religion as a form of wish fulfilment whereby humans long for a father figure to care for them, who controls the forces of nature and can help to control the forces within us (see Chapter 17).

CAROLINE
FRANKS DAVIS

Davis' Responses

Davis uses three different methods to respond to these challenges to the validity of religious experiences.

	Description-related challenges	Subject-related challenges	Object-related challenges
How the challenge can be overcome	Many beliefs about God seem incoherent and illogical, which means the religious experience also seems illogical. Sometimes change takes a long time; in fact, an observer may never witness a change in the experient. This does not take away from the claim of an experience happening. Memories of important and vivid moments such as a religious experience are less likely to be forgotten.	There is a common core of the revelation of God's nature in all religious experiences; claims of experiences are often centred on an all-powerful, all-loving 'being' connecting with humanity. Differences between them can be understood through the upbringing and cultural setting of the experient, but at their core there is something that unites them all.	Some may experience God while others do not, but this is not inconsistent with the nature of God and belief. If faith and an openness to receive an experience are accounted for, we can see how some may have an experience while others do not. Religious experiences may not prove the existence of God from one standalone event, but taken together with other experiences and other arguments for the existence of God, they can build a powerful case.
The words of Caroline Franks Davis	'Description-related challenges are not generally successful.'	'One must not assume some undetected (and probably undetectable) pathology in an otherwise healthy individual.'	'But [religious experiences'] most important place will be within a cumulative argument.'

> **TIP**
>
> Remember that Davis presents the challenges to religious experiences in order to rebut them, concluding that they are evidence pointing towards the existence of God.

Testimony and Credulity

Richard Swinburne (see Chapter 25) is an important influence on the ideas of Davis around religious experiences. Davis builds on his principles of **testimony** and **credulity**, and the idea of a cumulative argument for God's existence.

> **ESSENTIAL!**
>
> The principle of **credulity** states that we should believe that things are as they seem, unless there is some evidence to show we are wrong. We do this for other things we experience in our life, so why not for religious experiences?
>
> The principle of **testimony** states that we should believe others if they claim to have had a religious experience – unless there is a reason why we should not.

> **INSIGHT**
>
> Richard Swinburne is a Christian philosopher and theologian who defends theism and Christianity against the challenges posed by empiricism and, more recently, the New Atheist movement.

One prominent Christian apologetic writer who influenced Swinburne was C.S. Lewis. His non-fictional work defending Christianity, such as *Mere Christianity* (1952), influenced Swinburne's own *Existence of God* (2004). Lewis also used fictional stories to defend the Christian faith, most notably in the *Chronicles of Narnia* (published between 1950 and 1956), which contain many key Christian teachings.

INSIGHT

Lewis succinctly illustrated the defence of religious experiences used by Swinburne and Davis in his children's book *The Lion, The Witch and The Wardrobe* (1950), in which the youngest child in the Pevensie family discovers a new world beyond the back of the wardrobe. Her eldest siblings go to the Professor, who owns the house they are living in, to ask him what to do with her, as she is obviously lying or mistaken. He responds that they should believe her, through use of logic.

"'Logic!' said the Professor half to himself. "Why don't they teach logic at these schools? There are only three possibilities. Either your sister is telling lies, or she is mad, or she is telling the truth. You know she doesn't tell lies and it is obvious that she is not mad for the moment then and unless any further evidence turns up, we must assume that she is telling the truth'" (Lewis, *The Lion, the Witch and the Wardrobe*).

Understand Davis' Arguments
The Multiple Claims Challenge

One key challenge to the validity of claims of religious experience is that there are too many conflicting experiences from different religious traditions (and sometimes within the same tradition) for there to be any truth to the claims of God or the Divine that is encountered. In *The Evidential Force of Religious Experience*, Davis describes this as 'the challenge that since subjects cannot agree on a description of the alleged percept their experiences must be, at worst, illusory, or, at best, serious misperceptions. In any case, they are generally unreliable'.

Davis overcomes this by showing that there is a 'common core' in all religious experiences. This is supported by William James and Rudolf Otto (see Chapters 21 and 22), who highlighted commonalities between religious, and in particular mystical, experiences across different religious traditions. While the details may differ across experiences, these can be accounted for through cultural differences. The individual's upbringing, for example, will lead them to interpret an experience in a certain way, or they will be more able to experience something in one way than another. At their core will be a similarity, which for Davis points towards there being a theistic God.

Overcoming the Reductionist Challenge

Reductionist challenges to religious experiences claim that religious experiences can be understood through or 'reduced to' natural causes. These are presented most notably by Karl Marx, Émile Durkheim and Sigmund Freud, who each argued that religious experiences are, in some way, induced by society or the mind.

INSIGHT

Otto coined the term 'numinous' to describe mystical experiences where the experient is overcome with a compelling fear and awe at being in the presence of something 'wholly other'.

James categorised mystical religious experiences as being passive, ineffable, noetic or transient.

INSIGHT

'Perhaps the most popular current challenge to religious experience is the "reductionist" challenge' (Davis, *The Evidential Force of Religious Experience*).

Marx's view	Religion is used by those with power in society. They use religion to influence those without power and religious experiences are part of this influence. Experiences may be felt powerfully by the individual but they offer comfort and the hope of an afterlife where there is none. They have opiate qualities, as they do not remove the cause of the pain but they do create apathy.
Durkheim's view	Religion is a tool of society to help people feel connected to one another and agree on the values and norms of their society. Religious experiences have a part to play as they help people to feel connected to one another and share their commitment to their idea of 'God'. Religious experiences happen not because someone is experiencing God, but because they are experiencing a strong sense of meaning and reinforcement of these important messages of their society. Durkheim called this 'collective effervescence' and it is like the placebo effect.
Freud's view	Religion is a creation of the human mind. It is a symptom of the illness all humans suffer from – the guilt and disgust we have that is a by-product of the Oedipus complex. It is a collective (rather than individual) neurosis, and religion is one mechanism used to rid ourselves of it. Religion is a form of wish fulfilment and religious experiences are therefore induced by our own minds in order to give hope that these wishes are being fulfilled.

> **INSIGHT**
>
> 'Religious experiences are not the sort of thing which can easily be produced for observation in a controlled setting' (Davis, *The Evidential Force of Religious Experience*).

Davis rebuts these thinkers' views as simply theories on religion which are either non-empirical or no longer viewed as empirical (for example, Freud's view that religion is a collective neurosis). She also argues that they do not explain the wealth and diversity of religious experiences that humans have had – this links to the cumulative argument below.

The Cumulative Argument

Davis incorporates Swinburne's ideas into her theories by arguing that religious experiences contribute to an inductive and **cumulative argument** for the existence of God. This argument states that the wealth of religious experiences which have happened across time and cultures points towards there being some divine source to them all. She also argues that, taken in accumulation with other arguments for the existence of God, religious experiences help to build the case that God does in fact exist. 'A good case can often be made for highly ramified religious beliefs which do not depend on the evidence of religious experiences alone', she argues.

> **ESSENTIAL!**
>
> The **cumulative argument** says that individual events or arguments may not prove God's existence, but when taken together, they make a strong case.

> **WHAT DO YOU THINK?**
>
> Write down your thoughts on Davis' arguments and revisit them shortly before the exam to see if your views have changed.

> **TASK**
>
> Read Davis for yourself in the extract below. The notes in the margin will help you to grasp her views.

Read Davis for Yourself

In this passage from *The Evidential Force of Religious Experience* (1987), Davis outlines the importance of studying religious experiences in order to gain an understanding of key religious doctrines. The notes in the margin will help you to grasp her ideas.

CAROLINE FRANKS DAVIS

It is only comparatively recently in the history of civilisation that there has been widespread scepticism regarding religious experiences. Arguments against the plausibility of religious doctrines and reductionist accounts of religious experiences are now widely accepted, and many people lead atheistic lives which are to all appearances perfectly adequate. Therefore, religious individuals can no longer assume that experiences judged to be 'genuine' by fellow believers are immune from further attack. They are challenged on all sides, by philosophers, psychologists, sociologists, anthropologists, members of other religious traditions, and even by members of their own tradition with widely differing views. [*The Evidential Force of Religious Experience*] examines the value of religious experiences as evidence for religious claims. Its goal is to discover the role which religious experience can legitimately play in the defence of religious doctrines.

> Davis wants to tackle the recent scrutiny that religious experiences are held up to, and show that they can face this and still be taken as valid claims.
>
> This is a reminder of the important link between claims of religious experience and the teachings and beliefs of those faiths as a result.
>
> These are ways that religious experiences may be challenged by 'reducing' them down to a physical or natural cause.
>
> Davis is aware of anti-realist approaches to religion which would reduce religious experiences to symbols and subjective interpretations rather than as proof of a realist, objective God.
>
> Religious experiences are part of the overall defence of the existence of God when taken with other arguments.

Know Criticisms of Davis

Challenges to the 'common core' claim. A central part of Davis' support for religious experiences is her insistence that there is enough of a 'common core' of similarities between experiences across cultures and time to point to the existence of a theistic God. Welsh philosopher H.P. Owen challenged this, stating in a review of Davis' book that she was deliberately selective in her examples: 'My chief query concerns her appeal to a "common core" in reply to the "conflicting claims" challenge.'

This is a challenge posed by David Hume to accounts of miracles – that the claim of one miracle can conflict with the claim of another, leading the sceptic to question which can be true (if indeed either can be true). For many religious believers, miracles and religious experiences are central to the teachings of their faith, which are in direct contradiction to the teachings of another faith. One example is that Jesus' death on the cross and subsequent resurrection is central to Christianity's teachings, whereas it is crucially important within Islam that Isa was not crucified but miraculously saved from this, and ascended to heaven without dying.

Other scholars have criticised Davis for not accounting for enough of the challenges posed to the argument from religious experience. For example, the American philosopher Professor Pamela Sue Anderson said: 'What about the challenge – since Davis is concerned with challenges – of Ludwig Feuerbach?'

Feuerbach was a German philosopher whose critiques of religion influenced other atheistic writers such as Freud and Marx. He argued that religion (and therefore religious experiences) is a projection of our human wants and desires: for example, the longing for a loving father is satisfied through the belief in a father figure as God. This is similar to (and influenced the ideas of) Freud (see Chapter 17).

Naturalistic challenges. Scholars such as Richard Dawkins and Sam Harris would argue that all religious experiences have some natural, rather than supernatural, cause. This is evidenced through developments in neuroscience whereby religious experiences can be caused through stimulation of the temporal lobes of the brain (for example, the so-called 'God Helmet' experiment – see Chapter 19). While some thinkers, such as Ramachandran and Bishop Stephen Sykes may see this as how God has built brains, so that humans could have an experience with the Divine, for Dawkins, the evidence of a naturalistic cause rules out the need for something supernatural.

EVALUATION SKILLS

An answer to an evaluative question about a scholar is always deepened by demonstrating awareness of how other thinkers have disagreed.

INSIGHT

'Longing says: There must be a personal God, i.e. it cannot be that there is not; satisfied feeling says he is' (Ludwig Feuerbach, *The Essence of Christianity*, 1841).

INSIGHT

'The argument from personal experience is the one that is the most convincing to those who claim to have had one. But it is the least convincing to anyone else, especially anyone knowledgeable about psychology' (Dawkins, *The God Delusion* (2006)).

CAROLINE **FRANKS DAVIS**

Watch Out for Traps

Davis does not only set out the challenges to religious experiences. While Davis' categorisations of the challenges posed to claims of religious experiences are useful in setting out the case against religious experiences being proof of God, she counters these in her book. She believes that religious experiences still present a compelling case for the existence of a theistic God within an inductive, cumulative argument.

Davis does not claim that all religious experiences are genuine. Davis acknowledges that there will be people who lie, who are under the influence of drugs, who may be mentally ill, or who may just misunderstand an experience when they claim they have had an encounter with God. These are known as **subject-related challenges**. For Davis, however, this is not enough to discredit *all* claims of religious experiences.

Davis does not argue that religious experiences prove there is a God. Like Swinburne before her, Davis is using religious experience as part of an inductive argument for the existence of God. For Davis, the evidence from religious experiences points towards it being likely that there is a theistic God, and when this is accumulated with other arguments for that God's existence, the case becomes even stronger.

> **ESSENTIAL!**
>
> **Subject-related challenges** focus on the person who has the religious experience and may question their state of mind.

STRENGTHEN YOUR GRASP

1. Write your own explanation of Davis' defence of religious experiences. Include the following: description-, subject- and object-related challenges. Have examples for each of these and make sure you show how Davis rebuts them. Cover your notes and see what you can remember of these areas. This will help you prepare for an 'explain' question in the exam.

2. Make a list of the strengths and weaknesses of Davis' defence of religious experiences. How does her understanding compare and contrast with others – for example, Otto, James and Teresa of Avila? Give a ranking out of five for each of these strengths and weaknesses to help you select the evidence that you think will make the strongest points in an essay. This will help you prepare for an 'evaluate' question in the exam.

Exam Guidance A01

You may need to give an account of Davis' understanding and defence of religious experiences, and you may also be able to use her understanding in a more general question on religious experience. You should be able to explain the challenges to religious experience that Davis sets out, as well as how she then rebuts them. Be aware of how this is linked not only to other scholars concerned with religious experiences, but also to a discussion of religious language and empiricism.

Exam Guidance A02

Through considering the strengths and weaknesses of Davis' defence of religious experiences, you can evaluate how successfully she achieves her aim of defending them against the scrutiny and challenges she outlines.

24. R.F. HOLLAND

GET INTO HOLLAND'S WORLD

> **Quick Overview** R.F. Holland (1923–2013) was part of the 'Swansea School', which was a group of analytical philosophers based at Swansea University in the late twentieth century. He was known for his unflinching approach to philosophical questions – the most famous of which led to his understanding of 'the miraculous'.

R.F. Holland studied Classics at the University of Oxford, although this was interrupted during the Second World War when he signed up for military service and travelled to Africa and south-east Asia. On returning to academia, he took a particular interest in philosophical psychology. After hearing Ludwig Wittgenstein speak at Swansea University, he decided to form the 'Swansea Wittgensteinians'.

Holland was particularly influenced by Wittgenstein's later period of work, which focused on the use of language and the importance of the context for its meaning. We can see this influence in Holland's view of a miracle as an event seen to be miraculous by the person who experiences or witnesses it – their subjective interpretation of the event decides if it was a miracle or not, and it is not appropriate for another person to declare otherwise. In the same way, when we use religious language among a community of believers, we have our own subjective understanding of the terminology, which outsiders, who are not within our community, will be unable to understand or comment upon.

Holland took many influential academic positions across northern England through his career in philosophy, and he wrote many journal articles but only one book, *Against Empiricism* (1980). Perhaps his most famous essay, 'The Miraculous' (1965), in which he sets out his understanding of contingency miracles (see below), is our focus for this chapter.

Know Holland's Key Ideas
Interpreting Miracles

In contrast to an understanding of miracles as breaking the laws of nature, Holland views miracles as having natural causes. What makes an event a miracle is not necessarily the cause of the event but how these events are interpreted by those who experience or witness them. An out-of-the-ordinary coincidence can be seen by some to be the work of God, especially if this brings about some good for, or within, the person. This natural event may be seen as a sign of God's providence and protection for God's creation. The event is beneficial to the person in some way, rather than a natural event that may harm and destroy. Events that bring about a bad consequence for the person will not be interpreted as a miracle, or an act of a benevolent God.

> **INSIGHT**
> Holland was greatly influenced by Wittgenstein's Language Game theory of religious language (see Chapter 33) and viewed the meaning of a 'miracle' as being defined by the person who experiences it rather than those outside of the experience.

> **ESSENTIAL!**
> **Empiricism** is the belief that knowledge of the world is gained through use of our senses and experimentation.

> **INSIGHT**
> In Holland's view, religious believers will interpret an extraordinary event or coincidence as a miracle – proof of God's involvement in their life. The personal experience of a miracle is key to Holland's definition.

Although in the 'Know Criticisms of Holland' section we will see that many religious people would not accept Holland's understanding of miracles, his interpretation can be said to fit with some religious teachings.

- In the Qur'an, Muslims are told that there are 'Signs' or Ayah which show us that the Qur'an is true: 'He has subjected to you all that is in the heavens and the earth, all being from Him. Verily there are Signs in this for those who reflect' (Surah Al-Jathiyah Ayat 45:13).
- In the New Testament of the Bible, the Greek term *semeiois* is translated as 'signs', which are also seen as miracles: 'Fellow Israelites, listen to this: Jesus of Nazareth was a man accredited by God to you by miracles, wonders and signs [*semeiois*] which God did among you through him, as you yourselves know' (Acts 2:22).

William Lane Craig (see Chapter 2) interprets it in this way: a natural event is seen as a miracle of God because it works for the good of the prisoners who were wrongly held. This also relates to Paul Tillich's understanding of religious language (see Chapter 32).

Understand Holland's Arguments

IMPROVE YOUR UNDERSTANDING

Make sure that you know what Holland's example of the child caught on the tracks is and how this exemplifies his definition of a miracle.

Contingency Miracles

Holland's view of miracles differs from those of David Hume (Chapter 5), Richard Swinburne (Chapter 25) and Aquinas (Chapter 1), who viewed miracles as the **violation** of the laws of nature. In contrast, Holland defined them as the interpretation of an extraordinary event. In doing so, he placed the religious significance of the event squarely on the experient rather than the cause of the event itself.

TIP

Holland's view of miracles can be contrasted with the realist approach held by Thomas Aquinas.

Holland exemplifies this through the short story of a child being stuck on railway tracks while out with his mother. A train rushes towards the spot where the child is stuck. The train driver does not see the boy and vice versa. The mother yells at her son to move but he cannot. Suddenly, the train stops just before it hits the child. The mother views this event as a miracle. However, the train driver had actually fainted and the train had stopped automatically.

This is an example of a **contingency or coincidence miracle**. It is unclear from Holland's writing if he believed that God intervened or not. What matters is the *interpretation* of religious significance by the person who witnesses or experiences the event. We can see the influence of Language Game theory on this concept – the miracle makes sense and has meaning to all those who interpret it in the same way, due to the fact that they are playing the same 'game'. In this sense, the empirical proof of a miracle does not matter, but the interpretation of the event does.

> **ESSENTIAL!**
>
> **Violation miracles** are a realist understanding that miracles occur when the laws of nature are broken by God.

> **ESSENTIAL!**
>
> A **contingency or coincidence miracle** is an understanding or interpretation of an extraordinary event as an act of God by the person who experiences or witnesses it.

WHAT DO YOU THINK?

Write down your thoughts on Holland's arguments and revisit them shortly before the exam to see if your views have changed.

Read Holland for Yourself

In this passage from 'The Miraculous' (1965), Holland explains his example of the child caught on the tracks. The notes in the margin will help you to grasp his ideas.

> The mother thanks God for the miracle, which she never ceases to think of as such although, as she in due course learns, there was nothing supernatural about the manner in which the brakes of the train came to be applied. The driver had fainted, for a reason that had nothing to do with the presence of the child on the line, and the brakes were applied automatically as his hand ceased to exert pressure on the control lever.

The mother sees the event as a miracle. Others may not, but this is how she views the event.

Miracles, according to Holland, are not violations of nature, but coincidental natural events, with a beneficial effect interpreted to have been caused by God or the Divine.

Know Criticisms of Holland

Religious believers take a realist view of miracles. As this is an important part of their faith, the **realist** approaches of Swinburne and Aquinas may be more appealing to them. Holland's understanding of miracles leaves much to individual interpretation of events. On his understanding, the question remains as to whether God caused the event at all. In contrast to violation miracles, which may be witnessed by many and break the laws of nature, Holland's contingency miracles are subjective. For Holland, it is down to the individual believer to determine if something was a miracle or not.

The trilemma of C.S. Lewis. Lewis provided a criticism of the anti-real view of miracles with his 'trilemma': if Jesus himself claimed to perform miracles, was he lying, a mad man or telling an objective truth?

Stephen Law's 'Evil God' challenge. Critics use Stephen Law's 'Evil God' challenge to question why only the extraordinary events that have a positive outcome for the individual are seen as the work of a benevolent God. Could it not be that the extraordinary events that have a negative outcome for the individual can be seen as the work of a malevolent God?

Watch Out for Traps

Holland is not saying the religious believer is unaware that their miracle has a natural cause. For Holland, the believer is aware of the natural causes of extraordinary events. What matters is their interpretation of it, as in the case he gives of the boy on the train track. The event is believed to be a sign of God's love and power, which have a positive outcome for the child. The event could very well have natural causes, but the believer sees God as the architect of the timing of the natural event.

ESSENTIAL!

The **realist** view of miracles is that miracles are an objective event, independent of the mind that considers them, and that these are therefore caused by God.

INSIGHT

The 'Evil God' challenge is posed by philosophers such as Law to question theists about why the God they believe in is necessarily 'good' or 'omnibenevolent'. All the evidence used for this God could equally be used to show a 'bad' or 'evil' God instead.

TIP

Consider how adequate Holland's definition is for understanding what a miracle means to a religious believer.

STRENGTHEN YOUR GRASP

1. Write your own explanation of Holland's definition of miracles as contingent on the interpretation of the person who witnesses or experiences the event. Include the following: sign, miracle, contingency, positive. Cover your notes and see what you can remember of those four areas. This will help you prepare for an 'explain' question in the exam.
2. Compare the understanding of 'miracles' between Aquinas, Hume, Holland and Swinburne. What are the strengths and weaknesses of each one? Give a rating out of five for each understanding and write an explanation of why you chose one to be higher than the others. What would each of the scholars argue to the others about their understandings? Would some agree more with others?

Exam Guidance AO1

For an explain-style question you will need to know what Holland's definition of a miracle is and how this differs from the definitions given by Hume, Aquinas and Swinburne. You should also know his example of the boy caught on the train tracks and be able to show how this exemplifies his definition. Other examples of miracles would be useful to know for an 'explain' question, perhaps that of the earthquake in the book of Acts in the New Testament section of the Bible.

Exam Guidance AO2

For an evaluation-style question, decide how adequate and useful Holland's definition of miracles is. Consider this from the perspective of a believer as well as the perspective of a non-theist: does this make a difference to the usefulness of his definition? The 'Know Criticisms of Holland' section will help you to consider the weaknesses and stretch your thinking. Try writing responses to the criticisms as if from Holland's perspective.

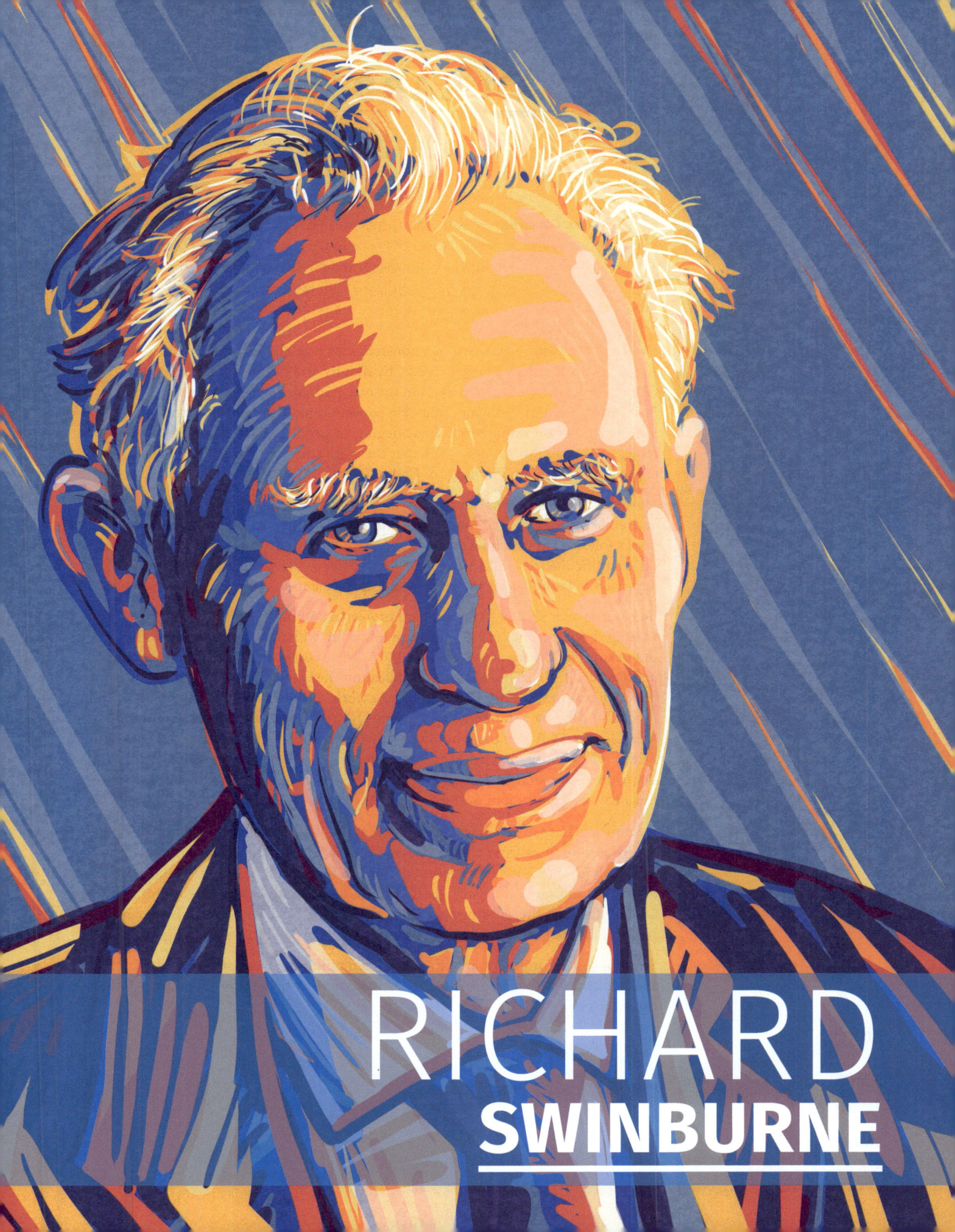

25. RICHARD SWINBURNE
GET INTO SWINBURNE'S WORLD

> **Quick Overview** Richard Swinburne (born 1934) is a key Christian apologetic scholar, and Emeritus Professor of Philosophy at the University of Oxford. He has faced many of the traditional criticisms of a theistic faith and offered alternative understandings for many philosophical problems.

Richard Swinburne was raised in a non-religious household and introduced to Anglicanism at school. He embraced Christianity and gained a scholarship to study Classics at Exeter College, Oxford but instead graduated with a first-class degree in Philosophy, Politics and Economics. He converted to Orthodox Christianity in 1995. During studies for his undergraduate degree, he developed an interest in the central issues of philosophy, including whether there are adequate reasons to believe in God, and especially in the main teachings of Christianity.

However, Swinburne was more focused on the philosophy of science at the start of his academic career. His first book, *Space and Time*, was published in 1968, and several more books followed in which he explored relativity theory and cosmology. This early focus on scientific theories influences Swinburne's later work, where he offered many theists an approach to faith that attempted to stand up to scientific scrutiny rather than avoid it.

Swinburne later shifted to focusing on problems within the philosophy of religion, writing about miracles (1971) and then following with his trilogy on the philosophy of theism; *The Coherence of Theism* (1977), *The Existence of God* (2004) and *Faith and Reason* (1981). Through these publications he wanted to show a natural theology, providing naturalistic arguments from the world around us for the existence of God, much like other key thinkers in philosophy have before, such as Thomas Aquinas (see Chapter 1). It is in these books that Swinburne sets out many of the theories to be discussed in this chapter. Swinburne later wrote specifically on the key Christian doctrines of atonement, the resurrection of Jesus and the problem of evil, showing the links between philosophy and theology.

Swinburne's later work also focused on the mind–body problem within philosophy, incorporating ideas from philosophers of the past on the relationship between the mind and the body alongside more recent understandings of the workings of the brain. He argues for 'substance dualism', where the mind and body are separate but influence one another through the workings of the brain. This further illustrates the interplay between philosophy and science, which has long been part of Swinburne's writings.

Swinburne's commitment to both science and philosophy as justified methods of enquiry about faith helps to reassure modern theists that their beliefs are coherent and can stand up to scrutiny.

INSIGHT

Richard Dawkins is a contemporary of Swinburne, and they have debated each other through publications and in person. Dawkins recognises that, even though they reach vastly different conclusions, Swinburne is committed to proper discussions of the existence of God rather than using 'flabby evasions' and 'obscurantism'.

Know Swinburne's Key Ideas
The God that Swinburne Believes In

In *The Coherence of Theism*, Swinburne set out his reasoning for why a belief in a theistic God is logically coherent and can be discussed through meaningful language. This significant contribution to philosophical discussions made Swinburne a voice of reasoned theism, providing solutions and responses to the problems posed to theistic belief from within philosophy. The book title does not imply that it is necessarily true that there is a theistic God, but that it can be a rational belief to hold and discuss.

INSIGHT

The Coherence of Theism was Swinburne's 1977 defence of how a belief in God can be rational and coherent. This includes his defence both of miracles and of religious language as meaningful.

Swinburne states that looking at a range of evidence can show that it is more likely than less that there is a God – and that this is the simplest and most complete answer.

A key element of Swinburne's defence of the existence of a theistic God is 'scientific principle'. When we are looking for a cause or reason behind a certain event, the simplest one will often suffice. Swinburne uses examples such as a detective sifting through evidence to find the likely criminal. The detective doesn't look for an over-complicated and convoluted solution, but simply follows the evidence. This mirrors the principle of Occam's razor – that simpler explanations require less verification and are therefore more likely to be true. For Swinburne, when faced with the philosophical problem of why there is a universe in the first place, and what caused life to develop and exist, an omnipotent and omnibenevolent God is the simplest and most complete answer. This has been challenged by scholars such as evolutionary biologist Richard Dawkins (see Chapter 19).

ESSENTIAL!

The **cumulative argument** for the existence of God states that 'God exists' is the best explanation for the universe, moral values and religious experiences, using a combination of varying arguments rather than an individual argument to prove God's existence.

Despite the flaws in the arguments for God's existence, including the cosmological and teleological approaches, religious experience and miracles (Swinburne does not view the ontological argument as convincing for the existence of God), taken together they make a viable case for God's existence. This is referred to as a **cumulative argument** for the existence of God, and has influenced many other scholars such as Caroline Franks Davis (see Chapter 23). Swinburne points to an orderliness that runs throughout the universe, which he says can only exist due to an omnipotent and omnibenevolent being. Interestingly, Antony Flew (see Chapter 27) converted later in life from atheism to deism, and credited Swinburne's arguments around the orderliness of the universe as a contributing factor.

The belief that there is an omnipotent, omnibenevolent and omniscient God means that philosophical problems arise as to how God can have all of these attributes at once. Scholars such as J.L. Mackie (see Chapter 13) suggest there can be no solution to this conflict. If God is all powerful, for example, does that mean that God can sin? Can God do the logically impossible, too? If God is all knowing, and knows the future, where does that leave human free will? What is the point of prayer? Finally, if God is all loving, why is there such suffering in the world?

Swinburne offers a solution to these apparent conflicts using his depiction of God as 'self-limiting'. This goes beyond a limitation to only do that which is logically possible, which other Christian philosophers had proposed. For Swinburne, if humans can have a loving relationship with God, his knowledge, power and revelations are deliberately limited. God has infinite knowledge, power and love, but for the sake of humanity he limits himself, as detailed in the table below.

Limited knowledge of the future	Limited intervention in the world	Limited revelation
God limits his omniscience so that he does not know all future events and actions. This allows for humans to be morally free, rather than acting out pre-destined plans that God already has knowledge of – meaning there would no longer be a free choice.	God could intervene at every moment, but does not do so. Therefore, we can have knowable natural laws and function as humans in making decisions about our lives. God can and does intervene on occasion, but only in extraordinary circumstances.	God does not give humans overwhelming evidence for his existence. Therefore, humans are still making personal choices for faith, meaning that this can be something genuinely chosen. This links to Swinburne's cumulative argument for the existence of God (see also Caroline Franks Davis in Chapter 23).

■ INSIGHT

Swinburne argues that God, out of respect for human freedom and choice, limits his foreknowledge, interventions and revelations in the world.

It is against this backdrop, or this 'wider knowledge' of the world and its relationship to God, that Swinburne presents his defence of theistic belief in both defence of miracles against the criticisms of David Hume (see Chapter 5) and against the challenges posed by the logical positivist movement.

Defining and Defending Miracles

The term 'miracle' stems from the Latin *mirus*, meaning 'amazing, wonderful and marvellous'. However, it has religious connotations within all faiths. Various attempts have been made within philosophy to define what we mean by a 'miracle'. With this problem in mind, before defending miracles from the criticisms of Hume (see Chapter 5), Swinburne set out his own definition.

Consider the various definitions of miracles below.

■ INSIGHT

Swinburne rejects Hume's definition of a miracle as a violation of a law of nature and presents a definition that miracles are 'non-repeatable counter-instances to the laws of nature' with a good outcome for the believer.

Aquinas	Hume	Swinburne	Holland
'That which has a divine cause, not that whose cause a human person fails to understand'	'A transgression of a law of nature by a particular volition of the Deity, or by the interposition of some invisible agent'	'An occurrence of a non-repeatable counter-instance to a law of nature'	'A remarkable and beneficial coincidence that is interpreted in a religious way'

For Swinburne, Aquinas' definition of a miracle (see Chapter 1) is insufficient, as highlighted by the 'God of the Gaps' theory – the idea that we use 'God' as an explanation for things that we do not yet know the scientific causes for. In the past, many things were understood to be supernaturally miraculous, but this is no longer the case.

Holland's definition of a miracle (see Chapter 24) would also be insufficient for Swinburne. By adopting an anti-realist view, Holland leaves the meaning of the miracle completely down to human interpretation, and this does not seem coherent with how religious people view the miraculous.

Finally, Swinburne disagrees with Hume's definition of a miracle (see Chapter 5). Hume understands it to be a violation of a law of nature alone – something that could hinder scientific progress. Swinburne always emphasised the close relationship between religion and science, viewing the two as symbiotic in helping us to understand God and the world, rather than working against one another.

INSIGHT

Swinburne presents religious faith as rational and sensible alongside our scientific understanding of the world, rather than in spite of science and its methods.

The table below outlines some key criticisms Swinburne presents of Hume's definition of a 'miracle'.

Stifling inquiry	Halting investigation	Undermining consistency	Encouraging the 'God of the Gaps' mentality
If extraordinary and unusual events are seen as 'miraculous', then we will have less motivation to inquire into them through empirical, evidence-based methods.	Once an event is seen as a miracle, then further investigations will be stopped – valuable scientific discoveries might be missed.	Science depends on an assumption that we have consistent and predictable natural laws, and if miracles are seen as exceptions that break these laws, then it makes the world appear inconsistent and unpredictable.	By defining miracles as breaking natural laws, we could simply be giving 'God' as a reason for something we do not yet understand. We should have the aim of exploring and explaining these events, rather than jumping to 'God' as a cause first.

Swinburne argues that it is better to see miracles as unique events that go against what we typically observe in nature. These he calls 'non-repeatable counter-instances' to the law of nature.

When something occurs that is against our usual understanding of natural laws, we can attempt to cause a repeat of the event. If it is repeatable, this can spur us into understanding the laws of nature in a new way (as it might not be an anomaly). If it is not repeatable, when all the conditions were the same as for the first event, it may indeed be a miracle.

By emphasising this non-repeatable aspect, rather than just a 'breaking of a law', Swinburne again brings us back to a scientific investigation of the event rather than just jumping to an assumption that an event is an action from God.

> **TIP**
>
> It is important to remember that, while Swinburne may be a Christian himself, he is not attempting to defend specific miracles through his definition. Instead, he is opening up the philosophical debate around miracles to show that it can be rational and sensible to be open to the possibility of miracles occurring. However, his principles of testimony and credulity are applied to the miracle claims within Christianity.

> **INSIGHT**
>
> Swinburne is concerned with showing that a belief in miracles can be a rational and logical position to take. He is not attempting to prove that miracles have occurred or will occur, but that it can be rational to believe that they have.

Swinburne believes that miracles are part of God's relationship with humankind. God is all-loving and has created humanity as a loving act. Therefore, it is rational to believe that God would (a) be able to suspend the laws of nature if needed through his omnipotence, and (b) want to intervene in the world to generate good outcomes for his creation. This, for Swinburne, is entirely within God's nature. It again highlights Swinburne's concern with showing that faith in God can be a coherent and logical position to take.

According to Swinburne, miracles can happen for two reasons:

- as an answer to prayer
- to 'signature' the teachings and lives of key prophets and figures, to show that they are indeed bringing a message from God to humanity.

It is clear that for Swinburne, a miracle is not simply where a law of nature has been broken, but that it has some religious significance and purpose. 'If a god intervened in the natural order to make a feather land here rather than there for no deep ultimate purpose, or to upset a child's box of toys just for spite, these events would not usually be described as miracles' (*The Concept of Miracle*, 1970).

Defending the Argument from Miracles

After defining miracles, Swinburne set out to defend the argument for the existence of God from the criticisms of key thinker, influential sceptic and empiricist David Hume (see Chapter 5). Hume had made five criticisms of the claims of a miracle occurring:.

- The balance of probability is weighted so far against a miracle occurring that it is irrational and unreasonable to believe that one has happened.
- There is not a 'sufficient amount' of educated witnesses to testify that a miracle has happened.
- Belief in miracles is mainly found in ignorant and barbarous nations.
- Miracles are exciting to think about, and believing a claim of a miracle can be a form of wish fulfilment.
- Multiple miracle claims from different religious traditions refute the validity of each other.

Swinburne takes Hume's first criticism and applies the reasoning that he has for believing in a God in the first place. For Swinburne, this significantly 'shifts' the weighting of the balance of probability. If someone already has a belief in an all-powerful and all-loving God, then it would not be so improbable that this God would intervene in the world. This God would have the power to intervene as well as the will.

Hume states that either the evidence for miracles is false and deceiving, or there is no valid evidence for such an event. Swinburne, however, extends what can count towards a miracle to include the following:

- our own memories of an experience
- witness statements and testimonies of what has been seen or experienced
- physical evidence of the event, in the place of the event, or medical proof
- a scientific understanding of what is thought to be possible and impossible.

Swinburne uses the principles of credulity and testimony (see below) to support the evidence given by witnesses. He then tackles the final criticism from Hume, that the miracles from one religious tradition will refute those of another due to conflicting claims.

> **INSIGHT**
>
> Hume's words (quoted by Swinburne) are as follows: 'In destroying a rival system it likewise destroys the credit of those miracles on which that system was established.'

Swinburne defends against this view, stating that miracles do not in fact refute one another but often have a common theme of benevolence and aid for a believer. This is not unlike Caroline Franks Davis' defence of religious experiences against the multiple-claims criticism.

Response to Logical Positivism

The logical positivist movement stated that all metaphysical claims, or 'God-talk', were nonsensical and meaningless. This was decided using the **Verification Principle**. The Verification Principle determines that for a statement to be meaningful it must be verified either analytically – that is, the truth of the statement is logically clear within the statement – or synthetically – that is, the truth of the statement can be checked or verified empirically.

A.J. Ayer (see Chapter 26) later distinguished between the strong Verification Principle, whereby synthetic statements can be tested first hand, and the weak Verification Principle, whereby it can be tested in theory to be empirically true. Antony Flew (see Chapter 27) refined this thinking, using terminology from the philosophy of science, emphasising that the meaning of a statement or proposition comes from the potential for it to be falsified, instead of the ability to verify this. This is known as the **Falsification Principle**. Both viewpoints had implications for all discussions around theology, philosophy and metaphysics, as many claims in this realm were nonsensical and seen as meaningless.

These views are not without their criticisms and Swinburne does not accept that these challenges *prove* that religious language is meaningless. Swinburne offers his own criticisms of the Verification and Falsification Principles (in his article 'God-talk Is Not Evidently Nonsense') in order to show that religious language does have meaning, and that a belief in an all-powerful and all-loving God is a rational position to take.

In *The Coherence of Theism*, Swinburne challenged the Verification Principle by noting that it does not pass its own criteria for what is meaningful. The principle cannot be empirically verified and is not analytically true (or true by definition). This is a major criticism and is covered in more detail in Chapter 26 on Ayer. Swinburne concluded that the Verification Principle is too rigid and restrictive in what it would deem 'meaningful' statements. Historical, artistic and emotional statements are deprived of 'meaning' by applying the principle, as are religious, ethical and metaphysical claims.

> **INSIGHT**
>
> The conflicting claims argument against miracles is also made against religious experiences, as an experience in one religion may counter that of another. Davis uses a similar response to Swinburne in arguing that there is a common core of messages at the heart of those experiences.

> **ESSENTIAL!**
>
> The **Verification Principle** is the idea that a statement can only have meaning if it can be empirically verified or is true by definition.
>
> The **Falsification Principle** is the idea that a statement can only have meaning if there is a possibility that empirical evidence could potentially prove that it is false.

> **INSIGHT**
>
> Swinburne rejects the central claim of the logical positivists that metaphysical, ethical and religious claims are meaningless. He criticises the Verification Principle at the heart of their method as well as presenting his own example – the Dancing Toys in the Cupboard – to show that language can have meaning even if it cannot be verified.

In 'God-talk is Not Evidently Nonsense', Swinburne gives examples of claims that can be made that cannot be empirically verified but can still have meaning.

Example 1	Example 2
The claim that there is a man-like being with no thoughts, feelings or sensations.	The claim that there are toys that get up and move around a room when everyone is sleeping.
'There is a being like men in his behaviour, physiology, and history who nevertheless has no thoughts, feelings, or sensations.'	'Some of the toys which to all appearances stay in the toy cupboard while people are asleep and no one is watching, actually get up and dance in the middle of the night and then go back to the cupboard, leaving no traces of their activity.'
There is no method of testing this claim empirically, as we cannot see or sense thoughts/feelings and sensations in someone else's mind.	There is no method of testing this claim empirically, as no one is witnessing the toys moving around and nor do they leave any traces.

Both of these claims, Swinburne argues, do not fulfil the criteria for meaning from either the Verification Principle or the Falsification Principle, and yet they can be understood and have meaning. Through this, Swinburne is illustrating that language can be meaningful even if it is not verifiable or falsifiable.

Understand Swinburne's Arguments

IMPROVE YOUR UNDERSTANDING

Make sure that you know how Swinburne defends miracles from the criticisms of Hume, and religious language from the criticisms of the logical positivist movement.

How Swinburne Defends Miracles against Hume

Why a miracle may have occurred. Hume's first criticism of the argument from miracles is what we may call the 'balance of probabilities'. He argues that it is far more likely that there has not been a miraculous event than that there has. Hume, as an empiricist, used **inductive reasoning** to say that because we have seen a certain action in nature occurring enough times, we accept this as a rule. The more we observe this rule, the more probable it is that this is happening and will occur.

Inductive reasoning means that we can make predictions of the future based on nature following certain rules that we have observed. It relies on nature following certain rules that we can observe empirically. It is more probable that the laws have not been broken than that they have.

For example, Christians may believe that Jesus rose from the dead, miraculously, but there have been billions and billions of people who have died and not risen from the dead, making this highly unlikely and improbable. Hume is not arguing that miracles such as this cannot happen, but simply that they are highly improbable and irrational to believe in.

> **ESSENTIAL!**
>
> **Inductive reasoning** is a type of logical thinking where specific examples or observations are used to create general conclusions and predictions.

Swinburne offers the following rebuttals to Hume's criticism.

Hume's empiricism	The problem of induction	Natural laws
Hume put forward his argument as an empiricist, that all knowledge is gained from experience. However, he did not follow the accounts of experiences of miracles enough.	Hume made an assumption having observed how things behave in the present or have behaved in the past, and how they will continue to behave in the future (see Chapter 5).	Hume's view of natural laws is outdated in comparison to contemporary scientific knowledge. He did not allow dynamic scientific inquiry, and how understanding of natural laws changes or expands over time.

For Swinburne, the existence of an omnipotent and omnibenevolent God is highly probable, as a result of his own cumulative argument for the existence of God.

If it is therefore highly probable that there is a God, and that this God is omnipotent, it makes sense that God could suspend the laws of nature if he wanted to. However, God cannot do this too often as it would interfere with free will. This logic fits with Swinburne's view that God's powers are **self-limited**. If God wanted to, he could interfere with every action, but for the sake of a relationship with humanity and our free will, he does not.

If there is good reason to believe (like Swinburne) that there is an interventionist God in existence, then there is good reason to believe this God will be able to, and want to, suspend the laws of nature for a miracle to occur. The weight needed to balance the probability of the miracle having occurred is not so great, as it does not rely heavily on the testimony of those witnessing the miracle.

INSIGHT

'If you have reason already to believe that it's quite probable that there is a God, then it's a serious possibility that the laws of nature only operate in so far as he chooses they should, then if you can show that this is the type of event he will bring about, then you only need a certain amount of testimony' (Swinburne, https://youtu.be/dmButXMCrZ4 interviewed on the show *Closer To Truth*).

Why we can accept witness accounts of miracles. The second part of Hume's criticism of miracles focuses on the testimony given by those who have witnessed or experienced a miracle. Hume boldly claimed that 'No testimony is sufficient to establish a miracle.' He questioned those who believe they have seen a miracle, suggesting that they are deceiving themselves or have been deceived. He also questioned the intelligence of those who believe them, and stated that those who have lower levels of education in the population are more likely to believe miracles.

Swinburne questioned Hume's 'sufficient testimony', in which Hume disregarded examples of miracles where there have been hundreds of witnesses. In his article 'Miracles' (1968), Swinburne challenged Hume's empiricist values: 'One wonders here at Hume's scale of evidence … is not Hume not just being bigoted, refusing to face facts?'

Swinburne also questioned the type of evidence that Hume suggested could potentially prove a miracle: that is, simply the written or verbal testimony of someone who had witnessed it. Swinburne drew comparisons between such a narrow array of evidence and that which a detective such as Sherlock Holmes would have and be able to analyse before making a judgement.

TIP

Remember that Swinburne's cumulative argument for the existence of God states that it is more probable that God exists if you 'add up' all the arguments in favour of God's existence. For example, the cosmological argument alone would not be enough proof of God's existence. However, the case is strengthened when this is taken together with religious experiences.

ESSENTIAL!

Swinburne resolves apparent issues with descriptions of God as all-powerful, all-knowing and all-loving by arguing that God is **self-limiting**. God limits his own power, foreknowledge and intervention in the world in order to have a relationship with free moral human beings.

Swinburne considered the well-known Christian miracle – the resurrection of Jesus.

> ³For what I received I passed on to you as of first importance: that Christ died for our sins according to the Scriptures, ⁴that he was buried, that he was raised on the third day according to the Scriptures, ⁵and that he appeared to Cephas, and then to the Twelve.
>
> ⁶After that, he appeared to more than five hundred of the brothers and sisters at the same time, most of whom are still living, though some have fallen asleep.
>
> ⁷Then he appeared to James, then to all the apostles, ⁸and last of all he appeared to me also, as to one abnormally born.
>
> (1 Corinthians 15:3–8, The Bible, New International Version)

Here, St Paul lists witnesses to the resurrected Jesus, numbering over 500. Would the accumulated evidence for each of these witnesses not count towards its being a probable miracle that had occurred? Note, however, that this does rely on accepting the Bible and Gospel accounts as a historical source, which Swinburne does after some investigation.

Central to the defence of miracles against Hume's criticisms are Swinburne's principles of **testimony** and **credulity**, which are also used in discussions around the claims of religious experiences (see Caroline Franks Davis, Chapter 23). He argues that we use these principles all the time in life, believing what people tell us and that things are as we are experiencing them. So why should we do anything different for religious experiences or, in this case, reports of a miracle?

Overall, Swinburne does not think that miracles alone can prove the existence of God, but they can act as an argument for it, in addition to other reasons. This forms Swinburne's cumulative argument for the existence of God. Each argument may have its flaws but, taken together, they present a compelling case for the existence of God – in the same way that ten leaky buckets can nevertheless hold a substantial amount of water.

ESSENTIAL!

The principle of **testimony** states that we should believe people who claim that a miracle has happened to them, unless we have other reasons to doubt their account of the event.

The principle of **credulity** states that if an event seems to have happened to us, then it probably has unless we have some other reason to doubt the event.

TIP

Swinburne's principle of testimony is an application of the theory of Occam's razor – that the most economical explanation for an event is probably true.

INSIGHT

Caroline Franks Davis (see Chapter 23) uses Swinburne's cumulative argument and principles of credulity and testimony to support the argument for religious experiences proving the existence of God.

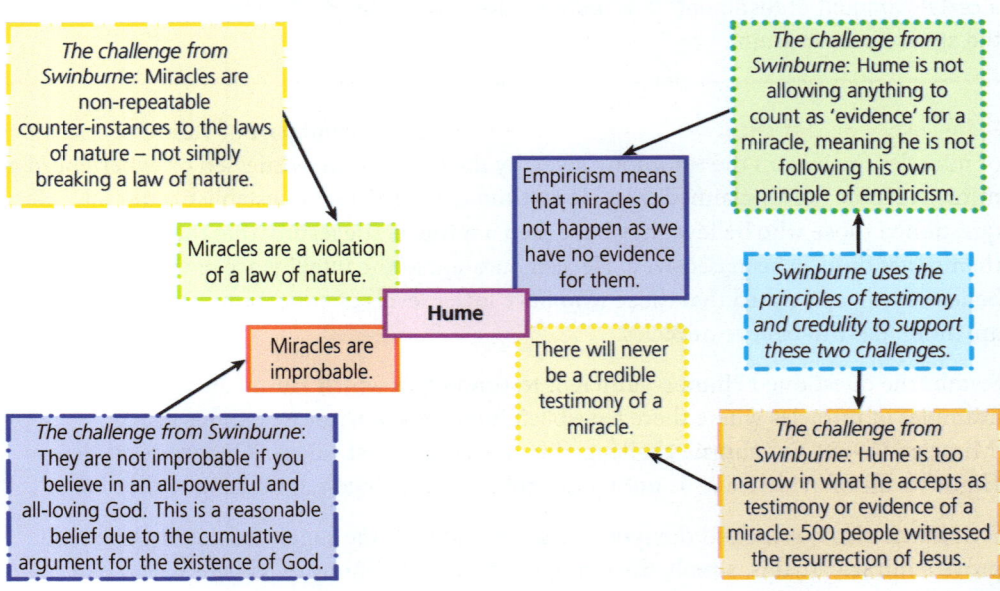

Swinburne's response to Hume on the topic of miracles

How Swinburne Defends Religious Language Against Logical Positivism

The logical positivist movement and later the *Falsification Symposium* questioned the meaningfulness of religious language in two ways:

- through the Verification Principle, which states that, to have meaning, propositions must be capable of being verified empirically
- through the Falsification Principle, which states that, to have meaning, propositions must be capable of being falsified.

These principles, according to the logical positivists, rendered all 'God-talk' meaningless. It is this argument that Swinburne refutes.

Swinburne highlights that many different kinds of statements are made every day and taken to be meaningful when they cannot be verified. This applies to historical statements that we cannot verify, as well as scientific ones. In addition, the Verification Principle is vulnerable to criticisms of inductive reasoning.

> **ESSENTIAL!**
>
> The *Falsification Symposium*, which began in 1955, was an academic conversation between Antony Flew, Basil Mitchell and Richard Hare on the meaningfulness of religious language and is explored in later chapters in this book.

TIP

Remember that the problem of induction, as first set out by Hume, is that assumptions about the future should not be made from what has been observed in the past. No matter how much we observe a certain thing, it does not logically follow – according to induction – that it will certainly happen in the future.

According to Swinburne, the strong Verification Principle 'is generally agreed to be false … It would show all universal statements to have no factual meaning; and since clearly some such statements have factual meaning, the theory must be false.'

In *The Coherence of Theism*, Swinburne gives as an example of a universal statement: 'All ravens are (at all times) black.' He argues that such statements cannot be conclusively verified: 'However many ravens you have observed to be black, there may always be another one and that may be white.' Therefore, 'Verificationism does not provide principles which are of use for settling the character of theological sentences'.

Swinburne argues that it is quite possible for people to have an understanding of terms and words that cannot be verified or falsified, and so religious language or 'God-talk' is not meaningless. People can use words and claims to describe 'states of affairs' that cannot be verified or falsified, but there is nevertheless an understanding of what the sentence or claim is conveying, therefore giving it meaning. In this way, for Swinburne, sentences can be significant and meaningful even when they do not fulfil the criteria for the logical positivists set out in the Verification Principle and Falsification Principle.

The Dancing Toys in the Cupboard

This is the most frequently cited of Swinburne's examples of why religious language can be meaningful, whether or not it can be verified or falsified. We are all able to have an understanding of what 'toys' are, what a 'cupboard' is, what 'dancing' is and what it would mean for this to happen 'when we are asleep'. Therefore, there is meaning in the statement that 'There are toys who come out of the cupboard at night when we are sleeping and we don't know they are dancing around us.'

We understand what those toys might look like, and how they might move around, but we do not have evidence for or against it. Therefore the meaningfulness of the language is not tied to the possibility of verifying or falsifying it. Religious language – 'God-talk' – can be meaningful because we understand the terms and concepts conveyed even if we cannot verify or falsify the statements.

The challenge from Swinburne: The problem of induction – 'all ravens are black' cannot be verified as we may find one white raven one day.

The challenge from Swinburne: The Verification and Falsification Principles are too narrow in what they accept as meaningful – historical, scientific and ethical claims can all be meaningful but do not fulfil the criteria needed.

The Verification and Falsification Principles show that religious language is meaningless (the logical positivist position)

The challenge from Swinburne: The Verification Principle cannot be verified – the claim that 'for claims to be meaningful they must be verified empirically or be true by definition' cannot be verified empirically, nor is it true by definition, so by its own standards it is meaningless.

The challenge from Swinburne: 'We can understand 'states of affairs' without being able to verify or falsify them, e.g. the Dancing Toys in the Cupboard.

Swinburne's response to the logical positivist argument that religious language is meaningless

WHAT DO YOU THINK?

Write down your thoughts on Swinburne's arguments and revisit them shortly before the exam to see if your views have changed.

Read Swinburne for Yourself
On Miracles

In this passage from his article 'Miracles' (1968), Swinburne addresses the challenges posed to miracles by Hume. The notes in the margin will help you to grasp his ideas.

> Swinburne criticises John Hick's understanding of miracles.

We have to some extent good evidence about what are the laws of nature, and some of them are so well established and account for so many data that any modifications to them which we could suggest to account for the odd counter-instance would be so clumsy and ad hoc as to upset the whole structure of science. In such cases the evidence is strong that if the purported counter-instance occurred it was a violation of the laws of nature … But for a violation of a law of nature to be a miracle, it has to be

> By this Swinburne is referring to God.

caused by a god, that is, a very powerful rational being who is not a material object …

If Hume were right to claim that evidence for the miracles of one religion was evidence against the miracles of any other, then indeed evidence for miracles in each would be poor. But in fact evidence for a miracle 'wrought in one religion' is only evidence against the occurrence of a miracle 'wrought in another religion' if the two miracles, if they occurred, would be evidence for propositions of the two religious systems

> Hume criticises miracles by stating that miracles from different religions will refute each other. Swinburne says that they do not.

incompatible with each other. It is hard to think of pairs of alleged miracles of this type.

… most alleged miracles do not give rise to conflicts of this kind. Most alleged

> For Swinburne, miracles are part of God's power and benevolence and will always bring about a good outcome for the individual.

miracles, if they occurred, would only show the power of god or gods and their concern for the needs of men, and little else … My main conclusion, to repeat it, is that there are

> Swinburne sets out the logical argument that there could be potential miracles that are accompanied by strong historical evidence – something Hume does not accept. Swinburne is not saying which miracles there has been strong historical evidence for.

no logical difficulties in supposing that there could be strong historical evidence for the occurrence of miracles. Whether there is such evidence is, of course, another matter.

RICHARD SWINBURNE

On Religious Language

In this passage from *The Coherence of Theism* (1977), Swinburne addresses the challenge to religious language posed by the Verification Principle and Falsification Principle.

> The first is the argument from examples; that if we consider any statement which we judge to be factual, we will find that it is confirmable or disconfirmable through observation (or experience in a wide sense). The trouble is, however, that there are plenty of examples of statements which some people judge to be factual which are not apparently confirmable or disconfirmable through observation.
>
> [...]
>
> Some of the toys which to all appearances stay in the toy cupboard while people are asleep and no one is watching, actually get up and dance in the middle of the night and then go back to the cupboard, leaving no traces of their activity. Now such statements are apparently unconfirmable – to all appearances there is no possible evidence of observation which would count for or against them.
>
> A man can understand the statement 'once upon a time, before there were men or any other rational creatures, the earth was covered by sea', without his having any idea of what geological evidence would count for or against this proposition, or any idea of how to establish what geological evidence would count for or against the proposition. Surely we understand a factual claim if we understand the words which occur in the sentence which expresses it, and if they are combined in a grammatical pattern of which we understand the significance.'

Annotations:
- Testing through the senses, empirically known.
- This is Swinburne's best-known example of a statement that can be made that is not verifiable but which is understandable and therefore can have meaning.
- Swinburne is referring to the Verification Principle and the Falsification Principle.
- We can understand the idea of there being a time when the whole earth was covered in water without necessarily knowing how this could be shown or disproved.
- We can understand the words and phrases used within a sentence, so we can say that it has meaning – even if it cannot be proven or disproven.

Know Criticisms of Swinburne

Issues with Swinburne's understanding of miracles. Some scholars criticise Swinburne's modification to Hume's definition of miracles. According to Swinburne, miracles are non-repeatable. This leaves the question of how we classify something that occurs more than once. A miraculous cure for a disease as an answer to prayer may be seen as a miracle by Swinburne. But what if it happens again to someone else? Does this prevent the act being a miracle because it has been 'repeated'?

What kind of God only answers some prayers? If we are to accept Swinburne's definition and defence of miracles, then we may also question the nature of a being that is picking and choosing who has a miracle and who does not. This could also feed into a key criticism of the arguments for the existence of God posed by the 'Evil God' challenge. This challenge states that if we accept the different classical arguments for the existence of God (for example, from design or cause), why do we then assume this is a loving and benevolent God? Surely it could be an omnipotent and omniscient, but evil or malevolent being? In fact, this may be a more logical solution to the 'problem' of evil and suffering. An evil God would allow and desire the suffering that people experience as part of that God's creation.

> **INSIGHT**
>
> The 'Evil God' challenge is a thought experiment that poses the question of why we do not believe in an all-powerful, all-evil deity with the same amount of conviction as we do an all-powerful, all-good God. The same evidence can be used to show that God is not loving: for example, with miracles only happening for some and not others.

Swinburne refines his definition of miracles (along with others) by stating that these are 'an occurrence of a non-repeatable counter-instance to a law of nature' (*The Concept of Miracle*, 1970) and their occurrence causes a good outcome for the individual or community involved – they are done with good intentions for a good reason. However, the seemingly arbitrary or partisan distribution of these miracles could point more towards a God with bad intentions. After all, there are many more people who ask, pray and plead for a miracle than those who have experienced one.

Issues with Swinburne's response to the logical positivists and the Falsification Principle. Scholars have raised several issues with Swinburne's 'Dancing Toys in the Cupboard' defence of the meaningfulness of religious language.

First, when used as an example of unverifiable statements, it could be argued that we could in fact set up tests to see empirically if the toys were moving around at night. The toys could be 'caught' moving at night with motion censored cameras or other 'traps', but religious experiences and other religious claims cannot be verified like this. It is not that we do not have the right camera to capture them, but that no camera ever could. Therefore, for many philosophers this is not a credible defence. Terms like 'God' and 'heaven', which cannot be empirically evidenced, are not the same as 'toys' and 'cupboards', which can.

Second, Swinburne's example shows that one may have an understanding of each of the components within a statement, such as 'toys' and 'dancing', even if we do not have evidence of them. Therefore the statement 'The toys are dancing when no one is looking' has meaning. Logical positivists, however, would not accept this because, even though the individual parts of a sentence may have sense, the sentence as a whole may be nonsense.

For example, consider the difference between:

The dog is in the garden.

and

The garden is in the dog.

Both contain 'dog', 'garden' and 'in', but one has meaning and the other does not.

When religious language is said to be meaningless by the logical positivists, it is not that the terms 'God', 'heaven' and 'soul' are misunderstood or without meaning, but that sentences *as a whole* that propose their existence are.

Watch Out for Traps

Swinburne does not say that any testimony or account of a miracle in scripture should be believed. Swinburne argues that it is rational and coherent to be open to the possibility of a miracle occurring through the principles of testimony and credulity as well as being part of a cumulative case for the existence of God. He does not argue that we should automatically believe miraculous accounts as true, only that we should be open to the idea that they could be, and then should judge the evidence accordingly. In Swinburne's understanding, Hume is starting from a position that it is irrational ever to believe a miracle could have occurred, no matter what the circumstance or evidence may point to.

Don't confuse the ideas of Holland and Swinburne on miracles. Both R.F. Holland (see Chapter 24) and Richard Swinburne are important scholars who question miracles. Swinburne's understanding of miracles fits into a 'violation' definition of miracles, from a realist position. There is an objective, real, omnipotent power that is causing the miracle by suspending, breaking or violating a usually understood law of nature. Holland's understanding fits into a 'contingency' definition of miracles, from an anti-realist position. The meaning of the 'miracle' comes from the interpretation of the event by the person who experiences or witnesses it.

Swinburne was not part of the Falsification Symposium. While Swinburne contributed to discussions around falsification and the meaningfulness of religious language, he was not officially part of the symposium. Make sure that you know which examples and stories are used by which scholars as part of this debate.

Antony Flew (part of the symposium)	Richard Hare (part of the symposium)	Basil Mitchell (part of the symposium)	Richard Swinburne (not part of the symposium)	John Hick (not part of the symposium)
Falsification Principle: The Invisible Gardener	'Bliks': The Lunatic and the Don	The nature of faith: The Partisan or the Mysterious Stranger	Unfalsifiable language can still be meaningful: The Dancing Toys in the Cupboard	Religious language will be eschatologically verified: The Celestial City

STRENGTHEN YOUR GRASP

1. Create a mind map of Swinburne's ideas on: the definition of miracles, Hume's criticism of miracles, the Verification Principle and the Falsification Principle. Explain how each point relates to belief in God. Refer back to your notes and add any extra information and examples in a different colour to remind you to revise this more thoroughly. This will help you with AO1 questions that focus on Swinburne's views.

2. Create a table showing the strengths and weaknesses of Swinburne's definition and defence of miracles and his response to the logical positivist movement's Verification and Falsification Principles. Which side of the table do you find more convincing? Considering the points you have on each side of the table, write a paragraph explaining how adequate you find Swinburne's explanation of religious belief to be. This will strengthen your AO2 answers relating to Swinburne's critique of religion.

Exam Guidance AO1

Swinburne's definition of miracles will be of use to anyone writing an AO1-style answer on definitions of miracles, particularly in terms of how it relates to and differs from those of Aquinas, Hume and Holland. Make sure you know how Swinburne's definition builds on and adapts Aquinas' and Hume's definitions, and how Holland's definition takes a completely different, anti-realist approach.

Swinburne's defence of the argument from miracles will be useful to anyone writing an AO1-style answer on the rationality of belief in religious miracles, not only in defence of the criticisms of Hume but also in relation to discussions around religious experience, and arguments for the existence of God more generally. Be sure of the reasons given by Hume for his view that any belief in miracles will be irrational. Remember the ways in which Swinburne refutes this view.

On religious language, Swinburne's criticisms of the Verification Principle and Falsification Principle will contribute to discussions around the meaningfulness of religious language, as well as the success of the logical positivist movement more generally. Be certain of Swinburne's use of the problem of induction as a criticism, as well as his example of the Dancing Toys in the Cupboard.

Exam Guidance AO2

When evaluating Swinburne's definition of miracles, ensure you know of the scholars who challenged him. Also critically compare his definition with the other realist approaches of Aquinas and Hume. In what ways, if any, is Swinburne's definition better, clearer or more coherent?

Swinburne's arguments in defence of miracles can be assessed through using the challenges posed to it and the 'Evil God' challenge as an extension. Ultimately, you may conclude that it depends on one's starting position as to how convincing, or not, you find his arguments to be.

Finally, essays evaluating Swinburne's contribution to discussions around religious language may highlight similarities with Hare and Mitchell (see Chapters 28 and 29), who also emphasise the significance of religious language, even though it may not be verified or falsified. Conclusions may be drawn that Swinburne is helpful in his criticisms of the Verification Principle more generally, and that even the main proponent of the logical positivist movement in the UK, Ayer (see Chapter 26), retracted his views later in life.

Evaluating Swinburne Today

In an exam, you could be asked to evaluate the adequacy or success of any of Swinburne's ideas as named in the specification. You can draw upon this section for ideas as you prepare, but note that Swinburne's theories cannot be addressed here in detail. You will be required to reach a judgement on the views that you present, but you do not need to reach the same conclusion as this reflection.

Richard Swinburne has never shied away from the difficult questions and challenges posed to religious belief. A strength of his approach to both miracles and religious language is that he faces those challenges head-on and seeks to give reasoned and well-thought-through replies as to why a belief in miracles can be rational and why religious language is in fact meaningful.

In this way, Swinburne provides the religious believer with the means to hold both faith and reason together, as many believers wish to in the modern world. Other religious philosophers in the past have taken a route of faith over reason, with fideism, in which statements do not have to stand up to rational scrutiny precisely because they are validated through faith. Swinburne does not take this approach: he firmly puts rationality and reason at the heart of his approach to faith. This is something that even his intellectual opponents recognise, as we see in the words of Richard Dawkins, 'Theology is a field in which obscurantism is the normal path to success … Richard Swinburne will have none of these flabby evasions.'

In addition, Swinburne's views present a bridge between the philosophical and the theological in that he takes philosophical arguments, such as those around miracles and religious language, and applies them to theological statements and beliefs. Philosophy has often been criticised or misunderstood as not relating enough to the real world. Through Swinburne's writing and examples, we see a clear link between key philosophical debates from the past (Hume) and the present (the Verification and Falsification Principles), and the beliefs and actions of religious communities today.

We may argue that Swinburne is right in his assessment of the Verification and Falsification Principles, although his example of toys in the cupboard is not without its criticisms. Swinburne's view that the Verification Principle does not help us sort meaningful from meaningless statements is now generally accepted in the philosophical world, with A.J. Ayer himself declaring later in his life that what he wrote in his book *Language, Truth and Logic* (1936) was mostly rubbish.

A key part of Swinburne's philosophy is a cumulative argument for the existence of God. He is not arguing deductively that there is definitively a God in existence, and that one single argument could convince us of this, but rather that there are many arguments which, taken together, show us inductively that it is more probable than not that God exists. Many may prefer this reasoning, as Swinburne acknowledges the flaws and faults with all the main arguments used, but concludes that taken together they make a compelling case for the existence of God.

This is likened to having several leaky buckets; on their own they may not hold much water, but together they will hold much more. This setting for his discourse on miracles makes for a much more appealing argument than the seemingly dogmatic approach of Hume. However, the approach has not been without its critics: the Antony Flew, a critic of theism, argued that ten leaky buckets are not in fact any more desirable than one: 'If one leaky bucket will not hold water there is no reason to think that ten can.'

As we have said above, Swinburne uses the language of reason and rationality to make his points, arguing that the simplest argument for the universe and all life and events within it is a loving and powerful God. Dawkins does not agree:

> *A God capable of continuously monitoring and controlling the individual status of every particle in the universe is not going to be simple. His existence is therefore going to need a modicum of explaining in its own right (it is often considered bad taste to bring that up, but Swinburne does rather ask for it by pinning his hopes on the virtues of simplicity). Worse (from the point of view of simplicity), other corners of God's giant consciousness are simultaneously preoccupied with the doings and emotions and prayers of every single human being.*
> (Dawkins, *The God Delusion*)

A key element of Swinburne's defence of the argument from miracles is the use of the principles of testimony and credulity, which rest on a basis of empiricism. These claims are made due to what the individual or community has experienced. However, this can be criticised as we know we cannot always trust our senses to tell us what is really going on. We could therefore judge that Hume's approach, which considers human wishful thinking and excitement at the thought of the miraculous, is stronger.

Swinburne also refutes Hume's assertion that miracles from multiple religions will cancel each other out. Without knowing which miracle is genuine, how can we accept those that conflict with one another? Swinburne's point, which Caroline Franks Davis makes relating to the same criticism of religious experiences, is that there is a common theme that runs through the miraculous, which fits the idea of a loving and omnipotent God.

Not only can this be criticised through the 'Evil God' challenge, as above, but it seems to work as a justification for personal miracles as an answer to prayer but is harder to reconcile with the second reason that Swinburne gives for miracles occurring. Swinburne states that miracles may happen in order for God to 'signature' the prophets and messages sent for humanity. The miracles associated with the religious innovators and prophets of the world religions, however, show that there is not necessarily a common core or theme, unless we take a more subjective, pluralistic view.

For example, within Christianity a key miracle is that Jesus was crucified and then rose again, whereas in Islam an accepted miracle is that Isa was miraculously saved from being crucified and ascended to heaven without ever dying. We can also take the example of the willingness of Abraham/Ibrahim to sacrifice his son, and the child being miraculously replaced by an animal. Was this Isaac or Ishmael? Depending on the religion, you have a different answer.

Swinburne offers a rational approach to faith which many within the faith will welcome. However, whether this is enough to convince those who have no faith that a belief in miracles can be rational and that religious language can be meaningful remains to be seen.

26. A.J. AYER

GET INTO AYER'S WORLD

> **Quick Overview** British empiricist Sir Alfred Jules Ayer (1910–89) popularised the ideas of the Vienna Circle on logical positivism and the Verification Principle. He was the second president of the British Humanist Society and a critic of the interwar governments of the UK, who he believed didn't do enough to support the poor and vulnerable in society, though he supported the government as an intelligence officer during the Second World War.

Sir Alfred Jules Ayer was the twentieth-century philosopher who seemed to break the mould of his predecessors. Perhaps the first true 'media philosopher', he gained celebrity status through appearances on a television show, *The Brains Trust*, and was honest about enjoying the moments when fans would stop him in the street and ask for an autograph.

Ayer was an only child who spoke of a strong connection to his maternal grandfather. Being the eldest grandchild, he looked up to his grandfather as a role model, which resulted in his drive to 'achieve'. Many who met Ayer described him as 'clever' because he was quick to understand and analyse whatever he encountered.

After studying at the University of Oxford, he had planned to spend some time at Cambridge learning from Ludwig Wittgenstein, who was lecturing there, but he was encouraged by his teacher Gilbert Ryle to investigate something exciting happening in Austria – the Vienna Circle. This was a movement that took some inspiration from Wittgenstein's ideas, although he was not part of their discussions. The circle was made up of both philosophically minded scientists and scientifically trained philosophers who met under the leadership of Moritz Shlick during the years 1924–36. They discussed **empiricism** and how this related to new movements in science and philosophy. Ayer took part in the discussions towards the end of the circle's life, in 1933, and while admitting that his command of the German language was limited, he was a quick learner and was able to follow what was being said quite well.

Ayer was hugely impressed with the movement and soon after wrote *Language, Truth and Logic* (1936), which popularised the Vienna Circle's ideas in the UK. He wrote the book when he was 24 and published it when he was 25. Yet the ideas contained in the book were so influential that they were deemed iconoclastic in terms of the challenge they posed to religious language, and all 'God-talk'.

In his later years, Ayer stated that 'much of the book was full of rubbish'. The logical positivism and Verification Principle set out in the book were, however, hugely popular approaches during the 1920s and 1930s, and they continue to influence discussions around philosophy and language today.

> **ESSENTIAL!**
>
> **Empiricism** is the idea that our knowledge of the world comes from our senses and scientific testing.

> **TIP**
>
> The Vienna Circle included Moritz Shlick, Hans Hahn and Otto Neurath, but not Wittgenstein – he influenced the Vienna Circle and logical positivism but was not part of the movement.

Know Ayer's Key Ideas

IMPROVE YOUR UNDERSTANDING

Make sure that you can explain what the Verification Principle is and how it can apply to religious language, or 'God-talk'.

Empiricism and Hume's Fork

Ayer was an empiricist; this meant he believed that all knowledge about the world could be derived from our senses. The work of David Hume (see Chapter 5) greatly influenced Ayer – specifically 'Hume's fork', with which Hume separated ideas into relations of ideas, and matters of fact.

- Relations of ideas have self-evident truth claims – they are true by their very definition. A famous example is 'a bachelor is an unmarried man'; there is no way that this cannot be true, as an unmarried man is, in fact, the definition of a bachelor. Relations of ideas are **analytic statements** and are knowable a priori.

- Matters of fact are not true by definition, but because of how they relate to the world. They can be verified or tested through empirical testing. They are **synthetic statements** and are known a posteriori.

Hume's fork sought to show that knowledge worth having had to fit into one of these two groups.

INSIGHT

'If we take in our hand any volume; of divinity or school metaphysics, for instance; let us ask, Does it contain any abstract reasoning concerning quantity or number? No. Does it contain any experimental reasoning concerning matter of fact and existence? No. Commit it then to the flames: for it can contain nothing but sophistry and illusion' (Hume, *An Enquiry Concerning Human Understanding*, 1748).

The Vienna Circle and Logical Positivism

Two hundred years after Hume was working, a group of philosophers and scientists meeting in Vienna to discuss philosophy and science embraced Hume's fork in their development of **logical positivism**. They were echoing discussions about science that were happening all across Europe at the same time. Building on Hume's fork and Wittgenstein's 'Picture Theory' (see Chapter 33), they had a shared view of philosophy that applied logical positivism.

INSIGHT

Wittgenstein wrote in *The Tractatus* (1921): 'What can be said at all can be said clearly, and whereof one cannot speak, thereof one must be silent.' This resonated with the logical positivist movement and inspired their conclusions around religious language. But while Wittgenstein's ideas helped to inspire the Vienna Circle, Wittgenstein did not share or endorse their conclusions.

ESSENTIAL!

Analytic statements are statements which are true by definition, through a priori reasoning.

Synthetic statements are statements which are true through empirical evidence, through a posteriori reasoning.

ESSENTIAL!

Logical positivism was a philosophical movement which arose out of the discussions of the Vienna Circle, whose ideas were popularised by A.J. Ayer in the UK. The logical positivists argued that religious language was meaningless.

Wittgenstein's **Picture Theory** is the idea that statements are meaningful when they relate to something in the real world.

Ayer used what he understood of logical positivism to set out his view on the meaningfulness of statements in *Language, Truth and Logic*. For Ayer, the only claims that can have meaning are those that can be shown to be true or false using scientific method (synthetic statements) or logic (analytic statements). Brian Magee, an important British philosopher who interviewed Ayer for his popular TV show *Men of Ideas*, said 'Logical positivism had seductive appeal and therefore an enormous vogue because it was clear-cut, easy to grasp, and provided all the answers' (*Confessions of a Philosopher*, 1997).

The Verification Principle

Ayer built on the ideas of the Vienna Circle and logical positivism with his formulation of the Verification Principle. This principle states that a statement can only be meaningful if it can be verified. Analytic statements are true by definition, whereas synthetic statements are empirically verifiable.

Consider these examples:

- A triangle has three sides – this is true by definition (analytic).
- It is raining outside – I can look outside and see this (synthetic).

This has implications for religious discussions, which are not true by definition and are about metaphysical things that cannot be verified or tested using our senses. Consequently, according to Ayer, since religious statements cannot be verified, they do not have meaning.

Consider these statements:

- God exists.
- There is an afterlife.
- There are angels in this room around us.

None of these statements has meaning for Ayer, as they cannot be empirically tested and therefore verified.

Ayer drew a distinction between 'strong' and 'weak' Verification Principles:

- The strong Verification Principle is the idea that statements can only have meaning if they can be empirically tested.
- The weak Verification Principle is a development of the Verification Principle which allows for statements to have meaning if, in theory, they can be empirically tested.

Consider Ayer's own example – the statement: 'There are mountains on the dark side of the moon.' Ayer was writing at a time when no one had seen what was on the dark side of the moon; in theory, however, someone could go and see it and verify the statement.

As statements about God, and therefore much of religious language, cannot be either strongly or weakly verified, Ayer argued that they are meaningless: 'God-talk is evidently nonsense' (Ayer, *Language, Truth and Logic*).

WHAT DO YOU THINK?

Write down your thoughts on Ayer's arguments and revisit them shortly before the exam to see if your views have changed.

TIP

The Verification Principle has implications not only for religious language but for all statements that we do not have the ability to verify.

INSIGHT

The Verification Principle states that a statement is meaningful if it can be empirically verified by empirical observations. According to Ayer, there is no way in which we could verify the truth or falsehood of propositions such as 'God is good' or 'Murder is wrong'. A statement of a metaphysical nature cannot have meaning.

Read Ayer for Yourself

In this passage from his book *The Central Questions of Philosophy* (1976), Ayer sets out the Verification Principle and how it could be applied to religious language. The notes in the margin will help you to grasp his ideas.

Margin notes	Passage
The statement has some meaning or sense.	A sentence is factually significant to any given person if, and only if, he knows how to verify the proposition which it purports to express – that is, if he knows that observations would lead him, under certain conditions, to accept it as being true or reject it as being false. Meaning was also accorded to sentences expressing propositions like those of logic or pure mathematics, which were true or false only in virtue of their form, but with this exception, everything of a would-be indicative character which failed to satisfy the verification principle was dismissed as literally nonsensical.
There would be some way to use our senses, to prove that it is true or not (i.e. empirical proof).	
The statement has meaning if it can be verified to be true or not; here Ayer is not saying that all true statements are meaningful but that what matters is if whether the statement can be verified to be true or false.	
Any statement that cannot be verified, either strongly or weakly, is meaningless and has no sense attached to it.	

In this passage from *Language, Truth and Logic* (1936), Ayer applies the Verification Principle to religious statements.

Margin notes	Passage
This is a statement about something beyond the physical universe, something relating to a realm that we cannot understand empirically; this is what Ayer refers to as 'God-talk'.	For to say that 'God exists' is to make a metaphysical utterance which cannot be either true or false. And by the same criterion, no sentence which purports to describe the nature of a transcendent god can possess any literal significance.
A transcendent God is beyond and outside of the universe and therefore cannot be empirically verified, so any statements about the nature of that God are meaningless.	
Having sense, meaning or a relation to something that can be tested in the world.	

EVALUATION SKILLS

An answer to an evaluative question about a scholar is always deepened by demonstrating awareness of how other thinkers have disagreed.

INSIGHT

'The Verification Principle was neither analytic nor empirically verifiable, and therefore, according to its own criterion, it was meaningless' (Magee, *Confessions of a Philosopher*).

Know Criticisms of Ayer

The Verification Principle fails its own test for meaningfulness. Scholars such as the American philosopher and arch-critic of the logical positivism movement Willard Quine have pointed out the failings of the Verification Principle. In fact, Ayer himself stated later in life that the 'fad' of logical positivism had long passed in philosophy.

The statement that 'Statements should be verifiable to have meaning' cannot be verified, so, therefore, by its own standards it is meaningless. This shows an inconsistency and incoherence in the Verification Principle, which implies that religious language is meaningless; if we are judging statements by the ability to verify them, we do not need to accept the Verification Principle itself.

In addition, critics of the Verification Principle, such as South African theologian Vincent Brümmer, state it is an error to consider religious statements to be the same as scientific or historical statements of fact. It may be that scientific facts are seen to have more meaning, but that does not mean they do. Kinds of meaning and their importance to the person using them could vary. There is meaning to be found in statements relating to great works of art, for example; they may have meaning, but they cannot be empirically verified. The same could be said for religious language as well.

Eschatological verification. Philosopher John Hick (see Chapter 16) takes Ayer's idea of weak verification and suggests that 'God-talk' is in principle verifiable when we die. He uses the example of two people walking towards a celestial city to exemplify this. They do not know if there is a city at the end of the walk – one believes there is, the other that there isn't. When they die, they will know for sure. This, for Hick, shows that the Verification Principle can apply to 'God-talk' – we will be able to verify it one day, when we die – and therefore it has meaning.

Alternative understandings of religious language may be stronger than Ayer's. Ayer's and the logical positivists' understanding of religious language is not the only way to approach the meaningfulness of religious language. This exact discussion was at the centre of the Falsification Symposium, and through this discussion Richard Hare offers a way to view religious language as both non-cognitive and unverifiable, but with meaning (see Chapter 28).

Hare introduces the idea of a 'blik', which is an unverifiable worldview or 'lens' with which we understand and assess all the information we receive about the world around us. This shapes and influences our understanding of what is happening to us, and yet we cannot see the 'blik' itself. Religion is one such 'blik', which therefore has meaning and significance while not being empirically verifiable.

> **TIP**
>
> The main criticism of the Verification Principle is that many statements that we hold as meaningful cannot be verified – for example, historical facts. It does not apply just to religious statements.

Watch Out for Traps

The Verification Principle did not prove that there is no God. 'God does not exist' is no more meaningful than 'God does exist', according to Ayer's Verification Principle. For Ayer (and the logical positivists), all propositions that cannot be verified are meaningless. Therefore, statements about what God and the afterlife are, are just as meaningless as statements about what they are not. The idea that all 'God-talk' is nonsense includes discussions around what God is, as well as discussions around what God is not.

Ayer did not believe religious language is meaningful because it is emotional for believers. Ayer developed a meta-ethical theory of emotivism (which is covered in the Ethics section of your course). He argued that even if the believer feels a great emotion connected to propositions relating to their religious beliefs, this still does not make such propositions meaningful because they cannot be verified in reality or in principle. The chapter on Ayer in the *Key Thinkers: Ethics* book from this series discusses his emotivism in more depth.

Ayer did not argue that only true statements are meaningful. While philosophy is often concerned with the accuracy of statements and propositions, Ayer is not arguing that only statements that are true are meaningful. A statement could be verified in reality or principle, for example, and still be found to be false. There would be meaning or sense to that statement, even if it were not true. For Ayer, a meaningful statement does not equal a truthful statement; instead, it is something that can be verified.

Consider this statement: 'I have black hair.' I could tell you this, but if we met in person, you would be able to see for yourself that the colour of my hair is not black. You would then have verified my statement. The statement therefore has meaning, even though it is false.

> **STRENGTHEN YOUR GRASP**
>
> 1. Write your own explanation of Ayer's view of religious language as meaningless. Include the following: logical positivism, strong Verification Principle and weak Verification Principle. Cover your notes and see what you can remember of these areas. This will help you prepare for an 'explain' question in the exam.
>
> 2. Make a list of the strengths and weaknesses of Ayer's view of religious language as meaningless. Ensure you have notes on the different critics of Ayer and the logical positivist movement. Give a ranking out of five for each of these strengths and weaknesses to help you select the evidence that you think will make the strongest points in an essay. This will help you prepare for an 'evaluate' question in the exam.

CREATE YOUR OWN QUESTION

Read this chapter and use command words such as 'examine', 'explain' or 'compare' to create your own AO1 question. For an AO2 question, make a one-sided statement about Ayer's views, put the statement between quotation marks and follow it with the phrase, 'Evaluate this view.'

Exam Guidance AO1

While many students will learn and apply Ayer's Verification Principle to both Religious Language and Meta-Ethics courses, it is important to know not only how these are linked but also how they are different. Compile notes on both logical positivism and strong and weak Verification Principles. You should be able to exemplify these with examples of specifically religious language. Know key criticisms of the Verification Principle and how they fit in with later work on the Falsification Principle (covered in later chapters of this book). Implications for religious language must be drawn out – don't just repeat the definition of the Verification Principle.

Exam Guidance AO2

You may be asked to evaluate Ayer's views in particular, or you may be asked a more general question on the meaningfulness of religious language. Know the strengths and weaknesses of both the strong and weak Verification Principles and come to your own conclusion as to how convincing you find the theory to be. You may like to bear in mind that Ayer himself claimed later in his life that his book *Language, Truth and Logic* was 'mostly false'.

To analyse and evaluate Ayer's view more thoroughly, compare and contrast the Verification Principle with other approaches to religious language in this book: for example, the ideas of the contributors to the Falsification Symposium (Flew, Mitchell and Hare) as well as Hick's celestial city. Alternative approaches to religious language, such as analogy (Aquinas and Ramsey), religious language as symbolic (Tillich and Randall) and religious language as a form of Language Game (Wittgenstein, see Chapter 33) may be more useful and adequate as approaches than Ayer's Verification Principle and the ideas of the logical positivist movement in general.

27. ANTONY FLEW
GET INTO FLEW'S WORLD

> **Quick Overview** Antony Flew (1923–2010) was an English analytic philosopher and a central figure in the Falsification Symposium, who took the ideas of Karl Popper from the realm of science into the religious realm. He was an advocate of negative atheism before changing his position and adopting deism later in life.

As the son of a Methodist minister and preacher, Antony Flew was raised within the Christian faith and attended a Church school as a child. By the age of 15 he had decided there was no God, and for most of the rest of his life he was a negative atheist – asserting that the burden of proof of God's existence rested on the theist who believed it, not the other way around. He believed that discussions should start with an assumption of no God unless proven otherwise.

Flew's academic studies were paused during the Second World War, during which time he learned Japanese and was a Royal Air Force intelligence officer. He was posted to Bletchley Park towards the end of the war.

After the war, as an undergraduate at the University of Oxford, Flew regularly attended meetings of the Socratic Club. He said in a later interview that he only happened to attend as the meeting was held in a pub near to his university accommodation. The most convincing Christian apologetic arguments he heard during these meetings came from the novelist C.S. Lewis, but Flew was not persuaded to return to the faith.

INSIGHT

The Socratic Club was a student club that met between 1942 and 1954 to discuss Christianity and the intellectual challenges to faith. C.S. Lewis was a Christian author and a member of the Socratic Club at the same time as Flew.

It was during this time that Flew wrote the article 'Theology and Falsification' as part of the Falsification Symposium, in which he built on the ideas of Austrian-British philosopher and social commentator Karl Popper around falsification and the scientific method. He criticised statements about God's existence as nonsense because they would never be falsified by the religious believer. He was also critical, at the time, of the idea of life after death and the free-will defence to the problem of evil.

INSIGHT

The free-will defence is offered by theists to explain why a loving and all-powerful God would allow suffering to happen in the world. In order for humans to have free will, they must have the freedom to choose between bad and good actions. If we could only choose actions that do not cause suffering, we would not have free will. This means that some actions will cause suffering. God allows this in order to have a relationship with us, and to enable us to be judged fairly for the afterlife.

INSIGHT

'The onus of proof must lie upon the theist' (Flew, 'The Presumption of Atheism', 1972).

> **ESSENTIAL!**
>
> **Deism** is the belief that a supreme being or higher power created the universe, but it does not reveal itself to its creation, nor does it intervene in the world.

As one of the UK's most notable atheist thinkers, Flew took part in a university debate on the existence of God with Christian apologist William Lane Craig in 1998, and was a signatory to *The Humanist Manifesto* in 2003. In 2004, however, Flew changed his position on the existence of God to **deism**, and particularly the Aristotelean idea of God. While this shocked many and caused some controversy, for Flew this was in line with his commitment to follow where the evidence took him. The discoveries of science had shown him that there was some order and cause behind the complexity of nature.

Know Flew's Key Ideas

IMPROVE YOUR UNDERSTANDING

Make sure that you know how the Parable of the Invisible Gardener relates to the Falsification Principle.

The Falsification Principle

Karl Popper (1902–94) developed the **Falsification Principle** in the scientific method as a way for the scientist to show that their hypothesis (idea or explanation for an event) has meaning. He developed the principle to help distinguish between science and pseudo-science. By 'pseudo-science' Popper meant referring to claims and ideas that are presented to appear like science, when in fact they are not. Popper presents astrology, parapsychology and alchemy as examples of fields that appear to present 'scientific truths', but which do not pass the test of the Falsification Principle.

> **ESSENTIAL!**
>
> The **Falsification Principle** states that for a theory to be considered scientific it must, in theory, be able to be proven false.

> **INSIGHT**
>
> Karl Popper uses the Falsification Principle to demarcate science from pseudo-science. It is an important part of the scientific method, but not the scientific method in its entirety.

Popper emphasised the importance of falsifying a hypothesis rather than just confirming it, for several reasons:

- It helps to counter 'confirmation bias', where we look for evidence that supports ideas that we already hold.
- It encourages objectivity, so that scientists are open to criticism and different ways of approaching their hypothesis.
- It can stimulate new scientific ideas, as theories are open to being disproved and new theories discovered.

Most importantly, it can help with the problem of induction. To use Popper's example, when considering a statement such as 'All swans are white', you could search for white swan after white swan in an attempt to prove the hypothesis. However, all it would take to falsify the statement is one black swan, thus showing the power of falsification in the scientific method.

Flew, a contemporary of Popper, applied this principle to religious claims. He argued that religious statements are often stated in such a way that they cannot be falsified through empirical evidence. When considering the problem of evil, for example, as something which may for many atheists show there is no God, theists will often maintain that God is working in mysterious ways or is beyond our understanding. Other examples are outlined in the table below.

'God is loving and powerful'	'Prayer is effective'	'I have had a religious experience'	'God's nature is beyond human understanding'
Despite the existence of suffering and evil in the world, theists often argue that God is beyond human understanding. Therefore the claim is unfalsifiable.	We cannot test empirically how effective a prayer is. There are often other explanations and natural causes. Therefore the claim is not falsifiable.	There are so many other possible causes and interpretations for the experience that it cannot be falsified.	This statement shows that beliefs and statements about God are unfalsifiable as they are beyond the capability of humans to investigate.

Ultimately, according to Flew, religious believers are not open to any evidence which could disprove the existence of the God they believe in – meaning statements about those beliefs are meaningless.

The Parable of the Invisible Gardener

The Parable of the Invisible Gardener was originally written by John Wisdom in 1944. It was developed by Flew to apply the Falsification Principle to statements of religious faith. You can read the parable in full later in this chapter, but in summary, two explorers discover a jungle clearing and discuss the possibility of a gardener tending to it. After setting traps to gather some evidence of the gardener, the sceptical explorer states that the gardener does not exist because of the lack of evidence. The other explorer continues to believe there is a gardener, but adjusts the nature of that gardener so that each failed test still allows for the gardener's existence. The conversation ends with a frustrated and despairing sceptic asking, 'What remains of your original assertion?'

Flew is claiming with this parable that religious believers change their beliefs about God to allow for God's existence whatever the question or challenge they are given, thus showing that their beliefs are unfalsifiable and not assertions about reality at all. When the gardener is said to be invisible and intangible, no empirical testing or observations can prove the gardener's existence.

Death by a Thousand Qualifications

The phrase 'death by a thousand qualifications' is related to a form of torture where someone is executed by a thousand cuts. Flew uses the phrase to show how what starts as an assertion, a truth claim or statement of fact about the existence of God is reduced bit by bit, through the modifications and allowances that believers give to God's nature, until it is no longer a statement of fact at all but just an unfalsifiable belief.

> **INSIGHT**
>
> 'What would have to occur or to have occurred to constitute for you a disproof of the love of, or the existence of, God?' (Flew, 'Theology and Falsification', 1950).

> **INSIGHT**
>
> The traps set by the explorers in the parable are examples of empirical testing.

> **INSIGHT**
>
> 'A fine brash hypothesis may thus be killed by inches, the death by a thousand qualifications' (Flew, 'Theology and Falsification', 1950).

> **INSIGHT**
>
> Flew was challenged by Richard Hare and Basil Mitchell through the Falsification Symposium. The Falsification Symposium was a discussion between Flew, Mitchell and Hare on the meaningfulness of religious language.

Consider a discussion between a theist and an atheist around the problem of evil. While the theist may start with an assertion of an omnipotent and omnibenevolent God, it is not possible to falsify this assertion by the existence of evil and suffering in the world, as the theist changes the definition of omnipotence or omnibenevolence to suit the existence of great suffering. Any challenge that the atheist presents to the theist for the existence of God can be explained away in such a manner, as if the goal posts are changed as we play the game.

WHAT DO YOU THINK?

Write down your thoughts on Flew's arguments and revisit them shortly before the exam to see if your views have changed.

Read Flew for Yourself

In this passage from his book *Theology and Falsification* (1968), Flew sets out his version of the Parable of the Invisible Gardener. The notes in the margin will help you to grasp his ideas.

> This represents the world.
>
> This shows that the world has beauty and chaos. Arguments from design may be presented for the flowers, but what arguments can give reason for the weeds?
>
> The traps set to provide proof of the gardener represent empirical testing and searching for evidence of God in the world.
>
> The believer has changed their idea of the gardener (God) to suit the evidence that has come to them, so now the traps would be no use to provide proof of that gardener.
>
> Here the sceptic is showing that the idea of the gardener has changed. The possibility of the gardener as invisible and intangible was not mentioned before the traps were set, but only after the traps did not catch him.

Once upon a time two explorers came upon a clearing in the jungle. In the clearing were growing many flowers and many weeds. One explorer says, 'Some gardener must tend this plot.' The other disagrees, 'There is no gardener.' So they pitch their tents and set a watch. No gardener is ever seen. 'But perhaps he is an invisible gardener.' So they set up a barbed-wire fence. They electrify it. They patrol with bloodhounds. (For they remember how H. G. Well's *The Invisible Man* could be both smelt and touched though he could not be seen.) But no shrieks ever suggest that some intruder has received a shock. No movements of the wire ever betray an invisible climber. The bloodhounds never give cry. Yet still the Believer is not convinced. 'But there is a gardener, invisible, intangible, insensible to electric shocks, a gardener who has no scent and makes no sound, a gardener who comes secretly to look after the garden which he loves.' At last the Sceptic despairs, 'But what remains of your original assertion? Just how does what you call an invisible, intangible, eternally elusive gardener differ from an imaginary gardener or even from no gardener at all?'

Know Criticisms of Flew

As part of the Falsification Symposium, Flew's fellow philosophers Richard Hare (see Chapter 28) and Basil Mitchell (see Chapter 29) gave their own criticisms of Flew's application of the Falsification Principle to religious language. They both criticised Flew for misunderstanding what religious faith meant for individuals.

Mitchell's Parable of the Mysterious Stranger. Mitchell's parable (outlined in Chapter 29) shows that religious believers do consider and allow evidence against their beliefs, but they weigh this against reasons for their faith and judge overall that they should stay faithful. Mitchell distinguished between a detached observer (as in Flew's parable) and a believer (as in his own parable). Mitchell showed that believers are indeed aware of the evidence that may count against their beliefs, most notably the problem of evil.

However, having weighed up all of the evidence, they decide, through a commitment of faith, that the God they believe in does exist. Flew's alleged misrepresentation of faith is something that fellow symposium contributor Richard Hare also highlighted.

Hare's concept of 'bliks'. Hare used the concept of 'bliks' to highlight that Flew had misunderstood how religious language functioned. As religious language does not provide a 'scientific' statement, only a statement relating to someone's unshakable 'blik' (or worldview), it cannot be verified or falsified. Hare stated that religious believers are not detached observers (as Flew's explorers are), but that they have some connection and investment in what happens in that garden.

Criticism of Flew's representation of faith. Fellow philosopher William Lane Craig, with whom Flew debated in 1998 on the existence of God, criticised Flew's representation of religious faith. This criticism stemmed specifically from Craig's own perspective as a Christian apologist. Flew stated that religious believers are not open to any evidence being able to falsify their beliefs. Craig countered by pointing to St Paul in the New Testament section of the Bible, who states that if the body of Jesus were to be found, this would disprove the resurrection claims of Christianity, therefore providing a way of falsifying the central assertion in Christianity that Jesus rose from the dead.

Watch Out for Traps

Don't claim that Flew invented the Parable of the Invisible Gardener. The parable was first put forward by leading British philosopher John Wisdom in 1944; Flew made some changes to the parable, as shown below.

	Wisdom 1944	Flew 1968
Where does the parable take place?	Garden	Jungle
What do the explorers discover?	Untended garden	Clearing
Who is reasonable out of the explorers?	Both men are reasonable	The sceptic is described as reasonable

Individual statements and assertions are not what mattered to Flew. While Flew gave examples of assertions and statements of religious belief, it is the mindset as a whole that he criticised with the Falsification Principle, not the individual statements. The overall reluctance to admit something that might falsify the belief is why it fails to assert anything about reality.

Flew did not only criticise liberal religious beliefs. While there are clear parallels to liberal 'qualifications' of the idea of God, Flew's parable also applies to traditional and fundamentalist beliefs. For example, any religion that asserts an omnipotent, omnibenevolent God must have some solution to the problem of evil – the 'weeds' that the gardener allows to grow. The theodicies that will be presented to explain why a particular God allows suffering will be a form of qualifying or changing the parameters of the discussion around who or what that God is.

> **INSIGHT**
>
> Liberal Christianity is an approach to Christian faith where the literal truths of the Bible are not as important as the symbolic or metaphorical messages. Paul Tillich was an important liberal Christian thinker who viewed religious language as symbolic (see Chapter 32).

> **TIP**
>
> Hare's use of the term 'blik' to describe the worldview or schema within which a religious person is using their language is described in detail in Chapter 28.

> **INSIGHT**
>
> 'It is because I mind very much about what goes on in the garden in which I find myself that I am unable to share the explorer's detachment' (Richard Hare in Flew and MacIntyre, *New Essays in Philosophical Theology*, 1955).

> **INSIGHT**
>
> William Lane Craig is a Christian apologist who defends Christianity using reason and philosophical argument (see Chapter 2).

> **STRENGTHEN YOUR GRASP**
>
> 1. Write your own explanation of Flew's challenge to religious language via the Falsification Principle. Include the following: the Falsification Principle, the Parable of the Invisible Gardener, the problem of evil, and death by a thousand qualifications. This will help you prepare for an 'explain' question in the exam.
> 2. Make a list of the strengths and weaknesses of Flew's view of religious language. Ensure you consider the challenges from the other members of the Falsification Symposium and religious believers such as Craig. Give a ranking out of five for each of these strengths and weaknesses to help you select the evidence that you think will make the strongest points in an essay. This will help you prepare for an 'evaluate' question in the exam.

Exam Guidance AO1

For an explain-style question you should have an understanding of Flew's version of the Parable of the Invisible Gardener, how it relates to religious belief, and how it can be applied to discussions around the meaningfulness of religious language. You should understand what is meant by the phrase 'death by a thousand qualifications' and be able to exemplify it with examples from discussions involving religious language. In addition, you should know and understand the Falsification Principle and how this is linked to, but different from, the Verification Principle. This may be useful for a specific question on falsification or more generally for a question on the meaningfulness of religious language.

Exam Guidance AO2

For an evaluate-style question you need to come to a conclusion as to how far you agree with Flew's approach to religious language, namely his criticism that religious assertions cannot be meaningful as they are not falsifiable. Consider each of the criticisms of his view – how convincing do you find them and how would Flew justify his position in response? How successfully do you think religious believers can defend their assertions from this theory? In addition, you should consider how the Falsification Principle compares and contrasts with the challenges of logical positivism and Ayer's Verification Principle. Finally, how does this theory apply to the varieties of religious faith and expression in the world? Is it more damning of a liberal faith where God is 'qualified' out of existence?

28. RICHARD HARE

GET INTO HARE'S WORLD

> **Quick Overview** Richard Hare (1919–2002) was a key contributor to the Falsification Symposium and was also known for his discussions of ethical ideas. He presented an anti-realist view of religion and defended the meaningfulness of religious language through his theory of 'bliks'.

A Christian thinker, Richard Hare studied Classics at the University of Oxford and when the Second World War broke out he volunteered to join the Royal Artillery. As a pacifist, he was conflicted, as he saw the need to fight against a regime that was causing enormous suffering in the world.

He was taken as a prisoner of war during the fall of Singapore. This experience had a lasting impact on his moral philosophy, which he believed should be able to guide people through the toughest of situations. Hare is noted as an ethical writer, specifically for his writings on preference utilitarianism and the meta-ethical theory of prescriptivism.

While teaching at the University of Oxford, Hare was involved with the Falsification Symposium. While he offered a defence of the meaningfulness of religious language to those who use it, he was greatly influenced by the ideas of A.J. Ayer and keen to show that all 'God-talk' was not nonsense.

Know Hare's Key Ideas
'Bliks' – the Way We View the World

Ayer (see Chapter 26) and Flew (see Chapter 27) challenged the meaningfulness of religious language by arguing that 'God-talk' is both unverifiable and unfalsifiable. They supported the position that, while religious language is cognitive, it is meaningless. Hare presented an alternative way to think about religious language – that, although it is unverifiable and unfalsifiable, it still has meaning for those who use it.

Hare introduced the term **'blik'**, which is a word from Dutch meaning 'sight' or 'glance'. Each of us have 'bliks' which filter and categorise what we see and experience of the world around us. The 'bliks' that you have determine your worldview; you start with this before you start to analyse the world around you. We accept the things which fit with and confirm our 'bliks', but we reject or explain away the things that don't. Religious language, therefore, has great meaning and significance for the believer, as long as it fits in with their 'bliks' or worldview.

> **INSIGHT**
>
> Hare responded to the challenge laid down by Antony Flew in the Falsification Symposium with his own theory of 'bliks', or the way we see the world being both unfalsifiable and also meaningful.

> **ESSENTIAL!**
>
> **'Bliks'** are unfalsifiable beliefs that shape our worldview. A person's 'bliks', or ways of viewing the world, give it meaning – even when others do not share the same view.

> **INSIGHT**
>
> 'Bliks' shape how we interpret every piece of data or information that we observe. 'Bliks' can be sane as well as insane, religious and non-religious.

Understand Hare's Arguments

IMPROVE YOUR UNDERSTANDING

Make sure that you know how Hare's story of 'The Murderous Dons' exemplifies his theory of 'bliks'.

The Parable of the Murderous Dons

Hare used his own parable of a student suffering from paranoid delusions, who is convinced that his university lecturers are trying to kill him. No amount of evidence that is presented to him will persuade him otherwise. His statements about the belief that they are out to kill him have meaning to him and have a great influence on his life and actions to the point where he refuses to attend lectures. But they are not verifiable or falsifiable.

Hare referred to an example of one of his own 'bliks' – that driving a car is safe. He put his trust in the safety of his car each time he drove it, even though plenty of evidence existed of the harm that could come to him if he crashed. Hare agreed somewhat with Flew's thesis (see Chapter 27) that religious language is not asserting anything about the world. However, he disagreed that this makes religious language meaningless. This language is meaningful as an expression of a worldview (although it cannot be falsified).

INSIGHT

Hare distinguished between sane 'bliks', such as his own trust that the car he drove was safe, and insane 'bliks', such as the student's delusion that his tutors were trying to kill him, but he did not explain the difference between the two.

WHAT DO YOU THINK?

Write down your thoughts on Hare's arguments and revisit them shortly before the exam to see if your views have changed.

Read Hare for Yourself

In this passage from the article 'Theology and Falsification: A Symposium' (1971), Hare explains the 'blik' of a student suffering from paranoid delusions, who is convinced that his university lecturers are murderous and intent on killing him.

> This is the 'blik' that the student sees all evidence through.

> Dons are university lecturers, originally at collegiate universities (such as the universities of Oxford, Cambridge and Durham), but it could refer to lecturers anywhere.

> The belief that the dons are murderous is so strong for the student that no evidence presented to him will dissuade him otherwise – in fact, he reinterprets any evidence to the contrary to fit his 'blik'.

[A certain student] is convinced that all dons want to murder him. His friends introduce him to all the mildest and most respectable dons that they can find, and after each of them has retired, they say, 'You see, he doesn't really want to murder you; he spoke to you in a most cordial manner; surely you are convinced now?' But the lunatic replies, 'Yes, but that was only his diabolical cunning; he's really plotting against me the whole time, like the rest of them; I know it I tell you'. However many kindly dons are produced, the reaction is still the same.

Know Criticisms of Hare

Religion is a mental illness? Hare's example is unsuitable as it makes the mentally ill student analogous to the religious believer. Many religious believers (Hare was Christian himself) would not accept that religious belief is like a mental illness. Many religious believers do not see their faith as a mere 'worldview' but take a realist approach, meaning they believe there is an existent, objectively real God or ultimate being. By giving religious language meaning through reducing religions to 'bliks', Hare risked losing much of the meaning that religious believers gave to the language in the first place.

Watch Out for Traps

Don't claim that 'bliks' are always religious. While the theory of 'bliks' is used here to defend the meaningfulness of religious language, we all have 'bliks' about a variety of things, religious and not. For example, someone may not fully understand how an aeroplane actually flies but have a 'blik' that it is safe to travel in one, explaining away any evidence of crashes rather than allowing them to change their view. Hare's 'bliks' could apply to atheist views about the world as much as to theist views. In fact, Hare used the example of how some will see order in the universe, pointing to a greater being, whereas others will see the same order and view it as chance.

STRENGTHEN YOUR GRASP

1. Write your own explanation of Hare's defence of religious language through the theory of 'bliks'. Include the following: 'bliks', worldview, the Falsification Symposium and convictions. Cover your notes and see what you can remember of those four areas. This will help you prepare for an 'explain' question in the exam.
2. Write a list of the strengths and weaknesses of Hare's understanding of religious language. Pay particular attention to how he is attempting to defend the meaningfulness of religious language in the face of the criticisms of the Verification and Falsification Principles. Give his view an overall rating out of five for how successful he is in this defence, and compare it with Flew and Mitchell when you have completed your work on their views.

Exam Guidance AO1

You should be aware of Hare's understanding of 'bliks' and how he illustrated them with his examples of the university student suffering with mental illness and the dangers of driving a car. You should also be able to give other examples that demonstrate how this concept can be related to both sane and insane worldviews and to religious worldviews. Ensure that you know how this is a defence of the meaningfulness of religious language, even though it is unverifiable and unfalsifiable. Make sure you know what examples and parables are given by each of the Falsification Symposium members.

Exam Guidance AO2

Consider how far Hare's theory of 'bliks' goes to defending religious language from the challenges of verification and falsification. Does he show that religious language can have meaning, as it does to those with a certain 'blik', or is religious language still open to the criticism of Ayer and Flew from verification and falsification? Consider how successful a religious believer would find the explanation to be and how authentic Hare's understanding is of genuine religious utterances.

29. BASIL MITCHELL
GET INTO MITCHELL'S WORLD

> **Quick Overview** British philosopher Basil Mitchell (1917–2011) was the final contributor to the Falsification Symposium. A devoted Anglican Christian who was a fellow and tutor at the University of Oxford, he also served as a member of the Church of England's working party on ethical questions.

Basil Mitchell was confirmed into the Christian faith but also had an awareness of other faiths from an early age, including Sufism, as his father was a Sufi disciple. As a child, Mitchell attended Sufi sessions of worship (a mystical approach to Islam where individuals may have religious experiences through worship), which had a **universalist** approach using texts and teachings from across various religious traditions. While studying classics at Oxford, Mitchell was awarded a scholarship to study Indian philosophy and began to learn Sanskrit. Mitchell served in the Royal Navy during the Second World War and the evil and suffering that he witnessed during wartime influenced his philosophy on his return to teach at Oxford.

> **ESSENTIAL!**
> **Universalists** believe that all of humanity will be saved, not just those who are of a particular religion.

Know Mitchell's Key Ideas

■ **IMPROVE** YOUR **UNDERSTANDING**

Make sure that you know how the Parable of the Partisan/Mysterious Stranger exemplifies Mitchell's defence of the meaningfulness of religious language.

The Parable of the Partisan

In response to both Antony Flew (Chapter 27) and Richard Hare (Chapter 28) within the Falsification Symposium, Mitchell defended the meaningfulness of religious language through his Parable of the Partisan (also known as the Parable of the Mysterious Stranger). His defence showed that those who held religious beliefs to be true were aware of how this belief or assertion might be falsified. However, their commitment to the belief (that is, their belief in God) helped them to retain their faith despite evidence that might be said to go against it.

> ■ **INSIGHT**
> The parable is clearly linked to the problem of evil, which is the challenge to the existence of God through the existence of evil and suffering in the world.

The parable tells of a freedom fighter in the Second World War who meets a mysterious stranger. The stranger tells the fighter that he is the leader of his side in the war (the Resistance) and that, although his actions might make it seem at times that he is on the side of the enemy, those actions are part of a bigger plan, and the leader will really always be on the side of the freedom fighters.

The hidden meanings of the parable are explained below.

Element of the parable	How this could relate to religious belief
The leader of the Resistance	God or a divine encounter of some kind
The partisan (or freedom fighter)	The religious believer
The other fighters who did not meet the leader of the Resistance	Those who do not believe, who did not have an encounter with God or some form of the Divine
The leader meeting the partisan	A conversion or religious experience of some kind
When the leader of the Resistance seems to be fighting for the other side	When people suffer on earth and question why God has either allowed or caused such suffering
When the partisan declares, 'The stranger knows best'	When religious believers say, 'God works in mysterious ways'

Through the parable, Mitchell showed that religious believers are open to challenges to their faith. They understand why some may question the leader of the Resistance when so many actions seem to go against the claim that he is on their side. Importantly for Mitchell, even though there is evidence to the contrary, religious believers still hold their beliefs as a commitment to their faith – not because they refuse to accept that there could be any evidence against it.

Understand Mitchell's Arguments

Mitchell was writing following his experiences in the Second World War. His contemporaries – A.J. Ayer, Flew and Hare – were also part of the war effort. The Parable of the Partisan was in part a response to the age-old problem of evil, and it would have been well known to his audience.

A response to the challenges of the Falsification Symposium. A criticism of Hare is that he fails to account for why and how people may change between 'bliks' (see Chapter 28). Similarly, a criticism of Flew is that he seems not to appreciate the power of the initial encounter with the 'invisible gardener' that may have caused the explorer to retain faith in the face of evidence to the contrary (see Chapter 27). Mitchell's parable is an acknowledgement of religious experiences or encounters as powerful reasons why believers will hold on to significant 'articles of faith' despite evidence to the contrary. He used the problem of evil as an example of the kind of issues a believer must grapple with to retain their faith.

Stories such as the 'test of faith' of the prophet Job/Eyyub show that these questions and possible falsifications have been part of religious faith for millennia. Although they could be evidence against the existence of God, the believer chooses to retain their faith due to their commitment and the power of the initial encounter. This shows how assertions relating to 'God-talk' can be meaningful, as the believer is aware of how they could be falsified but still chooses to retain their faith.

■ **INSIGHT**

'Despite being tempted to lose faith in the stranger, as he sometimes sees him appearing to help the enemy and sometimes not, the fighter always says to himself, "The stranger knows best"' (Mitchell, 'Theology and Falsification: A Symposium', 1971).

> **INSIGHT**
>
> The story of Job/Eyyub is found in Judaism, Islam and Christianity. The prophet is praised by God for being a faithful servant, and then Satan/Shaytan challenges God by stating that it is only because he has blessed him with a good life that he has stayed faithful. God then allows Satan/Shaytan to remove these blessings from Job/Eyyub, causing great suffering. Job/Eyyub remains faithful to God, however, proving that his faith is strong, the blessed life is restored and he is shown to be a man of great faith precisely because of the challenges to faith that he faced.

> **WHAT DO YOU THINK?**
>
> Write down your thoughts on Mitchell's arguments and revisit them shortly before the exam to see if your views have changed.

> **TASK**
>
> Read Mitchell for yourself in the extract below. The notes in the margin will help you to grasp his views.

Read Mitchell for Yourself

In this passage from 'Theology and Falsification: A Symposium' (1971), Mitchell explains how the faith of the believer in his Parable of the Partisan differs from the explorers in Flew's Parable of the Invisible Gardener.

> Here Mitchell is showing that religious beliefs are open to being falsified. Believers are willing to accept that there is evidence against their religious assertions, but overall they still retain belief due to their investment and commitment to them.
>
> Mitchell is showing how his partisan is different to the explorer in Flew's Parable of the Invisible Gardener. The partisan has a commitment, whereas the explorer views the garden without an investment in the existence of the invisible gardener.

The theologian surely would not deny that the fact of pain counts against the assertion that God loves men. This very incompatibility generates the most intractable of theological problems–the problem of evil. So the theologian does recognize the fact of pain as counting against Christian doctrine. But it is true that he will not allow it – or anything – to count decisively against it; for he is committed by his faith to trust in God. His attitude is not that of the detached observer, but of the believer.

> **EVALUATION SKILLS**
>
> An answer to an evaluative question about a scholar is always deepened by demonstrating awareness of how other thinkers have disagreed.

Know Criticisms of Mitchell

The Parable of the Partisan relies on an initial encounter with God or the Divine. Mitchell's parable seems feasible if a powerful religious encounter or religious experience is considered a basis of religious faith, in the face of evidence to the contrary. But how are these encounters responded to by those who may not have had them? This also leaves Mitchell's view open to the criticisms of the validity of religious experiences in the first place.

Flew's 'death of a thousand qualifications' still stands. Flew argued that religious believers can explain away any evidence that contradicts the existence of their God (see Chapter 27). Despite the challenges posed and questions raised about the existence of God, the believer can change the nature of that God to mean the challenge no longer applies.

Watch Out for Traps

Mitchell did not defend all religious statements. Mitchell did not defend unquestioning faith or religious statements made without an awareness or acceptance of evidence to the contrary. Unlike Hare's student with mental illness (see Chapter 28), who is unwilling to accept evidence against his claims due to his 'blik', Mitchell's partisan is fully aware that the actions of the stranger are contradictory to the initial claim of being a leader of the Resistance. Mitchell defended religious assertions from the perspective of those who are open about the struggles of faith, and yet retain a commitment to it.

> **STRENGTHEN YOUR GRASP**
>
> 1. Write your own explanation of Mitchell's defence of the meaningfulness of religious language. Include the following: the Falsification Symposium, the Parable of the Partisan, and the problem of evil. Cover your notes and see what you can remember of those three areas. This will help you prepare for an 'explain' question in the exam.
> 2. Create a list of the strengths and weaknesses of Mitchell's approach to religious language. Which of the other key thinkers in this book would support or criticise his position? This will help you with an 'evaluation' question in the exam.

Exam Guidance AO1

For AO1-style answers you could use Mitchell and his Parable of the Partisan in discussions about the meaningfulness of religious language specifically as a challenge to the logical positivists and the Falsification Principle. You should know the parable and how it relates to religious language, especially to discussions around the problem of evil and the assertion that 'God loves us'. You might also use it in a question relating to religious experience and the problem of evil more generally.

Exam Guidance AO2

For AO2-style answers you will need to consider the strengths and weaknesses of Mitchell's approach to religious language and how this compares and contrasts to the views of the other members of the Falsification Symposium. You will need to reach your own judgement as to how successfully Mitchell defends the meaningfulness of religious language by showing that religious believers who are willing to accept evidence may falsify their assertions, but overall will choose to remain committed to their faith.

30. IAN RAMSEY

GET INTO RAMSEY'S WORLD

> **Quick Overview** Bishop Ian Ramsey (1915–72) contributed to twentieth-century discussions around the meaning and interpretation of religious language through his theory of models, qualifiers and disclosures. He developed Aquinas' analogy by proportion and was heavily influenced by the ideas of Ludwig Wittgenstein.

Ian Ramsey was born in Lancashire into a working-class Christian family. He won a scholarship to attend the University of Cambridge, where he developed his interest in metaphysics and the relationship between religion and science. Ramsey studied at Cambridge at the same time as Ludwig Wittgenstein, and it is clear that Wittgenstein influenced Ramsey's ideas about religious language. Ramsey later took up various clerical roles within the Church of England, and was made bishop of Durham in 1966.

Through his work, Ramsey's main aim was to provide a counter-argument to logical positivism and the subsequent rise of atheism by providing philosophical grounds for religious language retaining its meaningfulness in spite of the criticisms it faced. According to Ramsey, there is an understanding of the existence of 'I', even though the self is an empirically elusive concept. Therefore, why reject the statement 'God exists' for its empirical elusiveness? Ramsey believed science and religion to be alike. Therefore, it could be entirely rational for someone to hold religious belief and discuss these beliefs meaningfully.

After his death, Ramsey's dream of a permanent centre as a space for the investigation of interdisciplinary areas was realised in 1985 with the Ian Ramsey Centre for Science and Religion at the University of Oxford. The centre provides a forum for discussions around theology and ethics in relation to ongoing discoveries in medicine, technology and science. It perpetuates Ramsey's aim to show that science and religion need not be in conflict.

Know Ramsey's Key Ideas

IMPROVE YOUR UNDERSTANDING

Make sure that you know how Ramsey views religious language as non-cognitive and analogical, and how he uses the ideas of models, qualifiers and disclosures to explain this view.

Two Types of Language

In his book *Religious Language: An Empirical Placing of Theological Phrases* (1957), Ramsey distinguished between two types of language – ordinary and religious. Ordinary language is straightforward, observational and makes sense. Religious language, because it is about metaphysical claims, will seem 'logically odd' as it is about God, which is outside of ordinary, observable experience. While it is 'logically odd', this does not make it meaningless, as it points towards something of God's nature as 'an attempt to be particular about the divine mystery'. If we judge religious language in the same way that we do ordinary language, we are making an error.

The influence of Wittgenstein (see Chapter 33) on Ramsey can be seen here with his assertion that questions around metaphysics will remain a 'divine mystery' unlike normal mysteries or questions about the world that we can investigate empirically (scientifically). The great 'divine mystery' means that we cannot make cognitive or factual statements about the nature of God. This does not mean that we cannot say anything about God's nature, however, as through analogy we can point towards it, and through experiencing personal disclosures we can gain a deeper connection to the nature of God with the religious language we use. Although religious language is not making factual statements in the same way as ordinary language is, it is still meaningful. For Ramsey it held meaning, as God could be understood through analogy.

Models and Qualifiers

The similarities of, and relationship between, science and religion were important for Ramsey. He explained that both use models to show difficult concepts. For example, a physical model of the double helix can show what the structure of DNA looks like. Science also uses words in a similar way to models: for example, the term 'wave' in discussions of 'light waves' or 'sound waves'. We may not see a light wave with our eyes, but we can understand something of how it works through knowing the shape of the waves on the sea.

In a similar way, religious language uses models – terms that can be understood from our own experiences that relate to what God is like. We are aware that the term we use is not an exact description of God, but we can anchor our idea of God in the experiences that we have of the world. Ramsey develops Aquinas' use of analogy (see Chapter 1) through the use of models and **qualifiers**. We use a word in ordinary language as the model and qualify this with an adverb or adjective to show that it is meant in a different way. For example, in the phrase 'Heavenly Father', 'Heavenly' is the qualifier and 'Father' is the model (ordinary language). Other qualifiers are 'all' (omni-), 'infinite' and 'eternal' (see the table below).

Term about God's nature	Model (how it relates to human experience)	Qualifier (how it is shown to be different from human experience)
Omnibenevolent	Benevolence – love	Omni – all
Omnipotent	Potency – power	Omni – all
Heavenly Father	Father – protection and love for his children	Heavenly – not of this world, in the same sense as a physical father
Good Shepherd	Shepherd – caring for the flock of sheep	Good – caring and loving for all of humanity as members of the 'flock'

> **TIP**
>
> Remember that Ramsey used the idea of models and qualifiers to show how religious language, which he admitted was 'logically odd', conveys meaning about the metaphysical.

> **INSIGHT**
>
> According to Ramsey, religious language is 'logically odd', but that does not make it meaningless. Questions around metaphysics (and therefore religious language claims) will always remain a 'divine mystery'.

> **TIP**
>
> Ramsey's view of religious language as analogical is much like the approach of Thomas Aquinas (see Chapter 1).

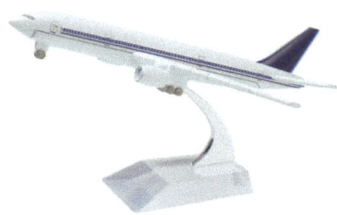

> **ESSENTIAL!**
>
> **Qualifiers** are adverbs or adjectives attached to models to show how the model is different from human experience, as we cannot experience the metaphysical directly. For example, 'omni' is an often-used qualifier to the model of love, power or knowledge, as in 'omnipotent'.

> **ESSENTIAL!**
>
> A **disclosure** is a breakthrough moment when religious language helps the believer to have some understanding of God, although it will always remain a 'divine mystery' to some extent.

> **INSIGHT**
>
> We will discuss how Ramsey's writing makes an assumption of belief in the 'Know Criticisms of Ramsey' section later in the chapter.

Disclosures

For Ramsey, religious language can point to an understanding of God, beyond the words that are used. The qualified models can help us to understand something of God's nature, although we will never know it fully. These moments, when we reach an understanding of God through religious language, are similar to a 'lightbulb' moment or the sun breaking through the clouds. Ramsey called them **disclosure** moments. Through these disclosures, we can grasp at something beyond our human experience.

One example Ramsey uses is of a teacher drawing a polygon with four sides on the board. The teacher then increases the number of sides to 16, 50 and so on until at a certain point the polygon appears to be a circle to the student observing. Close up, the individual straight lines would still be visible, but to all intents and purposes the drawing looks like a circle. However, these moments, Ramsey believed, do not give a full and total account of God's nature, as this is and will always remain a mystery while we are on earth, and he states: 'They disclose but do not explain a mystery' (*Models and Mystery*, 1964). In other words, our language will not be able to explain or express who or what God is, but it can point us towards it and help us to have some insight through analogy.

> **INSIGHT**
>
> Ramsey's example of a polygon with an increasing number of sides eventually looking like a circle is equivalent to a disclosure moment, as the viewer sees a deeper or greater meaning than the literal experience in front of them.

> **WHAT DO YOU THINK?**
>
> Write down your thoughts on Ramsey's arguments and revisit them shortly before the exam to see if your views have changed.

Read Ramsey for Yourself

In this passage from his book *Religious Language: An Empirical Placing of Theological Phrases* (1957), Ramsey explains the links between models, qualifiers and disclosures. The notes in the margin will help you to grasp his ideas.

Ramsey uses phrases such as 'light breaks' or 'penny drops' to describe moments when something is disclosed to a believer about the nature of God, and the believer is able to grasp something of the divine mystery. >	Whether the light breaks or not is something that we ourselves cannot entirely control. We certainly choose what seem to us the most appropriate models, we can operate what seem to us the most suitable qualifiers; we can develop what seem to us the best stories, but we can never guarantee that for a particular person the light will dawn at a particular point, or for that matter at any point in any story. Need this trouble us? Is not this only what has been meant by religious people when they have claimed that the 'initiative' in any 'disclosure' or 'revelation' must come from God.
Appropriate models are the terms and images we use from ordinary human language and human experiences relating to God, which must be accompanied by qualifiers. >	
Suitable qualifiers are the adverbs and adjectives we add to those terms to signify that God is beyond and outside of our human experience, although the models point us in that direction. >	
'Disclosure' is Ramsey's term for when religious language can show a glimpse of the nature of God, a piece of the divine mystery, to the person who has the experience. This cannot be God in totality, due to our finite nature, but it is an understanding nonetheless. >	

In this passage, Ramsey reminds us of the limits of language when discussing 'God'.

> Let us always be cautious of talking about God in straighthood language. Let us never talk as if we had privileged access to the diaries of God's private life … so that we may say quite cheerfully why God did what, when, and where.'

- Whenever we use language to describe 'God' we must remember that it can never be a full description of God, as God is so far beyond the limits of human language and expression.
- We cannot presume that our earthly minds with experience only of this world, can understand God, who is beyond this world. Statements about God must therefore be metaphysical, and while they have some meaning they cannot be the totality of God.

Here Ramsey explains further the significance of the term 'God' to the religious believer and how it is understood through qualification.

> For the religious man 'God' is a key word, an irreducible posit, an ultimate of explanation expressive of the kind of commitment he professes. It is to be talked about in terms of the object-language over which it presides, but only when this object-language is qualified; in which case this qualified object-language also becomes currency for that odd discernment with which religious commitment, when it is not bigotry or fanaticism will necessarily be associated. Meanwhile, as a corollary, we can note that to understand religious language or theology we must first evoke the odd kind of situation to which I have given various parallels.

- A fundamental starting point that cannot be broken down into smaller pieces. It cannot be reduced and is taken as a basic assumption.
- Ramsey is showing the importance of the term 'God' to a religious believer; it is something beyond our usual language. Ramsey admits that this language will be 'logically odd', but this does not mean it is without meaning.
- The language we use to talk about things, events and people in the world around us. Language about God must differ from this. Although we may use the same terms and descriptions in everyday language, the words are qualified when speaking of God in order to make that distinction.
- The 'models' we use are language that we can associate with our own experiences, but this must be 'qualified' when speaking about God and other metaphysical claims as God is beyond our usual experience.
- Ramsey is advocating an intellectually driven type of religious faith. He sees the so-called conflict between religion and science as somewhat overstated, and the Ian Ramsey Centre for Science and Religion set up after his death still seeks to encourage engagement between them.
- Religious language for Ramsey is analogical, and will never be able to reveal the full 'divine mystery', but through using models and qualifiers we are able to get some 'disclosures' about the nature of God.

Know Criticisms of Ramsey

Criticism of analogy. One major criticism of Ramsey's view is that we have no way of knowing if analogy is the best way to talk about God. A key part of his view is that God will ultimately remain a 'divine mystery' and cannot be known fully. This means we cannot know if the analogies we use are the correct ones.

Prominent Christian philosopher and defender of theism Richard Swinburne (see Chapter 25) would argue that analogy is not necessary, but that we are using terms such as 'good' about God univocally – meaning we know that it means the same thing but in a different context. In *The Coherence of Theism* (1977), Swinburne wrote: 'Surely a word is being used univocally if it denotes the same property, even if having that property amounts to something very different in different things.'

> **INSIGHT**
>
> Swinburne openly criticised Ramsey's use of models and qualifiers in *The Coherence of Theism*: 'This account of religious language is a somewhat vague one and does not answer in detail such crucial questions as when models and qualifiers are used legitimately, and when they are not.'

> **ESSENTIAL!**
>
> Using a term **analogically** means that we understand the word to be a comparison to something similar, but different. For example, 'God is good' means that I know what 'good' is for me as a human, and God's goodness will be similar to, but different from, what human goodness is.
>
> Using a term **univocally** means that we understand the term to have the same meaning in different contexts. For example, in the phrases 'a blue pen' and 'a blue car', blue is being used in the same way, for the same meaning, despite the different object.

From a non-theist perspective, empiricist David Hume (see Chapter 5) criticised the use of analogies to talk about God. He believed that the strength of an analogy lies in the similarities between the two things you are comparing. To compare human experience with some metaphysical being is not appropriate, according to Hume, as we cannot know empirically what 'God' or 'divine mystery' is. Ramsey's use of qualifiers shows how different the metaphysical claims are from the human experience, leaving it open to Hume's criticism.

Hume criticised the design, or teleological, argument in particular when he challenged the idea that religious language is analogous. For example, with Paley's analogy (see Chapter 3), we are making assumptions that the universe is like a watch, when we have no idea if it is like a watch at all. As an empiricist, Hume is concerned that we should have evidence for the claims we make, and since we cannot have evidence of the start of the universe, it is wrong to assume it is anything like the creation of a pocket watch: 'The dissimilitude is so striking, that the utmost you can here pretend to is a guess, a conjecture, a presumption concerning a similar cause' (Hume, 1935).

An assumption of God's existence and nature. Both Ramsey and Aquinas made an assumption of God's existence and nature by viewing religious language as analogous. This may be of use to those within a faith who profess to know and have a relationship with God, but it is less useful for those who do not. Wittgenstein's Language Game theory correlates to this, as religious language has meaning only for those who agree with its assumptions as part of their language game. This theory is explored in Chapter 33.

> **ESSENTIAL!**
>
> The **'Evil God' challenge** is posed to theists who assume that the God defended by the classical arguments for God's existence is 'good' rather than 'evil'.

In addition, this is not only an assumption that there is a God but also about what that God is like. The philosophical thought experiment, the **'Evil God' challenge**, highlights that assumptions are made about God's nature when the classical arguments for God's existence are used. Both Aquinas and Ramsey assumed that God is 'good' and 'loving', when there could be just as much evidence showing that God is not.

Direct revelation is the best way to understand God. Other Christian scholars, such as the Swiss theologian Karl Barth, criticise any use of analogies as they believe that knowledge of God can only come from revelation. This ensures that God does not collapse into human categories, and into our limited human understanding. Responsible talk about God, according to Barth, can only come from God's self-revelation to humanity, not from our flawed attempts to understand him from our own experiences.

Watch Out for Traps

> **INSIGHT**
>
> 'God reveals Himself. He reveals Himself through Himself. He reveals Himself. If we really want to understand revelation in terms of its subject, i.e., God, then the first thing we have to realize is that this subject, God, the Revealer, is identical with His act in revelation and also identical with its effect' (Barth, *Church Dogmatics*, 1932).

Not all religious language leads to disclosures. For Ramsey, religious language has the capacity to lead to disclosures around the nature of God and the divine mystery, but this is not guaranteed. However, religious believers will often state that those disclosures are in fact an act of God, causing a breakthrough in their understanding.

Religious language is not empirically verifiable. Ramsey acknowledged that we cannot experience God in the same way as we do the world – it is beyond our investigations – which is why metaphysical questions will remain a 'divine mystery'. Ramsey agrees with the logical positivists that religious language is therefore non-cognitive; however, he does not agree that it is therefore without meaning.

Religious language is not meaningless. Ramsey stated that talk about God and metaphysics is 'logically odd' but that does not mean it has no meaning. The meaning lies in what the words and terms point towards, rather than what they can be empirically proven to represent.

> **STRENGTHEN YOUR GRASP**
>
> 1. Write your own explanation of Ramsey's analogical approach to religious language. Include the following: models, qualifiers and disclosures. Have examples for each of these three areas and make sure you can link them to Ramsey's ideas. Cover your notes and see what you can remember about them. This will help you prepare for an 'explain' question in the exam.
> 2. Make a list of the strengths and weaknesses of Ramsey's understanding of religious language as analogical. Ensure you consider how other philosophers may view his understanding. For example, how does Ramsey's models and qualifiers theory compare and contrast with Aquinas' theory? How have other Christian philosophers challenged him and how would the logical positivists respond? Give a ranking out of five for each of these strengths and weaknesses to help you select the evidence that you think will make the strongest points in an essay. This will help you prepare for an 'evaluate' question in the exam.

Exam Guidance AO1

You will need to be able to give an account of Ramsey's model and qualifiers understanding of religious language, how it relates to Aquinas' understandings of analogy and how it is an attempt to defend the meaningfulness of religious language against the criticisms of the logical positivism movement. You should be able to give examples of religious language which exemplifies the models and qualifiers that are central to Ramsey's theory. You should also compare and contrast his views with other understandings of religious language – the *via negativa* and religious language as symbolic are different from Ramsey's view, which you need to understand.

Exam Guidance AO2

By considering the strengths and weaknesses of Ramsey's approach to religious language, you can evaluate how successfully he achieves his aim of defending the meaningfulness of religious language in the face of logical positivist and atheist challenges. Consider how successful Ramsey's approach is in comparison with other understandings of religious language that philosophers in this book have put forward. An important challenge to Ramsey's theory is that it does not really add anything to Aquinas' discussion of religious language.

31. JOHN HERMAN RANDALL JR
GET INTO RANDALL'S WORLD

> **Quick Overview** John Herman Randall Jr (1889–1980) was an American philosopher and contemporary of fellow liberal Christian thinker Paul Tillich. Like Tillich, he believed that religious language was symbolic, although unlike Tillich, he did not think that symbols pointed to an external ultimate reality or 'God'. Instead, he thought that they should be understood purely through the functions they perform, for those who use them.

John Herman Randall Jr grew up in New York City in the early twentieth century, at a time when the city was bustling with new inventions and ideas. His family home was close to the prestigious Columbia University, where he studied. Randall lived at home while attending Columbia. Being at home as a student and surrounded by intellectual conversation, he was able to discuss philosophy and theology with his beloved father. His father, a minister in the Church, was open about his liberal stance on religion and saw this as the continuation of the faith of the early Church fathers in contrast to the distinctly modern manifestation of fundamentalism. As a signatory of the 1933 Humanist Manifesto, Randall might be viewed as an opponent of religious belief. There are certainly issues with his view of religion for many who have faith. However, he was characteristically enigmatic when asked by his students what he actually believed, his response being 'It depends what you mean by God.'

Randall was greatly influenced by Aristotle and derived from him a certain optimism about the usefulness of language and the social sciences, which enable us to make sense of the world around us. The supposed conflict between religion and science is something Randall sets out to debunk in his writings. This encouraged him to study the early philosophers more, and in 1960 he published his well-received book *Aristotle*.

Another influence on Randall was Friedrich Schleiermacher, the father of modern liberal Protestant Christianity. Schleiermacher viewed religion as being primarily about human experience, with associated teachings, beliefs and doctrines being of secondary importance. He spoke of an 'Infinite in the midst of our finite nature', which influenced Randall's theory of religious language as symbolic.

During the 1930s, Randall was instrumental in helping refugees from Nazi Germany secure teaching positions at Columbia University, and some of these people became his close friends, like fellow philosopher Paul Tillich. After officially retiring, Randall co-taught at the university with Tillich.

Know Randall's Key Ideas

Symbols as Truth?

Central to Randall's theory is the understanding of religious language as non-cognitive (non-factual and emotive). This, for Randall, solves the apparent conflict between religion and science, as they are completely different modes of discussion about the world. Randall did not view religious language as a means of giving factual truths to the believer. He was anti-realist about theological discussions, meaning that he did not believe that 'the Divine' exists independently of the human mind. Instead, it is a symbol of the intellect (mind) for a religious dimension. While seeing religious language as non-cognitive, however, Randall still believed that it was meaningful.

While Randall's views may at first seem to resemble those of Sigmund Freud, who viewed religion as a creation of the human mind (see Chapter 17), there is a significant difference between the two. For Randall, religion was necessary and a force for good rather than simply an 'illusion' that should be removed as society progresses. Like his contemporary and friend Tillich (see Chapter 32), Randall distinguished between **signs** and **symbols**. Signs represent something other than themselves. For example, a red stop sign always represents the command to stop your vehicle. Symbols, however, are not simply representing something – they are revealing something about existence.

Randall also distinguished between cognitive symbols and non-cognitive symbols. Cognitive symbols are factual symbols which reveal a factual truth about the world, such as scientific theories or equations. Non-cognitive symbols, on the other hand, do not provide any empirical or factual knowledge; they reveal a different kind of truth to the believer. This is why Randall viewed religious language as non-cognitive. For Randall, symbols were purely the mechanism whereby humans are able to express and understand a divine aspect of the human experience. His view of cognitive and non-cognitive symbols is summarised in the table below.

Signs	Cognitive symbols	Non-cognitive symbols
Represent something else, which can 'stand in' for or swap with that thing	Reveal a factual truth about the world, used in the natural sciences	Reveal something about existence, help us to see something or understand something about life
Thumbs up means 'I'm OK' Red light signals the need to stop 'The cat is on the mat', therefore I can see a cat on the mat	$F = m \times a$ Newton's laws of motion The sum of the squares on the sides of a right-angled triangle is equal to the square on the hypotenuse Pythagoras' theorem	'God is love' reveals more of the importance of love to us The Khalsa symbol in Sikhism evokes the importance of justice and equality

INSIGHT

Randall viewed religious language as symbolic – non-cognitive, but meaningful. He believed that all of religion and religious language was myth. Religious symbols and writings such as holy scriptures are narratives used to explain or support a belief system.

INSIGHT

'Religious beliefs, though far indeed from being "meaningless", do not possess what is ordinarily meant by cognitive value' (Randall, *The Role of Knowledge in Western Religion*, 1958).

ESSENTIAL!

Signs are used when one thing directly represents something else (e.g. red = stop, green = go). Signs can be seen as pointers to show or tell you something.

Symbols participate in the reality they are pointing to, allowing a connection to be made. They can be seen as bridges between the person viewing or using the symbol and what they represent.

TIP

Randall's view can be contrasted with that of Freud, who understood religion to be an illusion and a symptom of a collective neurosis that humans suffer.

JOHN HERMAN
RANDALL JR

What Is Religion?

Religion and spirituality are woven into cultures and societies in ways that can lead us to believe that religion is a central part of our nature as humans. Randall emphasised the distinctly human activity of religion and the essential functions it fulfils in society. He did not focus on the teachings and revelations of religion, but on the role and function religion has for everyday human actions and emotions.

For example, some religious festivals are celebrated at key parts of the year, such as when crops are harvested or when days start to lengthen in mid-winter. These are symbolic of important moments in the life cycle of the celebrants, not necessarily instructed from a 'higher power', but born out of the human emotions and activities themselves.

Music, art and poetry can perform a similar function and humans turn to them in times of great elation, distress and need. Their power lies not in a literal or factual representation but in the emotion and reaction they evoke in us as humans. For Randall, the power of the myth similarly lies in what it evokes in humans.

INSIGHT

'We can assume that all religious beliefs without exception are "mythology". That is, they are all religious "symbols". If such symbols can be said to possess any kind of "truth", they certainly do not possess the literal truth of the factual statements of the descriptive sciences or of common sense' (Randall, *The Role of Knowledge in Western Religion*).

INSIGHT

'Religion gives men more and how much more only the participant can realise. In this it is like art, which likewise furnishes no supplementary truth, but it does open whole worlds to be explored, whole heavens to be enjoyed' (Randall, *The Role of Knowledge in Western Religion*).

Understand Randall's Arguments

IMPROVE YOUR UNDERSTANDING

Make sure that you know what symbols, the order of splendour and an anti-realist view of God are, and how they relate to discussions around the meaningfulness of religious language.

INSIGHT

- For Randall, there is no external, objective reality of 'God' or 'the Divine': these are symbolic of human desires, wishes and emotions.
- Religion and myths are positive for humankind as they help us view existence in a new and enlightened way. They allow us to reflect upon the 'order of splendour' in awe.
- Religious language is meaningful but in a different way from factual, empirical statements.

The Function of Symbols

It is important to remember that for Randall (unlike for Tillich), non-cognitive religious symbols do not reveal something about an essence or being beyond humans (a God or divine being) but are a wholly human construction. Randall took an anti-realist approach to statements relating to God and metaphysics. To him, symbols had four important functions for the individual and, perhaps more importantly, for the communities of people who use them.

> **INSIGHT**
>
> Randall stated that religious language was symbolic and fulfils four functions: evoking emotion, bringing communities together, expressing the non-literal and bringing the religious dimension into human experience.

1. Symbols arouse emotions in those who use them.

2. The symbols function as a method of bringing a community together. Randall used the example of how religious language has united people into larger communities than they may have been in before. For example, people may initially feel connected to the community where they live, as they live close by other people and share activities in their life. Through religious symbols, the community is enlarged to include everyone in that religion, not only through what the symbols mean but also through the actions that accompany them. An example is the Muslim idea of the Ummah, the bringing together of many groups of people who were originally tied to separate tribes and clans. Through symbolic praying towards one point, The Ka'ba, no matter where a Muslim is in the world, they can feel a connection with others.

3. Symbols communicate in a way that literal language alone cannot. Religious experiences were considered to be impossible to put into words by scholars such as William James and Rudolf Otto (see Chapters 21 and 22). Therefore, those who have religious experiences can use religious language symbolically to convey what has happened to them. Religious language can express truths about reality that cannot be put directly into words. In this sense, religion as a symbol goes further than the symbolism found in art, as it 'makes us see something about our experience and our experienced world'.

4. Finally, religious symbols help the believer to understand something about life that is beyond what can be disclosed through art, music or literature alone. Randall uses the phrase the **'order of splendour'** of the world. The symbols teach the believer how to find 'God', which Randall stated is a clarification of their own life, or an accessing of the divine dimension within it.

> **WHAT DO YOU THINK?**
>
> Write down your thoughts on Randall's arguments and revisit them shortly before the exam to see if your views have changed.

> **ESSENTIAL!**
>
> Randall's phrase the **'order of splendour'** means that symbolic language can cause us to see our existence and reality in a new light, evoking a sense of awe and wonder within us.

Read Randall for Yourself

In this extract from *The Meaning of Religion for Man* (1968), Randall discusses religious practices. The notes in the margin will help you to grasp his ideas.

> Randall was primarily interested in the lived experience of religion. He considered the doctrines and teachings of different faiths as secondary.
>
> Religious language is symbolic. Rather than revealing facts about the world, the religious symbols perform certain functions for those who use them, such as evoking emotions.
>
> Religion is a construct of the human mind – this does not have to be a negative conclusion, as for Freud, but it is nonetheless criticised by religious believers (see 'Know Criticisms of Randall' below).
>
> Here Randall reminds us that religious language, beliefs and practices all come from human desires, wants and emotions.

Religious practices furnish the means of expressing any deeply felt emotion – not only men's aspirations and loyalties but also their baser passions, prejudices and hatreds … In one sense, religions are little better than the turbulent human life they express; they are the most intensely human of all the activities in which men engage. It is hardly intelligent to blame the mirror for what it reflects or to think by breaking it to transform the scene.

In this extract from *The Role of Knowledge in Western Religion* (1958), Randall discusses the relationship between religion and art:

> Symbols do not bring something new into the world but show us what is already there, which we might not have seen or known.
>
> Here Randall is comparing religious language to art, music and paintings, but he goes on to say how it is different.
>
> For Randall, symbols evoke emotion but also action, spurring humanity on to be better and make a better go of life.
>
> An important function of symbols for Randall is the human emotional response they evoke.
>
> Randall's term for the divine dimension that humans can reflect upon (US spelling is retained here). This may be experienced as 'awe' and wonder.
>
> It is important to remember that Randall is not stating that there is 'a God' that exists objectively, but that the term 'God' is an often-used symbol as a result of human experiences.

The work of the painter, the musician, the poet, teaches us how to use our eyes, our ears, our minds, and our feelings with greater power and skill … It shows us how to discern unsuspected qualities in the world encountered, latent powers and possibilities there resident. Still more, it makes us see the new qualities with which the world, in cooperation with the spirit of man, can clothe itself … Is it otherwise with the prophet and the saint? They too can do something to us, they too can effect changes in us and in our world … They teach us how to see what man's life in the world is, and what it might be. They teach us how to discern what human nature can make out of its natural conditions and materials … They make us receptive to qualities of the world encountered; and they open our hearts to the new qualities with which that world, in cooperation with the spirit of man can clothe itself. They enable us to see and feel the religious dimension of our world better, the 'order of splendor,' and of man's experience in and with it. They teach us how to find the Divine; they show us visions of God.'

Know Criticisms of Randall

ESSENTIAL!

Logical positivism was a movement in the early twentieth century which viewed all statements that could not be verified as meaningless.

The challenge of logical positivism and materialism. According to Randall, the language of symbols is inherently non-cognitive and does not provide factual knowledge which can be gained through our senses alone. This conflicts with the **logical positivists**, as this means it is neither verifiable nor falsifiable. For logical positivists such as A.J. Ayer (see Chapter 26), this renders the language meaningless. More modern examples of this approach include the materialism of New Atheists such as Richard Dawkins (see Chapter 19), who would argue that untestable symbols are not necessary to give our life meaning, or to show us truths about reality. This can be achieved through the arts as well as the natural sciences.

> **INSIGHT**
>
> 'The feeling of awed wonder that science can give us is one of the highest experiences of which the human psyche is capable. It is a deep aesthetic passion to rank with the finest that music and poetry can deliver. It is truly one of the things that make life worth living' (Dawkins, *Unweaving the Rainbow*, 1998).

This is not how many religious believers view religion. Many religious believers have a **realist** view and would not agree with Randall's non-realist approach to their strongly held convictions that there is an objectively existing 'God' or Ultimate Being. While there may be many passages within scriptures, such as in the Bible, that can be read symbolically, there are others that do not seem to be meant in this way, such as Jesus stating 'I am the way, the truth and the life, no one gets to the father except through me' (John 14:6). According to John Hick (see Chapter 16): 'The Divine, as defined by Randall, is the temporary mental construction or projection of a recently emerged animal inhabiting one of the satellites of a minor star. God is not, according to this view, the creator and the ultimate ruler of the universe; God is a fleeting ripple of imagination in a tiny corner of space-time' (*Philosophy of Religion*, 1970).

Other scholars view religious language as cognitive rather than non-cognitive. For example, Caroline Franks Davis (see Chapter 23) states: 'We must defend the proposition that religious experience and religious utterances can and ought to be treated as capable of having cognitive content.'

The meaning of symbols changes drastically over time. A criticism of the thinking of Tillich and Randall is that symbols can and do change drastically over time, depending on the context and cultures in which they are found and used. If meaning can be changed so significantly, how can it remain meaningful? A well-known example is the Swastika, an ancient symbol associated with the Dharmic religious traditions, and meaning universal harmony and peace. The symbol was adopted by the Nazi Party during the twentieth century and took on a drastically different and negative association.

Watch Out for Traps

Religious language as symbolic. One common misconception about theories that see religious language as symbolic is that they are only referring to pictures as symbols. While pictures can be powerful symbols (for example, the Crucifix and the Star of David), viewing religious language as symbolic encompasses all metaphysical language, including statements about God or an Ultimate Being, prophets, religious experiences and an afterlife. For Randall, all of this language is symbolic as it reveals something about human nature and experience, rather than some objective reality of 'God'.

Religion as a negative thing. A further misconception is that, like Freud, Randall views religion as a negative thing for humanity. Randall viewed religion as myth, something wholly subjective and a creation of human minds, but that it is an essential part of what it means to be human. This is because it helps humans to access a 'religious dimension' to explain our existence and to see our lives from a different perspective.

Confusion between Randall and Tillich. Take care not to confuse the ideas of Randall and Tillich. While they both view religious language as symbolic, there are significant differences in their approaches. The table below can help you to distinguish between them.

> **ESSENTIAL!**
>
> A **realist** view of God contrasts with Randall's views and regards God as an objective reality, external to human ideas and emotions.

> **INSIGHT**
>
> Hick challenged the logical positivists by arguing that believers will have 'eschatological verification' of God's existence when they die. Essentially, they will only know when they die if heaven exists. Therefore, it is possible for God's existence to be weakly verified.

	Randall	Tillich
The idea of God	Anti-realist view of God: 'God' is a human construct drawing us to a religious dimension of our thoughts.	Realist view of God: God or the Ultimate Reality exists beyond human consciousness.
What term represents 'God'?	Order of splendour	Ground of being
Religious language	Religious language is completely subjective.	Religious language is not completely subjective.
	Religious language is completely non-cognitive.	Religious language is partially cognitive and partially non-cognitive.
How many functions do symbols have?	Four	Six

STRENGTHEN YOUR GRASP

1. Write your own explanation of Randall's analogical approach to religious language. Include the following: symbol, non-cognitive, functions and religious dimension. Have examples for each of these and be sure to link them to Randall's ideas. Cover your notes and see what you can remember of these four areas. This will help you prepare for an 'explain' question in the exam.

2. Make a list of the strengths and weaknesses of Randall's understanding of religious language as symbolic. Ensure you consider how other philosophers may view his understanding. How does Randall's symbolic language compare and contrast to Tillich's, for example? How have other Christian philosophers challenged him and how would the logical positivists respond? Give a ranking out of five for each of these strengths and weaknesses to help you select the evidence that you think will make the strongest points in an essay. This will help you prepare for an 'evaluate' question in the exam.

Exam Guidance AO1

You will need to be able to give an account of Randall's view of religious language as symbolic and meaningful. You should be able to explain both how Randall's view is anti-realist and also the four functions of symbols that he identifies: evoking emotion, bringing communities together, communicating beyond the literal, and enabling humans to access the religious dimension. You should be able to give examples that exemplify Randall's view of religious language as symbolic. You should also be able to compare and contrast Randall's views with those of other thinkers as regards their understandings of religious language: for example, Tillich's view of symbols, Aquinas and Ramsey on analogy, and the approach of the logical positivist movement.

Exam Guidance AO2

Through considering the strengths and weaknesses of Randall's approach to religious language, you can evaluate how successfully he achieved his aim of defending the meaningfulness of religious language in the face of challenges from logical positivists and New Atheists. Consider how successful Randall's approach is compared with the understandings of religious language that other philosophers discussed in this book have put forward.

32. PAUL TILLICH

GET INTO TILLICH'S WORLD

> **Quick Overview** Paul Tillich (1886–1965) was a German philosopher and critic of the Nazi Party in Germany during the Third Reich. He taught at the University of Chicago while in exile. His writings had a great influence on Christian thought in the later part of the twentieth century, and the minister and activist Martin Luther King Jr was influenced by him.

Paul Tillich was born into a Protestant family in Germany. The Higher Biblical Criticism of the late nineteenth century had brought into question the claim that the Bible was the direct word of God and caused many theologians to reconsider how the texts were meant to be interpreted. This, along with other liberal Christian interpretations by scholars such as Friedrich Schleiermacher, who believed that religion should be understood as 'the infinite within our finite experience', greatly shaped Tillich's views of religion.

As an army chaplain during the First World War, Tillich witnessed great suffering and this caused him to ask many questions about the nature of existence and faith. Dogmatic and literal interpretations of religion would no longer provide the answers in a world capable of causing such suffering.

Tillich greatly emphasised freedom through his writings, and while teaching at Frankfurt University he wrote a pamphlet on the importance of freedom in the face of the threat from the rising National Socialist (Nazi) Party. However, the pamphlet was instantly censored and Tillich became the first non-Jewish academic to be banned from teaching at universities in Germany. Eventually, he moved to the USA and befriended John Herman Randall Jr. They both developed theories about religious language being symbolic.

INSIGHT

'Man is man because he has freedom, but he has freedom only in polar interdependence with destiny' (Tillich, *Systematic Theology*, 1951).

Tillich was recognised by many other influential Christian thinkers as straddling both faith and reason in modern times. As Martin Luther King stated: 'He helped us to speak of God's action in history in terms which adequately expressed both the faith and the intellect of modern man.'

Know Tillich's Key Ideas

Christian Existentialism and the Ground of Being

Tillich both accepted and rejected the label of existentialist. Nevertheless, **existentialism** had an impact on his theory. He saw 'truth' not as something separate, that humans learn about externally, but as something learnt through individual experience. It could be differently experienced by different people at different times.

Martin Luther King said of Tillich (in October 1965, during the battle for civil rights): 'His Christian existentialism gave us a system of meaning and purpose for our lives in an age when war and doubt seriously threatened all that we had come to hold dear.' Tillich focused on sin being separation, meaning that segregation and alienation are evil.

In his book *Systemic Theology*, Tillich speaks of 'God' as transcendent and the reason and basis for all of existence. He argues that human language is insufficient to explain or even name him, her or it. This chimes with the theories of William James and Rudolf Otto (see Chapters 21 and 22) on religious experiences as ineffable and encountering something 'wholly other'. Language can never be literally applied to metaphysical (supernatural) claims and they must always be seen as in some way symbolic, even if they are not presented as such.

The German theologian and biblical scholar Friedrich Schleiermacher (who was an important influence on Tillich) viewed humans as finite beings experiencing the infinite. Tillich's term for this infinite essence is the **'Ground of Being'**. This could be understood in terms of the reason and cause of all existence, as well as the continued maintenance of those in existence. That which 'ultimately concerns' is what we put our faith in and what we are committed to. Tillich viewed all humans as having 'ultimate concerns'. However, these concerns can be idolatrous when they are not aligned with the 'Ground of Being' in some way. Tillich gave examples, including the nation or a head of state becoming the 'ultimate concern'. This was particularly poignant, as he was a critic of the Nazi Party; he could see the dangers of making finite, human constructions the focus of worship or 'ultimate concern'.

Signs and Symbols

Consider any religious service or ritual. Many symbols will be visible throughout, including the shape of the building, the sculptures within it, and the pictures and calligraphy on the wall. Water, light, smells and sounds are incorporated and physical actions represent spiritual processes. A mosque may have a dome-shaped roof to symbolise Tawhid or the one-ness of Allah. Iconography may be included in a Greek Orthodox Church to symbolise the stories of important saints. The Star of David might be visible at the entrance to a synagogue, representing God's covenant with humanity.

Much like these physical symbols of God, religious language contains plenty of symbolic language, as it is discussing the metaphysical realm which is beyond our usual human experience. Therefore, we must recognise the limits of our human language in understanding and conveying it. Tillich, like Randall (see Chapter 31), would argue that all of religious language should be understood as symbolic.

Tillich distinguished between symbols and signs. While both may point to something beyond themselves, only symbols 'participate' in what they point to. He used the example of red traffic lights, which point to the instruction for a vehicle to stop. The traffic light is 'just a sign'. A country's flag, on the other hand, is a symbol because it represents and participates in the power of that nation or monarch.

ESSENTIAL!

Existentialism is the philosophical belief that the world can be understood through personal and individual experience.

ESSENTIAL!

The **'Ground of Being'** is the name that Tillich gave to 'God'. He considered the human term 'God' as being insufficient to encompass its reality.

INSIGHT

A key quote from Tillich is: 'Man's ultimate concern must be expressed symbolically, because symbolic language alone is able to express the ultimate' (*Dynamics of Faith*, 1957). 'Ultimate concern' was Tillich's terminology for what each human has as the focus of their faith, commitment and hopes – this may be religious or secular. For Tillich, this should be aligned with the 'Ground of Being'.

TIP

It is unclear exactly how symbols 'participate' in what they point to, as Tillich claims. This is a criticism some scholars have of the theory (see the 'Know Criticisms of Tillich' section in this chapter).

Even though a religious symbol participates in or has a relationship with 'God' or the Ground of Being that it points us towards, Tillich was concerned that people might become idolatrous and confuse the symbol with the ultimate. An icon of a holy saint, a statue of a goddess, the historical figure of a prophet and even the church traditions themselves are not to be worshipped in the place of the Ground of Being.

Understand Tillich's Arguments

IMPROVE YOUR UNDERSTANDING

Be certain that you understand the following ideas: what symbolic language is, the meaning of the Ground of Being, what it means to say that a symbol 'participates', and how this relates to discussions around the meaningfulness of religious language.

INSIGHT

For Tillich, 'God' is a term used as a symbol for the 'Ground of Being' – the foundation of all being, rather than a 'presence'. All religious language is symbolic and points us towards the Ground of Being. Symbols are more significant than signs as they participate in that which they point to.

A Universalist Theory

Essential elements of Christianity are centred on symbolism. For example, since the time of early Christianity, new members to the faith have been welcomed through the practice of baptism. There is no literal (actual) sin present on the person (a new member of the faith) which is washed away through the rite with water, yet it is a symbolic representation of cleansing. Tillich understood all religious language through this non-literal representation.

Tillich's examples of religious language as symbolic are mainly taken from Christianity, although he believed that his theory applied to all religious expressions. Despite Tillich being a realist about the existence of the Ground of Being, his theory can be understood as universalist, in that he is accepting of all and any expressions of religious symbolism rather than adopting an exclusivist position where only Protestant Christianity is seen as the correct understanding of 'God'.

> **ESSENTIAL!**
>
> A **cognitive** view of religious language means a factual or literal belief in the words, which can potentially be shown to be true or false. Religious language or texts would be presented as true by believers, or accused of being false by non-believers.
>
> A **non-cognitive** view of religious language means a 'non-factual' understanding of the religious words used. Here, the religious language holds meaning of a different, more emotional nature.

Cognitive or Non-cognitive?

Scholars have debated whether Tillich's understanding of religious language as symbolic is **cognitive** (factual language) or **non-cognitive** (non-factual language involving feelings and emotions). On the surface, it may appear to be non-cognitive, as there is no way of knowing the correct or factual interpretation of symbols. However, unlike Randall, Tillich stated in a realist sense that there is a Ground of Being with whom we should be ultimately concerned. This is a religious claim of a cognitive nature.

The Six Criteria for Symbols

We have seen that Tillich viewed religious language as symbolic, as a kind of religious experience which connected humanity to 'God' or the Ground of Being without the limit of our mere mortal, human understanding.

> **INSIGHT**
>
> Tillich stated that symbols differ from signs as they participate in what they point to. He stated six criteria to help develop this distinction.

For Tillich, symbols could be understood through the six criteria that they fulfil. These are detailed below.

The criteria of a symbol	Tillich's example	In Tillich's words (from *The Dynamics of Faith*)
1. They point to something beyond themselves.	A red stop sign is not a symbol, but simply a sign.	'Decisive is the fact that signs do not participate in the reality of that to which they point, while symbols do. Therefore, signs can be replaced for reasons of expediency or convention, while symbols cannot.'
2. They participate in what they point to.	A flag participates in the power and dignity of the nation.	'This leads to the second characteristic of the symbol: It participates in that to which it points: the flag participates in the power and dignity of the nation for which it stands … An attack on the flag is felt as an attack on the majesty of the group in which it is acknowledged. Such an attack is considered blasphemy.'
3. They open up levels of reality which otherwise are closed to us.	A picture or a poem	'The third characteristic of a symbol is that it opens up levels of reality which otherwise are closed for us. All arts create symbols for a level of reality which cannot be reached in any other way.'
4. They open up dimensions of the soul which correspond to those aspects of reality.	A play	'The symbol's fourth characteristic not only opens up dimensions and elements of reality which otherwise would remain unapproachable but also unlocks dimensions and elements of our soul which correspond to the dimensions and elements of reality.'
5 and 6. Unlike signs, symbols are not planned and they grow and die in time.	A king	'They grow out of the individual or collective unconscious and cannot function without being accepted by the unconscious dimension of our being. Symbols … have an especially social function … Like living beings, they grow and they die. They grow when the situation is ripe for them, and they die when the situation changes.'

> **TIP**
>
> To understand Tillich, it is crucial to understand that symbols participate in what they point to: for example, the Star of David is part of Judaism, not just an identifier of the faith.

■ INSIGHT

Tillich acknowledged that the meanings associated with symbols can change over time. This can also be a key criticism of his theory, which is outlined in the 'Know Criticisms of Tillich' section later in this chapter.

■ WHAT DO YOU THINK?

Write down your thoughts on Tillich's arguments and revisit them shortly before the exam to see if your views have changed.

Read Tillich for Yourself

■ TASK

Read Tillich for yourself in the extract below. The notes in the margin will help you to grasp his views.

In this extract from *Dynamics of Faith* (1957), Tillich discusses the nature of faith.

> The reason for this transformation of concepts into symbols is the character of ultimacy and the nature of faith. That which is the true ultimate transcends the realm of finite reality infinitely. Therefore, no finite reality can express it directly and properly. Religiously speaking, God transcends his own name. This is why the use of his name easily becomes an abuse or a blasphemy. Whatever we say about that which concerns us ultimately, whether or not we call it God, has a symbolic meaning. It points beyond itself while participating in that to which it points. In no other way can faith express itself adequately. The language of faith is the language of symbols. If faith were what we have shown that it is not, such an assertion could not be made. But faith, understood as the state of being ultimately concerned, has no language other than symbols. When saying this I always expect the question: Only a symbol? He who asks this question shows that he has not understood the difference between signs and symbols nor the power of symbolic language, which surpasses in quality and strength the power of any nonsymbolic language. One should never say 'only a symbol,' but one should say 'not less than a symbol.'

- All faith involves symbolic language. We cannot express the infinite in our finite (limited) terms and experiences.
- The term 'God' is considered to be insufficient language for the transcendent being but it is the term that people most commonly use. It is simply a 'human' word and symbolic language is required to help us express what 'God' is like.
- Throughout Tillich's theory we see his concern that people should not become idolatrous, worshipping the symbol or even the name of God instead of the Ground of Being. Tillich uses the 'Protestant Principle' to explain that humans are limited in what they can express about 'God' and should recognise that limitation.
- This is what makes a symbol more than a sign. There is some connection and relationship with what the symbol points to, the significance of which may be known to those in the community of believers and not to those outside.
- While all religious people would accept there is some symbolic language in their faith, for Tillich, the whole language of faith is a language of symbols.
- If a believer thinks that their faith is being belittled by being labelled symbolic, Tillich argues that they do not fully understand what symbolic language is. There are key differences between signs and symbols that Tillich outlines in his six criteria.

Know Criticisms of Tillich

Tillich's understanding of religious language as symbolic is circular and philosophically confusing. Paul Edwards, an Austrian-American philosopher and contemporary of Tillich, wrote a critique of Tillich's views in an article called 'Professor Tillich's Confusions' (1965). Here Edwards accepted that metaphor and symbol are used throughout religious language but argued that they have to be reduced to something other than a metaphor or symbol to have any meaning. There must be some clear and objective 'thing' to which they point, otherwise they are 'circular' and take us nowhere. By this he means that the symbol is not pointing to any 'thing' at all – despite what Tillich is arguing. The symbol is only really pointing to itself. Symbols cannot be falsified or verified due to their subjective nature and therefore do not 'convey any facts'.

Important doctrines in religion are seen as factually, not symbolically, true. Another critic of Tillich's theory about religious language being symbolic was the American philosopher William Alston. He argued that if we do accept the symbolic interpretation, then statements such as 'Jesus has paid for our sins' and 'There is an afterlife' lose their significance for believers. Religious believers may see some of the scriptures and practices as symbolic, but there are central, key doctrines which they hold as objectively true, and Tillich's theory does not seem to allow for this. The Tillich theory does not offer a way of knowing if the symbol in question is even the correct one, or if it represents 'God' in the correct manner. Therefore, it is meaningless.

Is Tillich an atheist? Tillich's view of 'God' as the 'Ground of Being' and all biblical statements as symbolic has led to accusations from some within the Evangelical Protestant community that he is not Christian or even a theist but perhaps a pantheist (one who believes that the universe is God, and God is the universe) or even an atheist.

> **INSIGHT**
>
> 'Tillich is a complete atheist who lost his belief while completing his higher education. Intellectually he despises Christianity ... Still, being the son of a clergyman and having a fondness for religious life, Tillich [will] have his cake and eat it too. He is going to remain with the Church for the purpose of undermining Christianity from within' (Leonard F. Wheat).

Watch Out for Traps

Misconception about religious symbols. A common misconception about theories that see religious language as symbolic is that in talking about symbols they are only referring to pictures. While pictures can be powerful symbols (such as the Crucifix and the Star of David), understanding religious language as symbolic encompasses all metaphysical language. This includes statements about God or an Ultimate Being, prophets, religious experiences and an afterlife. For Tillich, all of this language is symbolic and it reveals something about the Ground of Being, as people align their 'ultimate concern' with it.

Tillich is not arguing that there is no God. While Tillich's views of 'God' may be unorthodox and vastly different from literal interpretations of scripture, he does hold that there is some-thing or some-one in existence, albeit this concept is beyond our human capabilities to express fully. In this sense, he is a realist about the existence of God, and some scholars argue that this ultimately makes his theory of religious language as symbolic a cognitive one.

Confusion between Randall and Tillich. Take care not to merge the ideas of Randall and Tillich. While they both view religious language as symbolic, there are important differences in their approaches. A useful activity would be to make a list of the similarities and differences between their approaches.

STRENGTHEN YOUR GRASP

1. Write your own explanation of Tillich's symbolic approach to religious language including: symbols, ultimate concern, Ground of Being and 'participate in'. Have examples for each of these and link them to Tillich's ideas. Cover your notes and see what you can remember of these four areas. This will help you prepare for an 'explain' question in the exam.

2. Make a list of the strengths and weaknesses of Tillich's understanding of religious language as symbolic. Consider how other philosophers view his understanding. How does Tillich's view on symbolic language compare and contrast to Randall's? How have other Christian philosophers challenged him and how would the logical positivists respond? This will help you when preparing for an 'evaluate' question in the exam.

Exam Guidance AO1

You will need to be able to give an account of Tillich's view of religious language as symbolic and meaningful, and should be able to explain his realist views about the existence of 'God' and how he viewed symbols differing from signs. Be ready to give examples that exemplify his view of religious language as symbolic. You might need to compare and contrast Tillich's views of religious language with those of others (for example, Randall's view of symbolism, Aquinas' and Ramsey's thoughts on analogy, and the approach of the logical positivist movement).

Exam Guidance AO2

By considering the strengths and weaknesses of Tillich's approach to religious language, you should be able to evaluate how successfully he achieved his aim of defending the meaningfulness of religious language in the face of challenges from logical positivists and atheists. Consider how successful Randall's approach is compared with the understandings of religious language that other philosophers discussed in this book have put forward.

33. LUDWIG WITTGENSTEIN
GET INTO WITTGENSTEIN'S WORLD

> **Quick Overview** Ludwig Wittgenstein (1889–1951) is considered by many to be the greatest philosopher of all time. He taught at the University of Cambridge and his work is generally separated into early and later periods, which have significant differences between them. This is especially the case in terms of whom they influenced. His Language Game theory is set out in his posthumously published book *Philosophical Investigations* (1953).

Born into a wealthy Austrian family, Ludwig Wittgenstein was homeschooled until he was 14. He had a stutter and found it hard to 'fit in'. He was fascinated by engineering and had a brilliant mathematical mind. He attended the University of Cambridge to learn the language of mathematics from Bertrand Russell (whom he viewed as the pinnacle of logic at the time). Russell viewed Wittgenstein as either a 'man of genius or an eccentric' and encouraged him to pursue philosophy. The two men maintained a correspondence and friendship for many years, until Wittgenstein strayed into what Russell saw as unnecessary theories.

Wittgenstein fought during the First World War and was taken as a prisoner of war. While imprisoned, he wrote *The Tractatus Logico-Philosophicus* (known as '*The Tractatus*'). He was concerned with how language functions and its relationship to the surrounding world. It was in *The Tractatus* that Wittgenstein set out his Picture Theory of language. He built on the work of the empiricist David Hume (see Chapter 5) when he stated that 'What can be said at all can be said clearly, and what cannot be said must be passed over in silence.' This theory went on to influence the Vienna Circle and the logical positivist movement.

TIP

Wittgenstein's early period of work was influenced by the ideas of David Hume (see Chapter 5) and Immanuel Kant (see Chapter 11).

After the war, Wittgenstein took on various roles – a gardener at a monastery, a school teacher and a hospital porter – but the bulk of his time was spent lecturing at the University of Cambridge. He stated that he was most useful to those who had a kind of mental cramp, and that he would be their 'masseur'; if they did not have the cramp, he would not be of use.

When the fascism and antisemitism of the National Socialist (Nazi) Party took hold in Germany, Wittgenstein became a British citizen. In his second book, *Philosophical Investigations*, Wittgenstein deviated from many of the ideas in *The Tractatus* and set out a new way to understand religious language, as a language game.

Know Wittgenstein's Key Ideas
The Role of Language

In the introduction to *The Tractatus* (1921), Bertrand Russell, Wittgenstein's teacher and friend, stated that 'The essential business of language is to assert or deny facts' and this is central to Wittgenstein's early approach to the meaning of language. In this earlier work, Wittgenstein set out his Picture Theory of meaning. Words should correspond to what we know of reality. Wittgenstein built on the ideas of another German philosopher, Gottlob Frege, who argued that individual words lack meaning; they only make sense when grouped in sentences.

> **INSIGHT**
>
> According to Wittgenstein, 'What can be said at all can be said clearly, and whereof one cannot speak, thereof one must be silent' (*The Tractatus*). By this, he did not believe that discussions around philosophy, ethics and aesthetics were unimportant – only that they could not be spoken about with any meaningfulness.

The Picture Theory of language: the words we use correlate to something in reality.

In the Picture Theory, the only language which has sense is that which relates to something in the 'real world'. This means that there are many metaphysical and religious statements that would be nonsense and it rules out many discussions of philosophy, ethics and aesthetics. This theory was taken up by the logical positivist movement.

In his later work, Wittgenstein moved away from the Picture Theory of words to viewing language as a tool. He believed that the meaning of language stemmed from how it is used by those who speak and use it rather than what it corresponds to in the world. A word can be used as a 'tool'. It can have multiple meanings depending on the context of when and how it is being used. To understand the meaning, we therefore must understand the full context of the community of speakers.

> **INSIGHT**
>
> In later years, Wittgenstein formulated a new understanding of religious language – that the importance of the language used lies in its use and context.

Wittgenstein explained that there are multiple (not single) meanings for words, and that these overlap with each other depending on the situation. He labels this 'family resemblances'. For example, the word 'game' may appear to have the simple meaning of playing something with others in a competitive way. However, when scrutinising different types of games (video games, professional football competitions, chess or hopscotch in a playground) you can see many differences between them. Reaching a single definitive meaning of 'game' is impossible, although the activities have enough in common with each other to share the word.

Language Games

In Wittgenstein's view, to understand what language means, we must look to how it is being used. The terms and phrases we use will depend on how and where we are using them. Wittgenstein calls these different settings and situations '*Lebensformen*', which translates as 'forms of life'. The language we use will make sense to those who are in the same *Lebensform*, and will not make sense to those outside of it.

In *Philosophical Investigations* (1953), Wittgenstein compares this to a human not being able to understand a lion – 'if a lion could speak, we could not understand him'. This may seem intuitive to many, but it was revolutionary in comparison not only to Wittgenstein's earlier work but also to the work of philosophers before him.

It is understood that the best way to learn a new language is to use it in context, with other speakers. Idioms, slang and turns of phrase do not make sense unless they are used in context. Consider the term 'bishop'. Within Christianity, it refers to someone with a certain authority in the leadership structure of the Church of England. In a game of chess, however, a bishop is a piece that moves across the board diagonally. Thus, every language game has to be understood from the inside. One 'form of life' will not be able to understand the language use of another.

Much like 'bishop' can mean something in a game of chess, and something different in the Church of England, so each language game has its own rules and agreements for use.

INSIGHT

It is unclear from his writing if Wittgenstein saw each religion as a different 'form of life' from atheism. However, his approach has nevertheless often been applied to discussions around religious 'language'.

This theory has clear implications for the importance of context and translations when considering holy books and scriptures. However, the links to religious language go even further.

Language Games Applied to Religious Language

While the logical positivist movement argued that religious language is meaningless and nonsensical, Wittgenstein did not see it as the job of philosophers to make that judgement. Their task was to see how the language is being used. To judge the language used within a religious 'form of life' according to the standards and scrutiny of a scientific 'form of life' is a complete misunderstanding of how the language is functioning. Philosophers should look to the role of the terms as they are being used by people within that language game to understand their meaning.

> **INSIGHT**
>
> For Wittgenstein, religious language is non-cognitive and meaningful as part of a language game.

Understand Wittgenstein's Arguments

> **IMPROVE YOUR UNDERSTANDING**
>
> Make sure that you know what Language Game theory is, what 'forms of life' are and what examples could be given to show that religious language is part of a language game.

Language games allow for a consideration of the context and use of religious language. The logical positivist movement could be criticised for being too scientific and clinical in its discussions of religious language. People who use religious language often have emotions attached, and feelings of community, hope and support. Using a Language Games theory to understand this religious language can seem more helpful, as it takes account of the context of the words, and their meanings for those who use them.

Wittgenstein believed language to be a public act. There could be no private language, as language is spoken between people who ascribe meaning to the terms they use. This meaning, rather than the words in isolation, is most important in the language game of religion.

> **INSIGHT**
>
> A key supporter of Wittgenstein, Welsh philosopher D.Z. Phillips, argued that philosophers have to consider the context of religious language and what the believer says and does in connection with their statements and beliefs.

Wittgenstein believed that language is a public act and that there is no private language.

Problems in philosophy occur when we misunderstand the 'rules of the game'. Take, for example, the sentence 'God exists.' While this is not a factual, cognitive statement for Wittgenstein, it still has meaning. It means far more than simply 'There is a God in existence.' To the religious believer, it comes with connotations of entering into a whole life of faith. The non-believer will not understand this precisely because they are not in the same game.

INSIGHT

Wittgenstein's Language Game theory is anti-realist in its approach to metaphysical claims. The meaning of terms and phrases in religious language comes from their use, rather than their corresponding to some external object in reality.

To be tied up in arguments and discussions around the truthfulness of such a statement as 'God exists' is unnecessary, according to Wittgenstein. There is no objective 'God' or being that we can prove either to exist or not – it simply does not matter. This makes truth relative to the groups of people who are talking within their game. What is meaningful is what is 'true for me' and will not be meaningful for you if you are not in the same game as I am.

INSIGHT

Wittgenstein's Language Game theory presents truth as relativist – it depends on the context, culture or perspective of those involved. It also holds a coherence theory of truth whereby the truth comes from the group of 'players' in the game agreeing with each other.

Religious language is often tied to a commitment and action. English philosopher R.B. Braithwaite (a contemporary of Wittgenstein) developed the 'meaning in use' principle of language games to emphasise that people partake in a religious language game as a result of a commitment, and this can have a great impact on their life. By stating that 'God is love', a Christian believer is stating a commitment to live an agapeistic life (a life of the kind of love Jesus displayed for humanity – unconditional and wanting the best for all). Religious language is, according to Braithwaite, a collection of stories that are not meant in a literal, cognitive sense but are inspiration and encouragement to live out the commitment that has been made. These stories are to be 'entertained' rather than believed.

INSIGHT

'A religious belief is an intention to behave in a certain way (a moral belief) together with the entertainment of certain stories associated with the intention in the mind of the believer' (Braithwaite, 'An Empiricist's View of the Nature of Religious Belief', 1955).

WHAT DO YOU THINK?

Write down your thoughts on Wittgenstein's arguments and revisit them shortly before the exam to see if your views have changed.

Read Wittgenstein for Yourself

In these passages from *Philosophical Investigations* (1953), Wittgenstein explains the family resemblances between 'games'. The notes in the margin will help you to grasp his ideas.

> Between different games there will be some language that is used in the same way, but other language that is used differently. Only the players in the game have a full understanding of this.

> Wittgenstein is showing that terms are not identical in meaning when they are used in different games or forms of life, but they are similar enough to resemble one another.

> Words may be exactly the same when spoken in different contexts or language games but they can (and will) mean very different things depending on who is using them and for what purpose. For example, you may have a mouse with your computer as well as a mouse in the kitchen cupboard; the setting determines the meaning.

> Central to Wittgenstein's Language Games theory is the use of words; the use of the words in a situation determines its meaning.

> By using the locomotive (train) example we can imagine we are suddenly immersed in a different language game and we will see the tools (hear and experience the language being used) but not actually know how to use them until we have learnt the particular uses for them. This is why people across different language games are unable to understand each other fully.

Look for example at board-games, with their multifarious relationships. Now pass to card-games; here you find many correspondences with the first group, but many common features drop out, and others appear. When we pass next to ball-games, much that is common is retained, but much is lost. Are they all 'amusing'? Compare chess with noughts and crosses. Or is there always winning and losing, or competition between players? Think of patience. In ball games there is winning and losing; but when a child throws his ball at the wall and catches it again, this feature has disappeared. Look at the parts played by skill and luck; and at the difference between skill in chess and skill in tennis. I can think of no better expression to characterize these similarities than 'family resemblances'; for the various resemblances between members of a family: build, features, colour of eyes, gait, temperament, etc. etc. overlap and cries cross in the same way. And I shall say: 'games' form a family.

[…]

Think of the tools in a tool-box: there is a hammer, pliers, a saw, a screwdriver, a ruler, a glue-pot, glue, nails, and screws. The functions of words are as diverse as the functions of these objects. (And in both cases there are similarities.) Of course, what confuses us is the uniform appearance of words when we hear them spoken or meet them in script and print. For their application is not presented to us so clearly. Especially when we are doing philosophy! It is like looking into the cabin of a locomotive. We see handles all looking more or less alike. (Naturally, since they are all supposed to be handled.) But one is the handle of a crank which can be moved continuously (it regulates the opening of a valve); another is the handle of a switch, which has only two effective positions, it is either off or on; a third is the handle of a brake-lever, the harder one pulls on it, the harder it brakes; a fourth, the handle of a pump: it has an effect only so long as it is moved to and fro.

Know Criticisms of Wittgenstein

Interfaith dialogue is possible. According to the Language Game theory, in which users of the language both have knowledge of, and accept the meanings of, the terms and phrases used, non-players of the game should not be able to hold meaningful conversations with those in that game. In terms of religious language, this should mean that non-religious people, or people not within a particular religious tradition, should not be able to have meaningful conversations across the divide, and should not be able to find common ground between themselves. But this is not the case, as interfaith dialogue is successful in many situations in the world and shows that common ground can be found. The website 'A Common Word' by English academic and theologian Dr Timothy

Winter at the University of Cambridge, is an example of interfaith dialogue between Muslim, Christian and Jewish people. Through it, Winter seeks to foster an 'Abrahamic Hospitality' between the traditions.

Language Game theory will lead to dangerous unquestioning faith. Some critics of Language Game theory, such as the American professor and philosopher Kai Nielsen, argue that by isolating religious language games apart from any external analysis and scrutiny, a certain Wittgensteinian fideism is formed. In his article, 'Wittgenstein and Wittgensteinians on Religion' (2000), Nielsen argues that according to Wittgenstein 'no philosophical or other kind of reasonable criticism, or for that matter defence, is possible for forms of life or, indeed, of any form of life, including Hinduism, Christianity and the like'. Critics such as Neilsen argue that religious claims need to be held up to scrutiny just as other non-religious claims are. It could lead to harmful superstitions, pseudo-religion, extremism and fanaticism if there is no objective reference point by which to judge the forms of life and language used within the 'game'. Supporters of Wittgenstein, most notably Phillips, counter that this is an unfair caricature of his view.

Wittgenstein's theory is anti-philosophy. Karl Popper criticised Wittgenstein for being anti-philosophy. Popper proposed that Wittgenstein's discussions were circular and self-serving. He only met Wittgenstein once – they had a ten-minute discussion in a postgraduate seminar room at Cambridge University, where Popper was adamant that philosophy was an important endeavour and provided a basis for moral and ethical codes. Wittgenstein reportedly waved a hot poker in the air as he gesticulated, and asked Popper to provide him with one example. 'To not wave a hot poker in an academic's face,' he replied.

> **INSIGHT**
>
> For Popper, Wittgenstein's playing with words and semantics was time and energy wasting, and prevented philosophy from fulfilling its purpose: 'Wittgenstein very fittingly compares a certain type of philosopher with a fly in a bottle, going on and on, buzzing about. And he says it is the task of his philosophy to show the fly the way out of the bottle. But I think it is Wittgenstein himself who is in the bottle and finds his way out of it and I certainly don't think he has shown anybody else the way out' (quoted in Magee, *Modern British Philosophy*, 1971).

Likewise, French philosopher Alain Badiou accused Wittgenstein of being an anti-philosopher. He picks up on the most famous line from *The Tractatus* and critiques it: 'It is quite simply false that whereof one cannot speak thereof one must be silent. It must on the contrary be named' (*Manifesto for Philosophy*, 1999).

Even Wittgenstein's first philosophical inspiration, Bertrand Russell, suggested that it was because Wittgenstein had become tired of hard thinking that he wanted to make it an unnecessary activity: 'The later Wittgenstein seems to have grown tired of serious thinking and to have invented a doctrine which would make such an activity unnecessary' (*My Philosophical Development*, 1959).

Watch Out for Traps

Stating that religious language is non-cognitive does not mean that it is not true. A common misconception is that 'cognitive' language is true, and 'non-cognitive' language is not. By calling religious language non-cognitive, Wittgenstein stated that it could not be shown or proven to be true or false. To call a statement 'cognitive' does not guarantee that it is true but says that in theory it could be shown to be true. For Wittgenstein, we cannot know the 'truth' of a religious statement other than the use of the statement for those who are using it. This is a criticism of the Language Game theory made by religious believers. To a religious believer, the truth of their claims often does matter, and will possibly be of central importance.

INSIGHT

Caroline Franks Davis (see Chapter 23) highlights this criticism: 'On the language game view, there ought to be not just one language game called "religion" but one for each different religious tradition. The radical cultural relativism thus envisioned ought to preclude any dialogue between the traditions. Such dialogue has, however, proved possible. Certain religious insights are considered superior to others on the basis of criteria which we apply to non-religious insights as well' (Davis, *The Evidential Force of Religious Experience*, 1987).

ESSENTIAL!

Fideism is the belief that faith is more important than reason when searching for religious truths.

ESSENTIAL!

Viewing religious language as non-cognitive means that it is not literally true or false; in fact, we cannot make that judgement about it.

> **INSIGHT**
>
> 'When if all possible scientific questions be answered, the problems of life have still not been touched at all ... There is indeed the inexpressible. This shows itself; it is the mystical' (Wittgenstein, *The Tractatus*).

Language game does not mean word games or trickery. Word games are tricks and amusements that people may use such as puns, jokes and silly stories. This is not what Wittgenstein suggested with his Language Games theory. He used the term 'game' to refer to a set of rules, an agreement between players, which allows the terms within it to have meaning for those who understand and agree to those rules, much like in a game of chess or cricket.

Don't argue that Wittgenstein agreed with the logical positivists. Wittgenstein's early work was a huge influence on the logical positivist movement. Key thinkers including A.J. Ayer ranked him highly, though Ayer stated, 'My admiration for him falls short of idolatry.' However, Wittgenstein's later work marks a divergence from the central tenets of the logical positivist movement. Even in the early period *The Tractatus* (from which the infamous 'remain silent' quote is taken) we see an acknowledgement from Wittgenstein that science and therefore the Verification Principle can only take us so far.

> **STRENGTHEN YOUR GRASP**
>
> 1. Write your own explanation of Wittgenstein's Language Games theory. Include the following: anti-realist, non-cognitive, forms of life, and language games. Have examples for each of these and make sure you link them to his ideas. Cover your notes and see what you can remember of these four areas. This will help you prepare for an 'explain' question in the exam.
> 2. Make a list of the strengths and weaknesses of Wittgenstein's understanding of religious language as part of a language game. Ensure you consider how other philosophers may view his understanding. How does Wittgenstein's Language Game theory compare and contrast to other understandings of religious language as analogical, symbolic and meaningless? Give a ranking out of five for each of these strengths and weaknesses to help you select the evidence that you think will make the strongest points in an essay. This will help you prepare for an 'evaluate' question in the exam.

Exam Guidance AO1

You will need to be able to give an account of Wittgenstein's view of religious language as part of a language game. You should be able to explain how he views religious language as non-cognitive but meaningful for those who are playing the game. You should be able to give examples of religious language that exemplify his view of religious language as a language game. You should also be able to compare and contrast his views with other understandings of religious language, such as Tillich's view of symbols, Aquinas and Ramsey on analogy, and the approach of the logical positivist movement.

Exam Guidance AO2

Through considering the strengths and weaknesses of Wittgenstein's approach to religious language, you can evaluate how successfully he achieves his aim of defending the meaningfulness of religious language in the face of logical positivist and atheist challenges. Consider how successful this is in comparison with the other understandings of religious language that philosophers in this book have put forward.

Acknowledgements

Photo credits

Full-page illustrations produced by Chantelle and Burgen.

Photos reproduced by permission of **p.11** © Isabell/stock.adobe.com; **p.13** © Savcoco/stock.adobe.com; **p.15** © The Picture Art Collection/Alamy Stock Photo; **p.31** © Vipman4/stock.adobe.com; **p.35** © Andrii/stock.adobe.com; **p.38** © Mark Garlick/Science Photo Library; **p.45** © Photocreo Bednarek/stock.adobe.com; **p.48** © GIS/stock.adobe.com; **p.60** Classic Image/Alamy Stock Photo; **p.67** © Gorodenkoff/stock.adobe.com; **p.74** © Gareth Southwell/Cartoonstock.com; **p.75** © Tomasz Zajda/stock.adobe.com; **p.80** © Feng Yu/stock.adobe.com; **p.87** © Fotopogledi/stock.adobe.com; **p.91** © Lukasz Janyst/stock.adobe.com; **p.93** © Digital Storm/stock.adobe.com; **p.98** © PRISMA ARCHIVO/Alamy Stock Photo; **p.106** © Martin/stock.adobe.com; **p.110** Reproduced by permission of Our World In Data; **p.116** Avalon Fund and Patrons' Permanent Fund; **p.118** © WavebreakMediaMicro/stock.adobe.com; **p.132** © Panitan/stock.adobe.com; **p.133** © T and Z/Shutterstock.com; **p.134** © Nicholas Felix/peopleimages.com/stock.adobe.com; **p.142** © Godong/Robertharding/Alamy Stock Photo; **p.144** © Lorenza Ochoa/Shutterstock.com; **p.150** © Vitstudio/stock.adobe.com; **p.151** © Oleksii/stock.adobe.com; **p.157** © Creatikon Studio/stock.adobe.com; **p.164** © M-Production/stock.adobe.com; **p.170** © Techtopia Art/stock.adobe.com; **p.172** © Mojo_cp/stock.adobe.com; **p.174** © Andrei Nekrassov/stock.adobe.com; **p.176** © Choat/stock.adobe.com; **p.179** © WALT DISNEY PICTURES/Album/Alamy Stock Photo; **p.184** © Dragan Boskovic/stock.adobe.com; **p.189** © Snaptitude/stock.adobe.com; **p.206** © SASITHORN/stock.adobe.com; **p.212** © Gorodenkoff/stock.adobe.com; **p.221** © Serhii/stock.adobe.com; **p.225** © Dezign56/stock.adobe.com; **p.226** © Chris/stock.adobe.com; **p.231** © Martialred/stock.adobe.com; **p.239** © Nadia Koval/stock.adobe.com; **p.246** © KBL Studio/Shutterstock.com; **p.247** © PhotoBank/stock.adobe.com; **p.248** © Drobot Dean/stock.adobe.com.

Text acknowledgments

p.32 Craig, William Lane. (1979). *The Existence of God and the Beginning of the Universe*. Here's Life. **p.82** Malcolm, Norman. (1960). 'Anselm's Ontological Arguments' in *The Philosophical Review* 69 (1) pp.41–62. **p.104** Mackie, J.L. (1955). *Evil and Omnipotence*. Oxford University Press. Reproduced with permission of The Licensor through PLSclear. **p.107** Rowe, William. (1979). 'The Problem of Evil and Some Varieties of Atheism' in *American Philosophical Quarterly* 16 (4) pp.335–341. **p.111** Paul, Gregory S. (2007). 'Theodicy's Problem: A Statistical Look at the Holocaust of the Children and the Implications of Natural Evil for the Free Will and Best of All Worlds Hypothesis' in *Philosophy & Theology* 19 (1–2) pp.125–149. **p.121** Hick, John. (2010). *Evil and the God of Love*. Palgrave Macmillan. Reproduced with permission of The Licensor through PLSclear. **p.198** Swinburne, Richard. (1968). 'Miracles' in *Philosophical Quarterly* 18. **p.214** Flew, Anthony. (1968) 'Theology and Falsification' in *University Discussion*. **p.234** Randall Jr, J. Herman. (1958). *The Role of Knowledge in Western Religion*. Starr King Press. **p.241** Tillich, Paul. (1957). *Dynamics of Faith*. Harper & Row.

Index

actual infinite 31
Adams, Douglas 40
aesthetic principle 39–40
Al-Ghazali 29–30
analogy 12–13, 19, 23–4, 44, 86, 227
Anselm *see* St Anselm
anthropic principle 38–40
anthropomorphism 12
anti-realism 14
apophatic approach 12
a posteriori knowledge 10–11, 16–17, 22, 30, 36, 39, 48, 80, 92, 206
a priori knowledge 10, 16, 30, 48–9, 65, 68–9, 74, 80, 92, 206
Aquinas, St Thomas 9–25
   criticisms of 20–4
   exam guidance 26–8
   existence of God 10–12, 16–19
   language as analogy 12–13, 19, 22–4
   miracles 14, 20, 23, 190
   nature of God 12–13, 15, 23
   social and historical context 9
archetypes 142–3
Aristotle 10, 12, 14–15, 18, 20, 73
art, and religion 234
aseity 67
atheism 43–4, 72, 99, 101, 105, 145–6, 148, 153, 174
Augustine *see* St Augustine
Ayer, A.J. 193, 205–10
   criticisms of 208
   exam guidance 210
   social and historical context 205
   Verification Principle 206–8
Berkeley, George 43
best possible world hypothesis 110
bliks 215, 217–18
Buddhism 100, 142
Cartesian Circle 77
cataphatic approach 12–13, 19
causal arguments 10

causation 21, 49
child mortality 109–11
Christian apologist 29
circular logic 22, 69
cognitivist approach 13–14
collective unconscious 141, 144
contingency 11, 18, 80
contradiction 9, 25, 33, 47–8, 80, 93, 102, 106
Copernicus 91
cosmological arguments 10–11, 17, 21, 44, 45–6, 54–5
Craig, William Lane 29–34, 215
   criticisms of 32–3
   exam guidance 34
   existence of God 31–2
   Kalam argument 29–31
   social and historical context 29
creatio ex nihilo 29
critical realism 175
cumulative argument 180, 189
Darwin, Charles 37, 38, 60–2
   criticisms of 61–2
   exam guidance 62
   social and historical context 60
   theory of evolution 37, 60–1
Davis, Caroline Franks 174–82
   criticisms of 181
   exam guidance 182
   on religious experiences 174–81
Dawkins, Richard 37, 148–54
   criticisms of 153
   exam guidance 154
   God Hypothesis 149–51
   social and historical context 148
deductive arguments 16, 30, 65
deism 211
Descartes, René 43, 72–8, 92–3
   criticisms of 76
   exam guidance 78
   existence of God 74–6
   social and historical context 72
design argument 35–7, 99, 150
disanalogy 44, 88
doubt 73–4

dysteleological argument 22
empiricism 43, 47, 54, 87, 92, 98, 140, 149, 206
Enlightenment 35
Epicurean hypothesis 19, 45, 51
Epicurus 98
   criticisms of 99–100
   exam guidance 100
   problem of evil 98–100
   social and historical context 98
epistemic distance 17
equivocal language 12
eschatological justification 119, 121
ethics
evil 98–111, 114
   eschatological justification 119, 121
   first/second order 119
   and free will 115–18
   moral 100, 116, 121
   natural 100, 109, 116, 121
   see also suffering
'Evil God' challenge 228
evolution 150
   Darwin's theory of 37, 60–1, 148
   natural selection 60, 150
   theistic 38–40
existence 11, 25
   modes of 81
   necessary 67, 69, 75, 79–83
   see also God: existence of; necessary being
ex nihilo nihil fit 11, 18, 25
fall, the 116
fallacy of composition 21
fallacy of false dilemma 102
Falsification Principle 193–7, 211–14
Falsification Symposium 197, 211, 214, 217, 220–1
felix culpa 117
fideism 251
Flew, Antony 211–16
   criticisms of 214–15
   exam guidance 216
   Falsification Principle 213–14
   social and historical context 211

free will 102–3, 110, 115–18, 120, 211
Freud, Sigmund 132–8, 145, 180
   criticisms of 136–7
   exam guidance 138
   religion as neurosis 135
   religion as wish fulfilment 134–6
   social and historical context 132
   tripartite mind 133
fundamentalism 151
Gaunilo 66, 86–9
   criticisms of 88
   exam guidance 89
   Lost Island Parody 86–9
   social and historical context 86
God
   existence of
      Aquinas, St Thomas 10–12, 16–19
      Craig, William Lane 31–2
      Descartes, René 74–6
      Hume, David 44, 49
      Malcolm, Norman 79–82
      Paley, William 36
      St Anselm 65–8
      Swinburne, Richard 189–96
      Tennant, F.R. 39
   nature of
      Aquinas, St Thomas 12–13, 15, 23
      Hume, David 49
      Swinburne, Richard 190, 192
God Hypothesis 149
Goldilocks zone 38–9
Gould, Stephen Jay 149
Hare, Richard 217–19
   bliks 217–18
   criticisms of 218
   exam guidance 219
   social and historical context 217
heresy 72
Hick, John 13, 29, 114, 119–24, 130, 209
   problem of evil 119–22, 127
   social and historical context 114
hierarchy of souls 15
Holland, R.F. 183–6
   criticisms of 185
   exam guidance 186
   miracles 183–5, 190
   social and historical context 183
Howard-Snyder, Daniel 107
Hume, David 21–2, 24, 32, 43–59, 228
   causality 49
   criticisms of 52–3
   exam guidance 56–8

   existence of God 44, 49
   Hume's fork 48, 206
   miracles 46–7, 51–2, 53–4, 190–6
   nature of God 49
   problem of evil 98–9
   social and historical context 43
Huxley, Thomas 61
illusion 133–4
imago Dei 15, 118
inconsistent triad 101–3
individuation 140, 142–3
indubitable knowledge 73
inductive arguments 10, 16–17, 22, 36, 39, 44, 48, 53, 194–5
inductive leap 20, 37, 44, 46, 47
industrial revolution 35
infinite regress 10, 18
infinite universe 30–1
innate ideas 73
Irenaeus *see* St Irenaeus
issue of causality 21
James, William 156, 161–7, 179
   criticisms of 165
   exam guidance 167
   on religious experiences 161–4
   social and historical context 161
Jung, Carl 140–6
   criticisms of 145
   exam guidance 146
   role of God and religion 142–4
   social and historical context 140
Kalam argument 29–31
Kant, Immanuel 23, 49, 80, 91–7, 142
   criticisms of 95
   exam guidance 97
   modes of knowledge 92–4
   social and historical context 91
knowledge
   categorisation 48, 92
   see also a posteriori knowledge; a priori knowledge
language *see* religious language
Leibniz, Gottfried Wilhelm 53, 77, 110
Lewis, C.S. 185
Locke, John 43
logic
   analytic statements 206–7
   circular 22, 69
   modal 81
logical positivism 151, 193, 197, 205–8, 234
Mackie, J.L. 100, 101–4

   criticisms of 103–4
   exam guidance 104
   problem of evil 101–3
   social and historical context 101
magisterium 149
Malcolm, Norman 79–85
   criticisms of 82–3
   exam guidance 84–5
   existence of God 79–82
   social and historical context 79
mandalas 142, 144
Marx, Karl 180
McGrath, Alister 148
miracles 14, 20, 23, 46–7, 51–2, 53–4, 150, 183–5, 190–8
Mitchell, Basil 220–3
   criticisms of 222
   exam guidance 223
   religious language 220–2
mystical experiences 9, 156–9, 162–4, 168–71, 174–81
natural selection 60, 150
natural theology 35
necessary being 11, 18, 21, 23, 25, 46
necessary existence 67, 69, 75, 79–83
Nietzsche, Friedrich 146
noumena 91, 142
Occam's razor 21, 22, 33, 46, 50, 189
Oedipus complex 135, 136
omnibenevolence 77, 99, 101, 109, 117, 118, 121, 124, 214
omnipotence 77, 99, 101–3, 109, 118, 121, 124, 128, 192, 214
omniscience 26, 77, 102, 104, 117–18, 124, 190
ontological arguments 64–8, 75, 77, 79–82, 92–3
original sin 116
Otto, Rudolf 156, 168–73, 179
   criticisms of 171–2
   exam guidance 173
   on religious experiences 168–71
   social and historical context 168
Paley, William 35–7, 44
   criticisms of 37
   design argument 35–7, 150
   exam guidance 37
   existence of God 36
   social and historical context 35
paradox 93
Paul, Gregory 109–12
   criticisms of 111

exam guidance 112
   innocent suffering 109–11
   social and historical context 109
phenomena 91, 142
Plantinga, Alvin 88, 103, 110
Plato 115
Popper, Karl 48, 151, 211, 251
potential infinite 31
pragmatism 161
prayer 157
primal horde 135
Protestant Reformation 156, 159
Ramsey, Ian 224–9
   criticisms of 227–8
   exam guidance 229
   religious language 225–7
   social and historical context 224
Randall, John Herman Jr 230–6
   criticisms of 234–5
   exam guidance 236
   religious signs and symbols 230–5
   social and historical context 230
rationalism 43, 74, 92
realism 14, 20, 161, 175
reason 9–10, 15, 43, 64
reductio ad absurdum 10, 17–18, 81, 87
religion, defining 232
religious experiences *see* mystical experiences
religious language 12–13, 19, 22–4, 197–9, 207, 209, 217, 220, 225–7, 230–5, 238–42, 246–51
revelation 9, 64, 228
Rowe, William 105–8
   criticisms of 107
   exam guidance 108
   existence of God 105
   problem of evil 106–7
   social and historical context 105

Russell, Bertrand 21, 33, 48, 93, 246
sceptical theism 107
scepticism 47, 54, 59, 73, 101
scholasticism 29
science, and religion 149–54, 161–2, 225
scientific method 207, 211
secularism 153
signs and symbols 231–5, 238–42
solipsism 54
sophistry 48
St Anselm 25, 64–71, 79–80, 87
   criticisms of 68–9
   exam guidance 70–1
   existence of God 65–8
   social and historical context 64
state of actuality 10
state of potentiality 10
St Augustine 114–17, 122
   criticisms of 124
   exam guidance 127–8
Steady State theory 29
St Irenaeus 110, 115, 118–20, 123–4
   criticisms of 125
   exam guidance 128–9
suffering 100, 105–7, 109, 118–26
   see also evil
Swinburne, Richard 188–204, 227
   criticisms of 199–200
   exam guidance 202
   existence of God 189–96
   miracles 190–8
   nature of God 190, 192
   social and historical context 188
symbols 231–5, 238–42
synthetic knowledge 92
teleological arguments 12, 17, 19, 22, 35, 44–5, 53
   see also design argument

temporal effects 31
Tennant, F.R. 38–41
   criticisms of 40
   exam guidance 41
   existence of God 39
   social and historical context 38
   theistic evolution 38–40
Teresa of Avila 155–60
   criticisms of 159
   exam guidance 160
   mystical experiences 156–9
   social and historical context 155
theistic evolution 38–40
theodicy 110, 114
Tillich, Paul 237–43
   criticisms of 242
   exam guidance 243
   existentialism 238
   religious signs and symbols 238–42
   social and historical context 237
transcendence 31
transverbiations 156
truth *see* knowledge; rationalism; Verification Principle
universalists 220
universe, causes of
   Craig, William Lane 30–3
   Hume, David 44–6
univocal language 12
Verification Principle 52, 193–7, 205–8
visions *see* mystical experiences
Wittgenstein, Ludwig 106, 183, 245–52
   criticisms of 250–1
   exam guidance 252
   religious language 246–51
   social and historical context 245